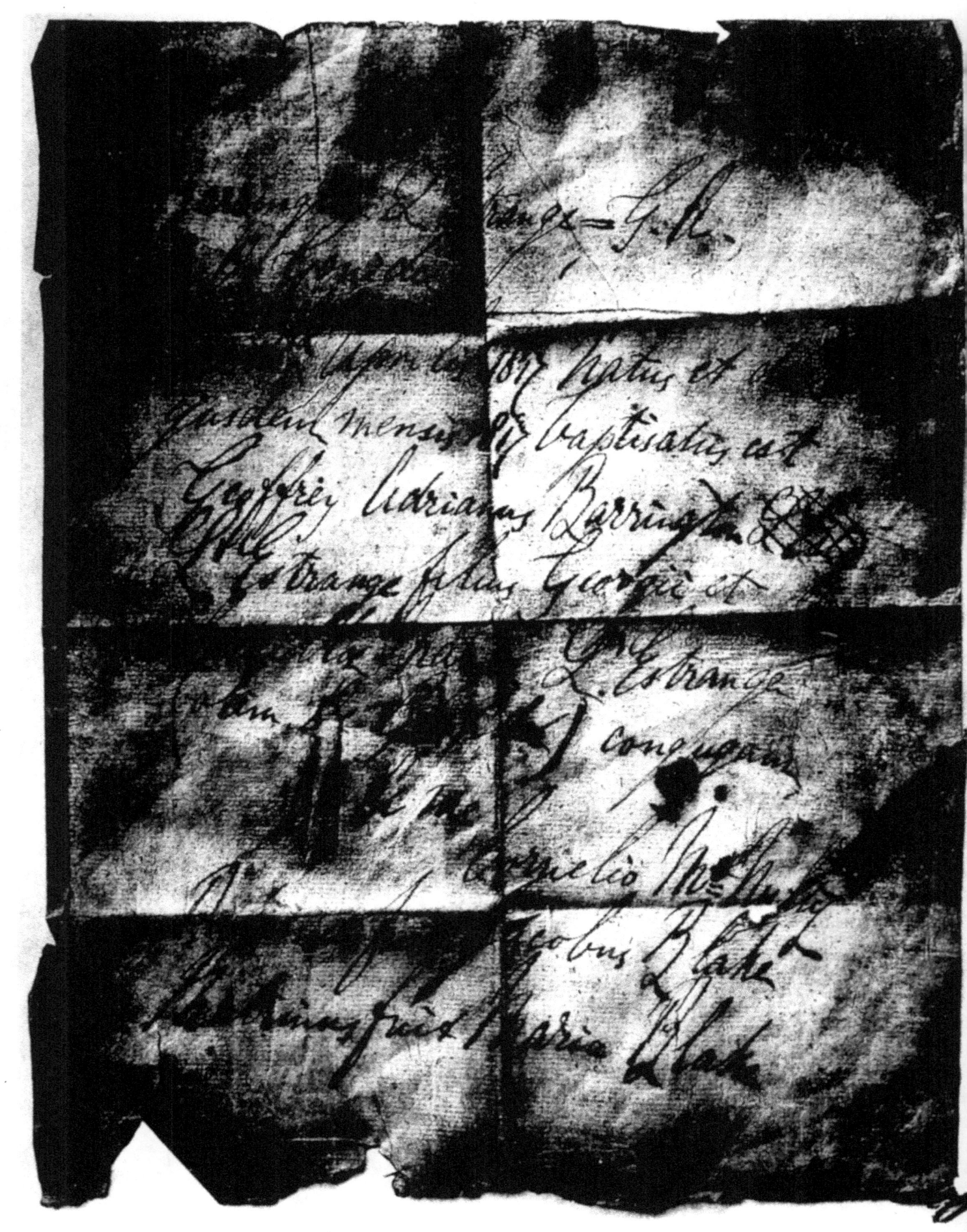

SEE PAGE 451.

No. 747.

BEING

THE AUTOBIOGRAPHY OF A GIPSY.

EDITED BY

F. W. CAREW, M.D.

———

BRISTOL:
J. W. ARROWSMITH, 11 QUAY STREET.
LONDON:
SIMPKIN, MARSHALL, HAMILTON, KENT & CO. LIMITED.

CONTENTS.

Chap.		Page
I.	NO. 747	1
II.	A FAIR START	13
III.	I LOSE MY FATHER AND START WITH MY MOTHER FOR DEVONSHIRE	23
IV.	I MAKE THE ACQUAINTANCE OF SOME OF MY RELATIONS	32
V.	FERNLEIGH COMBE	44
VI.	UNDER THE GREENWOOD TREE	56
VII.	"'TIS MY DELIGHT OF A LIKELY NIGHT"	67
VIII.	MY COUSIN TENNY KLISM	80
IX.	PASSON MARK	89
X.	A CUP OF TEA WITH MY GRANNY CHARLOTTE	103
XI.	DIES CARBONE NOTANDA	121
XII.	THE LIBRARY AT NETHERLEIGH COURT AND ITS OCCUPANTS	128
XIII.	THE STORY OF A BLIGHTED CAREER	142
XIV.	LIFE AT THE PARSONAGE	152
XV.	A SCRAMBLE WITH A SCRATCH PACK	
XVI.	THE SHINGLES BELOW BRENT HEAD	17
XVII.	THE AFFRAY IN HAWK'S WOOD	19
XVIII.	I LEAVE THE PARSONAGE	200
XIX.	I MAKE THE ACQUAINTANCE OF MANTIS LOVELL	212

CONTENTS.

Chap.		Page
XX.	MR. JOHN SHICE, M.R.C.V.S.	223
XXI.	THE L'ESTRANGES OF NETHERLEIGH COURT	235
XXII.	I ENTER THE SERVICE OF SIR GEORGE L'ESTRANGE, AND ACCOMPANY MR. GEOFFREY TO CAMFORD	244
XXIII.	LIFE AT CAMFORD	253
XXIV.	MATRIMONY AND GREEN SEAS	266
XXV.	A CRUISE AMONG THE WINDWARD ISLANDS	278
XXVI.	A CHAPTER OF MY LIFE WHICH MAY WELL BE SKIPPED	293
XXVII.	TWO DREAMS AND THEIR CONSEQUENCES	308
XXVIII.	I FIND MYSELF ONCE MORE IN WESTPORT	319
XXIX.	THE LOVERS' WALK	327
XXX.	I RE-ENTER SIR GEORGE'S SERVICE	339
XXXI.	LIFE AT NETHERLEIGH COURT	351
XXXII.	THE BARON TAKES ME INTO HIS CONFIDENCE	368
XXXIII.	A FINE OLD COUNTY SKELETON	379
XXXIV.	I AM ENTRUSTED WITH AN IMPORTANT COMMISSION	395
XXXV.	SOME PASSAGES FROM THE LIFE OF MR. JAMES WOOD	406
XXXVI.	I FIND OUT 'HOW THE LAND LIES'	420
XXXVII.	THE MISSION HOUSE IN NELSON STREET	433
XXXVIII.	"KOOSHTO BOK!"	444

N.B.—The covers in which this work are bound give a general idea of the colouring of the convict uniform, with the shoulder-badge, broad-arrows on back and chest, and transverse bands of red on the blue stockings. The figure **6** *denotes the term of imprisonment, the letters* **LD** *the date of the conviction, while* **747** *is the convict's number in the prison register.*

ERRATA.

Page 41, *line* 18, *for* 'others' *read* 'otters.'
,, 65 ,, 18, *for* 'just' *read* 'first.'
,, 106 ,, 14, *for* 'Mapas' *read* 'Malpas.'
,, 203 ,, 16, *for* 'distinction' *read* 'destruction.'
,, 227 ,, 14, *for* 'Mrs. Scott' *read* 'Mr. Scott.'

No. 747.

OR,

THE AUTOBIOGRAPHY OF A GIPSY.

CHAPTER I.

No. 747.

WHAT could possibly induce me, Francis Wylde Carew, M.D., Vice-Chairman of the Local Board and Hon. Secretary of the United Braun, Cran, and Lyd Fishery Association, to jeopardise my social status and cast, by implication, a stigma upon the offices which I had hitherto filled with credit to myself and the satisfaction of my neighbours, by collating and editing the Recollections of an individual, a considerable portion of whose life—according to his own confession—had been passed in more or less open violation of the first principles of law, order, and morality, is a problem which is likely to exercise the minds of my good friends and whilom patients, the gossips of Braunton Tracey, for some little time to come.

As a matter of fact the solution, though simple enough, is by no means obvious, and were I to attempt to explain to them that the highly respectable middle-aged individual whose habit it is to trot about the country lanes on a confidential cob every whit as sober-looking and respectable as his master—the very incarnation, in fact, of smug equine Philistinism—had once been hand in glove—as my poor father used wrathfully to declare—with every Gipsy, tinker, and idle, poaching vagabond throughout the country side, and by reason of the shibboleth which, as a lad, he had taken such pains to acquire to the exclusion of more profitable studies, a welcome visitor at every roadside camp-fire from London to the Land's End, the explanation would most assuredly have the effect of still further mystifying those whom it was intended to enlighten.

Yet so it was. And every now and again the old leaven of rigidly suppressed, but never wholly eradicated, Bohemianism rises to the surface, causing a temporary ferment which, however, decreases in duration and intensity with advancing years. It may, therefore, be understood how the discovery of a certain long-forgotten manuscript to which I shall shortly have occasion to refer at greater length, sufficed to arouse the innate nomadic predisposition which still hides its tatters beneath the sober garb of conventional broadcloth, and beguiled me into becoming the chronicler of an obscure waif, whom chance or destiny appear inseparably to have connected with the fortunes of a family whose vicissitudes form one of the saddest pages of our county history.

Between the years 1860-70 it had been my lot to be connected in a professional capacity with a Government establishment situated in a certain county on the South coast, no less remarkable for the exhilarating sense of physical well-being which its climate is wont to induce, than for the excellence of its mutton, and the benighted condition of its agricultural population.

Although, perhaps, to the hypercritical, the establishment in question may have lacked some of the luxuries and refinements of the palatial *caravanserai* which, in compliance with the daily increasing demand for superior accommodation, have sprung up, mushroom-like, throughout the length and breadth of the land, and was, moreover—in the opinion of the grumblers aforesaid—open to the objection that individual comfort had been somewhat ruthlessly subordinated to economical and sanitary considerations, I think I may venture to assert, without being suspected of undue partiality, that the general arrangements were excellent, while the inmates enjoyed many of the advantages of a first-class Marine Club, without having to undergo the invidious formality of a ballot or being subjected to the legalised blackmail of an entrance-fee.

To discard the periphrastic subtleties affected by the alumni of the Gladstonian cult for the more vigorous Saxon of the late senior member for Birmingham—as my favourite penny-a-liner hath it—I was surgeon to the convict establishment at Moorport, and I was not altogether in love with the appointment, experiencing, as I did, the unenviable sensations of a square peg which, by force of circumstances, is compelled to accommodate its angularities to the restricted circumference of a round hole. Moorport proper—I need scarcely observe that the Public Works, as they are somewhat euphemistically termed in 'professional' circles, were not included in this designation—was as dreary a little seaport as could well be imagined, its sole imports being convicts, and its exports dressed stone and wheatears *au naturel*, which—the wheatears, not the convicts—were trapped in large quantities by the natives and sold in the neighbouring market-town. It may readily be understood that the position I occupied was an unenviable one at best, and that to a man of more sanguine temperament or ambitious disposition it would have proved almost insupportable; but the appointment was a fairly remunerative one, and although a younger son of what is somewhat grandiloquently termed a 'county family,' the pecuniary was the only point of view from which I could afford to regard it. Since then times have changed with me for the better, but to this day I never ride past the gloomy precincts of our county gaol without instinctively quickening my pace, and I look back to the time I spent at Moorport with that vague feeling of unavailing regret so often experienced by those who have been compelled to pass some of the best years of their lives in a savage country—far removed from the humanising influences of society and civilisation.

Luckily for me, perhaps, I was content to take life pretty much as I found it, and in addition to my professional avocations I was a bit of a naturalist, a bit of a geologist, a bit of a philologist; in fact—as good-natured friends were never tired of remarking—a Jack-of-all-trades and master of none, an enthusiastic rider of hobbies, and a dabbler in a dozen or more 'ologies,' the pursuit of which, if not calculated to confer any distinct benefit upon posterity, possessed the negative recommendation of being altogether unobjectionable and helped to pass the time away. Naturally of an unsuspicious disposition, my sympathies were easily enlisted—a combination which, to a certain extent, unfitted me for the post I then occupied, since it laid me open to the attacks of designing malingerers, who very soon discovered that I was not only loth to turn a deaf ear to their complaints, but constitutionally incapable of saying "No" with the sharpness which so often passes muster for firmness of character.

During the term of my residence at Moorport I had ample leisure and opportunity for investigating the various phases and phenomena of moral obliquity which can only be studied with success by one who is brought into daily and hourly contact with the criminal classes, and it has since occurred to me that the very defects of character which I exhibited, combined with my Bohemian proclivities, may unconsciously have aided me in obtaining an insight into the inner working of the convict mind which would have been religiously barred against a person possessing the qualifications I lacked.

As soon as they discovered that my interest in them was of a purely philosophic nature, and that although I never invited their confidence, I never betrayed it when volunteered, my patients would sometimes insist upon unburdening their minds to me in a manner which, however flattering as a mark of their appreciation of my sense of honour, was, necessarily, not without its embarrassments. For anyone possessed of a keen sense of humour, these interviews were seldom without their ludicrous side, as, for instance, when a brawny convalescent in abbreviated drapery and a fortnight's beard, crawled from his mattress and going down on his marrow-bones, besought me, with tears in his eyes, to post a letter to a friend outside—in Moorportese 'to mail a cross-stiff to a pal.'

This, I may explain *en passant*, can only be effected by the connivance of a 'screw,' or warder—who, when accessible to a bribe, is termed a 'right-screw'—and costs from five shillings to a pound, according to the prisoner's circumstances. The 'right-screw' receives money from the convict's friends outside, and keeps up a running-account with the prisoner—having previously 'napped his regulars,' or deducted his commission, which averages from one-third to half of the sum received—supplying him with tobacco for chewing, spirits, and other luxuries, until his credit is exhausted.

To return to my interesting patient whom I have left shivering in a devotional attitude.

"Them bloomin' screws"—he was saying, "is so precious greedy, a pore cove aint got no sort 'er chance along of 'em. Truck sticks to their 'ands like cobbler's-vax, and has for the ready——" when my assistant entered unexpectedly, accompanied by one of the warders. No courtly gallant surprised at the feet of his mistress could have exhibited a more commendable self-possession than did that poor, suffering malefactor. "You see, Doctor"—he continued, all in the same breath and without any inflection of tone, pointing to his ankle which had been damaged in the quarries, the while an angelic smile irradiated a naturally repulsive countenance and his dexter eyelid underwent an almost imperceptible contraction, " hit 'll almost bear me now, and I 'opes to get back to vork by the hend o' the veek. Vith luck, that's to say——" he added, with a scowl at the unsympathetic warder whose sudden entrance had interrupted the little comedy, and hobbling back to his mattress, retired beneath his blanket.

The bulk of my professional experiences were, however, of a very different character. During the second year of my stay at Moorport I was called in to attend a poor fellow who had been badly injured in the quarries by a mass of stone falling on him. Had it not been for the quarries, no community in the kingdom could have shown a cleaner bill of health, but accidents—which the nature of the work rendered unavoidable—were continually occurring, and of the fifteen to thirty daily inmates of the infirmary, quite two-thirds were suffering from injuries of a more or less severe character. The measured tramp of the bearers soon became as familiar to me as the postman's knock, while the hastily improvised bandages saturated with blood, the nerveless arm dangling over the side of the stretcher, or the jacket mercifully thrown across the head and shoulders to hide the poor scarred face and the dull eyes which kept staring straight up to heaven, showed, only too often, that the reprieve had arrived unexpectedly at last, and that the soul was even then in the presence of the Supreme Judge, from whose sentence there is no appeal.

In this particular instance I found that the man had sustained a compound fracture of the left thigh, the ankle was also crushed, a couple of ribs on the same side were damaged, and in addition to his other injuries he was rather badly cut and bruised about the head. As far as I could judge of him, in his then shattered condition, he was a well-proportioned, intelligent-looking fellow of medium height and about fifty years of age, with jet-black bristles—hair, I had almost said, but the Moorport barber had been busy with the comb and scissors—strongly-marked eyebrows of the same colour, dark greenish-brown eyes with a steely glint in them, regular features inclining to the aquiline, an unusually swarthy complexion, and what used to be known to the *habitués* of the Prize-ring as a 'snake' head.*

In addition to the contusions caused by his recent accident, I noticed an old scar upon the left temple, and two or three small, white cicatrices upon the knuckle of the right hand, which showed that it was not the first time he had been in the wars. The skin was of that golden-olive hue which is seldom seen except among natives of a warmer clime, and wherever it had been exposed to the combined action of sun and wind, instead of burning to the regulation brick-dust colour which is one of the distinguishing marks of a Moorport resident, it had acquired that unmistakable black-brown tint which is only to be seen to perfection, in England, among the Gipsies of the full-blood, while a peculiar depression or indentation in the region of the temples, following the line of an imaginary hat-brim, confirmed my supposition as to the nationality of my patient.

Now craniology had been one of my pet 'ologies,' and when *afficionado* to Gipsycraft and an occasional sojourner among the tents of the Egyptians, I used to flatter myself

---

* A 'snake' head meant a dark, well-shaped but rather low-browed head which, when well set upon a strong but flexible neck, was popularly supposed to indicate the possession of an unusual amount of pluck and 'devil.' It was more frequently found among men of Gipsy or Jewish extraction, and it is probably an analagous idea which prompts country horse-dealers to describe a dark-coloured animal with an unusually neat but rather wild-looking head, as having a 'Gipsy-head.'—Ed.

that I could tell to what tribe a Rom'nichal belonged by the shape of his skull. In some of these tribes—the Boswells, for instance—the distinguishing characteristics are very well defined, and although I made a bad shot at the man's tribe, my surmise as to his being not only a Gipsy, but a West-countryman, ultimately proved to be correct.

Preparatory to reducing the fracture I was about to administer an anæsthetic, when the patient motioned my assistant back, and said in a low voice:—

"I'd rather not have any of that, sir, if you don't mind. It isn't the first time I've been handled by a doctor, and I can stand it pretty well, and if you'll give me a drop of brandy I shall be right enough."

Setting his strong, white teeth like a vice, he underwent the trying ordeal without a murmur, although the heavy drops of moisture which gathered on his brow bore ample testimony to the agony he was enduring. As soon as the worst of it was over and we had made him as comfortable in bed as circumstances permitted, he said to me:—

"If it isn't against the rules, sir, I should like my wife to be informed of my accident, and that I'm going on all right."

I told him that I would make a note of it in my report, and that I had no doubt that his request would be complied with, but the man's Spartan indifference to pain, coupled with the unusual consideration he had manifested for his wife, did not fail to impress me favourably, accustomed as I was to the physical sensibility and moral apathy of the average convict, while his well-modulated voice and respectful behaviour conveyed the impression that he had not been altogether a stranger to the society of gentlefolk—in fact I put him down at once as a gentleman's servant who had annexed the family plate or hypothecated her ladyship's jewellery, and, as events will show, I was partly right and partly wrong.

In due course an official enquiry was held as to the cause of the accident, when the following particulars came to light. The convict Samson Loveridge, No. 747: aged 53: married: had been sentenced at the Central Criminal Court, with two others named Ralli and Wilson, to six years' penal servitude for forging and uttering two £50 notes on the

Bank of England. Had arrived from doing 'separates' at Pentonville September, 186—, as a first-class prisoner. Gratuities due up to present date £8 16s. 3d. Conduct-marks in book of warder of working-party averaged 'good' to 'very good.' Prison character 'exemplary.' Had not forfeited any of the time which is deducted from the full sentence for discharge on ticket-of-leave—a rather exceptional circumstance, especially when we take into consideration the surly temper of some of the warders, who, in order to acquire the reputation of being smart officers, are addicted to reporting the most trivial misdemeanours on the part of new arrivals.*

A short time previous to the accident it had come to the knowledge of the Prison authorities that, owing to the tyrannical conduct of one of the warders in charge, one of the working-parties had agreed to mutiny, but on the eventful day the guard had been doubled and the little affair had not come off. For some reason or other the ringleaders had suspected No. 747, who worked in their gang, of 'rounding' on them—as a matter of fact without the slightest foundation—and they determined to 'sarve him out' as they call it. The party was employed in lowering some heavy blocks of stone by means of chains and pulleys, and it was No. 747's turn to receive the blocks below and cast off the coupling-chains. With diabolical ingenuity the cowardly ruffians contrived that the couplings should give way suddenly—a favourite device when they bore a grudge against a mate—and without a moment's warning the huge mass of rock came thundering down with a run amidst a cloud of dust and flying splinters—the result being that their intended victim barely escaped with his life.

His recovery was, naturally, a tedious business, and although he proved, on the whole, an exemplary patient, I found that he was of a most excitable disposition—the least item of good news being sufficient to induce a high state of elation which, in turn, was succeeded by a corresonding period of depression. When in good spirits—and,

---

* In the words of an old lag :—" The screws is bound to report some on us, and as we old 'uns, as knows the ropes, is most in general the best-be'aved, and it don't pay 'em to report their reg'lar customers, they naterally takes it out'er the joeys—and I don't blame 'em, neither."—ED.

to do him justice, he was never sulky or ill-tempered—he would rattle away to a sick companion by the hour together, and finding that he had received a very superior education, with a view to affording him some occupation for his spare time, I encouraged him to attempt to set down on paper the story of his life and experiences which will be found in the following pages.

Having provided him with the necessary materials, I left him to his own devices, but although I could see that his vanity was gratified at the idea of becoming an author, for some days nothing further came of it.

"You see, sir,"—he would say, "although I can tell a story well enough when I'm in the humour, I've always led an active life and never been accustomed to writing, and I don't rightly know how to begin—besides, nobody would care to hear about the sayings and doings of a man like me."

In order to encourage him, I told him that people did not always want to read about the manners and customs of their own class, but liked a little variety, sometimes.

"Well, sir,"—he replied, "there may be something in that, and if you'd give me a fair start and write the first chapter or two, I think I could manage to get along"—but this was just a little more than I had bargained for, and I explained to him that if I were to do so, he would lose whatever credit might attach to the performance, promising, however, at the same time to "give him a fair start," as he called it—and in this way the story of the convict's life and experiences came to be written.

Upon his recovery it was deemed expedient to transfer No. 747 to Dartland. On the evening previous to his departure I had taken leave of him, and he had delivered his manuscript—of which he was inordinately proud—into my safe keeping, but on the following morning, as I was passing through the entrance-gates, I met him crossing the yard, on his way to the station, in charge of a couple of warders. To anyone who understands the passionate intensity of feeling which so frequently underlies the stolid exterior of our English Gipsies, the scene which followed—no less characteristic of the one, than embarrassing to the other, actor—will be intelligible enough. As I was about to pass by with a nod and a word of encouragement, he stepped quickly aside and planted himself full in my path. Throwing back his head and stretching out his right hand—for in consideration of his good conduct and the injuries he had received, the handcuffs had been dispensed with—palm uppermost, to the full extent of his arm with the slightly theatrical gesture which characterises the Gipsy mode of shaking hands, he looked me straight in the face, and said in a voice which—to use a hackneyed phrase—trembled with suppressed emotion:—

"*'Duvelesti, Rye!* * You've been a good friend to me, and I hope you won't refuse to take my hand. Good-bye, *mi pal*, and *kooshto bok!*" †

In order properly to appreciate the situation it should be recollected that this little scene was enacted in the presence of at least half-a-dozen witnesses, and that I was fully alive to the ridicule to which this ebullition of genuine feeling on the convict's part must necessarily expose me.

The story got wind, sure enough—a little joke went a long way at the Public Works—and it was some time before I heard the last of "my pal." It should, however, in justice to the poor fellow, be explained that there was no intentional disrespect in the use of the phrase, '*mi pal*' being pure Romany and a contraction of the obsolete '*meero prala*,' 'my brother'—the ordinary form of salutation—and used in that sense by the Gipsy convict who, soon after his arrival at Dartland, was released upon a ticket-of-leave. We have never met again in the flesh, but I was afterwards told that he had emigrated with his wife and youngest boy—his eldest son being already in New Zealand—to Melbourne, where he started business as a livery-stable keeper and horse-dealer, and was doing very well when I last heard from him.

A year or two later I resigned my appointment and took over a country practice in my native county, but finding myself shortly afterwards in comparatively easy circumstances, I gave up practising altogether, and purchasing a small property not a hundred miles from Exeter, devoted myself to other, and more congenial, pursuits. One wet afternoon about a year ago, while occupied in routing out a cupboard full of old papers, pamphlets, and literary odds and ends of

---

* "God bless you, sir!"
† "Good-bye, my brother, and good luck to you!"

all sorts, I came upon the *disjecta membra* of the convict's manuscript, and finding time hang rather heavy on my hands during the long winter evenings, I thought I would amuse myself by trying to knock it into some sort of shape.

Living, as I did, in the county where many of the events mentioned in the manuscript had taken place, I soon became alive to the advisability of concealing the identity of the principal actors; but, with this exception, I have left things pretty much as I found them, contenting myself with correcting the orthography, altering the construction of sentences where I deemed it expedient, and occasionally clothing the author's ideas in language a little better suited to the requirements of polite society. In undertaking the self-imposed duties of editor, I not only enjoyed the advantage of being personally acquainted with one of the leading characters of Loveridge's story, but of having access to several letters written by that gentleman during his travels in the West Indies and America to friends in England, and of comparing them with the statements contained in No. 747's manuscript.

The history of the L'Estranges, like the majority of similar stories contained in Burke's *Vicissitudes of Noble Families*, is a sad one, and as long as any representative of the Devonshire branch survived, it would have been in the worst possible taste to revive a scandal which had been allowed to die a natural death, but now that the estates have passed into other hands and the incident alluded to in these pages has become public property through the medium of a *cause célèbre*, the necessity for reticence no longer exists.

I believe that I am correct in stating that of the more prominent figures of this narrative, only two are alive at the present day, although the last time I dined at the Two Services—which, by the way, must be close on fifteen years ago—I sat at a table near to that at which Oscar Jansen, the 'wicked Baron' of Loveridge's story, was entertaining two young friends who evidently belonged to the *jeunesse dorée*. He appeared to be flourishing like a green bay-tree—although, perhaps, the entire absence of verdure from the Baron's composition scarcely justifies the comparison—and as his hospitality was, as a rule, but as bread cast upon the waters, it is more than probable that, long ere this, those devoted youths have had their eyes opened to the true character of their entertainer.

Having been from my childhood upward a persistent devourer of light literature and entitled to describe myself as 'an old subscriber' to the principal circulating libraries in London and the provinces, experience thus gained, combined with a desire that readers of this rambling story should be made acquainted with its *raison d'être*, has decided me to avoid prefixing this introductory chapter with the obnoxious word 'Preface'—rightly abhorred and rigidly eschewed of all good Christians—and I can scarcely do better than conclude it with a summary of Samson Loveridge's character from the pen of one who knew him, perhaps, even better than he knew himself.

"Like the majority of us"—writes Mr. Cecil Blount, "poor Samson was a curious mixture of good and evil, and if in his case the latter appeared to predominate, it should be remembered that, during his childhood, he was brought into daily contact with people who would be considered by the 'unco guid,' if not by the great mass of respectable Philistinism, to have been little better than thieves and outlaws. He was devoted, body and soul, to his master's interests, could be trusted with any amount of money, and was out and away the best travelling servant I ever came across—in fact, throughout the whole of our travels, he officiated as paymaster to our entire satisfaction. He possessed a queer, magpie-like habit of picking up odd scraps of information, a retentive memory, a natural aptitude for acquiring a foreign *patois*, and a supply of chaff and *argot* at once cosmopolitan and inexhaustible."

"Old Sir George used to say that, for an Englishman, Loveridge was an excellent valet—which, coming from him, meant a good deal—and he was certainly one of the best men on a rough horse I ever remember to have seen. He had all the personal vanity and admiration for fine clothes, horses, etc., which characterise his race, and being utterly devoid of what we are accustomed to term 'principle'—an expression, the meaning of which it would be almost impossible to convey to a Gipsy—he was continually getting into scrapes which a less mercurially disposed individual would have experienced but little difficulty in avoiding."

And now, having furnished a brief explanation of the circumstances under which these Recollections have found their way into print, and afforded some sort of clue to the character and antecedents of the author, I will leave No. 747 to tell his own story after his own fashion.

July, 1890.—F. W. CAREW,
    Braunton Tracey,
        N. Devon.

CHAPTER II.

A Fair Start.

WHEN I was nineteen or twenty years of age and apprenticed to Sellars and Sons of Westport, I could run any distance, from one mile to five, as well as here and there one, and for two years I held the long-distance championship of the West of England against all comers, but, practice and train as I would, I was never any good at sprint-races. This was owing, not to any real deficiency in pace, but to my being a bad beginner. In long-distance races, as often as not, we started by mutual consent and there was always plenty of time to get the steam up, but when it came to jumping off the mark at the crack of a pistol, I was all abroad 'like a dog at a fair, looking seven ways for Sunday'—as my friend and trainer Joe Barton used ruefully to remark—and now, although in the present instance I am aware that the same excuse scarcely holds good, inasmuch as I have a long journey before me, my old infirmity still seems to cling to me like a burr to a homespun jacket,—the words trip glibly enough from my tongue when the fire is roaring up the chimney and I have a glass in my hand, but when it comes to writing them down in cold blood it is quite another matter, and at the end of a week I am no further advanced upon my journey than I was at the beginning of it.

When I was quite a youngster and travelling with my

people and some of the Locks in Gloucestershire, I very well remember being sent out with some of the other *chavvies* to *lel* some *pawni** from a spring near the camp, and being told that the shallow runlet near Ullen Farm was the beginning of the great river Thames, but it was not until many years after that I happened to cross London Bridge for the first time, and as I looked down at the mighty tide rushing between the piers, I couldn't help wondering whether any of the foul and sewage-tainted water had really come from the little spring far away among the Cotswolds. And now, towards the end of a not uneventful career, in which it has been my lot to traverse the shady as well as the sunny side of life's highway, I find it as difficult to carry my thoughts back to any given period of my childhood, as for the current of a river, swollen and discoloured with heavy storms and the pollution of great cities, to identify itself with the pure and limpid waters of the mountain spring from which it takes its source.

So much by way of preliminary canter, and now in order to make a real start, I will state that, at the earliest period to which I am able to refer with any certainty, my name was Samson Loveridge—Sammy for short—and that I was proud of it. For we Loveridges had gained a reputation in the West Country not only for our ability to inflict, but for our readiness to endure, the severest physical punishment whenever—as continually happened—we were called upon to tackle a rough customer at sight—qualities which secured for us a comparative immunity from molestation at the race-meetings, *velgoroos*,† and gatherings of a similar nature which we attended in the regular course of our business.

Like all the other *chavvies* I was a dark-eyed, brown-skinned, wiry young shaver, rough and hardy as an Exmoor pony, and with about as much conception of the abstract principles of right and wrong as a fox-cub. I possessed, however, one advantage over the latter quadruped, inasmuch as I was well aware that it was unadvisable to annex the game or poultry of our more immediate neighbours—an imaginary radius of from ten to fifteen miles being the limit within

---

* Children to fetch some water—all Gipsy words which occur in this work are spelled phonetically.—ED.

† Fairs.

which expediency imposed a certain amount of restraint upon our naturally predatory instincts.

It was always a word and a blow with all of us, young and old, male and—I regret to say—female, but it was the best possible training for the rough life we led, and as my poor, dear, old *Poori-dye* * used to chant:—"We aint *kaired o'goodlo* nor yet *o'lon*, and a tough skin carries the sway when we're *oprey* the *drom*."† In these days things were very different with us to what they are at the present time, I can assure you, and although ninepence may go as far now in buying food as a shilling did then, a man could make a couple of pounds a week by hard work where he wouldn't earn fifteen shillings now. The *tem* was not so *moolo*,‡ for there was always some sport or another going on, racing had still a firm grip of the West of England, prize-fighting shared the popular favour with cock-fighting, wrestling, and single-stick, waste lands and *chichikeni dromior* § abounded, and if you chose to pitch your tent upon the strip of greensward by the high-road and *hatch adoi* ‖ for a month, there was no one to say you 'Nay'—provided only that the lord of the manor stood your friend. They tell me that things are very different now,¶ and that I might travel from Bristol to Bodmin without meeting half-a-dozen true-bred, black old Romanys. When I was a lad, a country-town that couldn't boast of an annual race-meeting was accounted a very one-horse place indeed, and at Bridgwater, Barnstaple, Dulverton, Exeter, Taunton, Tiverton, South Molton, and twenty other small towns that I could mention, both during the race-week as well as at the large cattle and hiring-fairs, there was generally a 'turn-up' before the company separated, and the squires and farmers were always ready to put their pieces on my uncles Neptune or Sylvester, or on Tenny Klism, Perin, or young

---

* Grandmother.
† "We ain't made of sugar nor yet of salt, and a tough skin carries the sway when we're upon the road."   ‡ Country was not so dead-alive.
§ Grassy lanes leading nowhere in particular.   ‖ Stop there.
¶ Owing to the daily increasing vigilance of the Rural Police, consequent upon successive outbreaks of *pleuro-pneumonia*, it is a hard matter nowadays for a 'traveller' to find a resting-place for the sole of his foot in the West of England. Most of the Smiths from Cornwall sailed for New York in July, 1886, whither they had been preceded by many of the Stanleys and Coopers. The fruitless endeavours of the so-called Greek Gipsies to reach the promised land of America, affords another instance of the great Westward migration.

Vester, whenever either one of them took off his shirt and put up his hands within the magic circle against stout Tom Padley—afterwards guard of the 'Flying Times'—Thady Sullivan, the *Hindity Crink*,* iron-armed Jack Cabbage, or last, but not least, quick-tempered but warm-hearted Charley Hicks, the highflier,†—Plymouth Charley, as we used to call him—who enjoyed the reputation of being the cleverest light-weight in the West of England.

Charley was a *posh-rawt*,‡ one of the half-scrag, and made a pretty fair livelihood by hawking fish and rabbits about the small towns and villages. He was married to Selina Smith, youngest daughter of old Launcelot Smith of Barnstaple, and travelled the country with a light, two-wheeled trap—a regular poacher's mail-cart—drawn by a raw-boned, Roman-nosed 'flying dromedary' that could do his fifteen miles an hour when warmed up. In order to enable him to put the steam on downhill when carrying a bit of contraband and, consequently, in a hurry, he had invented a patent skid consisting of a piece of board about eighteen inches long, which hung from the back of the trap by a couple of short ropes—like a child's swing—and just trailed on the ground, and when he came to a steep pitch, he would hand Lina the reins, drop the break overboard, and lowering himself from the back of the trap, would take his stand upon the plank without slackening speed.

I have only to shut my eyes to see them as they used to come swinging down Hangman's Hill at the rate of twelve miles an hour, enveloped in a cloud of dust, Lina's black curls flying wildly in the breeze, the reins hanging loose on the old roan's back, and Charley skating behind and steadying himself by holding on to the tail-board of the trap, and as his keen, hard-set mug comes back to me I instinctively look down at the knuckles of my right hand, where three small, white scars show up, clear and distinct, through the brown skin. I will endeavour to tell the story of how I acquired these not dishonourable wounds, and if in its narration I relapse, now and again, into the old familiar way of speaking, I must crave your indulgence.§

 * * * * * *

 * Irish tinker. † Hawker. ‡ Half-blood.
 § In this and many other instances I have exercised my editorial prerogative in omitting some irrelevant anecdote, description, or reminiscence.—ED.

A FAIR START.

And now I must get back again to my family affairs, for talking about fighting always warms my old blood like a glass of port-wine, and, when once started, my tongue runs away with me like Billy Allen's blind pony. I have already stated that my name is Samson Loveridge, and that I was proud of my *cognomen*, but I may add that I was no less proud of my *prenomen*—for Samson, I must tell you, was an old family name. There had been Samsons who had been *nashado*,* Samsons who had been *bitchered pawdle*,† Samsons, in fact, who, in unconscious imitation of their illustrious namesake, had most of them made it a point of honour to die in their boots. My great-grandfather—the last Samson of our family in the direct line previous to my appearance on the scene—had terminated a somewhat chequered career by hanging himself in the lock-up at Winchester, in obedience to the impulse which prompts those of our blood who find themselves laid by the heels without hope of escape, to spare their relations the disgrace attendant upon death at the hands of the public executioner.‡

His fate was comparatively fresh in my memory, for my grandmother, old Charlotte Loveridge, could recollect travelling up from Brighton—where she had been staying with some of the Lees near the *Beng's choomba* or Devil's Dyke—for the express purpose of attending his trial. My ill-fated progenitor was by profession a *vafro-luvvumengro*, or 'smasher,' of the first water, and there were very few sections of the statutes relating to the "making, counterfeiting, tendering, uttering, or putting-off, of false or counterfeit coin," or to the "impairing, diminishing, or lightening of the King's current gold and silver coin," that my great-grandfather had not infringed. At shortening, sallying, trucking, gladdering—to descend from gentle Romnimus to base-born Kennick §—shoful-pitching, fawney-rigging, and the thousand and one ingenious little devices whereby the impecunious endeavour to augment their

---

* Hung.   † Transported.

‡ A connection by marriage of Loveridge's committed suicide in gaol in February, 1880, and another Gipsy of my acquaintance not only made a desperate attempt upon his own life under similar circumstances, but tore his wounds open after they had been sewn up by the surgeon. In both cases their relatives gave precisely the same explanation of their conduct.—ED.

§ A mixture of flash-patter and padding-ken talk—whence the name.

balances at their bankers', he was—as Passon Mark would have said—*facile princeps*, and in the course of a long and useful career he managed in his humble, unpretentious way to compile a record which, due allowance being made for the necessarily restricted sphere of his operations—would have borne comparison with some of the noblest conceptions of such past-masters of the craft as James Saward the 'Penman,' Ned Agar, or Charles of peaceful memory.

Had he confined himself to these comparatively harmless pursuits, he might have attained a patriarchal age—for my family, when not interfered with, were long-lived, as a rule—and, perhaps, like old Launcelot Smith, have died a churchwarden, but, unfortunately for himself, he was of an open and confiding disposition—though violent in his cups—and after a successful operation would betake himself to the nearest tavern, to which he was easily traced by the minions of the law.

It was at Winchester that, after a little commercial transaction—known among 'travellers' as 'trucking,' and simple enough, in all conscience, to the initiated—by means of which he had acquired some thirty 'hog,' or shillings, a pound of tea, two ounces of snuff, and half a pound of tobacco, at a comparatively trifling outlay, he had sought the seclusion of the Travellers' Rest—a public lodging-house, or pratting-ken, on the Southampton Road. Although naturally—as I have remarked—of an unsuspicious and peaceable disposition, and fond of children, the scarlet waistcoat of a Bow Street runner had invariably the effect of exciting his deeper feelings. To use my Granny's words:—"The old man was along of Sore-tailed Jack S——,* *ta lescro pal Mingo, a' peein' tatti-pawni sims dyescro tood.*† Suddenly the *Lullo-bengrees*,‡ who had been following them for days and had tracked them to Winchester, burst open the door and ran in upon them like the slow-going, true-scenting bloodhounds they were. "*De vauvere, Mingo ta lescro pal, sus moolo motto, awer Sam hoktered oprey*

* Old Jack S—— gained a precarious livelihood by attending fairs, race-meetings, etc., and allowing anyone to have three cuts at him with a stout cane for the moderate charge of one penny. Hence the *soubriquet*. His younger brother Mingo made a large fortune by coining, and his grandchildren received a college education.

† "And his brother Mingo, drinking brandy like milk." ‡ Red waistcoats.

ta dias de rawtfelo dikkimengro atoot yuv's sherro posh o yogengri saster. Moolerdas ajaw o Nashimescro, ta teero chuvveno Bauropooro-dad nasherdas yuv's kokero pa lescro menpangooshi kat o stardisko hev."

Old Charlotte used to relate this stirring episode of the family history with all the pride of a Highland crone telling her grandchildren how their forbears had fallen, covered with wounds and glory, as they charged the English bayonets at Culloden, and, to tell the truth, I had always been accustomed to regard my great-grandfather in the light of a very ill-used individual—such, I suppose, is the force of habit and early association.

* * * * * *

My name then, as I have already stated more than once, is Samson Loveridge, and I believe I was born in the little village of Renton, near the University town of Camford—not that it very much matters—where my father, William Loveridge, was foreman to Sitwell, the well-known horse-dealer. Sitwell—as I have heard my uncle Plato say—had picked him up at Barnet Fair, where he happened to see him take a rough four-year-old, bare-backed and with nothing to steer him but a halter, over a locked gate into a field, and back again into the road over a stiffish fence with a ditch on the landing side.

My father was quick enough to seize the opportunity of bettering himself—it would have been well for me if I had inherited his sound common-sense—and relinquishing the precarious avocation of small coper and colt-breaker for the regular employment which luck had thrown in his way, he quickly rose from rough-rider and under-strapper to breaksman and head-groom, until, at length, he became Sitwell's foreman with a comfortable salary.

In addition to being a naturally steady and respectable man, my father, like most of his family, could put up his hands when occasion required—qualities which, when combined, seldom fail to command respect. No class of the community is more quick to take the measure of a man's

---

* "The others, Mingo and his brother, were dead drunk, but Sam jumped up and hit the inspector over the head with the poker. So the Runner died, and your poor great-grandfather hung himself with his neckcloth to the window-bar of the lock-up."

foot than the whole tribe of outdoor and indoor servants, and when they find that he really means business and not only knows, himself, how things ought to be done, but *will* have them done that way and no other, after a few grumbles they settle down to their work and everything goes smoothly—but the moment they find that they can shirk their work or take a liberty, there is no more to be done with them, and they cease to be of any good either to themselves or to anybody else.

All the secrets of the swell dealer's stable were as an open book to one who, like my father, had from a boy been initiated into the darker mysteries of the professional coper. Although such operations as jipping,* nerving, bishoping, powdering a *nok*,† 'setting' a *bavol-gry* ‡ or 'bull-tit,' quieting down the too exuberant spirits of a *delemescro* § by 'loading' him with laudanum, sharpening up a stale old doghorse by the introduction of half-a-dozen small but lively eels into his internal economy, or even the surreptitious subcaudal insertion of a fid of the best Jamaica ginger, were not openly encouraged in Sitwell's establishment, yet he well knew that if there happened to be a screw loose in an otherwise faultless and high-priced hunter, he might safely trust my father not only to divert the customer's attention from the weak spot—wherein lieth the secret of successful horse-dealing—but at the same time to show off all the good qualities which the animal might really possess. Some customers take a deal of persuading, while others are best left to themselves, and a foreman who in his master's absence can tell when to talk and when to hold his tongue, keeps himself sober and respectable, and sees that his horses are turned out as they should be, is not to be picked up every day in the week, and, when found, is worth keeping.

Sitwell, himself, was a spare-built, long-waisted man of about five-foot nine, with a slight stoop, a pale, thickly-freckled face, foxy whiskers, and a pretty leg for a boot. The son of a small tenant-farmer in Kildare, he served his

---

*Staining a pair of suspicious knees or a bare place with Indian-ink to conceal a blemish. Every coper carries a 'stick of jip'—which can be bought at any wholesale stationer's—in his waistcoat pocket. The end of the stick is dipped in water and it is then ready for use. It has the advantage of not coming off on the would-be purchaser's fingers, like blacking does.

† Glandered horse. ‡ Roarer. § Kicker.

apprenticeship between the flags in his native country, and crossing St. George's Channel upon his father's death, soon acquired a rather questionable notoriety. Being qualified as a 'gentleman,' he did most of the dirty work for one or two well-known stables, never objecting to being put up on a 'wrong-'un,' and when his mount, after starting a hot favourite, walked in with the crowd amidst the execrations of its infuriated backers, Tom would gaze calmly round upon the sea of threatening, upturned faces—a trifle pale, perhaps, but bland and confident as ever—and if he happened to get a bit roughly handled before he gained the sanctuary of the weighing-room, he would make his appearance an hour later upon the steps of the Grand Stand, an enormous cigar between his lips and an expensive hot-house flower in his button-hole.

When he *was* put up on a good thing, his appearance in the pigskin had usually the desired effect of stalling off the general public, but when business was meant, mind you, and the money was right, there were few better men than Tom Sitwell either over the jumps or on the level. As so frequently happens, however, he never did himself much good at the game, and finding that he was neither getting any shorter in the tooth or narrower at the girth, and that he was no longer able to lay the razor quite so close, a lucky inspiration caused him to abandon the Turf for the neatly-plaited straw-edgings and red sand of the dealer's yard.

Starting with some half-dozen horses, in a few years he rose to the top of the tree and purchased a large business at Camford. He was generally to be found at the principal sales in London and the provinces, leaning back against the auctioneer's box, his thumbs hooked into the armholes of his waistcoat, one leg carelessly thrown across the other, his well-brushed hat tilted over his eyes, tooth-pick in mouth, and the inevitable flower in his button-hole, descanting volubly and in an apparently unprejudiced manner upon the manifold imperfections—real or imaginary—of some horse that he had come there on purpose to buy, and for which, needless to say, he had put in an outsider to bid. A past-master of the great art of 'crabbing,' he soon became the terror of the proprietors of the provincial Repositories, who knew that his ready tongue would soon knock the gilt off the gingerbread unless they made things pleasant for him.

I can just remember my father as he used to ride over whenever he had a couple of hours to spare, to the cottage which he rented for my mother about two miles out of Camford. I can just recall his dark, handsome face and supple, well-knit figure which the close-fitting stable-jacket, cord breeches, and well-cleaned boots and spurs set off to advantage. He would generally be mounted on some square-shaped, weight-carrying brown or lengthy, well-bred chestnut, showing all the bloom and polish for which Sitwell's horses were noted and for which none knew better than himself how to charge. The reins seemed to be lying loosely upon the horse's neck, and I used to wonder how it was that the great, powerful animals, so full of beans and courage, who always looked ready to jump out of their glossy skins at the least sound or movement, did not take advantage of his apparent negligence, and it was not until some years later that I found out what a firm seat and good hands could accomplish. It was my delight to be taken up in front of him, and my mother would stand at the cottage door and watch us as we walked or cantered along the strip of turf by the side of the road. They say that 'what is bred in the bone will out in the flesh,' and I certainly felt none of the nervousness which most children exhibit when they first exchange the rocking-horse for the genuine article, and I used to shout with delight when my dad would feel his horse's mouth, touching him at the same time with his heel, and causing the high-couraged animal to progress sideways with a delicious dancing motion, or to jump across the shallow gutters by the roadside with as much fuss and importance as if he were about to charge sixteen feet of open water.

CHAPTER III.

I Lose my Father and Start with my Mother for Devonshire.

MY mother's maiden name was Chilcott, and her family had long enjoyed a reputation for wealth and good looks among the wandering tribes of the Eastern counties, being all of them—men and women—tall, handsome people as you would wish to see. Her brothers, Harry, Wenty, and Obi, used to travel the district round Ipswich and Colchester along with the Shores, who were, taken all round, bigger and heavier than the Chilcotts, but not so good-looking.

Larry Shore—uncle of Jack Shore of Norwich—was considered at that time to be the best man of all the 'travellers' in England. He was a burly, black-whiskered, rough-looking chap, standing six-foot four in his boots, and weighing close on sixteen stone. He used to wear his long, curly, black hair nearly down to his shoulders, and when he fought, it had of course to come off, and being—like my namesake—very proud of it, the idea of losing it used to make him perfectly miserable. There he would sit in front of his tent, while his wife enacted the part of Delilah, and as the long locks fell to the ground he would whimper out:—"Oh dear! Oh dear! Just *dick* the *rinkeni bals*,* I do declare I must have a cry"— and cry he would, like any girl—especially if he had taken a glass—but when he tossed his hat into the ring and took his shirt off, the crying was mostly on the other side.

As I was saying, my uncles Harry, Wenty, and Obi, used to travel the Eastern counties playing the fiddle at gentlemen's residences, for they were the best Romany *bosh-killi-mengros*† in the country—playing either by ear or heart, as

* "Oh dear! Oh dear! Just look at the pretty curls."
† Fiddle-players.

we say. They had plenty of money and good clothes and never did any work to speak of, but wore handsome gold chains and rings, and when the girls went to a Gipsy *kelloben*,* they were dressed up to the nines in their silks and their satins—for all the world like quality folk. Their tents were seven or eight feet high, square shaped, with chairs and tables in them like a house—for the old people would often remain in one place for two or three months at a time, while their sons travelled the country with their wives and families. When, in the summer-time, they *hatched* their *tans*† in the neighbourhood of Camford, many were the carefully-attired young gentlemen who rode or walked out in the direction of the camp on the chance of exchanging a word or two with the handsome Chilcott girls —and I can assure you that the handsome Chilcott girls were quite capable of taking precious good care of their handsome selves.

One of the young gentlemen—Mr. Louis L'Estrange, the youngest son of Sir Pierre L'Estrange of Netherleigh Court, in the county of Devon—went further than the others, and abandoning all prospects of distinction at the University, entreated my mother over and over again to marry him— being willing to sacrifice his future prospects and risk his family's displeasure for love of dark-eyed Lelinda Chilcott. My mother, like a sensible woman, did not give him any encouragement. In the first place she didn't care for *Gorgios*, beyond exchanging a bit of chaff with them now and then and accepting any little presents they might be foolish enough to offer her, and in the second place she was engaged to my father at the time, and only waiting for a rise in his salary to marry him. The worst of it was that the more she laughed at her admirer, the madder and madder it made him, and when, at last, my mother went away with her people on one of their regular trading-tours, the infatuated young man left his college without leave and followed them from place to place, vowing that no one should marry her but himself.

Upon being informed by the Dean of St. Saviour's of his son's escapade, Sir Pierre left Netherleigh and posted up to Windsor—near which town the Chilcotts were encamped

* Ball.   † Pitched their tents.

on their way to Ascot races. The old gentleman had, no doubt, expected to find that my mother had been attempting to entrap his youngest son into a disgraceful marriage, and when he discovered the real state of the case, he was not only most grateful to her for her conduct throughout the affair, but was much struck with her quiet manners and good looks.

The L'Estranges were Roman Catholics, and Sir Pierre, anticipating some difficulty, had taken the precaution of bringing with him his household chaplain, who possessed more influence over the headstrong young man than anybody else. In the course of a stormy interview the two, between them, succeeded in bringing him to his senses, and, shortly afterwards, young Mr. L'Estrange was sent out to learn the management of an estate which Sir Pierre owned in Demerara, where he fell a victim to that scourge of our West Indian possessions, the Yellow-fever. How much of this story is correct, I have no means of judging, but I give it for what it is worth, just as I have always heard it told.

I should not have mentioned this little episode but for the fact that, upon the poor young gentleman's death, a will was found by which he bequeathed all his personal property and effects—which, after satisfying his creditors, amounted to some four or five hundred pounds—to my mother. His eldest brother, Mr. George L'Estrange, who was appointed executor, kindly offered to invest the money for her, and his offer being gratefully accepted, the incident formed a sort of connecting link between our humble fortunes and those of the L'Estranges of Netherleigh.

*   *   *   *   *   *

When I was about nine years old, my poor father died in hospital from the effects of internal injuries received several months previously while schooling a young horse, and my mother and I were left to face the world alone. I was scarcely of an age to appreciate to its full extent the magnitude of the misfortune which had befallen me, but my mother suffered terribly, and for some time after the sad event it seemed doubtful whether the shock might not permanently affect her reason. She took no notice of the neighbours who, in their homely way, looked in to volunteer assistance and express their sympathy, or of my boyish attempts at consolation, but would sit, silent and motionless, for hours together, refusing to take any nourishment or retire to rest.

A few nights after my father's death, being restless and unable to sleep—for I, too, was much affected, my childish grief finding easy vent in copious floods of tears—I crept, barefooted and in silence, down the steep, narrow staircase, and gently pushing open the door at the foot of the stairs, peeped into the parlour. Not a sound broke the perfect stillness of the summer night. Even the kitchen clock, neglected in the general grief, had ceased to tick, the only signs of life being shown by the cat, who lay crouched upon the dresser and glared at me with his fierce emerald eyes—aggrieved, apparently, at the unexpected interruption of his nocturnal sport. The mellow light of the harvest moon shining through the tiny diamond-shaped panes of the heavy lattice, traced an intricate diagram upon the broad stone flags, which, in turn, was rendered blurred and confused by the weirdly-working shadows cast by the trailing shoots of the monthly roses, which overhung the window and swayed to and fro in the night breeze. My mother sat perfectly motionless by the hearth in one of the two wooden armchairs which the cottage boasted. Her eyes were fixed with a vacant, lack-lustre gaze upon the dying embers, and her clear-cut features, refined by grief and fasting, as they showed up in strong relief against the pitchy darkness of the deep ingle-nook, seemed to my excited fancy to belong to an inhabitant of another and a purer world. Fearing to disturb her and experiencing a curious, half-guilty sort of feeling at having intruded upon her sorrow, I crept quietly back to bed and was soon asleep—but that scene is one of two which are inseparably connected in my mind with the name of mother. The other I shall come to soon enough.

The following morning her father, old Noah Chilcott, with his wife, daughters, and numerous belongings, arrived at Renton, and in the course of the next day some twenty or thirty Gipsy families—chiefly relations and friends of my father's—had pitched their tents upon the common to the no small consternation of the villagers. Upon the day appointed for the funeral, the body, dressed in a dark-green cloth hunting-coat, with breeches, boots, and spurs, was placed in a handsome coffin, and brought out from Camford to Renton in a hearse with white ostrich plumes, followed by two mourning coaches and a large number of people on foot, many of whom were, no doubt, urged by motives of curiosity. Upon reaching the cottage the coffin was taken out of the hearse, and carried to the churchyard by six men —amongst whom were my uncles Arno and Phineas, who lived not far off—wearing white silk hatbands, and white gloves. My mother's two unmarried sisters followed in one of the coaches, both dressed in white muslin, wearing long white veils, and carrying large posies of white flowers in their hands.

I believe that the people separated quietly after the burial, but, to tell the truth, I don't recollect very much about it. All I know is that some of my cousins, the Locks —who were a rough lot and had been drinking—came to blows with my mother's brothers, because old Noah Chilcott wouldn't allow them to make a bonfire of the cottage furniture upon the common. The old people—who were really well-to-do and who were credited by the country-people with the possession of fabulous hoards of golden guineas and silver plate stored away in stockings, crocks, tea-kettles, and similar receptacles—were delighted to find that their youngest daughter was not likely to prove a burden to them, and as she was determined to leave the cottage with a view to visiting her late husband's kinsfolk in Devonshire, they at once instituted a sale of the furniture and effects, and advised her to invest some of her money in the purchase of a *cuvva-bickenin' vardo*, or trading-van.

My mother, although prostrated for the time being by the shock of her husband's death, was a sensible woman enough, and taking her father's advice, purchased a *vardo**
and proceeded to lay in a good supply of the fancy-baskets, feather-brushes, mats, brooms, etc., which form the usual stock-in-trade of the travelling fraternity, and one fine morning we started on our long journey. The bustle and excitement of preparation had the effect of bracing her nerves and raising her spirits, and her fine constitution soon shook off the effects of the trial she had undergone.

* Van.

We had with us a *posh-rawt*, or half-breed, named Jesse Brown—a whitesmith by trade—and his wife. They accompanied us in their light cart drawn by an active pony, and, besides them, there was old Lisha Chilcott, a poverty-stricken relative of my mother's who was always glad of a job, and who led and looked after the van-horse and was supposed to make himself generally useful—and if the possession of a practical and comprehensive acquaintance with the relative strength of the malt-liquor retailed at the various *levinor-kers* * along the line of march, combined with a laudable anxiety to extend the scope of his investigations in that particular direction, even at the risk of some personal inconvenience, be accepted as a criterion of general utility, then old Lisha's services should indeed have proved invaluable.

Of course all this was a great change for me, for I had been attending the parish school for the last two or three years, and had it not been for my poor father's death, which altered all our plans, I should probably have been apprenticed to the village butcher, baker, or candlestick-maker, and have ended by marrying some cook or housemaid who had saved up a little money, and setting up an opposition establishment over the way. As it was, I need scarcely say that I was mad with excitement at the prospect of leading the real life of the road for the first time, and that I trotted along by Lisha's side much too proud to think of riding in the van, but long before we had got clear of the narrow country lanes and had struck into the great Western highway, I was lying fast asleep with blistered feet in the narrow bunk which formed my resting-place, thoroughly tired out with the unaccustomed exercise.

I can just remember that, on reaching the borders of Wiltshire, we were stopped by some constables who wanted to see our *slangs*,† and who proceeded to overhaul our belongings on the pretext of searching for some property which had been stolen from a neighbouring country-house, and that, near Chippenham, Lisha surprised two tramps in the act of robbing the van. My mother and I had gone into the town with Jesse Brown to try and sell some fancy-baskets, leaving the camp in charge of Lisha and Mrs.

---

* Ale-houses. † Hawker's licence.

Brown. It appeared that, as soon as our backs were turned, the old fellow made tracks as usual for the nearest *kitchema,** and having subjected the contents of the beer-engine to a pretty exhaustive analysis, was leisurely retracing his steps, when he was startled by the sound of screams proceeding from the direction of the camp. Full of beer and courage, he hurried back and found poor Mrs. Brown engaged in a rough-and-tumble upon the catch-as-catch-can principle with a sturdy tramp, while another of the same breed was busily engaged in ransacking the van. Lacking the gift vouchsafed his namesake of prophetic celebrity, he snatched up the *kekauviski-saster,*† which happened to be lying handy, and incontinently broke the head of tramp number one—felling him to the ground where Mrs. Brown who, judging from her physical conformation, appeared to have been specially designed by Nature to play the part of letter-weight, sat upon him severely.

Flushed with victory and armed with his formidable weapon, the old chap mounted the steps of the *vardo* with a view to ejecting tramp number two, but the rascal, alarmed at the defeat of his companion, lowered his bullet head and charged straight at the venerable Lisha—taking him just below the belt and causing him to execute a complete somersault backwards. By the time the old man—somewhat sobered by his involuntary gymnastics—had succeeded in collecting his scattered faculties and the small-change which had escaped from his breeches-pockets, the thieves had decamped, and Mrs. Brown, who in the meanwhile had been rather roughly handled, was feeling her face to make sure that her nose was still there.

Ah me! Shall I ever forget 'the days when we went Gipsying, a long time ago'? A long, long time ago in good truth it was, reckoning by the almanack, but it seems only yesterday that I was travelling the green West-country lanes. Shall I ever forget how we children, after wandering about the livelong day picking *kaulo-durrilor,*‡ and coming back with our hands and faces stained a rich blackish purple with the acrid juice, would be sent out again to collect kindling-wood for the fire? How we would creep into the hollow hedges and drag out the dried sticks and bramble-stems

---

* Public-house. † Kettle-iron. ‡ Black-berries.

until we had collected a goodly pile of brushwood, and how we would bind it together with a long, straggling, ragged-thorned briar-shoot, and tow it behind us down the dusty road to the *yoggin-tan** under the big oak-tree.

How, when our elders were clustering round the camp-fire, intent on supper, and the big watchman-beetles went droning by through the twilight with erratic flight, we would sneak away up the road, and mounting old Polly-count-the-milestones or China-eye, two or three together, would trot the long-suffering animals up and down the strip of greensward by the roadside, until the gruff voice of Neptune bade us desist, or fierce old Vester—dropping down on us like a blue-hawk on a nide of pheasant-chicks—would make his whip-lash curl round our bare legs, turning our rejoicing to lamentation, and causing us to fly for sanctuary to the shelter of Charlotte's tent.

How, when left in charge of the camp, we youngsters, arrayed in well-ventilated garments and shapeless felt hats two or three sizes too large for us, would produce our cherished fragments of clay pipe-stems, and strut up and down the road in front of the tents with a ludicrous assumption of self-importance, pausing, every now and again, to practice some new hornpipe step or double-shuffle, until, perchance, the sight of some well-dressed *Gorgio* would send us scurrying off intent upon the acquisition of stray *posheros*.†

But least of all shall I forget those frosty winter evenings when we used to snuggle together for warmth like a litter of puppies—for, as often as not, we slept under the *vardo* with nothing between us and the *shillo chick* ‡ but an old horse-rug, and, perhaps, a bit of sail-cloth stretched from wheel to wheel to keep off the wind—and listen to the heavy footfall of the men who had just returned from *poovin'* the *gryor*,§ and who, with legs swathed in hay-bands, were pacing up and down the road to assure themselves that there were no

---

* Camping-place—properly a place where fires are lit.
† Half-pence.   ‡ Cold earth.
§ Turning the horses out to grass—an operation usually performed at the expense of a neighbouring farmer. A padlocked gate is lifted off its hinges, and the horses turned in to graze until daylight, when they are driven out into the high-road before the farm labourers come to work.

baulos * abroad. They were a rough handful, some of them, and if a constable chose to be nasty instead of pocketing his *tringorooshi* † like a sensible chap, it was a chance if he didn't get a stone up against his head in some lonely lane of a dark night.

But the worst time for sleeping on the ground was about the last week in March or the first week in April—especially if you happened to be camped by the roadside between some old stone walls. You would be lying awake, perhaps, and you would hear a queer sort of hoarse, wickering, croaking noise all round you, and presently something chilly and slimy would flop up against your bare feet and give you the cold shivers—and then you would guess that the toads were on the march. If you poked your head out from under the canvas screen, you would see the ugly grey and brown-mottled brutes come hopping along the road in the moonlight two by two like the animals going into the ark, and carrying on all sorts of games—for they had just left their holes where they had been sleeping all the winter, and were off to spawn in the pools, and if you happened to be on their line of march they would come hopping, flopping, and sprawling over you, without as much as 'with your leave' or 'by your leave.' This would go on every night for about a week, and as soon as it was daylight we used to turn out and kill them by the score—for, you see, we didn't know any better—and folks passing by to market and seeing the bodies lying in the dusty road would wonder where on earth they all came from.

Although it is getting on for forty years since I was on the road, and although, since then, I have visited foreign countries and seen strange sights, the dank, fresh smell of decaying autumn leaves, a thin wreath of blue smoke curling up from a wood-fire, a tattered rag fluttering from a briar, a litter of freshly-cut shavings, a handful of grass carelessly thrown down by the way-side, or a roughly-executed cross traced with the finger in the dust at the cross-roads—the Loveridge *patteran* ‡—is sufficient to set my old heart a'beating, and brings back to my recollection many a long-forgotten incident of my far-away childhood.

* Swine—synonym for constable. † Shilling—three groats.
‡ A private 'sign' to show the stragglers which way to take.

CHAPTER IV.

I Make the acquaintance of some of my Relations.

WHEN we reached the steep hills, well-wooded valleys, green water-meadows, and softly gliding streams which form the amphitheatre in the centre of which the old town of Exeter is situated, we were met according to agreement by my uncle Plato Loveridge, and under his guidance we skirted the spurs of Exmoor, and crossing Cranmoor near Cranhead, struck the high-road which traverses the whole length of the Cran valley, amidst the northernmost recesses of which lies Netherleigh Combe, the head-quarters of my father's people when in Devonshire.

My uncle Plato was the second brother—Neptune being the eldest, Sylvester the third, Arno the fourth, Phineas the fifth, and my father the youngest. Arno and Phineas had married two sisters, and lived close to the river somewhere between Staines and Hampton. In the winter they mended chairs and wove baskets, while in the summer they attended the race-meetings in the Metropolitan district, travelling down to Kent for the *levinengrin'** in the autumn. They never came down Devonshire way, and were not considered to be much of a credit to the family, for besides marrying a couple of *pawno-moois*,† they were continually in hot-water, and were always sending to my father to borrow money to pay their fines—which, to do him justice, he never refused as long as he had it to give.

Plato was a powerfully-built man of about 40 years of age, slightly marked with the *boogones*.‡ A broad-brimmed hat —in the band of which was stuck the bright-coloured eye of a peacock's feather—overshadowed his rather handsome features, which were tanned to the colour of mahogany, and there was a general air of devil-may-care good-humour and

---

* Hop-picking. † White-faces—Gentiles. ‡ Small-pox.

rollicking swagger about him, which, with the merry twinkle of his dark eyes, combined to give the lie direct to the firmly moulded lines of the mouth and chin, and made him a universal favourite. He wore a bird's-eye neckerchief, a close-fitting cutaway coat with broad, stoutly-stitched seams, and an old pair of moleskin breeches and leather gaiters, while a characteristic finish was given to his costume by a pair of enormous silver-plated spurs with formidable rowels. He carried a dealer's brass-mounted, gut-and-whalebone whip, and bestriding a clever crop-eared cob with a wall-eye and hogged mane, he drove before him a couple of cart-colts that he had just purchased from a neighbouring farmer.

My uncle was the legitimate *gryengro** of the family, and carried on a thriving trade throughout the Western counties. Beginning life, like my father, as horse-breaker, rough-rider, and hanger-on at fairs and race-meetings, by the exercise of his shrewd wits he had gradually worked his way upward until he found himself in a position to start as a licensed horse-dealer, and it is only fair to state that he had maintained a reputation for straightforward dealing and integrity which had become almost proverbial, and which proved the best possible advertisement to him in his profession. If a farmer or tradesman required a cart-mare or nag-horse to run in a light van, he would go to Plato in preference to any of the small local dealers—for my uncle, being a good judge and always on the look-out, had the advantage of buying in the cheapest market and could afford to sell a useful animal at a fair price. He owned a small farm with a few acres of pasture-land near Bridgwater, from which place, as a centre, he travelled from fair to fair, buying principally three, four, and five-year-old cart and nag-horses, and sometimes supplying the Government agents with remounts for the cavalry.

Before he purchased the farm at Bridgwater he used to travel the country with his van and, perhaps, a dozen horses or so, worth from fifteen to fifty pounds apiece, and whenever a farmer, with whom he was in the habit of dealing, required a horse, Plato would call at his place and say:—
"I've got something here that's worth your buying. The price is so much. I'll leave him till I call round again in

* Horse-dealer.

two or three weeks time, and if he don't suit you I'll take him away or change him." The arrangement suited both parties, for the purchaser got a fair trial, and Plato would take any brute, however vicious or unsound—at a price—in part exchange, while, on the other hand, the farmer would allow him to turn his van and horses into a field at night, and supplied him with firewood and water.

His van, which was built in Plymouth, was considered to be the best on the road, and beat all the Leeds-made *vardos* to fits. It cost a hundred and forty pounds with nothing in it but the stove, and, when fully furnished, must have been worth close on three hundred. It was just like a piece of cabinet-work, without a knot in it from floor to roof, with the best of *sways** and carriage under-works. The doors, sashes, and fittings, were of polished mahogany, and the bracket-boards were ornamented with figures of St. George and the dragon carved in solid wood.

Although a shrewd, steady fellow in the main, Plato had his little weaknesses like the rest of us—a love of display being one of them—and late in the evening, after a big fair, I have seen him stand two or three pint pots on the table in front of him at a *levinor-ker*, and fill them to the brim with gold pieces.

"There," he would say, "there's a *peeaben* fit for a *kraulis*,† and I could fill half-a-dozen more if I had a mind. If you don't believe it, just step up the lane as far as my *vardo*, and I'll show you"—and it was no idle boast, although a foolish one, for he must have been worth some hundreds of pounds before he gave up travelling, and he made a sight of money afterwards.

Sylvester, the third brother, was also a *gryengro*, and, in partnership with his eldest brother Neptune, owned the ten or a dozen horses that were generally to be seen grazing in the neighbourhood of the camp or following the *vardos* to the different fairs. Unlike most of his brothers, Sylvester was a small man, but his pluck, good looks, and high spirits—which latter were continually getting him into trouble, especially after a successful cope—more than compensated for his want of inches. He was also a skilful smith and, on occasions, a desperate fighter, in both of which he was

* Springs. † "Drink fit for a king."

closely imitated by his eldest son—'young Vester,' as we called him.

My uncle Sylvester was deeply versed in all the mysteries of the coping craft, and, unlike his steady-going brother Plato, he not only trusted to Art to supply the deficiencies of Nature and repair the ravages of time and disease, but made the mistake of openly boasting of his ability to deceive the wariest customer.

If, for instance—as was frequently the case—he invested in a couple of dog-horses at knackers' prices—one a 'whid,' or *bavol*,* the other, we'll say, a chink-backed 'un—he would keep them on soft food for a few weeks, and after making them up and grooming them until they looked as fat and sleek in their coats as a couple of *poovo-baulor*,† he would send them into Exeter or some large country town on a fair or market-day. Here they would be led up and down the market-place or outside some Repository where a sale was taking place, 'on the drag,' ‡ by a very praiseworthy imitation of an unsophisticated chawbacon—their manes and tails neatly plaited with red and blue ribbons.

For the time being they were the property of Farmer Buckstraw, lately deceased, whose widow was anxious to dispose of them at any price as she was giving up the farm. Crafty old Vester never appeared on the scene until the last act, but directed operations from the tap-room of some neighbouring public-house, whither his dusky satellites brought him 'the latest' every now and again. After the intending purchaser had examined the good-looking but worthless brutes to his satisfaction, handling them all over, running them up and down, and giving them the orthodox punch in the ribs—for the bull-tit had been carefully 'set,' and the chink-backed 'un would go sound enough until subjected to the test of backing a load down-hill—the small, dark-complexioned man who represented Widow Buckstraw's bailiff would emerge from his lurking-place, and after a protracted bargaining—in the course of which he gradually allowed himself to be beaten down until he appeared to have considerably the worst of the deal—would pocket the greasy notes with much shaking of head and solemn asseveration

---

* Broken-winded horse. † Moles.
‡ On the off-chance of attracting the attention of a purchaser.

that "he really didn't know how he should face the poor missus with such a starvation price as that, and she a widder and most heart-broke"—with a good deal more to the same effect. Then my uncle and his pals would proceed to wet their luck, and that night there would be a *bauro chingaree** in camp, the probability being that on the following Friday most of the party would be charged with being drunk and allowing their horses to stray on the high-road—and by the time the heads had been plastered up and the fines paid, there wasn't much catch in it, as steady-going Plato was wont to observe.

When we came in sight of Fernleigh Combe, where the camp was pitched, young Vester—who came sprinting across the common at his best pace—was the first to greet us. He was as fair a sample of a young Rom'nichal of the full-blood as you would meet in a day's march, but his good looks were rather marred by the sullenness of his expression, and by a trick he had of glowering at a stranger, when spoken to, from beneath his bent eyebrows. His dark, close-cropped head was bare, a faded old *dockeri stook* † was loosely knotted round his throat, and he wore a long-sleeved waistcoat of shabby plush which had once been dark blue, with a double row of silver buttons shaped like horse-shoes—which had come to him through his mother, and of which he was very proud—tight-fitting cord trousers, and a pair of well-greased, heavily-nailed *chokkors*.‡ The carelessly tied neckerchief, long-flapped waistcoat, and heavy boots, gave him at first sight a rather loutish appearance, but, when stripped to run or fight, his supple, well-proportioned figure, combined with the free play of the muscles beneath the brown skin, would have delighted a sculptor, and had already been the means of enabling him to turn an honest penny by posing as model to wandering artists. That morning, as he came running to meet us, he might have been about seventeen years of age, and weighed under twelve stone, but when I saw him strip to fight his great battle in the Hurst, he stood five-foot-ten in his fighting-boots and weighed exactly thirteen-stone-four.

Although a good-tempered young chap in the main, he was subject to periodical outbreaks of temper, and while

* Free fight. † Yellow neckerchief. ‡ Boots.

these fits lasted, he would leave the camp and stay away for three or four days, which was, perhaps, about the wisest thing he could have done under the circumstances. He was very fond of the company of sporting men, and no sooner did he contrive to make a bit of money by hard work than he was certain to lose it in the toss-ring or betting at the races.

However, although a bit wild, he must have had his own peculiar notions of right and wrong, as the following anecdote shows. About three years after our arrival in Devonshire, a young chap named Matt Orchard came down from the Black Country to stay with his uncles—who generally travelled with us. He was about as desperate a young ruffian as ever I came across. If a constable collared him, he would flash his *churi** at him, as lief as not, and having been brought up in Birmingham, he was up to every fakement from 'trucking' to house-breaking. For some reason or another—possibly because my poor mother kept me dressed more tidily than the other boys, and I therefore suited his purpose better—Matt honoured me with his confidence, and for some time we carried on a very pretty little game unsuspected.

Before leaving Birmingham he had laid in a large stock of imitation-gold pins, the heads of which were made to resemble half-guinea pieces, and which cost about four shillings a gross, wholesale. When staying near a large market-town or fashionable watering-place, we would stick a dozen of these pins inside our waistcoats, and slipping out of camp, would loaf about some well-frequented thoroughfare in the suburbs until we saw a young farmer, well-to-do tradesman, or flashily dressed clerk coming along. Then we would take one of the pins, smear it with road-dirt, and running after our victim, would say:—"Pleas'sir, I d' think as this be yourn. We picked un up jest arter you 'd a' passed by."

Sometimes they would say:—"Well, my lad, this doesn't belong to me, but here's something for your honesty," sometimes they would give us three or four shillings for our find, and, sometimes,—such is the baseness of human nature—they would stick to it and tell us to go to the devil—a piece of advice which, in our case, was altogether superfluous. Of

* Knife.

course we had to shift our pitch and be careful not to try it on with the same party twice over, but it was a very pretty little game while it lasted, and we managed, on an average, to get rid of a dozen pins every week, and lived like *kooroboshnos* * on the proceeds.

However, we got spotted at last at Plymouth by one of those extra-clever gents who seem to find a pleasure in exposing the little foibles and weaknesses of their fellow-creatures. We were taking our ease at an inn in the suburbs of Devonport, and the *hanlo* † had just brought in a beef-steak fizzing hot from the gridiron and a quart of cider, when who should walk in but a military-looking gentleman followed by a *gav-moosh*. ‡

"You'll have to come along of me"—says the latter.

"What for, old lad-o-vax?"—says Matt, as bold as brass.

"'Taining money under false pertences"—answers the *baulo*, and he lays hold of Matt, tears his waistcoat open, and *latchers* the *busahor*.§ Matt reaches for the knife, but thinks better of it, and says he—"All right, Master, I'll go along o' you. Guv'nor"—to the landlord—"jest put that there steak by the kitchen-fire to warm. We'll be back in a brace of shakes."

So we goes before the *beshermengro*,‖ but, Lor' bless you, they couldn't do nothing to us, and they lets us go with a caution. When we gets outside, who should be waiting for us across the street but Vester? "Sammy"—he says to me, "*vel kerri langs mande*,¶ and as for you Matt, I'll have a word with you present."

Matt makes a face at him and slinks off to finish the steak all by himself, while I goes along of Vester—very much against my inclination. Well, he never as much as *cherrups* a *lav*,** but as soon as ever we gets outside the town, he sets to and gives me such a leathering as I never had before nor since.

"What's that for?" I blubbers out, for I was took quite aback. Vester he looks most as puzzled as I was—then he says, short-like, in a half surly, half shamefaced sort of a way:—"*Teero dad se moolo*" ††—and marches off with me

---

* Fighting-cocks. † Landlord. ‡ Constable. § Finds the pins.
‖ Stipendiary. ¶ "Come home along of me."
** Gives me a hint. †† "Your father is dead."

trotting after him like a little dog with its tail between its legs.

Although I failed, at the moment, to trace the precise connection between my father's death and the hiding I was getting, in course of time it gradually dawned on me, and I have no doubt that his well-meant attempt to keep me straight has been placed to the credit side of Vester's account.

  *   *   *   *   *   *

To return to our first meeting with our relations. As we turned off the high-road into the deeply-indented, wheel-marked track which led to the Combe, we were met by my uncle Neptune—the *sherengro*, or head-man of the tribe—who accompanied us to the camp and introduced us to the rest of the company. In addition to my uncles Neptune and Sylvester Loveridge with their respective wives Meralda and Triphi, there were *tannin'** in the Combe at the time of our arrival several of the Orchards, with their wives and families, two or three of the Burtons, Wisdom Boswell—a brother of old Charlotte's—with his wife Lucretia and his daughter Lementina, and a *churdo*, or half-breed, named Ned Stokes, a basket-maker by trade—but 'travellers' kept coming and going, staying a longer or shorter time as suited their convenience.

My uncle Neptune was a wiry, hard-bitten customer of about eight and forty, rather taller than his brother Plato, but not so heavily built, and looking less than his real height by reason of the slight stoop which so often becomes habitual to men whose occupations compel them to be constantly scrutinising the surface of the ground or the eddies of the running stream. He walked with long, springy strides, lifting his feet well off the ground at every step, his gait being altogether different to the rollicking, bow-legged swagger of burly Plato, or to the short, game-cocky strut of uncle Vester—and when one is lying in a tent, with one's ear close to the ground of a still night, one precious soon learns to distinguish between the measured footsteps of a *prastramengro*† and those of a pal, and, sometimes, it makes just all the difference. His unusually

---

* Tenting—camping.   † Policeman.

swarthy skin was burnt almost black from continual exposure to sun and wind, and he was not only of a darker complexion than his brothers, but a far 'deeper' Romany, and seemed almost to belong to another, and elder, generation. He was always holding up to derision the 'gorgeous' habits of the younger members of the community, and in common with his mother—old Charlotte Loveridge—and Wisdom Boswell, observed all the customs and traditions of our race.

In bad weather he would occupy himself in making and repairing his nets—and of these selfsame nets I shall have more to say later on.

There were plenty of otters in the Cran and its tributaries, which worked backward and forward from the distant springs of Cranhead to the tidal waters above Blackstow, and for these artful customers he would invent all sorts of pleasant little surprises. When they refused to enter the traps cunningly set at their landing-places just below the water-line, he would find out their favourite runs through the rushy 'bottoms' and thick scrub which bordered the river bank. Selecting a run which had the appearance of being well used, he would set a trap in the middle of it, and having covered it lightly over with leaves and mould, would place an old log across it—taking care, however, not to spring it during the operation. If it had not been for the log, the otter would have smelt the trap directly, but being compelled to raise his head in order to clear the obstruction, his keen sense of smell was effectually baffled. In the course of a day or two all taint had disappeared from the trap, and the log having been removed and placed across the run about a foot further on, the odds were that the next time the wily *matchinesko-jooko jessed dovo drom*,* he put one or both of his forelegs right into the *chauro* of the *tilomangri* † as he took-off to jump the log. The skins were cleaned and pegged out on boards, and when he had accumulated a sufficient quantity, he used to take them to the furriers at Bristol, where they fetched good prices.

With the exception of old Jasper Lee, the King of the Ratcatchers, my uncle Neptune was allowed to be the best trapper in the West of England, and used to contract to

---

* Otter came that way. † Plate of the trap.

kill down the rabbits on gentlemen's estates—as I shall have occasion to relate. He also supplied a couple of firms of whip-makers in Birmingham and London with yew and holly sticks, for which he received about sixpence apiece—the whips, when finished, selling at from ten shillings to a pound. When we were travelling about the country we were always on the look-out for likely sticks, and when they were felling timber Neptune used to *tipper* a *posh-korauna* to the *vesh-dikkimengro*,* and ask leave to take a look round to see if he could find a stick or two, and in this way—especially in Monmouthshire—he would often run against as many as a gross or two of nice yews and hollies. The wood-reeve had, of course, no business to allow him to take them, but as soon as we cut them, we used to shave a piece off the stub and also off the butt of the stick, so that it couldn't be replaced and identified.

But it was chiefly as a fisherman that he excelled. Like the others, he knew every submerged stump, rock, and hole in the river-bed from Cranhead to Blackstow, as well as the best natural bait for every day in the year—which he varied according to the weather and the state of the water—and if the hotel-keeper at Netherton required a nice dish of trout for some gentleman to take home with him just to show his friends what good sport he had been having, or a farmer sent word that he wanted a few for his missus who was ailing, they could always depend upon Neptune's bringing them up to the hotel or *givengro-ker* † next morning. I was never much of a fisherman myself, possessing neither the skill or the patience which the gentle art demands, but, as a boy, I was very fond of accompanying my uncle when he started up the river for a day's fishing.

When bent on one of these expeditions the old man—for he seemed very, very old to me, although scarcely past the prime of life—was always in the best of humours, and I had little difficulty in persuading him to relate his choicest stories of bygone smuggling and poaching expeditions intermingled with legends and *goodlis* ‡ couched in *poorodirest Romnimus*.§ I have only to close my eyes to see him now, as, sitting bolt upright, his back comfortably supported by the trunk of a

---

* Give half-a-crown to the wood-reeve.
† Farm-house.   ‡ Tales.   § Old-fashioned Romany.

wide-spreading oak which sheltered us from the blistering rays of the noonday sun, a jar of cider securely resting within the haven of his outstretched legs, he would place his short, black *swaegler** between his white teeth and proceed to fill it with exasperating deliberation, while I—an idle young shaver some ten or twelve years of age—lay stretched, face-downwards, at full length upon the rush-grown turf, my chin resting upon the upturned palms of my hands, and my eyes fixed with a look of eager anticipation on my uncle's swarthy visage.

He always insisted upon my dressing myself tidily whenever I accompanied him upon one of these expeditions, as we often came across some of the gentlefolk out for a day's fishing, and for this purpose he had presented me with an old tweed jacket and waistcoat—the gift of one of the sportsmen aforesaid, and much too small for either of my cousins—which, needless to say, I almost invariably forgot to put on. On such occasions—especially if it so happened that his supply of cider or tobacco was beginning to run short—he would pitch into me like one o'clock.

"*Shoonta tu, tawno bengalin!*"—he would growl. "*Soskey tu kek na rivessa dulla heesior savi mande diom tukey? Kek man pookerova tute kekni goodlior, t'sorlo. Bostramenga! Prast an sig kater tan, chiv lende oprey, ta an meero bauro, toovalesko-gunno ta pord oprey dovo panbengreski vellin!*" †

"*Parraco chavvi*" ‡—he would grunt, upon my return with the jar of cider and tobacco-pouch—the latter a present from his friend and patron the vicar of Netherleigh—and having taken a prolonged pull at the former, restoring it to its old resting-place with a deep sigh of satisfaction, and having replenished his pipe, he would perhaps proceed to relate how his father, Teerus Loveridge, when innocently taking a short-cut across Netherleigh Chase upon a certain rough night late in October, had been attacked by a savage stag. How, for upwards of an hour, he had successfully dodged the brute round a giant oak, whose branchless,

---

* Pipe.

† Listen, you young imp! Why don't you wear those clothes I gave you? I sha'n't tell you any stories this morning. Look alive, now! Run to the camp as quick as you can, put them on, and bring my big tobacco-pouch and fill up that cider-jar!"

‡ "Thank you, my child."

lightning-riven trunk and gnarled bark studded with hundreds of iron nails upon which successive generations of keepers had been in the habit of impaling the bodies of the vermin they had trapped, offered no hold for hand or foot, while the startled hinds, flitting phantom-like through the driving mist, hovered around and gazed wonderingly, with necks and ears outstretched, at the unwonted spectacle. How, at last, the stag had caught and pinned him against the rough bark, lacerating his ribs and tearing the very shirt from his back. How the resolute Gipsy had seized the savage brute by the horns, and drawing his clasp-knife, which he managed to open with his teeth, had stabbed him again and again in the neck until they fell, locked together in the death struggle—the stag never to rise again. How my grandfather had been picked up insensible the following morning by one of the keepers. How, strange to relate, a sack containing some two dozen dead rabbits had been found not far from the scene of action, and how, when taken before Sir Geoffrey L'Estrange, that good sportsman had presented him with a guinea to salve his bruises, advising him, however, at the same time, to steer clear of the chase for the future lest worse might befall him.

With story after story—related in language better suited to my comprehension than the 'deep' Romany which the old people were in the habit of using amongst themselves—he would beguile the long summer afternoon, until, just on the edge of night, the trout began to rise. Then, picking up his rod, he would glide, otter-like, into the stream, and wading thigh-deep and casting with practised hand, would jerk out trout after trout on to the bank behind, where I waited ready to disengage them from the hook.

His heaviest baskets were always made by using the grubs which we *chavvies* dug out of the wasps' nests which abounded in the dry banks. These he used to boil in milk to make them tough, picking them out of the comb as he required them, and in this state they would keep for a long time. Sometimes he would be out all day attending on gentlemen and watching them thrash away till their backs ached, while he smoked his pipe on the bank, and as soon as they had given it up as a bad job and he had pocketed his half-crown, he would commence operations on his own account, for "*hatch* till the *dood vels oprey**" was his motto—a regular old fly-by-night was Neptune. Having previously ground-baited two or three likely holes where the bank had been partially washed away by the winter floods, leaving an eddy or backwater, he would commence to fish with the grubs about eleven o'clock at night, when the trout had done rising at the fly, and would go on fishing until daybreak, invariably returning with a heavy basket.

For five years I sat—a ragged but attentive disciple—at the feet of this dusky Gamaliel, and when, very much against my inclination, I once more became a *kerengro*,† I had a hard job, indeed, to break myself of the habits I had thus unconsciously acquired.

CHAPTER V.

Fernleigh Combe.

FERNLEIGH COMBE, the head-quarters of our tribe when in Devonshire, is a secluded glen running at right-angles to, and opening out of, the broader valley of the Cran. It is effectually sheltered from the north-westerly gales which come roaring in from the Atlantic, by the extensive range of hills known as Brent Downs, while, to the south, it overlooks the sandy, bracken-covered wastes of Fernleigh Common, across which runs the high-road leading from the market-town of Netherton to the little fishing-village and harbour of Blackstow.

* "Wait till the moon rises." † House-dweller.

The common is bounded by the rapid waters of the Cran which, rising far away amidst the granite tors and peaty, moss-grown hags of Cranhead, during the lapse of centuries has scooped and honey-combed for itself a channel through the rocky strata of Cranmoor, chafing and foaming with impotent rage at every rock and boulder which bars its downward progress, leaping impetuously from ledge to ledge, and imitating and reproducing in its headlong career the boiling waves, eddying whirlpools, and foaming cataracts of a thousand miniature Niagaras. On leaving the moor and entering the valley—the precipitous sides of which are clothed with a dense growth of tough-leaved oak, silvery hazel, and holly beloved of woodcock—it is joined by its tributary the Nym, which mingles its peat-stained current with the clearer waters of the parent stream just above the hamlet of Cranmeet.

Fernleigh Common—as I have endeavoured to explain—is bounded by the river, and on the further, or southern, bank the ground rises abruptly to the height of two hundred feet or more. Upon the brow of the hill, towering above the undulating screen of variegated foliage which clothes its slopes, the west front and terraces of Netherleigh Court—the seat of Sir George L'Estrange—stand boldly out and appear, when viewed from opposite, almost to overhang the river bed. The reader, if he perseveres, will in due course be introduced to the inmates of the Court, but, for the time being, he must, perforce, be content with the society of humbler folk.

Let us follow the footpath along the river bank until we come to Netherleigh Bridge, with its massive lichen-covered buttresses of grey, weather-worn stone, and its three ivy-crowned arches. Leaving it on our right, we cross the high-road and take a short-cut across the rabbit-burrowed expanse of Fernleigh Common, where three or four donkeys and ten or a dozen horses are grazing in charge of a couple of dark-eyed, bare-footed *chavvies*. Tossing them a copper in response to their reiterated applications for a *poshero*, we turn to the left, and striking a wheel-marked track across the turf, follow it until it enters a narrow valley which, penetrating to the very back-bone of Brent Downs, eventually leads to the hamlets of

Buckland—where the lighthouse now stands—and Loxhoe, perched upon the verge of the cliffs which overhang the Bristol Channel.

The roadway—worn and washed by rain and storm and covered with loose stones—rises at a steep gradient as we advance, and is forced to twist and turn in order to avoid the slabs of rock which threaten to bar the path. To right and left the sides of the valley slope abruptly upwards, the sunlight being intercepted by the overarching branches of the straggling birches, oaks, and ash-trees, which root and run up like weeds in the rich but shallow leaf-mould. Above the narrow belt of vegetation the grey limestone crops out at irregular intervals, rearing its jagged crests along the whole length of the valley, and cutting the blue vault of heaven with its fantastic outlines. Here, in marked contrast to the spindly growth below, the yews spread and cluster in bushy tumps, while, far above, to right and left, the moor stretches away in a long succession of illusive skylines.

The Combe is the favourite resort of holiday-makers from Netherton, and at about half a mile from its entrance there stands a pretty, rustic cottage with bark-covered arbours lined with moss, inhabited by an old couple who are permitted by Sir George to retail tea, ginger-beer, and suchlike non-intoxicating beverages to the factory-hands and other visitors who drive out in cruelty-vans from the town. About a mile beyond the cottage one side of the valley has been quarried away, leaving an open space, or plateau, which has been used as a camping-place by successive generations of Loveridges, Burtons, and Orchards. About half a mile, again, beyond the camp, the road bifurcates, one branch—little more than a bridle-path—leading across the moor to Blackstow by a short-cut, while the other takes you past Blackrocks—a rough face of limestone where the yew-trees grow thickly and overhang the roadway—to Buckland Point, Loxhoe, and Brent Head.

The camp itself scarcely requires more than a passing word of description. Half-a-dozen vans, as many tents, pony-carts laden with sail-cloth screens and *koshters* for the cocoa-nut pitches, harness stowed away beneath the vans and carts, lurchers coiled up among the harness, tattered garments hung out to dry and rags fluttering from the bushes, circles of charred ashes, cocks and hens scratching about, a tame *kakaratchi** pecking at the *chavvies' nango-herrees*,† a film of blue smoke curling upwards from a couple of camp-fires, wood-shavings, scraps of white-metal, and wisps of straw *ad libitum* littering the ground—fill in the outlines of men, women, and children according to your fancy, and the picture is sufficiently complete for our purpose.

The scene is picturesque or commonplace according to the idiosyncrasy of the spectator, and the history of each individual round the camp-fire is correspondingly interesting or the reverse. I have already introduced you to some of the party, but there are others here whose stories might well point a moral although they may be scarcely calculated to adorn a tale. Take, for instance, that little black-complexioned, small-pox-pitted man—Black George, as he is called—with the closely-cropped iron-grey hair, who is sitting cross-legged in front of his tent, busily occupied in cutting skewers. His brother committed suicide in Exeter gaol while awaiting his trial on a charge of murder, and he, himself, was strongly suspected of being an accomplice. He could tell you, if he were so minded, as curious a story of treachery, jealousy, and revenge, as ever inspired a Corsican vendetta, with a woman at the bottom of it, as usual—in the eyes of the world as sordid and cold-blooded a murder as ever found a record in the pages of the Newgate Calendar.

Take again that woman who is sitting with her back towards us, and who, from her attitude, is apparently nursing a baby. If you will cross to the other side of the fire you will see that—to use the stereotyped novelistic formula—her features still bear traces of considerable beauty, that her dark eyes have a vacant, lack-lustre expression, that her long hair is plentifully streaked with grey, and that she is crooning to herself as she rocks to and fro something which, upon a closer inspection, looks uncommonly like a bundle of rags. The name she goes by is Sabina Burton, and her history—what is known of it, at least—would furnish ample material for a Transpontine melodrama. I will give you the outline, as before, and you can fill in the details for yourself.

* Magpie.   † Naked legs.

She is a strong-limbed, fine-figured woman, thirty-seven years of age, with a careworn face almost entirely devoid of expression and only redeemed from positive plainness by the splendid teeth, eyes, and hair, but twenty years ago she was considered to be the handsomest *Romani chi** in the West of England. At that time the Burtons were in the habit of passing the winter in Devonshire, their regular camping-ground being a wood belonging to Squire N———l of Battiscombe Park—a fine estate upon the shores of one of those estuaries which contribute so much towards the beauty of the South Coast. Squire N———l was a good-looking, pleasure-loving man of about eight and thirty, who had retired from the Guards with the rank of Colonel, and owned two of the smartest yachts—one a racer, the other a cruiser—of the R.Y.S. The rest of the family consisted of his mother—a stately, hard-featured dame, with silvery-grey hair, a crutch-handled stick, and a slight limp—and a younger brother who still held a commission in one of the Guards' regiments.

The first part of the story is easily told. The Squire is struck by Sabina's beauty, and the silly girl is flattered by his admiration. One fine day he takes her out for a sail in the yacht's boat, and the next that is heard of her is that she is living in London with carriages, horses, fine dresses, and jewellery, to her heart's content. In the spring of the following year they visit Paris, and in the autumn they travel up to Scotland, staying, amongst other places, in Edinburgh and Inverness, where—as was afterwards proved by the hotel-books—they pass as man and wife. Squire N———l rented a shooting on an island off the West Coast, and one of his yachts was always stationed there in readiness to take the party backwards and forwards to the mainland.

One dark night the yacht's boat got stove-in against the landing-stage. A strong tide was running and the Squire's body was never found, but Sabina and two of the sailors managed to cling to the piles and were eventually rescued. The captain of the yacht—acting, no doubt, under instructions—refused to give Sabina a passage back to England, but allowed her to take whatever she claimed in the way of

---

* Gipsy girl.

money and jewellery, and put her ashore at the nearest village, from whence she started on foot to Inverness.

As bad luck would have it she fell in with some Scotch Gipsy-tinkers—Nokkums as they call themselves, a mongrel breed—who robbed her of every farthing she possessed and otherwise maltreated her. She eventually reached Inverness in a pitiable condition, with scarcely a rag to *gaver* her *nangipen*, and here, to make matters worse, she gave birth to a male child. Some charitable people interested themselves in her case, and as soon as she was sufficiently recovered to take the road, they paid her coach-fare to the English border, from whence she started off on her long tramp to Devonshire, where she rejoined her friends,—and a precious hard time she had of it, I can tell you.

This, you would think, ought to have been about enough for one woman, but here the curious part of Bina's story commences. A pettifogging lawyer in Plymouth happens to overhear some of the gossip about the poor gentleman who was drowned, drives out to the camp, interviews Sabina, ferrets out all the particulars, gives it as his opinion that the child is heir to the Battiscombe estates according to the Scotch law—there had been some talk of a marriage before a blacksmith, jumping over a broomstick, or suchlike, the details of which I disremember—and offers to take up her case on speculation. Then what does the silly thing do but tramp off to Battiscombe, ring the front-door bell, and ask to see Dame N———l, under the impression—mistaken as it proved—that the old lady would receive her grandchild with open arms.

The result of that interview will never be known, for Bina and the child disappeared without leaving the slightest trace behind them. No search was made for her at first, as her people supposed that she had fallen in with some relations and gone off on the tramp, and it was some months before they began to realise that she was lost—the general impression being that she had committed suicide. The matter formed a nine days' wonder, and when the facts of the case became known, the tide of public opinion set strongly against Dame N———l, for having—as was supposed—spoken harshly to the poor girl and driven her to the rash act.

In course of time the affair was forgotten, but several years after, maybe eight or ten, old Harry Orchard—Longsnout, as we call him—was camped in Little Boy's Lane, about nine miles from P——, on his way to the September Fair. Not a quarter of a mile from the camp, and close to the high-road, there stood—and stands now, for the matter of that—a great, rambling, square-shaped block of buildings, something between a cavalry-barrack and a farm-house, where unfortunate creatures whom God had deprived of reason were put away. It was shut in on all four sides by a belt of trees, the windows were closely barred, and there was a general atmosphere of damp and gloom about the place which gave one the cold-creeps even on the finest summer day, while an occasional yell—half laugh, half scream—proceeding from one of the quadrangles in the interior of the buildings where the more violent patients were exercised, only served to intensify the feeling of melancholy which oppressed the beholder.

The madhouse had a bad name, and if you chose to believe half that the neighbouring cottagers told you, it must have deserved it. Some years subsequent to the date to which I am referring, the Commissioners refused to renew the license, the result being that the establishment was broken up and the buildings—for which no other use could be found—allowed to go to ruin.

When I was a youngster and camping with my people in Little Boy's Lane, I well remember exploring the gloomy buildings with some of the other *chavvies*. The flagged quadrangles were overrun with weeds, the rats squeaked and skirmished behind the wainscots, and the swallows darted in and out through the broken panes of the iron-barred windows. The padded-room, where the leather hangings had been torn down from the walls and the stuffing lay in mouldering heaps upon the floor, caused a delicious sensation of half-terrified anticipation to pervade our childish minds, and the excitement culminated with the discovery of several broken plaster casts of the heads of patients, taken after death, which strewed the floor of what had been the laboratory. One especially—a gigantic head of nearly twice the ordinary size, with a low, retreating forehead, blubber lips like a negro's, and ears sticking out at right-angles to the skull—I shall never forget, if I live to be a hundred. It was cracked in two, but we put the pieces in an old handkerchief and stole back to the camp.

As it happened, my *poori-dye* *—old Charlotte Loveridge—had gone off to a neighbouring village that morning in her little donkey-cart with her niece Lementina Boswell. Well, cousin Vester, he takes and sticks the head together, and stains the face dark, and blacks the hair and eyebrows and wkiskers, just like a regular old tinker. Then he bores a hole in the mouth and sticks a *swaegler* † in it, and jams an old *stadge*,‡ that we had picked up off a dust-heap, tight onto the head. Then he dresses up a figure in a waistcoat and an old pair of breeches, and lays it on my Granny's mattress in her tent, and covers it half over with her blankets. When the old lady came back that evening and went to her tent to shake up her mattress after supper, you could have heard her screams half way to P——. First she swore that the *pooro Beng* § was in her bed, and then she declared it was Black Pat, the mush-faker from Cork, drunk and snoring fit to bring the tent down, but when she found out the truth, she told Lementina to put the harness on her donkey, "she wasn't going to stop with a lot of nasty, low, mumping *churdos*" ‖ and the rest of it—such a row you never heard.

To return to Longsnout. I should mention that we used often to meet the male patients straggling along the roads in single file in charge of an attendant, but the women were always exercised in a large grass paddock surrounded by a high quickset hedge, in front of the Doctor's house. Well, as Harry was passing this field in his *vardo* the day after the Fair, a poor creature clambered over the gate in the hedge, and rushing up to where he was stood in the road, clung to him for protection. As you may imagine, old Longsnout—the respectable father of a family—was taken a bit aback, but he was fairly flabbergasted when the woman began to *rokker* Romany, but before she had time to say more than half-a-dozen words, the female attendants came up and tried to drag her away. But the more they pulled, the tighter she clung to Harry, and in the meanwhile Sinfi, seeing her husband in the arms of a female lunatic, gets out of the *vardo*,

* Grandmother. † Pipe. ‡ Hat. § Old Devil.
‖ Half-breeds—mongrels.

and in spite of the alterations which confinement had effected in her appearance, identifies the stranger as Sabina Burton, whose mysterious disappearance had created such a sensation in South Devon about ten years previously.

Then Doctor C—— comes up and explains that the poor woman—whom he calls Eliza Froud—had more than once tried to escape, and eventually Sabina is handed over to the attendants.

To make a long story short, as soon as they get back to Devonshire, Harry Orchard tells the Burtons what had happened, and within a month Pharoah—Bina's eldest brother—pitches his camp in Little Boy's Lane. In addition to the *vardo* he has with him a light tax-cart with a fast-trotting horse, and whenever the weather is fine, he takes the van along the road past the field where the women are being exercised, and loiters about in the hope of enticing his sister away.

For a week or more he carries on this game without any result, but one fine day, just as he was about to give it up as a bad job, he notices a commotion among the patients and a woman comes running across the field with a clear lead of some twenty yards or so. The female attendants are giving tongue like a pack of hounds as they follow, the lunatics are jabbering in a high state of excitement, and one of the gardeners—who is working in the Doctor's flower-garden and whose attention is attracted by the uproar—throws down his spade, and jumping the ha-ha, joins in the pursuit. Cutting off an angle of the field, he reaches the gate just as the poor, hunted creature tumbles over it, but Pharoah hits him 'Pom!' in the mouth and sends him to grass, lifts his sister into the tax-cart, and off they go at a gallop, leaving the boys to look after the *vardo*.

To the day of her death nobody knew the rights of Sabina's story, how she came to be placed in the private Lunatic Asylum, and who paid for her keep—for Doctor C—— was not the man to keep pauper patients. The fate of her child was never satisfactorily cleared up—many Gipsies will tell you that he is living now, and that they have met him—for her memory was a complete blank, but one curious thing Pharoah soon found out, and that was that she would walk ten miles round rather than cross a bridge—

especially near the sea, where the tide ran up. The only way to get her over was to put her inside the van, and there she would lie on the bed with her head muffled up in a shawl, hugging the rag-doll to her breast, and if there was no *vardo* to put her in, Pharoah used to bandage her eyes and lead her across—just the very same as you would put a restive horse into a railway-box. And that is as much as any 'traveller' can tell you of Sabina Burton's history—and enough too, I daresay you will think.

* * * * * *

To go back to my kinsfolk. When occasion served they were always ready to dance, drink, or fight with the best, and no class of the community knew better how to enjoy a thoroughly idle day. Upon a fine Sunday in summertime, like to-day, we used to turn out about six o'clock, and the men and boys would stroll down the Combe and across the common for a swim in the river. On these occasions there was generally some rather rough horse-play indulged in which, as often as not, ended in a fight. After disporting ourselves in the water, we used to run races on the bank to dry ourselves, our brown skins glistening in the sunshine while we made the valley echo with our shouts and laughter —greatly scandalising the holy fathers, one or two of whom were often to be seen at this early hour pacing with measured steps the trimly kept walks on the further side of the river.

For on the opposite bank of the Cran the grounds of Netherleigh Court sloped abruptly down to the water's edge, and towards the end of June were one mass of lilac and scarlet-coloured rhododendron blossoms. Along the well-gravelled walks which zig-zagged in and out among the dense masses of foliage, the priests—for not only the L'Estranges but the neighbouring families of Langrishe and Fazackerley were Roman Catholics, and the household chaplain at Netherleigh generally had a friend staying with him to help him with the services—loved to stroll, pausing, now and again, to admire the fragrant blooms as they expanded into fuller beauty beneath the glowing rays of the summer sun.

Sometimes the women would go down to the river to perform their ablutions—hidden from the inquisitive gaze of chance wayfarers across the common by the thick, scrubby undergrowth which clothed the steeply-shelving banks—and wash the family linen, and then, of course, the reverend gentlemen forsook the leafy groves and sought the seclusion of the chapel, passing the hours in pious meditation or stern religious exercises. At least we supposed so, and lynx-eyed old Granny Charlotte—who could never be induced to enter the water, but sat on the high bank smoking her pipe and making disparaging remarks anent the personal appearance of her female relatives—confirmed us in the supposition. Some of the younger and more irreverent of the party did, indeed, affirm—but why repeat the gossip so dear to female tongues, which, lurking like sting of asp behind the pearly teeth and smiling lips, is ever ready to dart forth and, with sublime impartiality, to destroy with subtly distilled venom the reputation of dearest friend or deadliest foe?

Returning to camp with that curious, indescribable feeling of mingled freshness and lassitude which usually follows a prolonged immersion in fresh water, we find our breakfast ready, and after that meal has been discussed, there is always plenty to be done. The horses have to be brought in from their feed, kept from straying, and their various ailments attended to. Tyres, spokes, and felleys, have to be 'faked up,' boots greased, firewood collected, water fetched, harness mended, and a thousand and one odd jobs attended to.

If we happened to be camped on a Sunday near some town or village where the clergyman of the parish was well known to us, one or two of the women might go to Church in the afternoon, while the patriarchs of the tribe, if the wind was chilly, would stretch a piece of sail-cloth across some *rans** stuck in the ground, and behind this temporary barricade they would crouch round the fire, occasionally peeping through the rents in the canvas at the sound of approaching footsteps, and criticising in no very friendly spirit the personal appearance and costume of the passers by.

"*Mi deari Doovel*,† I do sometimes wunner whatever we be a' comin' to!" exclaims old Teanni Boswell,—whose own head-dress resembles a Grenadier's busby flattened out and run to seed—as a good-looking, over-dressed servant-girl in all her Sunday bravery of broad-brimmed felt hat with

* Rods † "My dear Lord!"

drooping feather, tight kid-gloves, and imitation-gold locket, trips by in a hurry to meet the baker's young gentleman at the end of the lane, displaying a pair of undoubtedly useful, but somewhat elephantine, extremities as she daintily picks her way along the dusty road.

"*Dordi! Dordi! Dick lesti's peeris!** Reg'lar varmin 'starminaters I sh'ld call 'em"—chimes in sharp-eyed Beebee Oceana, spotting the weak point with the accuracy of a coping vet. "Lord 'elp the pore beetles when that pretty thing is about!"

With similar remarks and observations couched in an equally charitable vein, intermingled with despondent forebodings anent the *moolo*, or dead-alive, state of trade, and enlivened by professional reminiscences reflecting upon the gullability of mankind in general and of silly *gorgios* in particular, they would pass the afternoon pleasantly enough in unconscious imitation of their betters, while the girls and boys would play a game something between cricket and rounders—a couple of old hats placed about ten yards apart serving as wickets, into the crowns of which the bowlers endeavoured to pitch the ball,—and the young men and maidens of the tribe would start off on long nutting or black-berrying expeditions, making, the while, mental notes of the chief features of the surrounding country, especially with regard to its game-producing capabilities.

In the evening the men would stroll into the nearest town or village, where they discussed sport, trade, or local politics, and exchanged the gossip of fair and racecourse with the frequenters of the *kitchema* over a quart of cool ale, while the cunning dames, with eyes ever directed to the main chance, would allow themselves, under cover of the gathering gloom, to be coaxed into telling the fortunes of the credulous housemaids or factory girls. Many were the pieces of silver which found their way from the pockets of the foolish country wenches into the dusky palms of the reputed sorceresses on a fine Sunday evening, and if the poor, deluded creatures could only have understood the meaning of the jokes and laughter which circulated freely round the camp-fire at their expense, they would most assuredly have kept their hard-earned wages in their pockets.

* "There! There! Look at her feet!"

CHAPTER VI.

Under the Greenwood Tree.

IN those days—it must be remembered that I am speaking of close on fifty years ago—people were not so particular about giving leave to fish, and not only my uncle—who was in the habit of accompanying gentlemen and supplying them with flies, etc.,—but anybody who chose to leave his name at the head-keeper's cottage, was allowed to fish for trout in the Netherleigh water.

To my mind there are few pleasanter ways of passing a midsummer afternoon, than to lie idly stretched at full length, pipe in mouth, in the shade of a branching oak, watching the swifts as they skim the surface of the rippling stream, far too lazy even to get up and fling a stone at a water-hen who is paddling unsuspiciously within ten yards of our lurking-place. Save for 'the busy hum of insect-breathing life,' the voice of Nature is hushed in Netherleigh Chase.* The aristocratic red-deer, disdaining to associate with their plebeian relatives the broad-horned fallow bucks, are lying in small bands of from ten to twenty in the narrow rings of shadow cast by the elm-trees, in all the glory of sleek summer coats and velvety horns—perfectly motionless save for an occasional twitch or flick of ear or tail. An old hind, driven from the shelter of the tall ferns by the flies, trots mincingly across a sunlit glade—closely followed by her white-spotted calf—in search of cooler quarters. Even the

---

* Netherleigh Chase is described in old records as "a privileged place for receipt of deeres and beastes of the foreste," either by royal grant or—as is more likely—by immemorial usage. The "beastes of chase" are the "buck, doe, fox, marten, and roe." During the xviith century it was changed into a Park—still, however, retaining the old name—by enclosure with pales under a grant from the Crown. A chase, it may be explained, "is of a middle nature between a forest and a park, the chief difference being that it is not enclosed, fewer recognised officers belong to it, and it has no peculiar courts or laws."

few rabbits who have ventured above ground in quest of a breath of fresh air, seem loth to leave the shelter of the plantations, and sit listlessly within a yard or two of their holes, waiting until the evening dews shall have imparted a refreshing moisture to the sun-dried herbage. The only creatures seemingly endowed with the smallest particle of energy are three magnificent cock-pheasants who, as if aware that the hues of their burnished plumage derive additional lustre from the glancing rays, strut complacently to and fro in the very eye of the sun, and seem literally to revel in the tropical heat.

My uncle Neptune has dozed off to sleep with his pipe between his teeth, but being, myself, of a restless disposition and anxious for a story, I jerk a stone with a loud plash into the river. The effect is instantaneous.

"*Chavvi*"—says my uncle, waking with a start, " did *tute dick dovo matcho?* " *

"*Auvo kauko*"—I reply, looking preternaturally innocent, "*yur hoktered* the *vauver rikk, tuley* the *limmers.*"† Then as he proceeds mechanically to refill his pipe, I hand him a match and whine insinuatingly:—"*Pen mande* the *goodli* of *Josho Beshaley's moripen.*" ‡

Taking a preliminary pull at the cider-jar, my uncle settles his back comfortably against the tree, coaxes his pipe into full blast, and begins:—

"Well, then, *mi chavvi*, I'll tell you all about the *moripen*, and there's few knows the rights of it better nor me—'ceptin' them as done it—through my fust wife—your aunt Richenda as lies buried at Plymouth—bein' a Stanley of the ancientest breed, and cousin to poor Josho. You see, Josho were the lawful king of all the Rom'nichals in this here *tem* ontil they murdered him, and there ain't, not to say, no proper king now—although there's two or three as calls the'selves sich. They was lawfully crownded king and queen, him and his wife Rhody, by the Mayor o' Bath, for, you understan', he topped 'em all with his money—some thousands it were—but the next one come within a few hundreds of him. There was crowds of our people there for to see the crownation,

---

* " My boy, did you see that fish ? "
† " Yes, uncle, he rose the other side, under the bushes."
‡ " Tell me the story of the murder of Joshua Stanley."

bein' the First o' May, and they carried Josho and Rhody up and down the streets in two of them big baskets with handles to 'em,* all covered with flowers and ribbons."

"He'd got plenty of money, had Josho—bein' tarrible close at a bargain—and used to carry a tidyish bit of plate about in his *vardo*. Somehow or another it got winded about, and one mornin' just at the *sig* o' the *sala*,† as he were *hatchin'* near the corner of Beggar's Bush Lane, in Somersetshire, two chaps come up and forced the door open and held a loaded pistol to his head, and carried off every bit of it— silver tea-tray, teapot, jugs, spoons, and all. But Rhody, she *pallered* ‡ 'em unbeknownst right away to Bedminster, and when she sees 'em safely tiled down, she starts off for to fetch Mister Yetts, and they gets seven year apiece. *Tatcho's mi dad*." §

"Ah! he were as nice, Christian a sort of man as you need wish to meet, were Josho Beshaley, and carried on a big head a' horse-dealin'—takin' the sway right away from Bristol to the Land's End and back. He were a clever, knowledgable man with horses, and the best hand to *bishen* a *gry* ‖ as ever I see. There he'd sit with his file and his chisel, 'tick-tack! tick-tick!' and alter their tooth to any age so as to pass the farrier, and for fakin' a *nok* ¶ there never were his ekal. Yes, as I were a' sayin', he were as nice, Christian a sort of man as ever I knowd, and I shan't forget the turn it give me when I see the pore, dear King took out'er the water."

"We was down at Totnes Fair, your uncle Vester and me, and a lot more dealers. Josho had sold five or six horses and had a cheque for fifty pound and a bag of gold and silver in his pocket, and bein' a bit *boino*** after he'd had three or four quart, he didn't forget to flash it about— just the very 'dentical same as your uncle Plato. Amongst the others there was two men as we'll call M. S—— and B. C——,—that's near enough, for they're alive now,—both of 'em Romany dealers of the half-scrag. Now Josho had a fine grey horse there, as he'd refused a lot of money for, and they was tryin' to buy it of him, but they couldn't come

---

* Possibly sedan-chairs.　　† Day-break.　　‡ "Followed."
§ "As true as my father"—equivalent to "that's a fact."
‖ "Bishop a horse."　　¶ "Glandered horse."　　** "Boastful."

to no agreeability, and, at last, there was high words passed atween 'em."

"Presently, about ten o'clock, these two chaps gets up and walks out, and about half-an-hour later Josho says:—'I must be *jallin'*, *pals*'*—and we goes out and helps him onto his *kooshto roller*—for he were a bit top-heavy, though not to say *motto* †—and he rides off towards the bridge, while me and Vester and some half-a-dozen others, we stops to have another gallon."

"What do I mean by a *kooshto roller*? ‡ Well, it's like as this. If we was in a *kitchema* where there was a lot of Gorgios about and perhaps a constable as'd picked up a word or two of Romany, and I was arstin' you about a *gry* as had been *chored*, § I sh'ld say:—'*Chavvi* did *tute dick* the *vauver roller*? ‖ or, if it were a sheep as had been stolen, I sh'ld say 'the *vauver bokkra*,' instead of sayin' the *chordi gry* or the *chordi bokkra*,¶ so that nobody shouldn't understand what we was *rokkerin'* ** about. *Tatcho*,†† *mi chavvi*, that's deep travellin' talk, though it ain't, not to say, reg'lar Romnimus."

"Well, about twelve o'clock they turns us out, and we starts off across the bridge. In those days there was a *stiggur* ‡‡ at each end of it, and an extry *pannomengro* §§ was put on at fair time—but he'd a'gone home. When we gets onto the bridge the moon shone out bright, and there, right in the middle of the bridge, we see something white, all the very 'dentical same as a *bavolengro*.‖‖ I were a bit *trashado*¶¶ when I seen it, I ain't above confessin'—for I'd had a tightener—but Vester says:—'*Bavolengros* be d—d, come along. *Moosh* nor *beng* sha'n't *trasher mande*'***—and when we *velled adoorer*,††† what should it be but Josho's grey horse. Then we conceited that summat were *dosh*,‡‡‡ for the *gry* were all of a trimble. So we goes back and tells the man at the town-end of the bridge, and as soon as it come light we makes a sarch, and there we finds Josho a'lyin' in the water, with his pore, dear head all mashed to a pulp agen the cutwater. There was the cheque in his pocket, right

---

* "Going, brothers." † "Drunk." ‡ "Fine nag." § "Stolen."
‖ "Other horse." ¶ "Stolen sheep." ** "Talking." †† "True."
‡‡ "Gate." §§ "Toll-keeper." ‖‖ "Ghost." ¶¶ "Frightened."
*** "Man nor devil sha'n't frighten me." ††† "Came nearer,"
‡‡‡ "Wrong."

enough, and an old silk handkercher as had 'longed to his daughter as died—but the gold and silver were gone, every *poshero*." *

"Then, of course, there was a fine to-do, and the denouncement of the crowner's quest were that the pore, dear, King had been murdered. Rhody Stanley, she travels up to Bristol and goes to Mister Yetts, as lived close to the Red Cow Pit in Bedminster, and puts the case in his hands —for, you see, 'twere him as got back the plate for her, and, naturably, she put her dependance upon him. This here Mister Yetts were a sort of a Bow Street runner in a private way—same as might be these here detectitives—and he had a couple of cells in his house where he *pandloed* † them as he took, as you can see to this day. He were a tarrible clever gentleman, and never a sessions didn't pass but what he'd put away ten or, maybe, a dozen for murder, sheep-stealin', house-breakin', or forgery."

"Well, Mister Yetts he goes and he takes the two men as I've a'named to you, but he couldn't prove nothin' up agen 'em, and had to let 'em go, and, a year or two arter, this here M. S—— bust out and carried on a big head horse-dealin', and bought some house-property near the bone-factory at Exeter. And that were the end of pore Josho Stanley, the King of the Gipsies."

"What became of Rhody Stanley? Well, *mi chavvi*, she *merred* ‡ at Puriton, and Betsy Stanley died at Kewstock, near to Weston in Somersetshire, in the lane at the end of Squire Pickett's wood as runs down to the *lon-pawni*.§ If you walks down the lane you'll see a stone stile just oppersite the fisherman's cottage, and jest beyond the stile there's two postes druv into the ground agen the wall, and it were there she lain and died. The tent were pitched agen the wall, with the trench cut round it to carry off the water and the fire oppersite the entrance, and the lane bein' the parish boundary, there were a reg'lar combustion as to whether she were to be *poosheno* ‖ in Weston or Kewstock—but the *rashengro*, ¶ he lost the toss, and she were buried in the churchyard close by. Old Isaac Jowles—him as they've got drawed out with his creel on his back—died within a yard or two of the same

---

* "Half-penny." † "Locked-up." ‡ "Died." § "Salt-water."
‖ "Buried." ¶ "Clergyman."

place, and they took and buried him in Yatton churchyard along of his wife Merella and his two daughters, with this bit of a *goodli oprey* the *sherro-bar* *:—

> 'Here lie Merrily Jowles,
> A beauty bright,
> That left Isaac Jowles,
> Her heart's delight.'

"Then there was Josho's sons, Fellow and Billy, and his daughter Priscilla—pore thing—as died at Halwell, near Dartmouth. She were in a galloping declination and couldn't eat scarce nothin'. One day, early in the spring, she says to Josho:—'Father, I think I could fancy a bit of ducklin' and a few peas'—for, you see, she had an onnaturable craze for 'em, bein, out of season."

"'You shall *lel* 'em, *mi chi*,'† says Josho, 'if they cost a guinea apiece'—and he jumps on his horse and gallops off to Squire Newman's place—a very nice gentleman he were and always a good friend to our people, and when he went to foreign parts he promised to bring me back a present, but, as you have heard tell, he were shot in the wars—and he goes in and tells the Squire all about it."

"'Stanley'—says Squire Newman, 'go to the head-gardener, and if he's got a few early peas in the forcin' bed, you're welcome to all there is for your poor girl.'"

"Well, it so happened as there were just enough to make a dish, and Josho rides backs to camp, and they cooks 'em along of a ducklin'—but the pore thing couldn't relish but one nor two, and she dies that very same night as ever was. She'd left it as there were to be a silver fourpenny-bit under every nail in her coffin, and so 'twere done. Then they takes and burns everythin' as 'longed to her—and she had some beautiful dresses and things—all esceptin' a *kaisheni pongdishler*‡ as Josho kep' in conservation of her—the very same as we found in his pocket when we took him out of the water at Totnes—and when he were buried, pore dear man, his son Billy took and kep' it in rememberment of him."

"About the hangin' of Ryley Scamp? Well, you must know, *mi chavvi*, that Gilderoy Scamp were one of the

---

* "Inscription on the head-stone."
† "Have them, my girl."   ‡ "Silk handkerchief."

ancientest old Romanys in the country. He used to travel round about Maidstone, and one moonlight night he were coming back from the 'Three Bells,' between Strood and Maidstone, middlin' in drink, but not to say so that he couldn't see a hole in a ladder. It were a fine moonlight night, and as he were feelin' pretty comfortable, he takes and lays hisself down to sleep *tuley* the *bor**—same as I've done, myself, hundreds of times. When he gets up 'bout the time when the *cam* left the *pawni*,† he sees somethin' white a'flutterin' on the hedge oppersite him, and, sure enough, there was a lot of dish-clouts and baby-linen a' hung out to dry."

"Well, as I've told you, the old man didn't rightly know what he were a'doin' of, and he takes down three of these here napkins, and, says he to hisself:—'Gilderoy, these'll jest do nicely for your *chi*,‡ as is expectin' to be *chivved* to *vuddrus*'—and he takes and puts 'em in the pocket of his old velveteen coat, and when he gets home, he gives 'em to his wife to take care of."

"Next mornin' the woman of the *ker*§ misses the linen, and *bitchers* for the *prastramengro*.‖ 'Did you notice anybody about last night?' says he. 'Yes'—says she—'when I went up to bed about eleven o'clock, I looked out'er winder, and I seen a big, stout man in a keeper's coat pass by in the moonlight.' That were enough for the *baulo*, so he goes off to Dog Lane—about a mile'n a half from Pickerton Heath —where Gilderoy were *hatchin'*, and *latchers* the *cuvvas drey* the *tan*.¶ Then he goes back to the cottage, and arsts the woman whether she can 'denticate 'em. 'Yes'—says she, 'I'm a left-handed sewer, and when I was makin' 'em, I put the fust letter of my child's name—Dannle, as were to be— in the corner of 'em in red silk'—and there it were, sure enough."

"So they takes the pore, old man and tries him at the 'Sizes, and, long and by last, sentence of death were put upon him. At the *shoonaben*,** just as the *bauro-beshermengro* †† were a'puttin' the sentence onto him, Gilderoy, he takes out his big red silk handkercher and he wipes the death-sweat—

* "Under the hedge."   † "Sun left the water"—sunrise.
‡ "Daughter."   § "Cottage."   ‖ "Sends for the constable."
¶ "Stopping, and finds the things in the tent."
** "Trial."   †† "Judge."

for he were in mortal terror—off of his forehead. Then he rolls it up and tosses it to the usher, and says to him:— 'Give that to my poor missus in rememberment of me.' So the screw hands it to her across the dock. And now, *mi chavvi, rig covo in zee,** for it is a werry curious thing. When I seen that same handkercher some eight or ten year arter, it were jest as damp as if it had been layin' out all night in the dew—and if it were dried one day, it were jest as wet the next, and so it have alway re-mained. And when I told Father Denny, up to the Court, the story, he said as it were a merricle, and he told me about a vargin as he used to know as the same thing happened to, or summat werry similiar, but I disremember the pertic'lers now."

"It had been a heavy 'Sizes, and they was all to be tucked-up on Pickerton Heath where the gallows was derected. They drives out from Maidstone twenty-one of 'em—includin' the officers—in the Black Mariar, and each of 'em was allowed a pint o' beer and two-pennorth o' bread and cheese—but pore, old Gilderoy couldn't stomach his'n. 'Give it me'—says the man as were set next to him, as were a sailor and not easy upset—'one may as well die full as empty'—which were werry true. But pore, dear Master Scamp died tarrible hard, and when they cut him down, his *yakkors* was laid right out on his cheeks. I never see sich a sight before, and I don't care if I never don't again."

"Just before the trial, old Missus Scamp goes to the woman and offers for to pay the blood-money to buy him off, but the woman's husband says:—'No. He shall swing for it.' But wait a minute. Not very long arter—may be a year, may be two—this same man were comin' back from Strood market with a wagon full of samples of corn what hadn't been sold. He were a bit top-heavy, and when he come to Blue-bell Hill, close to 'Bell's Bower,' as they call it, where pore little Bell were murdered, he stumbles under the wagon, and the wheel—them *herrees* † down in Kent is about a foot broad in the tyre, and just about as much as a man can wheel afore him—passes right over his head and mashes him out as flat as a *hotchiwitchi* ‡ in a stone-trap. So, you see, God hadn't a' forgot him, nor it aint often as He do."

"About little Bell? What a boy it is for the horrors, to

---

* "Bear that in mind." † "Wheels." ‡ "Hedgehog."

be sure! Well, Honeywood the drover had noticed that each day as he passed a pertic'lar place in the road his dog begun to howl, just as they will sometimes when anybody's dead—I've a' knowd my own *jooko* howl tarrible o' nights when I've *pooshed a chavvi*.* So, one day he thinks:—'I'll just foller that there dog'—and he follered him through the gap in the hedge into the copse, and there, under a great hollow bush—what they call's Bell's Bower to this day—he finds the little boy a' lyin' with his pore, dear eyes pecked out, his nose cut off, and stabbed in a hundred places. It 'peared as how he'd been to call for his grandmother's parish-money, and that two of his tompanions had a' done it for the sake of the half-crown. One of 'em were hung at Maidstone, and the t'other were sent to the Penitentiary, and when he come out he were started off to Bermuda for stealin' three-pennorth of old iron."

"Tell you about the Brinkleys takin' the murderer up to Woodgreen? Well, it's the last I shall tell you to-day, for the trout'll be comin' on the rise present. There's three brothers of 'em, Walter, Jim, and Eddard, reglar *koorin' mooshor*,† weighs from fourteen to fifteen stone apiece, they does, but nice, quiet, despectable men as you'd meet anywhere—ontil they're put upon, that's to say. Well, '*prey yeck chairus* ‡ they was *hatchin'* close to the big brick-field at Woodgreen, and Jim and Walter they starts off at the *sig* of the *sorlo* to *lel* some *kosh* §—as they said—or else to *dick pauli* the *gryor* as they'd *pooved* the *rarde* ‖—as others said—but it don't much sinify. As they was a' *toovin'* their *swaeglers* ¶ they seen a couple of coves sneak into the brick-field in a dysterious sorter way, and they noticed as they was carryin' a heavy bag."

"'Hullo!'—says Jim Brinkley, 'these blokes aint upter no good'—so they *pallers lende*,** and present they sees 'em set the'selves down in a lonesome corner, and preceed to open the bag. And what d'ye think were in that *gunno*††? Well, I'll tell ye. 'Twere *sor pordo* to the *mui* with *ruppeni*

---

* "Buried a child."   † "Fighting men."   ‡ "Once upon a time."
§ "Day-break to get some wood."
‖ "Look after the horses as they'd turned out to grass over night."
¶ "Smoking their pipes."   ** "Follows them."
†† "Sack."

roys, chauros, ta corros. * Then they begins to divide the swag, but before long they falls to a' quarrellin', and one says to the t'other:—'If you don't turn up my fair share, I'll put the narks upon you. S'elp me never, I will, s'true as I'm a' standin' here.'"

"Well, long and by last they gets to high words, and Walter—a nice, quiet, peaceful-'spositioned chap he allers were—he whispers to Jim:—'It's about time we stepped in. They had ought'er be good for a *chinamongri*† apiece.'"

"'*Hatch* a *vongish!*'‡ says Jim, 'let's see what they'll do next. Perhaps they may bury it'—and that's where I blames him, as he didn't show hisself sooner. Well, the two *chories* § gives over quarrellin', aperiently, one of 'em gets up to light his pipe and stoops down under the lee of the *bor, avree* the *bavol*,‖ the other follows him, careless-like, with his hands in his pockets, and before you could say 'knife' he whips out a long-bladed, spring-backed *churi*,¶ and stabs his pal just in the neck, then in the side, and when he drops, he stands over him and drives the *churi* into him again and again—just as you might a fork into a tough beef-steak."

"It were all over before you could say 'God help his soul,' and the Brinkleys was too late for to save him. Then Jim stoops down and onlaces his boots—for they hadn't nothin' in their hands—and gives one to Walter, and they creeps on their hands and knees towards the murderer, as were tyin' up the sack. Directly he seen them, he done his push, but they was up with him in a minute, and he turns round upon 'em and faces 'em with the *rawtfelo churi drey lescro vast, dickin' sims o pooro beng yuv's kokero.*** Then Jim ups with his *chokkor*†† and knocks him down, and stands atop of him, *yeck peero oprey lescro men, ta yeck oprey lescro per*,‡‡ while Walter takes the knife away from him."

"'I'll give you twenty pound apiece if you'll let me nammus'—says the cove."

"'No fear, you ——'—says Jim, 'I'm a' goin' to take you to the station, so get up and come along of me. Walter'—says he—'you stop here and mind the *moolo*.'"‖‖

* "All full to the mouth with silver forks, plates, and goblets."
† "Five-pound-note."   ‡ "'Wait a moment!'"   § "Thieves."
‖ "Hedge, out of the wind."   ¶ Knife.
** "Bloody knife in his hand, looking like the devil himself."   †† "Boot.
‡‡ "One foot on his neck and one on his stomach."   ‖‖ "Corpse."

"Then Jim starts off with the murderer, and directly they gets outside the brickyard the chap draws another knife—a pocket-knife it were, this time—and attackts Jim, and cuts the palm of his hand open and lays all the sinneys bare before he could wrast it away, but, at last, he gets him to Whetstone and hands him over to the constable. Then the inspector and the doctor drives back to the brick-yard, and there was the poor chap with thirty-four wounds in him and the silver plate a' lyin' all around—but it were the fust blow as done it, so the doctor said. By that time the brick-layers had come to their work, and two or three on 'em carries him as far as the high-road—for the ruts were that deep he wouldn't have stopped in the trap for the jolting—and then they lifts him into the gig and drives him back to Whetstone."

"Jim had to 'pear five or six times at the 'quest and the *shoonaben*,* and what d'ye think he got for his trouble? Just five bob a time. The judge says to him:—'How much do you consider that you arns a day, my man?' and he answers like a fool:—'Sometimes two shilling, sometimes three or four, sometimes more and sometimes less, 'cordin' to sarcumstances'—instead of up and tellin' him that the valley of his time and what he arnd *a' bosherin'*† were oncalculable. So they give him the *pange collor*,‡ although Jim had paid 'em pounds and pounds in his time in fines."

"And what did the murderer get? He copped twenty years penal—*S'op mi deari Doovel* that's all he *lelled*,§ and as they walked him out, he turns round and he says:—'Thank 'ee, my lord, I can just about do that little lot on my berloomin' 'ead.' Yes, they're nice tender-'arted old ladies, is judges, if you happen to kill a man, but if you as much as pulls a stick out of a hedge or destructs the *tober* ‖ with your horse and van, it's twenty-three and six or two quid, as the case may be. They don't forget to pile it up. *Tatcho!* Hand me the rod, *mi chavvi*, they're beginnin' to rise at the head of the stickle."

---

* "Trial." † "Playing the fiddle." ‡ "Five shillings."
§ "So help me God, that's all he got." ‖ "Road."

CHAPTER VII.

"'Tis my delight of a likely night,
   In the season of the year;
For we can fight and run, my boys,
   And jump over anywhere."

THERE were plenty of rabbits on Fernleigh Common, and Sir George—always a good friend to us—used to *del mende mookaben** to kill a few, now and then, for our own use, as long as we didn't sell them or otherwise abuse the privilege. It was, as I have explained, to our advantage to keep in with the neighbouring gentry and farmers, and we never molested the game of the former or the pig-stys and hen-roosts of the latter, any petty larcenies being usually traced to low, wandering *peerdos* † or Irish hawkers—mumpers, frizzlers, and *Hinditi-koramescri*, as we called them—or, as often as not, to the farm-labourers themselves.

To their other avocations my uncles added that of professional warreners, and were often employed by landowners who kept no keepers—or whose keepers were too busy looking after the pheasants to have time to devote to the purpose—to kill down the rabbits by contract, and nothing *hunnaloed* ‡ Neptune more than to be called "an infernal old poaching scoundrel," by some short-tempered Squire unable to appreciate the nice distinction between a professional warrener and a professional poacher. The usual arrangement was that we were to have the option of purchasing whatever rabbits we might catch at from seven to ten shillings *per* dozen, and having separated them into three classes according to their condition, we sent them off to the dealers in the Midlands, who returned us from ten to fifteen shillings *per* dozen. A keeper was generally told off to superintend our operations and count the take, but he could not be everywhere at once and was generally open to reason, and when—as not infre-

---

* Give us permission.   † Tramps.   ‡ Angered.

quently happened—the foolish, buck-eyed *kaunengros* * ran their heads into the nets, together with any rabbits which we might have caught during his absence they were quickly *chivved tuley poov* † in a hollow bank or deserted 'bury,' to be left till called for, and were looked upon by us as a fair set-off against the wear and tear of nets and plant.

We went to work in a most methodical manner, very little being left to chance. Upon taking a contract to kill down the rabbits on a certain estate, our *sherengro* would start with his assistants for the scene of action—which was, as often as not, in a distant county—taking with them several hundred yards of netting, net-stakes, dogs, ferrets, etc., and followed by a couple of light carts driven by two of the women, containing the *kauvis, kekauviski-saster, pirrior, tans, ta ranior*.‡ Upon reaching their destination a dry camping-ground—near which water could be obtained—was chosen, sheltered as much as possible from the prevailing wind by a wall or thick hedge. The *vardos* were drawn up close alongside the hedge, the holes for the tent-rods bored in the ground with the *kekauviski-saster*, the tents pitched, the trenches dug, the fire lighted, and the big *pirri* set *a'bullerin'*.§ At daybreak the men made a careful survey of the scene of their prospective operations, noting the lie of the different coverts, the 'work' of the rabbits, and the direction of the wind, and having selected the most likely spot for the night's 'pitch,' Neptune would proceed to pace out the ground with the accuracy of a land-surveyor, with a view to determining the exact length of netting required.

As soon as this had been ascertained, the men returned to camp, and placing the requisite quantity of netting and stakes upon a light cart, drove back to the place which had been selected for the night's 'pitch.' Wherever the nature of the ground permitted it, the nets were set in the shape of a huge parallelogram formed of from six to fifteen hundred yards of netting. Selecting—according to the prevailing wind—whichever side of the plantation appeared to be the favourite feeding-ground, a man would walk from one end of it to the other, dropping as he went a small bundle of

---
* Hares. † Hidden under ground.
‡ Kettles, kettle-iron—a stout iron rod, pointed at one end and curved like a shepherd's crook at the other, by which the kettle is suspended over the fire—pots, tents, and tent-rods.   § Pot set a'boiling.

nets at regular intervals just outside the hedge or fence, while a second man followed him, carrying the net-stakes—the requisite number being dropped beside each bundle of nets.

On reaching the end of the covert—sufficient netting having been dropped to stretch from one end to the other—the men would turn their backs to it and march off into the open ground, at right-angles to the line of plantation. Continuing to drop the bundles of nets and stakes as they went, they would keep on in a straight line until they reached a spot distant some two or three hundred yards from the covert. Having thus traversed two sides of the parallelogram, they would again turn at right-angles, this time keeping a course parallel with the line of the plantation, dropping the nets and stakes as before and completing the third side. Then, turning their faces towards the plantation, they would march straight back to it, continuing to drop the nets and stakes as they went and thus completing the square or parallelogram.

Supposing the plantation to be three hundred yards in length, they would then have deposited twelve hundred yards of netting, forming a complete square, each side of which would average about three hundred yards in length.

The men would then proceed to set the nets along three sides of the square, pushing the stakes firmly into the ground and hanging the nets loosely upon them—the average height of the net being about eighteen inches from the ground. The nets which had been dropped along the edge of the covert were, of course, not set, but were left lying in bundles on the ground all ready to be run up directly the rabbits had come out on the feed. When the ground outside the covert happened to be covered with patches of gorse, bramble, or fern, a good deal of time was spent in cutting a clean track in which to set the nets without fouling. Having finished their work, the men would return to camp, leaving the nets standing with somebody to see that they were not interfered with.

After supper—according as the moon rose late or early—they would start off again for the plantation. By about eleven o'clock the main body of the rabbits would be well out on the feed, and as soon as they had assured themselves that this was the case, the men would creep noiselessly along in the shadow of the covert, and hastily run the nets along its entire length, thus completing the square and effectually preventing the rabbits from regaining the wood.

Every rabbit that happened to be out on the feed was now securely enclosed, and the work of slaughter commenced. The frightened animals, disturbed at their feed, came scuttling back to covert, only to 'snob' themselves in the meshes, when a sharp turn of the wrist dislocated their necks and put them out of their misery. Many of them, finding their retreat cut off, would break back for some other point, but the side-nets now came into play and prevented them from effecting their escape—in fact, as far as any chance of escaping went, they might just as well have been left until morning, were it not for the fact that if rabbits are left for any length of time undisturbed, they will set to work and quietly gnaw their way through the netting, not only getting away but causing considerable damage to the nets. For this reason, if rabbits are 'pitched out' by the keepers for shooting next day, they usually hang lighted lanterns on the net-stakes and keep somebody walking up and down to prevent the rabbits from gnawing their way through the nets and regaining the covert.

The professional poachers, who are unable to carry a large quantity of netting about with them without incurring considerable risk of detection, simply run a single line of netting along a plantation, thus losing all the rabbits which break back. Whenever two coverts lay within a convenient distance and opposite each other, we used to run two long lines of netting across the intermediate space, joining them at each end and thus enclosing the whole area between the two. We used to make a fresh 'pitch' every night, but, after a bit, the rabbits became too scarce and shy to repay us for the trouble of setting the nets—and trouble it was, and no mistake, for we were up all night and only got two or three hours sleep during the day, what with one thing and another. We then set to work and ferreted the woods and hedgerows from one end of the estate to the other, each man taking a separate beat and working from hole to hole in methodical fashion without leaving a single yard of ground unexplored.

In addition to the above-mentioned methods of destruction we had scores of wires set round the plantations, but we never used guns—the only instrument employed being a strongly-made earth-scoop shaped like a cheese-taster and fixed to a long handle which acted as a lever for prising up stones—as they only disturbed the game and spoiled the *shoshois* for the market. Frequently, when travelling about the country, we used to see the pretty *veshenengros* in their brown velveteens and leather gaiters shooting and banging away as if the whole place belonged to them, and we used to wonder what their masters could be about to allow it.

* * * * * *

My cousin Tenny Klism *—who lived away up in Gloucestershire and used to travel with us a good deal—had an air-gun, and when we were up Wiltshire and Hampshire way, on a moonlight night he would often bring in three or four thumping hares which he would manage to kill in the following manner. Taking up his position on the open downs, about three or four hundred yards from some plantation where hares were in the habit of lying during the day-time, he would select a well-used 'run,' and throwing himself flat on his face along it, would wait until an old hare came out to feed. *Kaunengros* can't see very well straight in front of them, and as she came loppeting towards him, he would give a low whistle, which had the effect of making her sit up on her haunches and prick her ears, when he would take a steady aim at the patch of fur on her chest, which showed snowy white in the bright moonlight, and roll her over in her tracks.

When out of our own district and not employed in a 'professional' capacity, I must confess that all was fish—or, rather, fur and feathers—which came to our nets, and few days passed without a *tawno bal*, a grey-coated *shoshoi*, or a plump *veshen-caunni*,† finding its way into the *pirri*. The best thing about the Wiltshire downs was that an extensive view could be obtained in every direction, so that they weren't able to jump atop of us without warning, and if

* Tenant Lock—a member of a tribe inhabiting Gloucestershire—Tenny being an abbreviation of Tenant, and *Klism* the Gipsy for a lock.
† Leveret, a grey-coated rabbit, or a plump pheasant.

a *yogengro* happened to put in an appearance unexpectedly, we could always take a short-cut across the turf, and a stern-chase is, proverbially, a long one. Sometimes, however, they would lie in wait for us, and coming back from Weyhill Fair in a light tax-cart I have seen many a pretty course and many a hare rolled over by our dogs, and the way old Vester would send the mare flying over the mole-hills which dotted the elastic turf in all directions when the *yog-mooshor** popped their heads out of a furze-bush, was a caution to weak nerves, and no mistake.

Neptune had a rare old dog called Bob. His father was a cross between a greyhound and a sheep-dog, and his mother was one of those rough-coated deer-hounds. If you took him to a gateway with a stiffish breeze blowing across the field towards him, if there happened to be a *kaunengro* lying within a couple of hundred yards, his old stump of a tail would stand out as stiff as a ramrod, and it took a good hare—a very good hare, mind you—to beat him, for he ran by nose as well as by eye and would bring them back in his mouth every time, if he couldn't manage to drive them towards the *vardos*. For night-work I never saw the beat of him, and if a hare-net had been badly hung in a gateway, he would run under it, whereas, if it was properly set, he would top the gate without disturbing it.

The way he and old Rough—Tenny's dog—would work the *kaunengros* on a twenty-acre piece was worth a journey to see. Supposing that there were eight or ten hares in the field, and a couple of gateways where the nets were set, instead of coursing them as hard as they could split—as a greyhound would—they would dash in and separate them and then stop: then they would move them on a bit and lie down if they found that the hares were going too fast: alternately hunting and crouching, turning and driving them towards the gateways, so that they should come to the nets one by one instead of in a drove, and give us time to set them again.

I mind, one time, we were crossing Pewsey Downs to Weyhill Fair along with some of the Ayres, and they had a couple of pretty smart *jookos*†—run cunning, both of 'em would, but not much count for night-work. The sun was

---

* Gun-men—keepers.   † Dogs.

just rising, and Horace Ayres shades his eyes with his hand and points away across the downs. "There she lies—" he says, and you could just see a bit of the white fleck on her belly as she squatted in her form on the side of the hill. Then he takes and slips a halter on to one of the colts, and gallops off and 'shoos' his two dogs on to her. She had about a hundred yards start, and it was as pretty a course as you need wish to see. They might have been away about a quarter-of-an-hour, and then we see the hare come back over the skyline, and the dogs left her and come and lays theirselves down by the *vardos*, dead-beat. Then Neptune takes old Bob and sends him after her, and he was away a matter of might be ten minutes. We all stood quite still and presently we hears "pit-a-pat, pit-a-pat," and back she comes again with Bob close behind her, and he takes and drives her right in between the *vardos* and kills her there under the horses' feet. Ah! he was a good-'un, was Bob, but when we went up Hampshire way we most in general left him behind at Chippenham—you see, he was just a bit too much of a popular character for quiet folk like us to travel with.

* * * * * *

About the out-and-outest Romany poacher ever I come across was Anselo Draper, whose people travelled the Staines and Egham district. He was in the habit of attending the pigeon-matches and of shooting against the farmers and tradespeople for a fat pig or a cup, just as the case might be—and when he did so, he generally used to win, for he was the quickest and cleanest shot I ever saw, and his sister Shuri was almost as good, though not better, as some folks said.

While walking through a thick fir-wood one of those little blue-rocks has darted out, zig-zagging between the poles, and I have seen Anselo throw up his gun and turn her over before she had clapped her wings six times. If a covey of partridges rose before him in the dusk, when anybody else would only hear a 'whirr' and just catch the flutter of wings, he would knock over his two birds, right and left, as easy as in broad daylight, and on a foggy afternoon in November, when you could scarcely see twenty yards before your nose, he and his son Pyramus—a grown man and a rough handful, like his father—used to play the very mischief with any well-stocked manor. They would make for the part of it where the game was the thickest, walking in line about thirty yards apart, and killing everything that got up, hares, pheasants, and partridges—for birds lie close in a fog and look bigger than they really are —till they had as much as they could carry.

Sometimes the pretty *yogengros* would turn out when they heard the shots, but, Lord love you, they might as well have hunted a shadow, and more often they preferred to stay by their firesides, for they knew that when Anselo and Pyramus were heavy loaded they would stop and fight or else drop and lie like stones in the middle of a field of turnips or a ditch, and if they took to their heels there wasn't a keeper in Norfolk or Suffolk could catch them in broad daylight—let alone a fog.

One of Anselo's favourite capers was to dress up as a *yog-moosh* *—velveteens, leather gaiters, and all complete— and he would then call round at the head-keeper's cottage to inquire if they wanted an under-keeper. Then he'd gammon the *sherro-veshenengro* † to show him his birds at feeding-time, and when next he and Pyramus travelled that road, they would make things very lively for the *veshen-caunnis*.‡ They pretty well cleaned out some of the best coverts in Norfolk, Suffolk, and Hertfordshire, and, at last, there were very few keepers but what got to know the two Drapers.

In the spring of the year, when eggs were worth ninepence apiece, Anselo would often pick up from fifty to a hundred a day—for he had an eye like a hawk, and knew exactly where to look for them—and these he carried inside his shirt, which was padded and quilted with cotton-wool after a very ingenious fashion by his sister Shuri.

One fine day in May three keepers lay in wait for him, and managed to jump atop of him just as he was stooped down to pick up some eggs in a strip of underwood close to the high-road. One tackled him on one side, and one on the other, while the third came on in front, but he hit

---

* Keeper—gun-man.   † Head-keeper—head-woodfellow.
‡ Pheasants—wood-hens.

them over right and left when they tried to close with them, and butted the third with his head, leaving him senseless in the middle of the road. The other two picked themselves up and followed him, but it was no go, for Ans'lo was a first-class runner and jumper, and could clear a five-foot bar in heavy boots—as I know to my cost, for although I beat him at running, I lost a sovereign to him one day at Westport over a high-jump. He got clear away at the time, but, a fortnight after, a constable takes him at Baldock Fair, near Hatfield, and they fined him close on ten pounds, which he paid, or he would have been sent to St. Albans— for, you see, the old *stardo* * at Hertford was closed.

"Call yourselves keepers?"—says one of the *pooknees*,† "a pretty set you must be for three of you to let one man go in broad daylight!"—but, Lord bless you, it would have taken three very smart men to capture Ans'lo, and they didn't go the right way to work. As he was leaving the court Lord Edward comes up, and, says he:—"Draper, if you'll come to me as second keeper, I'll give you thirty shillings a' week."

"Thank 'ee kindly, my lord"—says Ans'lo, "but I couldn't do it. I'll come as head-keeper if you wish it, but, you see, it wouldn't never do for me to have someone over me as, perhaps, didn't know more 'n half what I did"— but it might have been better for him if he had gone keeping, for the last time I saw him, poor chap, he was completely crippled with the rheumatics from lying out o' nights, and couldn't scarcely move hand or foot.

* * * * * *

During the month of February a good deal of very destructive poaching goes on—as often as not—unsuspected. The coverts have been shot through three or four times and a nice stock of birds left for breeding, while the keepers who have been up, night after night, ever since the previous June, are naturally inclined to take things a bit easy.

At this time of year live pheasants always command good prices for the aviaries. Three or four smart chaps will slip into a long, narrow belt of plantation where there is a good stock of hens, about an hour before daylight. They will

* Gaol. † Magistrates.

quickly set two or three dozen pheasant-wires in the likeliest 'runs,' and as soon as the birds come down from bough they will form line, and, starting at one end of the plantation, will beat quietly towards the other, zig-zagging about so as to make good the ground between them, and gently tapping the trees with their sticks to keep the birds on the move. The plantation being narrow, the frightened birds keep running before them towards the further end, and several of them are safe to run into the wires—the result being that when the keeper goes egg-hunting in May, he wonders what on earth has been shortening his hens so, and, as likely as not, ends by buying eggs off the very dealer who has purchased his hen-pheasants for the aviaries.

"Bless my dear life"—young Vester used to say, "I never sha'n't forget that mornin' up by B———. There was Tenny Klism, Harry Orchard—Longsnout, as we calls him—Perin, and me, and we'd a'nicked about a dozen pheasants a'creepin',* when, all of a sudden, the fine *yogengros* jumps atop of us. The others bolted different ways, and I *dels* the *moosh* as had a' collared me a *tatto yeck oprey* the *mooi*,† and done my push with Harry *a'slommin' mande*.‡ When I climbs the Park wall I looks round and I sees Longsnout *a'prasterin' tuley* the *choomba* with the *yogengros paul leste*.§ He were *a' rikkerin' yeck* o' the *gunnos oprey lescro dumo* ‖ with three or four hens and a cock in it, and they was a' bangin' agen his old ribs a good 'un. When he finds as the keepers is a' gainin' on him, he *mookers* the *veshen-caunnis avree* the *gunno yeck-paul-a'vauver*,¶ and the *pooro boshno*** goes straight up into the air like a sky-rocket 'ithout a stick—for his tail had stopped in Longsnout's hand—a' cock-cock-cockettin' fit to bust his blessed kekker-pipe. There I sets atop of that there wall a' larfin' till I cried, and when Longsnout reaches out his hand for me to pull him up, I were that helpless I falls right atop of him,

---

* This particular form of poaching is called 'creeping for pheasants, owing to the fact that the skilled operator usually blocks the pheasants 'runs' with a barricade of sticks and brushwood, leaving a small aperture—in which the wire is set—for the pheasant to creep through.

† "I hits the man a hot-'un in the face."   ‡ "A' following me."

§ "A' running down the hill with the keepers after him."

‖ "A' carrying one of the sacks on his back."

¶ "Lets the pheasants out of the bag one after the other."

** "Old cock-pheasant."

and a near miss it were the *yogengros* hadn't a' got us that journey. *Tatcho!*"*

* * * * * *

Although wary enough by day, partridges are the stupidest birds in the world at night, and the easiest to catch, and the prettiest way of catching them is to 'tunnel' them. You require five things for successful 'tunnelling.' A moonlight night, a field of short grass—the barer the ground, the better, for if the grass is long the birds will flush instead of running—a tunnel net, an old horse, and a covey of partridges.

The 'tunnel' consists of a number of hoops made of bent hazel—the largest hoop, which forms the mouth of the 'tunnel,' being about three feet in diameter, and the end hoop about one foot—over which the net is stretched. When set up it resembles a duck-decoy on a small scale, being funnel-shaped and extending a distance of thirty feet, and when not required for use it shuts up like an accordion and goes into a small sack which a man can carry under his arm.

The *modus operandi* is as follows. You choose a moonlight night the last week in August or the first week in September, and start off—two or three of you—leading an old horse, to look for a covey of partridges. You see the birds roosting on the ground, all clumped up together, as plain as possible in the bright moonlight, and as soon as ever you have spotted them you set up the 'tunnel' as near as you can to them without disturbing them, and run up a couple of wings of netting about eighteen inches high on each side of the mouth of the 'tunnel,' the whole apparatus, when set, exactly resembling the letter Y—the tail being the 'tunnel,' and the fork the two wings leading to it. Then you lead the *pooro gry* † up to where the birds are 'jugging'—taking particular notice to keep on the farther side of him—and as you approach them they will get up and begin to run in front of the horse. You keep edging and driving them towards the wings, and when they run against one of the side-nets, they follow it down to the mouth of the 'tunnel,' which they enter without hesitation under the impression that they are running through a gap in a hedge. Then you show

---

* "That's a fact." † Old horse.

yourself, and the frightened birds rush up the 'tunnel' and find themselves in a small purse-net at the further end. The mouth of the purse-net is tied together with a piece of twine, and having opened it, you shake the birds out into a bag, all alive and kicking. Then you start off to look for another covey, and if you are lucky you may get two or three more lots that night—but three coveys is considered a good night's work. If birds are plenty and you know your business, it is just as easy as decanting a bottle of port.

'Roosting-in' partridges and catching them in 'flight,' or 'drag,' nets—as some call them—is a very favourite game, and nothing clears a manor quicker. On the other hand it is easily prevented. In addition to bushing the fields a good keeper won't have chaps loafing about the estate of an evening watching the birds roost, and unless partridges are 'roosted in,' it isn't much use looking for them on a dark night.

About the first week in September two or three of us would take a quiet stroll through the fields, keeping, when practicable, in some public footpath, and each man would endeavour to mark down a good covey of partridges to their jugging-place in a pasture-field or clover-ley. As soon as the birds fly in off their feed and settle down to their roost, they clump up all together and will not move again that night unless disturbed by a dog or something, and having marked the exact line of their lay by some conspicuous object in the background which can be easily seen at night against the skyline—just as fishermen know their fishing-ground to a yard or two by some landmark on shore—we saunter quietly back to camp.

Between ten and eleven o'clock we start again with the net—about five-and-twenty yards by ten with a dragging-rope running the whole length of the net in front—and make for the field where the first covey has been marked down. Then, stretching out the net square on the ground and starting from the exact spot where the man stood when he marked them down, we lay hold of the rope and drag the net over the clover in the line of where the birds are roosting, while one or two more walk after the net—or 'tail' it, as it is called—and as soon as the partridges rise, which they do the moment the net goes over them, these men throw themselves on top of them and prevent their escape. If there is a good breeze blowing and the bearings have been properly taken, we probably get the whole covey, but a still night is no good whatever.

Whenever a patch of corn, barley, or oats has been left standing near a pheasant-covert, the birds are sure to beat away for it, and they will roost in it on the ground like partridges. Standing barley is the best for netting pheasants, and, next to that, a light crop of wheat—but very little can be done in heavy wheat, and oats play the very mischief with the nets owing to their fibres working into the meshes.

A good keeper will always drag any out-lying patch of wheat or barley where he knows his birds roost, and turn them down in some covert at a distance to save them from poachers, but some of the cunning ones, when they have got a party of gentlemen coming out to shoot next day and want to show good sport, will send out some young chaps to 'tunnel' or 'drag' for partridges on their neighbours' outskirts overnight, and having wrung the necks of the old birds, will turn the young ones down in a piece of standing barley in the middle of their own manor. Artful toads are those keepers.

'Dragging' a corn-field in the dark is by no means easy work, and novices at the game, instead of walking straight, will go over the same ground two or three times and only get a few birds where men who know their work would pick up from ten to twenty brace of pheasants. Everything depends upon the men who work the dragging-rope knowing each others' signals. One twitch of the rope may mean 'Hold-hard': two, 'Steady': three, 'More this way': four, 'Further your way,' and so on. It takes a goodish man to work a 'flight-net' over a corn field, and it is a terrible wet job owing to the heavy dew. It isn't a bit of good trying to catch partridges in this way in standing crops, for as soon as they 'flush' and strike the net as it passes over them, they drop again like stones and creep away between the stalks of corn or barley, but the stupid pheasants keep flapping and struggling against the meshes in their efforts to rise, and are at once pounced upon by the men who are 'tailing' the net.

CHAPTER VIII.

My Cousin Tenny Klism.

THE lurchers which followed our vans and which were generally to be seen lying curled up, dead tired and fast asleep, under an empty cart during the day-time, were clever enough in all conscience and could tell a *prastramengro's pirraben a posh-mea avree*,* but, for night-work, they were no better than the dogs belonging to the pitmen and mill-hands of the Midlands, many of which never see the daylight, but are kept in cellars and coal-pits in order to accustom them to the darkness, an incredible amount of pains being bestowed on their education.

You see, when a chap depends on his dog to help get him a livelihood, he can't afford to be whistling, and thrashing, and cussing, and holloaing at him in the field like a gentleman's servant who has very little else to do but break dogs, and is paid a pound a week for doing it.

My cousin Tenny Klism used always to bring a couple of these lurchers down with him when he came to stay with us —which he did whenever his medical adviser prescribed a change of air. Tenny was a fine, big chap, standing over six foot in his *holivas* † and broad in proportion—active as a cat and light-hearted as a kitten. He could jump a five-bar gate backwards and forwards at a walk, *koor sar a gry*,‡ and play the fiddle as I have seldom heard it played—the real, 'wild' music that poor Squire Allington delighted in. He was a light-hearted, convivial sort of chap, *kaumlo* of the *racklis* § and of good company, but the worst of him was that, directly he got a drop in him, he became noisy and quarrelsome, and being as strong as a bull and a desperate

---

* Constable's footsteps half-a-mile off.   † Stockings.
‡ Fight like a horse.   § Fond of the girls.

fighter, he was continually coming into collision with the powers that be.

His father, old Greenleaf Klism, had made a tidy bit of money *bickenin' gryor*,* and owned some forty or fifty acres of farm land near Monmouth, and when he died, he left Tenny upwards of eight hundred guineas, the farm, and a fine *vardo* which, with its furniture and fittings, was worth about another couple. As long as his mother lived, he did well enough, but when she died he married a woman named Annabel Musto, who was not only a good deal older than himself but an out-and-out bad lot. The language that woman would make use of on occasions was something terrible, and while Tenny has been leading the van-horse and smoking his pipe, I have seen her following him along the road raving and cursing at him like a madwoman, until I really expected to see her fall down in a fit.

After two years of constant nagging and quarrelling she left him for good and all, and travelled the country with old Jasper Lee, the King of the Ratcatchers. She used to say that she had only married Tenny out of respect for his well-known pugilistic powers, and when, like a good-natured chap, he knocked under to her instead of giving her a good leathering, as she deserved, she left him for a more masterful consort.

This she found in old Jasper, who had one wife already, but he proved equal to the occasion and soon had her as handy as one of his tame rats. They used to travel through the West of England once every year, killing the rats in the *filisins* and *givengro-kers*,† and I well remember old Master Lee as he sat, bolt upright, in his *myla-vardo*,‡ driving a pair of Jerusalem ponies, tandem-fashion, in rope harness with an old hunting-whip with which he also larrupped his consorts, who followed amicably together in a light tax-cart with the pots, pans, and tent. He was a thick-set, bull-necked old chap—like his brother Ruslo Lee—with an almost black skin deeply pitted with the *boogones*.§ He wore a greasy black velvet hunting-cap, an old bottle-green cutaway coat with crown-pieces for *crafnis*,‖ a waistcoat which had once been scarlet but which had turned a dingy mulberry colour,

---

* Horse-dealing.   † Country-houses and farm-houses.
‡ Donkey-cart.   § Small-pox.   ‖ Buttons.

with lion-shillings for buttons, and a pair of grimy cord trousers, as black as any stoker's, the knees of which were protected by an old pair of horse's knee-caps. He always made a great mystery of his art and would never work in company—which very possibly accounted for his success. He used to boast that there wasn't a rat in England but would come out of it's hole and talk to him—all I knew about it was that he used to rub his hands with some strong-smelling oils before handling his traps, which he baited with scraps of herring smeared with aniseed or carraway.

To return to my cousin Tenny. After his wife left him, he became more and more reckless and spent half his time in gaol, and most of his money in paying fines for assaults on constables and for allowing his horses to stray on the highway. He joined his brother Credit, and the two travelled the country together and made a living by *killin* the *bosh* at the *kitchemas* and *kellobens*,* setting up the cocoa-nuts at fairs and races, and *chinning busahor* for the *mausengros* and *feeders* for the *toveli-gueris*,† but he very soon came to the end of his money and at last he was obliged to sell the farm near Monmouth. When, one autumn, he came out of Southampton gaol—where he had been doing a stretch for 'trucking,' followed by an aggravated assault upon a constable—he was compelled to sell the van, and travelled westwards in a light cart, bringing his two dogs, Rough and Nelly—which he had kept to the last in spite of several tempting offers,—with him.

When he arrived at the Combe he was as lean as a wolf, and barely weighed twelve-stone-seven. He told us that he had been even lower than that, but that he had picked up a bit during the last two months, having managed to get on the blind side of the Governor. To give a Bowdlerised version of Tenny's story:—

"The Guv'nor he comes to my cell one day and:— 'Pannell,' ‡ says he, 'they tells me as you beant *trashado* by neither *moosh* nor *beng*, and are pretty *flick* of your *vasters*.§

---

* Playing the fiddle at the public-houses and dancing-saloons.
† Cutting skewers for the butchers and clothes-pegs for the washerwomen.
‡ Pannell was, probably, the *alias* under which Lock was travelling at the time of his arrest.
§ "'Frightened by neither man nor devil, and are pretty handy with your fists.'"

Now, I've got a cove in here ravin' mad, as we can't do nothen with, and none of the blamed screws don't care for to tackle him.'"

"'Right you are, my Rye'—says I with a wink at the head polis, 'but to tell you the downright truth I be that pore and weak along o' the bloomin' skilly that I ain't not to say fit to tackle a mouse, let alone a madman'—so, by long and by last, the Boss o' the *Stardo**—as were as nice, senserful a gentleman as ever you see—he takes me into the kitchen and tells the cook to look arter me, and I has a proper blow-out of butcher's meat and about a quart and a half of ale."

"'Now'—says the Boss, when I'd a' done myself pretty tidy, 'jest you come along o' me'—so I goes along o' he and two o' the blank screws."

"As we comes to one of the cells we *shoons* a termenjous *chingaree* † a' goin' on inside, and I guessed 's how it were the *diviou-yeck* ‡ a' playin'-up Pandemonium and Thomas. The screws they didn't care for to go inside to see what were the matter, for, you see, he'd *posh mored dui o' lende*,§ and they'd been obligated for to shove his vittels into the cell with a long stick—just the 'dentical same as they does to the tigers at the travellin' shows—and the cell were for all the world like a wild-beaste's den."

"'Now, Rye'—says I to the Boss, 'if you'll jest arst one of these gentlemen to onlock the door, I'll see if I can't come to some sort 'er understandin' with him'—so they slips the door open, cautious-like, and I steps inside."

"Directly I clapped eyes on him I seen how he warn't no more mad nor you nor me, but only a purtendin'. I knowd it by the way he took my measure all of a instant like, runnin' his eye over me as cool as a cowcumer, jest 's if we'd been a' goin' to shake hands inside the ropes. He'd a tore his beddin' and clothes *sor* to *cutters*,‖ and was a' dancin' on his mattress and a' yellin' blue murder. Thinks I to myself, 'You're a roughish handful for any man to tackle,' and I begun to fight shy of the job—for he were a great, upstandin' chap more 'n a inch taller nor me, with a stiff back on him like a sojer—but the door were shut behind

---

* "Prison."   † "Hear a tremendous noise."   ‡ "Mad-one."
§ "Half killed two of them."   ‖ "All to rags."

me and I hadn't much time to think, for, all of a suddent, he gives a orful yell and comes straight at me a' nashin' of his teeth and a'slobberin' *sims a diviou jooko*,* but I steps aside, quick like, and tips him the auctioneer on the jaw, sharpish, and down he goes of a heap. Then he picks hisself up and come at me again, but I props him in the same old place and downs him. Then he ketches holt o' me round the knees and pulls me down atop of him, and there we lays a' rollin' over and over on the floor a' scrappin' and a' tearin' like a couple of bull-an'-tarriers. Fust he gets me under—for I hadn't nothen to grup him by, for his *bals* were *moredo*† and havin' no clothes on he were as slippersome as a eel—and sarves me out shameful with his knee. It were nothen but the ale as kep' me goin', but at last I gets upsides with him, and when I *was* atop of him, *s'op mi deari Doovel* I made his blessed chump rattle agen the blessed floor a good 'un and no mistake. I could hear the Guv'nor as had his eye to the peep-hole *a' savvyin'* ‡ and a' chucklin', and presently he puts his head in, and, says he:—'Well, Pannell, and how's the patient going on?'"

"'Nicely, thanky, Rye'—says I, and then the screws come in and took and lain him on his little bed as peacerful as a infant, and begun to set things straight."

"Well, long and by last I was 'pinted to look arter him, but he were main vi'lent and wouldn't speak a word, and if my eye were off of him, he'd slip out 'er bed and 'tempt to run up the walls like a blessed monk. At last, one day when I'd been obligated for to down him, he busts out a' cryin' like a child, and says he:—'Look here, Pannell, I can't stand this here not no longer. You're the fust man as ever done me, but I give you best, for I've had pretty nigh enough on it.'"

"Then he told me 's how he'd a' been a Sergeant of Marines, and had been convicted of stealin' a cash-box from a gentleman's house, and when he got *staramescro*§ he detarmined to sham mad, so as to get removed to the County Lunatic 'Sylum, from which he could easily off it. Well, I were very comfortable as I was, for the Guv'nor he give me *pange collor a cooricus* for *dickin' paul' leste*,|| as well as

---

* "Like a mad dog."   † "Hair was shaved."   ‡ "Laughing."
§ "Imprisoned." || "Five shillings a week for looking after him."

the run of my teeth in the kitchen, so we jest agreed between us to say nothen about it. The Boss he'd come along and *pooker** how the cove were a' gettin' on, and I'd say:—'Thanky, Sir, he's jest had his bath nice and quiet and seems to relish his vittels and don't offer for to tear his clothes.' And whenever one of the bloomin' screws shoved his head in, the artful bloke would give a orful yell and go straight for him. As soon as I got my discharge they *bitchered leste* to the *diviou-ker*,† for he played it up worse 'en ever, and I heard since's how he got clear away within the week."

Tenny's two lurchers, Rough and Nelly, never left him night or day, and were always good for a *tawno bal* ‡ or a couple of *shoshois* § whenever he happened to take a look round of a night,—which, to tell the truth, was pretty often. Now old Squire Beaumont of Upcote had a fine *yogengro* named Ludlow, who fancied himself above a bit at wrestling and fighting, and who was always down on us like a hundred of bricks whenever he got half a chance, through having had a bit of a turn-up—just a couple of rounds, a *kaulo yak ta kek dushtopen* ‖—with Tenny in a *levinor-ker*, and having got the worst of it, as might have been expected.

Old Squire Beaumont was a bit of a character, and his three daughters were just as indisputably the three prettiest young ladies in Devonshire, as the Squire, himself, was the meanest man in the county—sneak the toasted-cheese out of a mouse-trap, he would. He used to come out hunting on an old flea-bitten grey, whose back was so hollow and hips so ragged that when you were walking behind him you could see nothing but the Squire's head and shoulders, and them humped up like a cat with the colic—old Jack-in-the-Box we used to call him—and when he drove the poor old brute into Netherton to attend the magistrates' meeting, or on any other business, he would make the groom walk him about for three or four hours to save sixpence for putting up. Upcote was a show place, but the establishment was conducted upon the most economical principles, the rabbits being made, if not to 'pay the rint,' like Paddy's pig—for the property was freehold—at all events to cover the

---

* Inquire.   † "Sent him to the lunatic-asylum."
‡ Leveret—little hare.   § Rabbits.   ‖ Black-eye and no harm done.

expenses of preserving and contribute largely towards the maintenance of the household. Every morsel of fur or feathers which was not consumed upon the premises, was forwarded *per* carrier to Exeter, and a favoured guest, indeed, might the visitor deem himself, whose arrival was celebrated by the production of a patriarchal cock-pheasant to grace the luncheon-table. Sir George L'Estrange—who was considered to have about the best pheasant-shooting in the county—always made a point of asking his neighbour to shoot the coverts, as their estates adjoined, but, although a very good shot, it was noticed that, somehow, the Squire always missed any birds flying towards Upcote, and next morning, wet or fine, he would turn out soon after daybreak with Ludlow and two or three brace of spaniels to beat the bounds, and in this manner would contrive to pick up a very fair percentage of Sir George's birds. Every autumn he made a point of attending the sheep-fair at Cranmeet Bridge, where he would purchase a score of broken-mouthed ewes off the moor. These delectable quadrupeds cost him from three to five and twenty shillings apiece, and having been duly killed and skinned, were put in the mash-tub to pickle, and, with the rabbits, formed the staple food of the household during the winter.

Somehow or other Ludlow—who was a man after the Squire's own heart—came to hear about the dogs, and, like the cowardly bully he was, he determined to have his revenge on Tenny for the licking he had received in the public-house. One fine Sunday afternoon in September, Tenny, Vester, and I, were strolling along the green-lane outside Squire Beaumont's park-wall with some of the children, who were picking blackberries, while Rough and Nelly skirmished about, pushing their inquisitive noses into every bramble-bush and patch of fern, after the manner of their kind. Suddenly I happened to look back over my shoulder, and caught sight of Ludlow's head disappearing below the coping of the park-wall, which was from ten to twelve foot high and hard to climb from the outside, but at certain places on the inside, where the ground was higher, the keepers had placed hurdles against it so as to enable them to take a look round.

I mentioned the circumstance to the others, and we

walked on about fifty yards and then wheeled sharp round, and, sure enough, we caught him again. We didn't think much of it at the moment, and walked on, but, presently, we noticed that old Rough was lagging behind, and as he didn't come to Tenny's whistle, we went back and found the poor brute rolling on the grass, apparently in the greatest agony. His legs were drawn up close to the body, while his backbone arched itself like a bow, and after a few convulsive struggles the old dog fell back stone-dead. We thought at first that he had been seized with a fit, and my cousin was just mad at losing him, but, a few minutes later, Nelly began to exhibit the same symptoms. Then we guessed at once that Ludlow—who knew that we were in the habit of coming along the lane on Sunday afternoons—had thrown some poisoned meat to the dogs as they passed, and knowing that tobacco was the best antidote for poison, we cut up what we had with us, and rolling it into balls, forced it down her throat. But the poison had got too long a start, or else —as was afterwards proved to be the case—the dose had been an extra strong one, and after lingering in torture for several minutes, the poor thing fell back dead within a yard or two of where her old companion was lying.

Those who fancy that rough chaps like us have no feelings, make a very great mistake, for there were big lumps in our throats and tears in our eyes as we stood and looked at the keeper's handiwork, and as for the *chavvies*, they *ruvved* * as if their little hearts would break. Tenny didn't say much, but he asked Vester to give him a back, and drawing himself up by the coping of the park-wall, he got astride of it and then let himself drop on the other side, but luckily, perhaps, for both, the keeper had made himself scarce. Then he climbed back again, and as we stood talking together in the lane, some gentlemen happened to ride by, and they advised us to have the dogs examined and apply for a warrant against Squire Beaumont's keeper—and this we determined to do. Next morning we put the panniers on Jenny and took the bodies over to Dr. Lyons of Blackstow—always a kind friend to any of our people and a very sporting gentlemen—and a *post-mortem* was held with the result that about six grains of strychnine was found in each of them—enough to have poisoned half-a-dozen dogs.

* Cried.

Our next step was to apply for a *goodlo** against the keeper, and this Sir George granted, but when the case came before the magistrates at Netherton, Ludlow—who was proved to have bought some strychnine in the town a short time previously 'to kill rats,' as he declared—brought a couple of under-keepers to swear that he was three miles away at the time, and the magistrates refused to convict.

I may tell you, by the way, that some extra artful keepers have a nasty trick of pushing a bit of poisoned liver down each pipe of the rabbit-buries where they have reason to suspect that poachers are in the habit of ferreting regularly —what they call 'baiting 'em.' Of a moonlight night, when the earths are not too extensive, the rabbits will bolt quicker than in the daytime, and it is enough to make a chap wild to feel the line slacken, and, when you pull it back, to see your poor 'camel'—that is worth, perhaps, ten bob to you— dragged out as dead as a nit, with a bit of poisoned liver inside of him. The keepers have a regular scale for strychnine, one grain for a ferret, two for a cat, four for a fox, and six for a dog—d—— all such chaps, say I, a *veshengro* should be a *yog-moosh*, not a *drabengro*.†

When the case was dismissed Tenny never *chirruped* a *lav*, but a few nights afterwards Ludlow was found lying in the road about a hundred yards from his own cottage, perfectly insensible and pounded almost to a mummy. Two of his ribs were broken and most of his front teeth were missing, and when he came out of the *naflo-ker*,‡ the feeling in the neighbourhood was so strong against him that even Squire Beaumont didn't dare to take him back. *Yuv kekker kedas chichi kooshtoben pauli, ta man shoondom yuv moolered adrey o bootiesti-ker.*§

* Warrant.

† A keeper (wood-fellow) should be a keeper (gun-man) not a poison-monger. ‡ Hospital.

§ He never did any good afterwards, and I heard that he died in the work-house.

CHAPTER IX.

Passon Mark.

IMMEDIATELY below the village of Cranmeet the narrow valley of the Cran broadens out into a succession of water-meadows, where attempts have been made to improve the naturally scant and rushy herbage by a system of alternate drainage and irrigation. With this end in view, a main-carrier has been made to intercept and carry off the surplus water from the Cran at an artificial weir specially constructed for the purpose at Cranmeet, and after irrigating the water-meadows by means of an ingenious arrangement of hatches and sub-carriers, it empties itself into the river at a bend in the stream about two miles lower down.

After an autumn flood the carriers are dammed back until they fill, and the farmers, lifting the side-hatches, allow the muddy waters to overflow the fields, leaving, as they subside, a fertilising deposit. Then it is that the foolish, headstrong salmon, intent on spawning and obedient to the resistless impulse which urges them ever upward and onward, enter the main-carrier at the bend where it empties itself into the river, and work their way upward through the water-meadows under the mistaken impression that they are taking a short-cut to the gravel-beds above, while the greedy trout, forsaking their hovers beneath the stubs and boulders in the river bed, follow their example, routing about among the submerged herbage to their hearts' content and reaping, for the time being, a plentiful harvest. But their enjoyment —like the majority of mundane pleasures—was short-lived, for the rapidly subsiding waters would leave them struggling in the deeper furrows, where they would burrow for shelter beneath the tussocks of rushy grass—only to be thrown out, high and dry, on the following morning by the merciless four-pronged 'tatur-fork of the keen-eyed farm-labourer.

Knowing this, the younger members of the tribe would often organise a nocturnal raid for the express purpose of anticipating the rightful occupier of the soil. As soon as the water began to clear and the overflow gradually subsided into the carriers, we would start at dead of night equipped with lanterns, gaffs, fish-spears, or anything that our ingenuity could fashion into a weapon of destruction. First of all we made our way to the irrigation-weir below Cranmeet and shut down the main-hatch, and the supply of water being cut off, the carriers began to fine down rapidly, causing the broad-backed salmon and dainty, red-spotted trout to seek the shelter of the deeper holes. Then, beginning at the lower end of the meadows, we would work our way upward, exploring every likely hole and water-worn bank of main and sub-carriers by the searching glare of the lanterns, and probing the rushy bottom with *matchinesko pusimangrior.**

Suddenly a frightened salmon would dart from his temporary lurking-place and rush madly up-stream, furrowing the shallow water of the carrier as he went and leaving a long series of mimic waves in his wake, while we youngsters—a dusky, bare-footed crew—would follow him at best pace along the bank, uttering subdued cries and capering with excitement, until Perin or Vester would get a chance of driving the deadly grains through him, when he was jerked out and promptly *chivved adrey* the *gunno.*† Sometimes half-a-dozen fish might be seen lying side-by-side in a deep hole where the gravelly bed had been washed away by the rush of water through the hatch, and when—after gaffing or spearing two or three of them—the water became too foul to see the others, they were poked out with long sticks and driven down-stream into an old bat-fowling net which, when set across the carrier with its bow firmly pressed against the bottom, formed a very handy instrument of capture.

It was exciting sport—or if it wasn't sport in the strictest acceptation of the term, we thought it was, which comes to very much the same thing—and a fleeting glimpse of the capering, dark-skinned figures with bare legs and fantastically tattered garments, tearing along the banks amidst sup-

---

* Fish-spears.   † Popped into the sack.

pressed cries of excitement, the rapidly-shifting light from the lanterns dancing, meanwhile, like *moomli-moolomengris** above the troubled waters, might, when combined with the midnight hour, the strange language, and the wildness of the surroundings, almost have justified a superstitious rustic on his way back from fair or festival, in supposing that the ghostly 'wish-hounds' were abroad, or that a troop of elves, escaped from their subterranean abode beneath the rugged boulders of Dartmoor, were holding high revel among the mist-veiled meadows of the Cran valley.

On reaching the water-meadows the river broadens out and dawdles lazily along at a more sober gait, as if half inclined to take an hour or two's siesta in the dancing sunlight after the exhausting course of gymnastics which it has lately undergone, winding and twisting in leisurely fashion like a glistening and plethoric serpent, and forming at the bends a succession of deep, still pools, the abode of antient and—truth to say—somewhat legendary trouts, whose noble proportions were only supposed to be equalled by the refinement of their tastes and the high standard of their education. Every now and again the smooth, dark current of the gliding stream would break into gurgling rapids or broadly smiling stickles, where the lusty trouts aforesaid, forsaking their lurking-places in the deeper pools below and emboldened by the gathering darkness, would suck down the luscious sedge-flies or powdery-winged moths as they floated past, dimpling the surface with oft-recurring rings.

Here, during the summer heats, the wild-eyed Devons with their small, blood-like heads, glossy dark-red coats, and shapely thoroughbred limbs, would stand, belly-deep, in the cool stream, lazily flicking the flies from their flanks with long, flexible tails, and occasionally stamping their feet—thereby causing the shoals of inquisitive but timorous minnows to seek the shelter of the deeper water, furrowing the surface of the shallows in their frantic haste.

Here, too, the tiny white-waistcoated water-ouzel—a younger brother, surely, of the weirdly-croaking bird who haunts the stony crests of Dartmoor—may be seen perched upon a partially submerged boulder in mid-stream, dipping and bowing with comically obsequious gestures, till, dropping

* Jack-a-lanterns.

from his perch, he runs into the bubbling waters of the stickle and disappears from sight as if intent on suicide, only, however, to reappear lower down—then, settling on some jutting ledge or lichen-covered stone, he bursts into song, trolling and piping with ever-varying note.

The summer-snipe, who has been perambulating the sandy margin, darts from the shelter of the overhanging bank at our approach and flits along with rapid, jerking flight, so close to the surface of the stream that every feather of his snowy breast and each beat of the dun-coloured pinions are mirrored and reproduced by Nature's camera with a minuteness of detail which puts to shame the latest developments of the photographic art, while, every now and again, the strong-billed, thick-set kingfisher flashes like an emerald beneath the overarching boughs, or poising himself for an instant, hawk-like, above the shallows, closes his quivering wings and drops like a gannet among the unsuspicious fry—a habit which, in dry seasons, often leads to self-destruction, owing to the bird striking his head against the bottom.

As the angler wends his restless way along the bank, cursing the weather or his want of luck—it is never his want of skill, be it observed—after the manner of his kind, but cheered, perchance, by the recollection that his companion has done even worse than himself, and fortified by the reflection that the shades of evening will surely cause his fortunes to amend, the solemn Jack-heron rises with heavy-flapping wings from a minute inspection of the stickles, and wings his way with a hoarse 'fra-a-nk' to his sanctuary amongst the lofty trees of Netherleigh Chase.

Turning a sharp bend in the river where a fringe of reeds screens the further bank, we—that is to say my uncle Neptune and a dark-eyed, brown-skinned young nipper of about twelve or thirteen—instinctively come to a halt as we catch sight of the figure of a man stealthily creeping on hands and knees towards the water. As we watch his proceedings—screened, ourselves, from observation by one of those unnegotiable, stone-fronted, razor-backed banks peculiar to the district—we notice for the first time the rings made by a rising trout, which dimple for a moment the oily surface of the stream. The fish is rising in a little eddy, or backwater, formed by a projection in the bank, and is methodically sucking down the flies as they work round out of the current—secure in the immunity which his almost impregnable position has hitherto afforded him from the insidious advances of the piscatorial fraternity.

It is a ticklish cast, for in order to bring the fly well over him, it must drop just six inches above and inside the spot where he is lying in the very shadow of an uncompromising-looking stub—a minute inspection of which would reveal the fact that several highly-finished specimens of the fly-dresser's skill are deeply embedded in its bark, or hang from neighbouring twigs like insects in a butcher-bird's larder, while a 'bleu-upraight,' attached to a frayed and ragged collar, sways to and fro with every breeze and bears mute but emphatic testimony to the hazardous nature of the enterprise.

Creeping as near as he dares to the edge of the bank, the fisherman raises the light rod, and with a few quick turns of the wrist—letting out line, the while, with his left hand—causes the casting-line to hover above the stream without touching the water, until he has got the exact length and strength. Nerving himself for the final cast, the line flies out straight and true and the tail-fly is about to drop, light as thistle-down, just six inches above the unsuspecting fish, when, suddenly, and with a prodigious amount of unnecessary fuss and clatter, flapping of wings, and beating of water, an apoplectic old water-hen bursts out of the reeds which fringe the opposite bank, within whose shelter her chicks—six tiny, black, fluffy balls—are securely floating, and succeeds, very effectually, in diverting attention from her interesting progeny.

The fisherman rises at once from his devotional posture and winds in his line preparatory to departing, the while a monosyllable—and that not a blessing, unless my ears deceive me—escapes his lips. There being no necessity for further concealment, we climb over the bank. The Parson—for a clergyman of the Church of England he is, despite his somewhat equivocal attire—recognises us, and calling us to him, gives me his basket to carry, lights his pipe, and accompanies us as far as the camp in the Combe for a chat and a cup of tea with my granny Charlotte.

The Rev. Mark Sealy, M.A., of St. Saviour's, Camford, and incumbent of the parish of Netherleigh in the county of Devon, is a remarkable man, and as he is to exercise a powerful influence over the bare-footed lad who trots behind him with the fishing-basket over his shoulder, he merits rather more than a passing word of description.

Mr. Sealy, or, as he is better known throughout the country side, 'Passon Mark,' is one of those spare-built, wiry men of about five-foot-ten, whom a judge of athletes and athletics would rightly credit with a superabundance of nervous energy combined with powers of endurance far above the average, despite the absence of any exceptional muscular development, and who, if they be so minded, can generally effect an insurance upon their lives on more equitable terms than the majority of men of twice their physical strength. At the period to which I am referring he must be about forty, but, unlike most men of similar physique and habits, he looks older than he really is, for the dark hair is plentifully streaked with grey at the temples, although the strong-growing whiskers show no sign of advancing age. The features are regular and refined, with the exception of the mouth and chin, which rather belie the purely intellectual cast of the upper portion of the face, while the eyes of a deep, blackish grey and the dark, straight line of the eyebrows, give additional character to a countenance which, whatever may be its defects, is at all events not deficient in firmness. The naturally swarthy complexion, bronzed by sun and wind, is as brown as any Gipsy's, and looks even darker than it is by reason of the stubbly growth which overruns the jaw and upper-lip, for only on Sunday and on Thursday, being market-day, does the Parson indulge in the luxury of a clean shave. Except when excited or in congenial society the general expression of the face is severe even to melancholy, while energy and determination are written in every line of the strongly-marked features—but for those who are acquainted with the true history and nature of the man, there is at times a wistful expression in the dark, fearless eyes which is infinitely pathetic.

The hot afternoon sun beats down upon an old, weather-stained hat of soft felt into which are stuck some dozen roughly-tied trout-flies, while the sunburnt neck—innocent of collar—is confined within the folds of a dingy and carelessly-knotted birdseye handkerchief. He wears a loose-fitting shooting-coat much frayed at the wrists and elbows and patched with leather on the right shoulder where it has been worn into a hole from constant contact with salmon-rod and gun-barrels, while his legs are encased in a pair of rusty-looking black-cloth trousers which, at some remote period, have evidently done duty in the pulpit. For convenience in wading he has rolled the last-mentioned garments up to the knees, and his stockingless feet are protected from thorn and stone by a pair of heavily-nailed shooting-boots—the unmistakable handiwork of the village cobbler—the seams of which are bleached and the leather turned a rusty brown from frequent immersion in bog and stream. The most confiding pawnbroker would most certainly not have advanced five shillings upon his raiment—unless, haply, a farthing had been judiciously inserted between the linings of the waistcoat pocket—but he who would judge by outward appearances alone, should serve a longer apprenticeship than the brief span of years allotted to the majority of us renders practicable, and, despite his neglected exterior, no braver or kindlier heart beat within the limits of North Devon than that of the Rev. Mark Sealy.

I shall never forget my first meeting with him, characteristic, as it was, of this singular man. It was during the winter following my arrival at Fernleigh Combe, and I was sitting by the roadside awaiting the return of some of our people who had been to a neighbouring fair, holding in a ragged handkerchief a couple of *tullo hotchiwitchis* * which I had ruthlessly dragged from their warm hiding-places under the shelter of a dry bank, where they lay snugly coiled up, deep-buried beneath an accumulation of dried sticks and autumnal leaves.

The prickly-coated little *pals-o-the-bor* † are in the finest condition for eating during the late autumn. Some dogs are wonderfully clever at finding them, but he who knows where to look for them needs no dog to guide him, and we used often to find ten or a dozen a day when their hiding-places had been left undisturbed for any length of time. We *chavvies* used to hunt for their 'runs' in summer, following

---

* Fat hedgehogs. † Hedgehogs—brothers-of-the-hedge.

them up to where the old mother lay coiled-up in her dome-shaped, water-proof nest with her dear, tiny *tawni-yecks* * all covered with fluff and soft white spines. The grumpy old paterfamilias—the *pooro jooko*, or old dog, as we call him—constructs a separate nest for himself at some distance from that occupied by his wife and family, so as to be out of the way of domestic disturbances, while a well-beaten track, or 'run,' connects the two establishments. Sometimes we used to hunt for adders under the stones on the moor—Scob Hill used to be a terrible place for them—and when we found one, we used to *chiv* it *adrey* a *gunno* and take it home and give it to cousin Lementina's pet hedgehog. Then the nasty *sap* † would strike at the *hotchi*, who retaliated by scrunching its ugly head between her sharp teeth, and then quietly set to work and eat every bit of it, beginning at the head and working down to the tail. If you find an adder asleep in the sun and take an ash-stick and draw a circle round it *adrey* the *chick*,‡ he can't for the life of him cross the line. But, as usual, I have wandered away from the subject in hand.

On the particular occasion to which I refer, Passon Mark—as the country folk called him—had evidently been having a day with one of the neighbouring packs of hounds, and was mounted on a weedy, breedy four-year-old on whose rough coat the drying sweat had formed a white, powdery scurf, and whose knees already bore the Devonshire Arms unmistakably stamped upon them. Bringing his tired nag to a standstill in the middle of the road, he fixed his keen glance upon me, and assuming an air of preternatural solemnity, addressed me in somewhat the following strain:—

"Tell me, my son, art thou an offshoot of that dusky Eastern brood which, leaving its home 'neath India's burning sun, hath overrun the Western continents, to find, at length, a resting-place 'midst Fernleigh's shelt'ring cleaves? Know'st thou the philosophic Plato, fierce Sylvanus, or Neptune, ruler of the finny tribes? With him I fain would speak."

For a moment or two I stood listening in amazement to the unfamiliar words, unable to catch their import, but my quick wits, sharpened by frequent encounters with the street-boys of Camford, soon told me that the strange gentleman

---

* Little-ones.   † Snake.   ‡ In the dust.

was trying to come it over me, and unabashed by his air of affected solemnity, I replied:—

"My name, Riley,* is Sammy Loveridge, and we're *hatchin'* 'long of uncle Neptune in the Combe, and if you want me to *tool* your *gry* or *rikker* a *chinamangri* to a *rawni*,† I'll do it as well as ere a boy in the camp."

I should, perhaps, explain that, when living near Camford, I had been used to run errands for the College gentlemen and to hold hacks and pony-traps at the cricket-matches, athletic sports, and race-meetings. The Parson appeared to be greatly amused at my reply, and tossing me a shilling in exchange for the two hedgehogs—which I have no doubt he liberated the moment my back was turned—told me to run up to camp and inform Neptune that he wanted to see him that evening. After that I saw him at intervals at the camp, to which he would come whenever he heard that somebody was seriously ill, and going into the tent, would sit down beside the straw mattress upon which the sufferer was stretched, and endeavour to convey to the ignorant, neglected mind the message of Forgiveness and Hope.

He was never one to rant at people either in the pulpit or out of it, in fact his enemies declared that the parish was in a shocking state of spiritual neglect—which might or might not have been true, not professing to be a judge of such matters myself—but I have always thought that as much may be done by one who, without any undue parade of religion or affectation of sanctity or asceticism, contrives to gain the respect and confidence of his poorer brethren and knows how to administer the word in season, as by the sleek and sanctimonious gentleman who, arrayed in glossy broadcloth and faultless linen, shouts 'Damnation' at his defenceless hearers from the pulpit, and then goes back to dine sumptuously at the Squire's house and listens approvingly, with unctuous smile, to the broad stories which circulate freely round the mahogany, or by the gaunt enthusiast who takes a delight in depriving himself of the necessaries of life, wears a sackcloth shirt next his skin, a blue ribbon in his buttonhole, and addresses every grimy coal-heaver and gin-sodden street-loafer as 'his dear brother in Christ.'

* A corruption of *Rye*—Sir, in use amongst West-country Gipsies.
† "Hold your horse or carry a letter to a lady."

Whether Passon Mark exactly hit off the golden mean is open to discussion, but the poor people swore by him. A firm believer in the good old British attributes of pluck and endurance as exemplified in the ordeal by battle, his sporting proclivities slightly exceeded the limits of modern muscular Christianity of even the most advanced type, and in these degenerate days would most assuredly have procured for him the attention of his diocesan. Mounted on some rough-coated youngster of his own breeding, his well-known face was often to be seen looking over the heads of the bystanders when two good men and true took off their shirts and agreed to have it out after the old English fashion, and he thought no more of riding fifty miles when a main of cocks was to be fought—especially if some of the combatants had chipped the shell in his own coops, for his breed of black-breasted reds was celebrated throughout the county—or to witness a bout of single-stick or wrestling between two local champions, than a popular curate would, nowadays, think of playing 'Kiss-in-the-Ring' at a choir-outing, or singing one of Santley's songs at a tea-fight. Nor was he a merely theoretical admirer of the Prize-Ring—with its exhibitions of bull-dog courage and lessons of self-restraint—but was, himself, a by no means contemptible exponent of the noble art, and although, as I have said, a spare-built man, he once administered a well-deserved thrashing to a pot-valiant bully who ventured to taunt the reverend gentleman about his partiality for field-sports and occasional attendance at the ring-side.

It came about like this—but as the story is Neptune's, not mine, I may as well give it in my uncle's words, just as he used always to tell it.

"You see, this here Ben Pierce—him as they called the King of the Drovers—had come from up-the-country through bein' wanted about a matter of some *vongur*—so I've heerd say—from the sale of some *baulos*, as 'd been 'trusted to him, and as he'd kep' back. He were a wilulent, contankulous, gurt chap, near on to six feet high, and big made all about, with a red face and sandy *bals*. I adnowledge as he c'ld put away more cider for a wager and use worser landwidge than ere a man in the county, and because he were allus a'roarin' and a'cussin', and a'strikin' folk unbeknownst, he took the sway over the others, and they called him the King of the Drovers. He were a treachersome, *narkeri* sort'er chap, and if he had a grudge agen a body, instead of challengin' him and fightin' of him fair and square, he'd bide his time till he were off his guard and then hit him, suddent, fit to stun an ox—and that's how he come to be tried for manslaughter at Bodmin."

"Well, you see, the *Rashai*—or, as I sh'ld say, Passon Mark—had ridden over to 'tend the sale of pedigree stock at Squire Stratton's up to Tordown—him as cut his throat, though why he done it, nobody knows, as were a werry rich man with a wife and fam'ly. Passon'd had a fall out with this here Pierce about some calves as he'd taken to Netherton market, and while he were standin' talkin' to some of the quality, up comes the King as drunk as a lord, and starts abusin' of him and usin' filthy landwidge. Then Squire Stratton's bailiff orders him off the place, and he shakes his fist in Passon Mark's face, and he says, says he:—'You'm fond enough of seein' other chaps fight, but you'm afeard to put up your dukes yourself.'"

"Passon, he laughs and he says:—'I dessay some people 'd say as it weren't quite my business. You're drunk now, but the werry fustest time as I ketches you in a quiet place, I'll give you a chance to see whether I can put up my hands or not.'"

"Well, maybe five, may be six months arter, the day before Norton Fair, Passon'd been fishin' near Cranhead, and as he were walking home along the highroad 'cross the moor, he heers a horse and trap behind him, and when he turns round, who sh'ld he see but Ben Pierce and four or five more drovers in a light spring-cart on their way to the Fair, which is held the fust Wednesday in April."

"When Passon Mark seen who 'twere, he steps into the middle of the road and stops the horse, and he says to the King, as were drivin':—'You rec'klet, my man, what I told you the lastest time ever I seen you, so come outer that there cart, for I never breaks my word.' But the King happened to be sober, and didn't seem to pertickler care for the job. 'Get outer the road'—says he, 'or I'm d———d if I don't drive over ye'—but the others wanted to see the fun and made him get down. Passon he lays his rod and basket by the side of the road, and takes off his coat and weskit and rolls up his sleeves and lays his *stadge* atop of his *chucko*. Then he says to the drovers:—' I only arsts for fair play. If you'll all stand back on the grass and leave the roadway to us, I'll be satisfied.'"

"So they sets to, and the fust round or two the chaps be'aved fair enough. Passon Mark were a beautiful boxer, fly to every move, for he'd larnt it all up to Camford Colledge from a perfessional, and time outer mind when he's been up at the camp and a couple of the youngsters were prac-tizing with the gloves, he'd put 'em on and show them a trick or two. The King weighed fourteen stone, and over, and were a round-armed hitter, and he rushed in and tried to beat down the *Rashai's* guard, but, so long as he'd plenty of room, Passon c'ld dodge and counter him. Then the chaps got excited and begun to crowd round, hollerin' for the King, and Passon he got it hot and heavy 'bout the head and shoulders, through not bein' able to get away, and I believe he'd a'been killed atween the lot of 'em if the coach hadn't happened to come by."

"The drovers was shoutin' and cussin' so, the guard were obligated for to blow his horn tc clear the road, but when Gentleman George saw what was up, he stops the coach, hands the reins to the box-seat, and tells the guard to stand at the horses' heads. Then he gets down and most of the passengers with him, and as Passon wouldn't stop, he gets the sponge outer the boot and washes his face, and they makes a proper ring. One of the gentlemen calls time by his watch, reg'lar, and they fowt on till they was pretty well beat and knocked about."

"Now I must displain to you that the *Rashai* were wun-nerful flick of his *tatcho vast*,* but when he begun the fight he come to the contermination not to use it onless he got a good openin', and kep' it up his sleeve—in a way of speakin' —a'purpose to *hokker* and *tadder* † the King, and make him think he'd only a left-handed hitter to tackle, but at last he saw his chance and upper-cut him a termenjous smack on the pint o' the jaw, and near as possible knocked him outer time."

"The King he come up next round a'shakin' of his head

* "Right hand." † "Deceive and draw out."

and a 'spittin' out blood—for his tongue were cut—but he'd had pretty nigh a belly-full a'ready, for he were a chicken-hearted one with all his bluster when he wern't *posh motto*.* He were werry careful of the *Rashai's* right after that, but at last he got his arm too high and left his side open, and Passon he *bongered* his *sherro* † and swung his right round and fetched him a reg'lar rib-bender in the proper place just over the spleen, and the King he throws up his hands and ketches at his breath and turns as white as a sheet. It ain't pleasant when you gets fairly pasted there, as I knows myself."

"That finished it. So they gives the King a drop of brandy and puts Passon Mark on the coach, and off they goes full gallop to make up time, and drops him at the cross-roads near Netherleigh. And after that all the other drovers turned on the poor King like a pack of curs, because he were a down pin, and it were who sh'ld be the fust to fight him. He smashed hisself up through falling' off a gun-carriage at Plymouth when in drink, and was a long time in hospital, and I can't rightly tell what become of him after."

Although one of the hardest men of his day to hounds and fond of a ride between the flags when at the University, his means did not admit of his hunting regularly, and it was only when hounds met within easy distance that he would mount one of his half-broken, three-parts-bred colts, and as long as it could raise a gallop his knowledge of country stood him in good stead and enabled him to show in front, but as soon as his nag's laboured gallop and heaving flanks proclaimed that its bolt was shot, he would reluctantly turn its head away from the hounds and make his way back to the little moorland Parsonage, vowing every time that it should be his last appearance in the hunting-field.

Passionately fond of riding across country and a finished horseman, he was anything but a houndsman, for as long as there was something to jump and something to jump it with, it was a matter of absolute indifference to him whether Lord Braunton's hounds were driving an old greyhound fox across the cramped banking-country to the south-west of Cranmoor, or whether Tom Ball's scratch pack were rousing an outlying stag from the hanging coverts of Fulford, Putcombe,

---

* "Half drunk."   † "Ducked his head."

or Hawk's Wood, or straggling like a skein of wild-geese across the vale in pursuit of the fragrant herring or surreptitious bagman.

It had formerly been the custom for the masters of the neighbouring packs to send notice to the principal resident in each parish of the meets for the following week, and old Mr. George Sealy had been in the habit of giving out the list of fixtures from the reading-desk—which not only ensured a good attendance on the part of the sporting farmers, but afforded the congregation a congenial subject for meditation during the drier passages of his discourse. But upon succeeding to the living at his father's death, Passon Mark, then fresh from Camford, set his face sternly against this practice and communicated the necessary information to the churchwardens at the conclusion of the service —an innovation which, at the time, was considered to be not only new-fangled, but to have a strong revolutionary tendency.

Were I to recount one tithe of the stories which, rightly or wrongly, were fathered on the worthy but eccentric clergyman—the best friend I ever had—I should need a volume as big as a family bible, but if anybody who is interested in the subject should find himself in the neighbourhood of Netherleigh, let him interview Samuel Buckingham, the oldest surviving yeoman-farmer, over a glass of whiskey, and I warrant him he will not be disappointed.

Postponing a more detailed description of the life and habits of Passon Mark—beneath whose roof it was my lot to pass four of the happiest years of my life—to a more convenient opportunity, I will, in the meantime, accompany him back to camp, where the reader shall be introduced to the oldest member of our family, my grandmother Charlotte Loveridge.

CHAPTER X.

A Cup of Tea with my Granny Charlotte.

WHEN the Parson, my uncle Neptune, and I reached the camp that hot summer afternoon, we found my grandmother smoking her pipe outside her tent and basking in the genial sunshine like an old brown lizard on a stone-heap. Despite her three score and ten years, she was still a hale, hearty old lady, considerably above the middle height, with a handsome, hard-set countenance, black, glittering eyes which could assume at will a stony, basilisk stare at the sight of an unwelcome intruder, or gleam and sparkle with unholy mirth. Her naturally swarthy skin, burnt to the colour of mahogany, was seamed and crossed with deep crow's-feet at the corner of the eyes, and her strong, regular teeth were slightly discoloured by the nicotine from the short cutty pipe which was seldom long absent from her lips.

Her grizzled hair, covered with a gaudy yellow handkerchief, was coiled and plaited after a fashion of her own. From her ears hung a pair of heavy silver earrings, and her brown, taper fingers with their long filbert-shaped nails were encircled by massive gold and silver rings—some of which were plain while others had been curiously chased by some bygone Gipsy *roopomengro*.* Across her shoulders was thrown a warm woollen shawl, the gift of some charitably disposed lady, for during the winter months she got a touch of the 'brantitis,' as she called it. Her dress was completed by a shabby black velvet body fastened with small silver buttons, and a skirt of some serviceable material cut sufficiently short to disclose a pair of well-turned ankles—the symmetry of which not even a pair of thick worsted stockings and heavy laced-up boots sufficed to mar.

* Silversmith.

According to her own account she was close on seventy at the time of our arrival in camp, and had been accounted in her younger days the handsomest Romany *chi* in the West of England. This might well have been the case, for many a woman of less than half her age might have envied her upright carriage and supple, well-proportioned figure, which time, itself, seemed powerless to affect—all I can say is that although I have seen scores and scores of ancient Romany dames in my day, I never came across a more thoroughly mendacious, brazen-fronted, deep old *chovahauni*[*] than my *poori-dye*[†] Charlotte.

She used to spoil us children dreadfully, and we were very fond of her, for she was just as full of tricks, and tales, and superstitions, and charms, as an egg is of meat. I never took much count of them, leaving that to the girls, but I used to listen with delight to her stories of successful impositions practised at the expense of credulous *gorgios*. According to her simple creed these latter had been created by the merciful dispensation of an all-wise Providence for her especial benefit, and she would fly into a perfect fury whenever Mr. Sealy hinted that the majority of her ingenious little devices such as *duidickaubin'*, *hokkerin'*, *dookerin'*, and *caurin'*,[‡] were nothing more or less, in plain English, than swindling, lying, and stealing.

"What? Me steal from de nasty, low creatures! I wouldn't demean myself for to do sich a thing!"—and the hot blood would mount to her withered cheeks while her deep-set eyes gleamed and scintillated with an unearthly light, and taking the pipe from between her teeth she would dash it to pieces on the ground in a perfect frenzy of virtuous indignation, causing the cross-grained lurcher puppy which she had been nursing in her lap to leap from her knees with a howl and retreat beneath one of the vans.

"Why, de silly things comes a' runnin' arter me a' beggin' and a' seechin' me to help 'em, and I does help 'em to de best of my debility, on de quiet, like—not bein' one to tell all de world when I conforms a 'nevolent action, like that there Mother Yabbicombe[§] up to Loxhoe. Steal? Krishna!!!"

[*] Witch.   [†] Grandmother.
[‡] Ringing the changes, blarnying, fortune-telling, and filching.
[§] A celebrated white-witch.

—and drawing herself up to her full height the old lady would stalk off to her tent and drop the canvas screen behind her, and no amount of persuasion would induce her to show her face again until her visitor had taken his departure.

Generally, however, in the course of the next few days Passon Mark would drop in, accidentally, with a small present of tea or tobacco, which invariably had the desired effect of mollifying her outraged susceptibilities, and the two would be the best of friends again.

Mindful of former benefits and solicitous—as touting tradesmen say—of future favours, the sight of the Parson was always sufficient to put the old lady in the best of humours, and upon our arrival at the camp she at once bestirred herself to get ready a cup of tea.

"Set ye down, *Rashai*,* set ye down while I *dels tute a tas o' muttramengri*.† That's right, *mi chavvi*—upset the *kauvi*‡ all over the shavings and put the blessed fire out. I never did see such a Malpas-child in all my born days——."

"And why do you call her a Malpas-child, Mrs. Loveridge?"—asks the Parson, always anxious to fathom the meaning of any queer-sounding expression which any of the party may chance to make use of. By that time an irregular circle had been formed round the fire, the interstices being filled by the dark, tangled heads of restless, inquisitive children and the lithe forms of obsequious, tail-wagging dogs, whose cringing demeanour and general readiness to efface themselves showed that they were perfectly conscious of their liability to forcible ejection at the shortest notice.

"Why, you see, Ryley, 'tis like as this"—bursts in Perin, Neptune's eldest boy, who is always ready to shove his oar in, "when we used to travel up in Hertfordshire——"

"*Tool te jib* § and bide till somebody arsts yer 'pinion"—growls Neptune, who is not in the best of tempers, "and take care I don't put my foot in yer mouth"—rather a hazardous experiment, by the way, since Perin, who is getting on for three and twenty, could have 'done' his respected progenitor without taking his coat off—"it's cackle, cackle, cackle, from mornin' till night, and anybody can't get in a word edgeways. As I were a' goin' for to tell you,

---

* "Parson."   † "Give you a cup of tea."   ‡ "Kettle."
§ "Hold your tongue.

Rashai, there was a gentleman named Squire Malpas lived in a fine, old-fashioned red house at S——. He'd got eight or nine farms and thousands and thousands of pounds in gold—and how d' ye think he lived? Why, just for all the world like one of these here hermikes as I've a' heerd tell on. It were like this, you see. He goes and falls in love with some young *rawni,* and because she wouldn't have him, he takes his solemn Natty Davis as how he wouldn't wear no clothes nor yet leave his house ontil they carried him out shoulder-high."

"There was a bit of a green oppersite the house, and there we used to camp—for he were very fond of travellers, and as long as he didn't catch you telling him no lies, you might have most anything out of Squire Mapas. I was *hatched adoi* only a few weeks afore he *moolered,* and I suppose as I were the last *Rom'nichal* as *rokkered* the poor dear gentleman. When he seen me there, he come and open the winder, and he says:—'How are you, Loveridge? Go round to the back of the house and I'll let you in.'"

"Well, Rashai, I goes round and there I finds 's how the best part of the roof were tumbled in. The door of the room were hangin' on one hinge, and there he used to sit upon a little wooden stool with *chichi* to *gaver* his *nangipen* but a *pooro ovle*—and a *vassavi, chickli yeck* at *dovo*,* for all the edges was wore into a fringe from draggin' on the dirty floor. He had been as nice-lookin' a little gentleman as ever you need wish to see, but his face and hands was as black as a tinker's and his hair were all down over his shoulders like a Injun's. I disposes, Rashai, as it had to do with the old Roman custom of sack-cloths and hashes, and all of the same head, so to speak, with this here wailin' and 'nashin' of teeth?"

"The room were full of books—for he were a wunnerful well deformed scholar of a man—and I sh'd say as there were all three or four load of empty gin-bottles lying' about. He'd a' trod out a reglar little 'run' between 'em s' far as the winder and back, and there was handfuls of silver three-penny-bits a' lyin' amongst the hashes in the fire-place, for, you see, whenever anybody come to the winder for a chat,

* "Nothing to cover his nakedness but an old blanket—and a wretched, dirty one at that."

he'd give 'em a glass of gin and a *trin-ora* *—and he didn't forget for to take a drop himself, bein' of a natchurably sociable 'sposition and most in general a bit top-heavy when I seen him. He esteemed 's how he give away four hunderd pound in charity every year—leastways, so he told me. I mind one time 's how the *Hindity-mescri* † as worked in the harvest-fields shot at him, and they was obligated for to put a couple of sentry-boxes near the house for the constables to *hatch* in. Yes, he were a wunnerful clever man to talk, and when they tried for to get the peroperty away from him, he *rokkered* that powerful that the *bauro-beshermengro bitchered* the *shoonomus*, ‡ and gave his denouncement 's how the Squire were perfectly impetent to manage his own affairs hisself."

"Well, Rashai, I goes in and sets myself down and *rokkers* to him for a couple of hour—for, bein' a bit of a scholard, myself, I were able to talk up to him—and he keeps arstin' me questions 'bout where I'd been travellin', cunnin' like, to try and find out whether I were tellin' him the Gorspel truth."

"'You tell me as you've been in Dorsetshire'—he'd *pooker*." §

"'*Auvo*, Rye' ‖—I'd answer, 'I knows every inch of the country from Yeovil to Lymington.'"

"'How far d'ye call it from Blandford to Wimborne?' he'd arst."

"''Bout a thirteen mile.'"

"'And how far d'ye make it from Blandford to Wareham?'"

"''Bout a fifteen mile'—I answers, and he thought as he'd a caught me."

"'How d'ye make that out?'—he says, turnin' on me quite sharp."

"'Well, it's like as this'—I *pens*, ¶ 'it's five-and-twenty mile by the highroad, but it ain't more 'n fifteen by the crossroads past High Woods and Charlborough and over Crawford Bridge'—and then he'd turn away and look at a book of the roads as he'd got in his hand all the time—unbe-

---

* "Threepenny-bit."   † "Irish"—dirty people.
‡ "Judge dismissed the case."
§ "Ask."   ‖ "Yes, Sir."   ¶ "Says."

knownst to me, as he thought—to see whether that were right or not. Lor' bless ye, it wouldn't never a' done to *pen leste hokkabens*,* even if you was in the habit of doin' sich a thing which, as you very well knows, Rashai, I aint."

"Quite so, Neptune, quite so"—blandly assents the Parson, "your reputation for mendacity is so thoroughly established as to stand in no need of any corroboration on my part."

"That's just what I always tells 'em"—bursts in my uncle, evidently flattered by this spontaneous testimony to his moral rectitude, and gazing beamingly around upon the small circle of attentive listeners as one who should say:— 'Remember Passon Mark's words the next time you hear any body call me a *rawtfelo hoffeno*'—"and when I got up to go, he gives me his hand, and he says:—'Good-bye, Loveridge, you'll never see me again. It's very nearly over'— and I felt like to *ruve*,† he looked that ill and lonesome, and I says:—'God bless you, Rye'—and come away, and the very next week I heerd as he were dead. And that's why we calls anybody a Malpas if they does anything queer—out of rememberment of the poor, dear Squire."

"Yes"—sententiously remarks old Wisdom Boswell, knocking the ashes out of his pipe against the sole of his boot, as he sits cross-legged by the fire, "there's some queerish customers among the Squires in that part of the country. D'ye mind the Reverend Squire Farrington, as lived near to Baldock, not very far from Squire Malpas? A very nice sort of a gentleman he were, and very good to us travellers, but a reg'lar queer one. He owned a fine *filisin*‡ with a park round it, and a *congri* § inside the park, where he used to perform the sarvices."

"One fine mornin' he climbs up into the polepit, and he says to the congeregashion:—'My good friends'—says he, 'I don't espect as there will be any more sarvices here'— and he takes off his gown, and out he walks. I suppose, Rashai, as he'd a' got tired of it and wanted to dismiss himself out of the ministry, and that were how he elected for to do it. He were mortial fond of music, and every traveller as could play the fiddle were always sure of a welcome and as much as he had a mind to eat and drink. I've been

---

* "Tell him lies."   † "Cry."   ‡ "Country residence."   § "Church."

there scores of times along of the Lees and Chillcotts—fine players they were, either by ear or heart. Sometimes they'd set down to play a tune out of a book, and then the Squire would jump up and say:—'No, d——n ye, no. That isn't what I want. None of that book-stuff for me. Give me the real, wild music'—you see, it were the reg'lar, nat'ral Romany music as he liked. Ah! he were a very nice gentleman were Squire Farrington, and I wish there were more of his sort about."

"Yes"—chimes in Neptune, "old Tom Chilcott were a fine player, and when Larry Lee drew a bow, you could answer for it—and that's what you want when you're dancin' a man for money. I mind dancin' a chap—Noah Burton it were—for a guinea, down to Exeter. Little Zacchy Petulengro* were to play the fiddle for us, but, somehow, I didn't like the derangement—for Zacchy know'd Noah a sight better nor he done me."

"'Let's dance it off to once'—says Noah."

"'No'—says I—for I didn't feel over and above grand, through havin' had a tightener the night before—'I'll dance you to-morrow at three o'clock, and that'll be better for the landlord, and per'aps it'll be better for you, and per'aps it'll be better for me'—which it were."

"Then I goes round to one of these here gaffs where they sings and dances, and I finds a Eyetalian with a orgin. 'Can you play the Plymouth hornpipe, my man?'—I arsts him. 'Yes'—he says, and he works it out beautiful and reg'lar, so's there weren't no gettin' away from it. 'You're the man for my money'—I says, and long and by last we 'grees to give him *pange collor*† for playin', whoever won. Noah, he broke down twice, and the gentleman as was humpire, he says:—'I've been countin' your steps, and you done thirty seven different ones.' Yes, Rashai, I can shake my leg a bit though you mightn't think it. Give me a light clog, and I reckon I can put as many steps into the Plymouth hornpipe as any man in the *tem*‡ excepting poor Dookey Cooper."

"Dookey Cooper?" enquires Mr. Sealy. "Is that any relation to Jack Cooper—the Valiant Gipsy, as they called him in the Ring?"

* "Zachariah Smith"—from *petul*, a horse-shoe.
† "Five shillings." ‡ "Country."

"*Auvo*, Rashai. Dookey were Jack's second son. Oliver were the eldest—him as dances at the music-halls, gaffs, and theatres—and Dookey were the second, a *gryengro* * by trade, and the best Gipsy dancer in the country. He married Plenty Lee, one of Ruslo's daughters, and she used to *kair a tat o' vongur a' dookerin'*,† and brought it all home for him to spend—which he weren't long a' doin', bein' as merry a chap as ever stepped. When he went round to the big race-meetings like Ascot and Goodwood, he were a reg'lar duke and no mistake—bottle-green cutaway with two rows of crown-pieces for buttons, and *bengri* ‡ with gold guinea-pieces, plush breeches, white stockings, and red maroccer ancle-shoes with silver buckles. He used to stop about Woodstreet in Epping Forest along of his son Solly and his daughter Patience. His mother—that were Jack the *kooromengro's* § wife—lived along of his brother Oliver at Harrow Green, but Jack's letters from Australia—the few there was of 'em—was derected to Woodstreet."

"Dookey, poor chap, used to take on these here apoleptic fits, and at last it weren't safe for to leave him, so Sol or Patience used always to bide long of him, one or t'other of 'em. One day, as bad luck would have it, they was both of 'em away together, and when they come back, they finds the poor, dear man lyin' right across the fire, and one side of him burnt all to cinders. So they buried him there, close to the Rising Sun, on the Bellevue estate."

"Did you ever see much of Jack Cooper himself?"—queries the Parson.

"Not a powerful great deal"—replies my uncle, *meero pal jindas leste ferreder ke mande,*∥ through his fust wife bein' Jack's niece. Run and see if you can't wake yer uncle, Perin. *Yuv's delled-akooshi drey lescro tan sims a pooro hotchi-witchi.*" ¶

A few minutes later my uncle Vester makes his appearance, rubbing his eyes and stretching himself after a roll between the blankets and looking—what with his black, stubbly chin, his ruffled locks, his expression of preternatural

---

* "Horse-dealer."   † "Make a lot of money by fortune-telling."
‡ "Waistcoat"   § "Prize-fighter's."
∥ "My brother knew him better than me."
¶ "He's gone to sleep in his tent like an old hedgehog."

acuteness, and the 'feathers'* clinging to his hair and whiskers—for all the world like a cunning old raven on the moult.

"You see, Riley"—he begins apologetically, as he catches one of the lurchers in the ribs with the side of his boot, and sitting himself down and crossing his legs, usurps its place in the circle round the fire, "I only got back late this morning from Lansdown Fair after three days on the road, so I just *hatched-akooshi* to *lel* a *bitti sovaben*."†

"Did *tute bicken* the *vauver roller?*" ‡ enquires Neptune in a stage whisper with an air of the deepest mystery.

"*Auvo pal. Ma rokker anglo o rashengro* §"—replies his brother with a scowl. "I were just tellin' Neptune's how I sold the *nok* ‖ as I bought off of Fenimore Lee."

"You'll get yourself into trouble one of these fine days"—observes the Parson, "but let's hear how you managed it."

"Well, Riley, I just give him a handful o' cayenne pepper to sniff at, just the very same as you'd take a pinch of *nokengro* ¶—but you wants to be very careful. You should hold your arm out, so—with the *lullo dantimengro*** in the palm of your hand. Turn your head away, and take pertic'-lar notice to keep up-wind of him, 'cos, when it rooshes out, if it takes holt on you it's sartin death. Then I plugged his nostrils up with tow, s' far's ever I could push it up outer sight. I got nine pound for him—I give thirty shillin' and a quart o' cider—and I sold a *whid*†† to Nelson Dufty on Bedminster Down. I was camped there up on the Knubbers, and he come along in the evenin' and he says to me:— 'What'll you take for that brown mare of yourn?'"

"'Fourteen pound—no less'—I answers."

"'I'll give you ten'—he says. Thinks I to myself 'I wish I had your money,' but I makes believe to drive her off away from him, just for to *tadder leste*."‡‡

"'Well, come'—says he, 'I'll give you twelve'—a' follerin' of me up the road."

---

* "Particles of the barley-straw which formed his bed."
† "Lay down to take a nap."   ‡ "Did you sell the other—stolen—horse?"
§ "Yes, brother, don't talk before the clergyman."
‖ "Glandered horse."   ¶ "Snuff."   ** "Red-pepper."
†† "Broken-winded horse."   ‡‡ "Draw him on."

"'No'—says I, 'thirteen pound, nineteen shillin' won't buy her, for she's a rare worker.'"

"'Chuck a sovereign back for luck, and it's a bargain'—he says."

"'*Kekker*'*—I *pens*, for I knew I had him landed, 'I give twelve pound for her at Lansdown, but I don't objec' to stand a shant of gatter'—so he gave me the fourteen *bar* and took her away. Next mornin', just as I were pulled out into the road ready to start, he come up to the *vardo* and he says to me:—'I wish as you'd step down to my yard and look at that mare. Her flanks is a' heavin' like a pair o' bellus, and she's a' blowin' fit to put the fire out. Have she got a windball into her?'"

"'Not she'—I says—which were true enough—'onless you've a' give her one?'"

"'Then whatever's the matter with her?' he arsts, for he aint not to say much used to horses—if he knows which end of 'em bites, it's 'bout as much as he do know."

"'Well'—I answers, and I couldn't for the life of me help *savvyin'*, † 'I shouldn't wonder if she wer'n't a bit touched in the wind. Leastways that's what the chap as I bought her off told me.'"

"Then he chucks his hat down on the ground and begun dancin' and cussin', and wants to fight me. 'Keep cool, my lad'—I says, 'and put your hat on while it fits you. In ten minutes you might want a shoe-horn to put it on with'—and the Gorgios as were standin' by begun laughin' at him and chaffin' him, so he picks up his hat and goes back home like a senserful feller—for he know'd as it wer'n't no good a' tryin' to come it over me."

"And how did you manage to stop her blowing?"—inquires Mr. Sealy, who is not above picking up a wrinkle.

"Well, Riley, the *ferredest cuvva* ‡ to 'set' a whid, *bavol*, or bull-tit—whichever you likes to call 'em—is to pick a few sackfuls of the tenderest leaves off of a ash-tree, and give 'em nothin' else to eat for three days—that'll *bakken* 'em and set 'em as tight as wax. Then I gives 'em a pint of sweet oil and just a bite of clover. Some gives 'em a handful of shot done up in lard, but it's very dangersome—'specially if you don't happen to sell 'em right away—for they're as like as

* "No."   † "Smiling."   ‡ "Best thing."

not to fall down dead when they comes to work. Some gives 'em two-pennorth of paregoric and a few beans, but onless you keeps 'em constant on the move they're terrible apt to lie down, and then you've a job to get 'em up again, and, besides, a dealer's sure to lift up their eyelid and see by the yaller colour of the eyeball as they've been *drabled*.* A good thing—'specially in winter when you can't get no ash-leaves—is to give 'em a pound or two of black sugar and four pound of bran damped up together, that 'sets' 'em and opens their pipes, and it's a fine thing to travel on. My father used always to stick 'em with the fleam in the rough of the mouth till the blood come, and then give 'em a haporth o' starch and a feed o' beans, and let 'em swaller their own blood mixed with the beans and starch—and a very capitable thing it is, too."

"The Complete Horse-Coper, by Professor Sylvester Loveridge—popular edition, edited by the Rev. Mark Sealy, M.A."—laughs the Parson in his half-joking, half-sarcastic way, "I wonder if it would sell. In the meanwhile I'll trouble you for another cup of tea, Mrs. Loveridge. Continue your lecture, Vester."

"Well, Riley, as I were a' sayin, the worst of givin' them opium or laudanum is that it makes 'em so sleepified and turns the whites of their eyes yaller. I prefers to give a *delemescro*† a quart of old ale with a ounce of snuff in it, and sometimes I cuts some of the rasty fat off of a side of bacon, and balls 'em with it. That'll keep 'em quiet for a bit, just the very same as a handful of *ballovas* ‡ shoved into a horse's mouth will make him quit canterin' and fidgettin' in harness, and settles him down to his trot. A horse's eyeball oughter be a bluey, slatey colour without any checks or creases—'specially yaller creases, them's megrims."

Here my uncle pauses in order to take a pull at the cider-keg, and then proceeds like a giant refreshed. "D'ye *jin* what a 'bobby-horse' is, Riley? That's the same as a 'chink-backed 'un.' You can most in general tell 'em by a little lump in their spine where the mischief is. Twist 'em sharp round with the halter, and their quarters'll drop down just as if their *dumo sus poggered in dui*.§ They can pull a

---

* "Hocussed."   † "Kicker."   ‡ "Lard."
§ "Back was broken in two."

load up-hill right enough—and that's how I allus likes to show 'em—but if they tries to back it down-hill, over they goes to once. It's just the same when your horse ricks his back a' jumpin'. Take a big lump of Rooshian taller and rub it well in all along the spine from withers to quarter. Then pour some strong vinegar over it and rub it in so hard as ever you can, till it's all worked of a slush together. Then take and kill a sheep and clap the warm skin over the loins —that'll fetch him up if anything will. A 'nappy' horse is when they've got these here little lumps along the neck and withers about as big as a nut. They breaks out either side, and if you works 'em hard, they're as like as not to croak. A 'beany' horse is when they goes dotty on one *peero* * and you puts a little bit of sharp flint between the toe and the shoe of the t'other foot to make 'em go level."

"Some'll shave the t'other foot down to the quick, but I prefers to take the shoe off and prick 'em in the toe till the blood comes, and then put it on again—then they'll go alike on both and there aint nothing to show. I do declare it's mortial dry work a' talkin' this hot weather."

"Keep it up, Vester, keep it up"—says Passon Mark encouragingly, as my uncle appears inclined to slow down, "your works only require oiling."

Another long drain at the keg and the veteran coper resumes his lecture. "If a *grasni* † don't *panni* proper, give her three pennorth of cayenne in lukewarm water, and if a *gry* don't *mutter*, give him a bit of saltpetre about as big as a nut. If a *grasni's* two or three *dood tawnifake*, half an ounce of cayenne and a pennorth of salts'll slip it better nor anything. D'ye *jin*, Riley, the headest *cuvva* for *creminor* ‡ in horses—'specially for these here bots? Get my mother here to give you some wood-laurel. 'Tis a sort of a small bush with smooth leaves like a orange-leaf, and the rankest pisin. Keep the horse fastin' and don't give him no corn, but let him have three leaves the fust day with a lock of nice hay, two leaves the second, and one the third. Six leaves is counted deficient to cure any horse, and it's better nor smokin' 'em with a bacca-pipe,—same as I displained to you *vauver divvus*."§

* "Foot."   † "Mare."   ‡ "Best thing for worms."
§ "The other day."

"Suppose now"—suggests the Parson with that bland and confidence-inviting air which stands him in such good stead when bent on drawing out some particularly wary customer, "you were to find a stray horse, and were to take him to a fair and sell him to pay expenses. How would you alter his appearance so as to spare his former owner—if he should happen, by chance, to be present—the mortification of seeing his old favourite sold?"

"Well, Riley"—replied my uncle, "if I were to happen to run agen a come-by-chancer I sh'd crop his ears or dock his tail or hog his mane, 'cordin' to the sort of him, and if he had a long jacket on him I sh'd boil some rosin and vinegar together and dab it on wet—that loosens the hair—and pluck him as clean as a goose. Then, if he were a dark-coloured 'un, I sh'd take two pennorth o' copperas, some lokemove, and a little sweet ile—it don't do to use turps, 'cos of burnin' the skin—and mix it up and work it in with a stiff brush all over till he come out grey, but if he were a light-coloured 'un, I'd mix up four pennorth o' lamp-black with liquefact and ile, and turn him out black or magpie so's his own dam wouldn't rekernise him twelve hours arter."

"I mind a grey horse, as I'd made a nigger of, as I sold to a carrier in Barnstaple, and for five weeks he worked twice a day past the door of the farmer as bred him, without his ever suspectin' nothing. There's plenty of these here Gorgios as calls thesselves copers and fancies they knows everything, as can dock or crop a horse and alter his teeth and paint his marks out, but when it comes to puttin' a new tail on or turnin' a white 'un into a black 'un, why they aint no more account nor a infunt."

"And how do you manage to make the dye stand the water-brush for any length of time"—enquires the Parson, looking for all the world as if butter wouldn't melt in his mouth, but inwardly as keen as mustard to learn the *bauro hokkani*." *

"Well, you see, Riley"—replies my uncle with a furtive but comprehensive wink which escaped the notice of the Parson while it included the rest of the assembled company, "it's like as this"—the Parson pricks his ears—"If

---
* The great secret.

I were to tell you that, you'd know a'most as much as I done, and that wouldn't never do. There's jest two or three little things as we Rom'nichals likes to keep to ourselves, or else we shouldn't be no better nor Gorgios, and that's one on 'em"—murmurs of assent from the circle round the fire, 'Oh, he's *gozvero* * is Vester!'—'you don't ketch him a'noddin''—"I took a little horse up to Lansdown with me—but now I think I'll just take another pint and turn in between the *koppas*,† for I can't rightly keep my eyes open."

"And how about Jack Cooper, the Valiant Gipsy?"—says Mr. Sealy, covering his disappointment by opening up another subject.

"Well, Riley, it's a bit too long a *goodli*‡ now, but if you like I'll come up to the *rashengro-ker* § one evenin' and tell you all about him from the time he fowt his fust battle till he got the *chiv* to *pawni*,|| and how I lent him my fightin'-boots—reg'lar proper laced-up *chameski chokkor* with *busahor*¶ to 'em—to *koor* in, when he lost the great fight to Bishop Sharpe, for, you see, he had a' took five hundred for to lose. I says to him when I were a' lacin' of 'em up:—'Jack, I've a matter of twenty *bar* about me. What am I to do with it?' 'Don't arst me no questions, my lad'—he answers, short like. That were enough for me, Riley, as you may dispose, so I goes and maces five quid more off of Matthias Cooper and five off of Isaac Herne, and I puts all the thirty on the Bishop. It come off all right as you d' know, but I tell you it made me feel real *naflo* ** to see it, and how the gentlemen did 'hoosh' at him, to be sure. 'For shame, Jack'—they said, 'we shouldn't never have thought it of you!'—for he'd always been a great favorite with the nobs. And when it were all over I took the boots and ripped 'em up with my knife, and chucked 'em away—for I thought they'd bring me *vafro bok*†† if I fowt in 'em after. There was always half-a-crown apiece for every Romany at the ring-side when Jack fowt, for, you see, he liked to have his pals to shout for him—it just makes all the differ when you gets in a tight place. Some time after,

---

* 'Cunning.'   † "Blankets."   ‡ "Story."   § "Parsonage."
|| "Trip to sea"—transportation.   ¶ "Kid boots with spikes to them."
** "Sick."   †† "Bad luck."

when he was driving down to fight O'Leary, I was hangin' on behind, and one of the swells says to Jack:—'What do you think about it yourself, Cooper?' 'Sir'—says Jack, 'I shall kill him; I know I shall, I feel it that strong on me'—and, as you know, Riley, he killed the poor man dead. He felt the *dook** powerful strong on him that day, did Jack, but he never done no good after. And now I'll say 'Good-evenin',' for I aint so limber as I used to was, and I feel as stiff as a hunted hare."

"'Talkin' of fightin'' begins Neptune, whose tongue, once started upon a congenial topic, would go on wagging like the pendulum of an eight-day clock, "one of the best fights I ever see were that atween old Ruslo Lee and Beiram Burrell. You see, Rashai, 'twere like as this. Master Lee had always had the denouncement of bein' the best man in Derbyshire, Lincolnshire, and Nottingham, and this here Beiram had beaten the same men in less time, so that, altho' they'd never met, Ruslo were mortial jealous of him—which were only natchurable under the sarcumstances. Ruslo were one of the blackest old Romanys in the *tem*, a stocky, bull-necked old chap, not so wunnerful tall, but thick-through like the butt of a oak-tree—same as his brother Jasper. Beiram were a bigger man all about, with arms on him like legs o' mutton, over fourteen stone and twenty year younger. He were one of these here *posh-rawts*,† a travellin' smith by trade and had been sparrin' in the booths all his life, and down to every move, but a very quiet, despectable chap in company—ontil he were put upon that's to say. As clever and pretty a two-handed fighter, he were, as ever I see, could cut pints with it and chuck nothing away, and when it come to a half-arm rally, he would stay with 'em—not like some of 'em as spars all over a forty-acre field and can only fight when they've got the lead—for his heart were good, but he weren't up to the chuckin' game, and that's how Berkeley Ryles come to beat him, same as he done Caleb Hearne and Jonathan Brinkley, but he hadn't got a sound finger the last time I seen him—Berkeley, I means."

"Well, Rashai, there was me and Beiram and Bully Stevens and Arno Boswell and Septeerus Smith—about a dozen 'travellers' altogether—a'settin' in a little *kitchema* ‡

---

* "Destiny." † "Half-breeds." ‡ "Inn."

about ten mile this side of Horncastle, the day after the big August Fair, *a'peein' a corro levinor*,* when the door opens and who sh'd step in but Ruslo Purrun† and his daughter. After we'd passed the time o' day, he turns to Beiram and he says:—'What may your name be, my man?'"

"'My name be Burrell'—answers Beiram."

"'It is, is it?'—says Ruslo. 'then you're the 'dentical man I'm looking' for. I've been follerin' of you these three weeks, and now that I've found you, I'll fight you for forty pound or whatever you're worth.'"

"Beiram, he sets there quite cool, and finishes his glass. Then he says:—'Master Lee, you sha'n't go away without your answer, but I'd rather stand a gallon of ale to the company than fight you'—for he were as nice, quiet a chap as ever you see, were Beiram—ontil he were put upon, you *jin*."

"'Let's see what you can put down'—says Ruslo, and Beiram takes off the wallet as he carried on his back, and flings it down on the table.

"'There'—he says, 'you'll find about three pound in coppers, some *vongashees*,‡ and a matter of fifteen pound in gold and silver.' You see, Rashai, Beiram were wunnerful clever at this here *caurin'*,§ and made a sight of money at it. He'd go into a jeweller's shop and arst to see some weddin'-rings, and by the time he'd done sortin' of 'em, there'd be two or three of 'em missin'—and the same thing with the small-change at the *booticas*.‖ I've seen him hold out twenty-four penny-pieces in his two hands, and keep his fingers stretched out straight the while—a'palmin' of 'em. Anybody with a bit of bluff can truck, gladdher, or sally, but it takes a perfessor to *caur*. *Tatcho*."

"By long and by last they 'grees to fight for twenty pound, and we all goes out into the orchard at the back of the house to see fair, and they strips and sets-to. Arno Boswell looked arter Ruslo, and I picked up Beiram. The fust round or two Master Lee hit my man tarrible hard in the face, and when I sponged him down, Beiram says:—'I shall have to do all I know to win this time, I see.' After the fourth round Arno says to Ruslo:—'You'll only smash your

---

* "Drinking a glass of ale." † Lee—a leek ‡ "Rings."
§ "Filching by sleight-of-hand." ‖ "Shops."

knuckles agen his head. Take my device and try to break his left arm just below the shoulder'—and Ruslo made that his mark and hit him on the same spot time arter time. When they'd fowt about forty minutes, it come on dark, so they leaves off and 'grees to start agen next mornin' at six o'clock."

"We was all camped together, and next day, soon arter daylight, Ruslo walks across to Beiram's *vardo*, and there he were with nothing on but his breeches and his boots onlaced, and his left shoulder were black and blue and pounded most to a jelly."

"'It ain't worth your while dressin' of yourself'—says Master Lee, ''cos I'm a'waiting to begin'—and he buckles in his leather belt and chucks down his hat—Romany fashion—and hands his shirt to his daughter. Then Beiram laces up his boots, and they sets-to again. When they'd a'fowt eight or nine rounds, Beiram says to Ruslo:—'Can't you hit no harder nor that, Master Lee? You be gettin' a bit slow.'"

"'Never you fear'—Ruslo *pens*, 'I ain't begun yet'—but, bless your soul, he weren't no good at all to the other, and at last Beiram catches him under the right ear and lays him out like a log. We all thought he were dead, for just a drop or two of black blood come away from his left ear, and he were quite dark in the face. Arno had to bite his ear, sharpish, to bring him to, and you might a'taken a pint and a half of clotted blood from between his waistband and his body. Beiram's left arm above the muskle were swoll up nigh as big as his head and all mortificated, so I goes out and kills a adder and slits him open and rubs the fat into his shoulder—but for a fortnight or more he had to wear his arm in a sling, and to this day when the east wind 's a'blowin', he can't scarcely use it nor yet get no rest o' nights."

"Then Master Lee's daughter—I can't mind her name, but she were the youngest of 'em—says:—'Father, didn't you allus tell me that, when a man licked you fair and square, I should have him for a husband?'"

"'*Tatcho, mi chi. Se cuvva ajaw*'*—Ruslo answers—for, you see, he couldn't go back on it, though he didn't want her to marry a tinker."

* "'True, my daughter, that is so.'"

"Then she walks across to where Beiram were stood, *ta yoi chivella laki's vast drey laki's putsi*,* and takes out a shammy-leather bag, and flings it at his head—in a way of speakin'—and says she:—'You'll find fifty pound there, Beiram Burrell, as I had from my mother. Take it, and me along with it. So they was *rommado*,† but they never got on well—owin' to the old man—and Beiram didn't treat her not to say over and above well, not bein' a reg'lar Romany bred and born, but one of these here half-baked travellers."

"Quite an Homeric combat"—observes the Parson, knocking the ashes out of his meerschaum preparatory to making a start.

"Never know'd him"—rejoins Neptune, "but I once fowt Meyrick Lock at Binegar Fair for five *bar*, and sent him to sleep inside of ten minutes."

"Well, Neptune, you shall tell me about that another time"—says Mr. Sealy, rising and stretching his legs, which have become cramped from sitting so long in one position, "and all about Berkeley Ryles 'what never was captured,' Larry Shore, Jonathan Brinkley, Big Tom Musto, and all the rest of them. And now it's about time for me to be off to the river again, or I shall miss the evening rise. *Kooshto bok*, Mrs. Loveridge, and *kooshto rarde*." ‡

* "And she puts her hand in her pocket."
† "Married."
‡ "Good luck, Mrs. Loveridge, and good night."

CHAPTER XI.

Dies Carbone Notanda.

A STRANGER striking inland and southward across the steep hog-back of Brent Downs in search of shelter from the violent squalls and chilly showers of combined rain, sleet, and spray, which come driving in from the Atlantic, might, as he sank the skyline, almost have imagined himself amidst the stern and desolate scenery of the Western Highlands.

Far as the eye can reach lies a vast, gently-undulating tract of barren heather, the monotony of which is only partly relieved, while the all-pervading sense of solitude and desolation is proportionately accentuated, by the huge granite tors—rough-hewn by the hand of Nature and toned down to the prevailing sombre tint by time and weather—which crop up at frequent intervals. Piled around their base in picturesque confusion lie clitters of grey stones of all shapes and sizes, which it requires no great stretch of the imagination to convert into the crumbling remains of some prehistoric fortalice.

In the hollows, where the drainage from the higher levels has cut a channel through the spongy soil, small oases of rushy grass assume an emerald hue as a fitful gleam of sunshine travels athwart the gloomy scene, brightening, for a moment, the dull olive-greys of the whortleberry-scrub, and affording to the eye a pleasing relief from the monotonous colouring of the surroundings, while here and there the surface of the moor is corrugated and intersected by ink-black peat-bogs and treacherous quagmires where the cotton-grasses wave their silky crests—a sure indication of the boggy nature of the soil beneath.

These morasses can only be traversed in safety by springing lightly from tussock to tussock of matted grass, causing the peaty water to squirt aside beneath the pressure, and the stranger, if himself a native of the northern wilds aforementioned, may find his first impression confirmed by the sight of several freshly-made tracks deeply cut in the dark, yielding soil, which will at once suggest the presence of red-deer, while, as if to complete the illusion, high overhead with wary neck outstretched to its full extent, a patriarchal black-cock which some poaching sheep-dog has routed out from his hiding-place amongst the whortleberry-scrub and matted grass, may be seen cleaving, with laboured, duck-like flight, the western gale—with two exceptions the only living object in that dreary landscape.

I, Samson Loveridge, mounted upon an animal if possible more ragged and poverty-stricken than myself, formed the principal exception—a small, insignificant specimen of humanity, but, with my unkempt black hair, tattered garments, and bare feet, thoroughly in keeping, from an artistic point of view, with the wildness of the surrounding scenery. I suppose I must have been a pitiful-looking object enough in all conscience, with no redeeming points save my dark eyes, white teeth, and clear, brown skin, but I had plenty to think about and more urgent matters than my personal appearance to occupy my attention.

It had been my duty the previous evening to *poov* the *gryor*, and to see that the more restless of them were securely hobbled. Amongst the others was a well-bred bay galloway of about fourteen hands, with long, rough coat, indeed, but whose neat and bloodlike head, thin neck, and flowing mane and tail, afforded a striking contrast to the decidedly plebeian appearance of our old white Polly-count-the-milestones, Ginger-Jack, and China-eye, whose respective duties it was to draw the heavy living-vans, or to that of the twelve or fourteen other nags of varying degrees of vice and infirmity who formed the bulk of our equine stock-in-trade.

The bay pony was—not to put too fine a point on it—a *chordi gry*,* and had only arrived the previous evening, having

---

* Stolen horse. *Chordi gryor* are seldom exposed for sale in the open market, being generally taken to the stables of some inn at a distance, and there 'swapped' for some animal of less questionable antecedents. Strange as it may appear, horse-stealing has never been more prevalent during the last fifty years than it is at the present day, and quite lately I have seen a couple of stolen horses openly sold at a well-known provincial Repository, to the no small delight of the select *coterie* who were 'in the know.'

been ridden into camp soon after dusk, bare-backed and all of a lather, by my uncle Vester. I had been ordered to hobble and turn him loose for the night with the others, preparatory to making certain indispensable alterations in his personal appearance with a view to rendering his identification by his late owner next door to an impossibility, and I had faithfully carried out my instructions, but on starting out at daybreak to round the horses up, I found that the new-comer had managed to slip or break his hobbles—which were old and rotten—and had made himself scarce, so, leaving the others grazing contentedly amongst the tall ferns which clothed the sides of the Combe, I started off in the direction of the moor above.

There had been a sharp white-frost over night, and at first the tracks were easy enough to follow, but as they approached the edge of the moor where the rushy grass and bracken began to intermingle with the stubbly growth of the heather, the sun, breaking through the dense mist which, closely packed like the whitest of white cotton-wool, filled every goyle and cleave of the valley below, first burnt the impress of the iron tips black and distinct into the frosty ground, then, rising higher and higher in all the glory of a cloudless October morning, obliterated them altogether. Knowing from experience that it would be worse than useless to scour the moor on foot, I returned to camp, and slipping a bridle on old Whistling Jenny and taking a spare halter with me, set out in quest of the fugitive.

Whistling Jenny was a black pack-mare, short-backed and sure-footed, who enjoyed the reputation of being able to smell a Revenue officer a mile off on the darkest night—a qualification which, however, was somewhat discounted by the fact that, owing to a chronic bronchial affection under which she laboured, the aforesaid officer received ample intimation of her whereabouts at something like the same distance. She was the joint property of our people and of old George Beer, who kept the Raven Inn at the little fishing port of Blackstow, and whose family, consisting of five hulking sons, earned a precarious livelihood as farmers, pilots, fishermen, smugglers, and—as some said—wreckers. Although at the time to which I am referring the lighthouse had not been built at Buckland Point, the latter occupation had gradually fallen away of late years, but in spite of the fact that a sharp look-out was kept at the newly-established coastguard stations along the coast-line, every now and again a cargo was run, and on these occasions our men and horses formed a ready means of transport to a secure hiding-place inland.

The weather had changed at mid-day with the turn of the tide, and all through the drizzling afternoon that followed I searched in vain every likely feeding-ground and sheltered hollow from Brent Head to Blackstow. The watery sun was already sinking in the West behind fast-gathering masses of threatening night-clouds before I discovered any traces of the fugitive, and following the fresh tracks, I came upon him quietly feeding amongst some scattered boulders. Catching sight of me at the same moment, he threw up his head and started into a trot, but his hind-feet kept treading on the broken hobbles which still trailed from the off-fore leg, pulling him up short at every other stride, so giving the old mare her head and ramming my heels into her ribs, I galloped alongside and soon succeeded in slipping the halter on to him.

With the exception of a crust of bread and a mouthful of cheese, not a morsel of food had passed my lips that blessed day, and the evening was closing in apace as I turned into the narrow bridle-path which formed the short-cut between Netherton and Blackstow. In the meanwhile the wind had risen with the turn of the tide, and heavy squalls accompanied by a fine, misty rain which soon wetted me to the skin, came driving over the Downs. As I shogged leisurely along, wet-through, tired-out, and hungry—*moccado, kinyo, ta boccalo*, as we should say—but cheered alike by the prospect of a hearty supper and by the reflection that I had escaped a no less hearty jacketing, my quick ears caught the dull 'thud! thud!' of a horse coming at full speed across the moor above. As the measured stroke of his hoofs upon the rough track—far behind me as yet but evidently quickly overtaking me—was borne to me by the freshening breeze, anxious no less to escape recognition than to avoid collision, I instinctively pulled the nags into the shadow of the overhanging bank on the off-side of the road, screening the *chordi gry* from inquisitive eyes by interposing old Jenny's carcase, then, dragging my tattered head-piece well down over my eyes, I turned round to identify the reckless horseman who was risking his neck and his horse's knees in the fast-gathering gloom.

To my surprise, as he dashed past, I recognised Mr. Lyons, the sporting doctor from Blackstow. Half turning in his saddle and taking a pull at his ewe-necked chestnut, he shouted something to me as he galloped by, the only words which I was able to distinguish being 'mother'—'accident'—'hurry'—then, touching his horse with the spur, he plunged forward and was quickly swallowed up by the driving mist.

Exempt as our people are, to a remarkable extent, from the petty ills and infirmities to which the ordinary house-dweller is subject, and which in many cases are brought on by want of exercise and confinement in stuffy, ill-ventilated rooms, we seldom call in the assistance of the regular medical practitioner save in cases of urgent necessity. It may, therefore, be imagined that the sight of the village doctor galloping at breakneck speed, coupled with the words of warning which had reached me above the rattle of hoofs and the growling of the rising storm, was calculated to send a cold thrill of terrified anticipation through my boyish heart. Hastily slipping over the shoulder of the stale old mare, I threw myself across the mettlesome pony, and sitting well back, with my legs and heels glued to his ribs, I followed at full speed in the doctor's tracks, leaving Jenny to find her way back at her own sweet will. Rattling down the stony road through the Combe at top speed, regardless of slips and stumbles, I soon arrived at the camp, where the doctor's weedy thoroughbred, enveloped in a cloud of steam and evidently cooked to a turn, was being led up and down by one of the children.

Throwing myself off the pony, I ran instinctively to my mother's van, but finding it deserted, I made my way to Charlotte's tent, round which a knot of women and children had collected. Just outside it, with their eyes fixed upon the screen which divided the outer from the inner compartment, stood my uncle Neptune, old Levi Orchard, and Wisdom Boswell, who had been the first to get back from Netherton market—the portentous air of sobriety and decorum which prevailed being in marked contrast with the bustle and disorder which usually characterised the return from market, fair, or race-meeting. As I pushed past them not a word was said, but Neptune patted me encouragingly on the back. The bowed heads and pitying looks only served to confirm the presentment of evil which oppressed me and caused me to hesitate, but I felt myself pushed gently forward, and lifting the canvas, my eyes fell upon a scene every detail of which will remain indelibly stamped upon the tablets of my memory to my dying day.

My poor, dear mother lay stretched upon the heap of barley-straw which served as mattress, the vivid crimson, black and yellow stripes of the rug which covered it bringing into startling relief the ghastly pallor of her olive skin, from which all traces of colour had fled. Her hair had escaped from its fastenings and partly concealed the face, while behind her, and half supporting her, knelt my grandmother, whose sturdy figure, swarthy brow, and grizzled locks contrasted strangely with the refined beauty of my mother's oval face and clear-cut features.

Kneeling beside her, with his back towards me, was Dr. Lyons, who was endeavouring by the application of a hastily improvised tourniquet to staunch the blood which trickled at every pulsation from a deep gash which almost severed the muscles of the left fore-arm. In the background were crouched two or three of the other women—old Trainette Burton, her daughter poor Sabina, and Oceana Orchard— while fierce Lucretia Boswell, from beneath the penthouse of whose bent eyebrows the light of battle was wont to flash, was timidly holding my mother's uninjured hand and sobbing like a child. The tent-cloth flapped and strained at the pin-thorns as the heavy gusts came driving down the Combe. A farthing-rushlight stuck in the neck of a bottle threw a sickly glimmer over the scene, and every now and again a dusky head, favoured by the dense shadow, would be cautiously thrust through the opening in the canvas, only to fade away into the outer darkness as a stray gleam from the flickering candle revealed its presence to Lucretia's watchful eyes.

The shadow of death was already upon her, but, as I crept forward, the old, soft light of love beamed for a moment from my mother's eyes, and her features—pinched and drawn with pain and the loss of blood—seemed to relax into a smile. But why should I endeavour to prolong a scene the chief features of which—however circumstances may cause its details to vary—must of necessity find their counterpart in the experience of most of us? I know not for how long I knelt in silence by my mother's side with burning eyes and a choking sensation in my throat—for, boy-like, dazed and stupefied with an unknown terror, I knew not what to say or do—but when at length the doctor rose and motioned to the spectators to leave the tent, I threw myself beside the lifeless body and sobbed as if my very heart must break.

* * * * * *

I afterwards ascertained that my mother, who had been left almost alone in camp with the children, had been occupying herself in chopping firewood, when, suddenly, the sharp-pointed head of the *chinamangri* had flown from the handle, inflicting a deep wound upon the left fore-arm which she had been unable to staunch.

We buried her in the churchyard at Netherleigh—where she had been in the habit of occasionally attending the services—and many years afterwards I placed a modest headstone above the spot where sleeps " Lelinda, the beloved wife of William Loveridge, and youngest daughter of Noah and Lavinia Chilcott, aged 31."

The sharpest mental agony—not infrequently accompanied by unavailing remorse and self-accusation—is common to all ranks of the community, but prolonged grief is a luxury which, perhaps fortunately for us, is denied to the poorer classes. The daily struggle for existence and the hard matter-of-fact necessity for prolonged bodily exertion—the natural outcome of a wandering, hand-to-mouth life—leave us but little leisure for nourishing a private sorrow.

In the same way, after a military funeral, the bayonets are fixed, the arms shouldered, the band strikes up a lively air, and the escort moves away from the burial-ground in quick-time. The tear which has trickled unobserved down the bronzed cheek is hurriedly brushed away, and the casual observer, unused to similar scenes, might be inclined to moralise upon the transitory nature of human affection. But those who have helped to lower their comrade into his last resting-place know well that, although the gap in their ranks will be filled up, the wound is no less deep or their regard for him the less sincere because, perforce, they must go through the daily routine with mechanical alacrity.

CHAPTER XII.

The Library at Netherleigh Court and its Occupants.

I THINK I have already mentioned that Sir Pierre L'Estrange had taken a great interest in my mother's fortunes from the time of his first meeting with her, near Windsor, on that memorable occasion when the Dean of St. Saviour's had summoned him post-haste from Devonshire, and ever since the old baronet's death his eldest son, Sir George—who had succeeded to the title and estates—had made a point of personally paying over the interest of the money to which she had become entitled under the will of his ill-starred younger brother.

It has since then occurred to me that as the whole of the small fortune thus inherited amounted to little more than four hundred pounds, and as Sir George was in the habit of paying us interest upon it to the amount of twenty pounds twice a year, he must either have invested her money very cleverly or else—and I have a shrewd suspicion that this was the case—have constituted himself our banker. It is true that he was popularly credited with a rent-roll of between forty and sixty thousand per annum, so that he could afford to be generous, but to do him justice he was always kindness itself, and although by no means a favourite with the neighbouring gentry, no landlord was more universally respected and beloved, not only by his own tenants, but by the poorer classes generally, than was Sir George L'Estrange.

In March and September I invariably accompanied my mother to Netherleigh Court to receive our half-yearly payment, and I can well remember seeing Sir George's young wife walking on the terrace, while her eldest son, Master Geoffrey, played about the garden in charge of his nurse, a handsome Normandy peasant who wore the quaint costume of her province.

Lady L'Estrange, whose history I shall be obliged to relate further on, was a fragile looking creature, with beautiful dark-brown eyes and the smallest hands and feet I ever saw. The sight of my mother with her clear olive skin to which the rich blood imparted a warm glow, her dark eyes, and jet-black hair confined within the folds of a bright-coloured handkerchief, may perhaps have reminded the young French lady of her country-women, for she would always call us to her and converse with my mother in pretty broken English, while I was encouraged to go through my steps for the edification of the future baronet. Upon our departure the gentle, delicate-looking lady would compliment me upon my dancing and would never fail to place a broad silver piece in my dusky paw, and my mother and I would retrace our steps to the camp wondering to what tribe of *vauver-temmeni* Rom'nichals * the dark-eyed nurse with the brown skin and high cheek-bones could belong.

A few days after my dear mother had been laid in her peaceful resting-place beneath the big yew-tree in Netherleigh church-yard, a well-mounted groom rode into camp and informed my uncle Neptune that Sir George wished to see him at the Court at eleven o'clock the following morning, and that he was to bring me with him.

Long before the hour appointed, my uncle and I were waiting in the court-yard—for we are an early-rising race, and having no regular work to do, are, for that reason, perhaps, generally pretty punctual at appointments, especially when there is a chance of obtaining an old suit of clothes or a pair of cast-off shooting-boots—and soon after the big

* Foreign Gipsies.

stable-clock, with its black face and gilded hands, had finished striking eleven, we were admitted by a supercilious footman in shirt-sleeves and pink-and-white-striped waistcoat, whose carroty locks had not at that comparatively early hour acquired the exquisite grey tint which, at a later period of the day, was wont to excite the admiration and envy of his rural compeers.

My uncle Neptune was got up for the occasion regardless of expense, and his face wore a jaunty, self-satisfied expression which nothing but an easy conscience, combined with a well-founded confidence in the artistic perfection of his attire, could warrant. His usually tangled and rebellious locks had been liberally anointed with *ballovas** and carefully parted and plastered down over his swarthy brow, from beneath which his dark eyes sparkled merrily, while his smooth brown skin and muscular, sunburnt neck, presented a pleasing contrast to the uncompromising stand-up collar of antique build which, for the nonce, encircled it. In place of the dingy old handkerchief which usually did duty for collar and neckcloth, he sported a brand-new yellow-fancy † artistically tied and fastened with a fox-tooth pin, his athletic figure being set off by a tight-fitting suit of shepherd's-plaid —the gift of some aristocratic but narrow-chested patron— the exiguity of the material being, however, more than compensated for by the exuberance of the pattern. His nether limbs were encased in a pair of well-worn cord trousers, very tight below the knee and very baggy above, and in his hand he carried a curly-brimmed white beaver hat, which had once adorned the knowing head of Charles Nelson of the 'Flying Times.'

Thoroughly pleased with himself and the world in general, as he passed through the servants' department he cast looks of unqualified approbation upon the well-favoured maid-servants, who giggled in return at the merry-eyed old gentleman, to the ill-concealed disgust of the supercilious menial aforesaid. For my part I was decently dressed in the old, dark-coloured tweed suit which Neptune had given me, and my granny Charlotte had clipped and combed my hair into a semblance of order.

* Lard.
† A yellow-fancy was a yellow handkerchief with a profusion of white spots.

It appeared that Sir George was engaged at the moment, so we were first of all conducted to the snug sanctum occupied by Mr. Adams the butler, and that portly individual proceeded to fill a brown earthenware jug with strong home-brewed ale, and at once plunged into an interesting conversation with my uncle. Now this may appear, at first sight, to have been a very great piece of condescension on the part of so exalted a functionary, but my uncle was a great crony of Adams', who in addition to being the model of a baronial retainer of the nineteenth century, was a thorough sportsman at heart and an enthusiastic naturalist—his pantry forming quite a museum of curious birds and beasts which he had not only shot, but stuffed, himself.

Here might be seen the ring-ousel, which frequents the higher ranges of Dartmoor, looking exactly like a common blackbird with a white patch on its breast: the clumsy-shaped, parrot-beaked cross-bill which, in very severe weather, is occasionally to be met with amongst the pine-trees during the period of its annual migration: a queer-looking, cream-coloured snipe which he had shot on Cranmoor: a pair of house-martins the exact tint of London milk: and a red-legged chough which a westerly gale had driven inland from the distant cliffs of Cornwall—while a golden-clawed peregrine from Lundy, a marsh-harrier, and a pair of buzzards, formed the gems of his collection. Numerous festoons of birds'-eggs hung from the ponderous beams which supported the low ceiling, and the prison-like aspect of the heavily-barred windows was enlivened by cages containing bullfinches and canaries, which piped and trilled as if for a wager. From beneath the cupboard where he kept his private decanter of old port, there protruded the venerable pied head of a badger, whose snarling lips disclosed a formidable array of sharp-pointed teeth, and who appeared only to be restrained by a strong chain and collar from making a snap at the calves of the inquisitive intruder.

The butler was a stoutly-built, fresh-complexioned Yorkshireman, with greyish-brown hair, whiskers carefully trimmed to the orthodox mutton-chop pattern, and clean-shaven mouth and chin. Notwithstanding a striking external resemblance to a certain well-known dignitary of the Church of England, he was, as I have said, a good all-round sportsman, and when the time approached for the decision of any of the so-called classic races, he might be seen scanning the betting-returns with anxious eyes, while the other inmates of the housekeeper's-room looked on respectfully, under the impression that he was engaged in a scrutiny of the railway share-lists—in some of which new-fangled ventures he was credited, rightly or wrongly, with having invested the bulk of his savings.

At length, in obedience to a summons from the library-bell, Mr. Adams assumed his swallow-tailed coat, and gracefully wiping his mouth with the back of his hand, preceded us across the entrance-hall and along a corridor. Then, halting in front of a massive oak door on the right-hand side, he tapped respectfully, and finally ushered us into Sir George's presence.

The library, or Justice-room, was a well-proportioned, square-shaped apartment, the walls of which were entirely hidden by dark oak panelling and book-cases. A heavy-piled carpet of rich but harmoniously-blended hues covered the greater portion of the floor, which was also of dark oak, waxed and polished like the coat of a well-groomed horse and slippery as ice—as I very soon discovered to my no small discomfiture. Two sides of the room were occupied from floor to ceiling by shelves containing a large and valuable collection of books, ranging from the black-lettered, vellum-covered folios and quaintly illuminated manuscripts of the Middle Ages, to the handsomely bound editions of the better-known modern authors, while one end was almost entirely taken up by the old-fashioned fire-place, with its deep recesses, hearth-stone, and quaint fire-dogs, across the backs of which a huge log was smouldering, and above this, again, was a massive and richly-carved oak mantel-piece bearing the L'Estrange arms and the date 1566 deeply cut in old English characters.

Over the door were fixed the branching horns of a mighty stag carrying seventeen points, the double brow-antlers being unusually long and curved, while the tines which formed the cups stuck out like the prongs of a hay-fork. This was the identical stag which my uncle, Teerus Loveridge, slew in single combat on a certain misty October night, as before narrated. The horns were affixed to a wooden shield, into which was inserted a silver plate commemorating the occurrence.

The side of the room immediately facing the doorway was almost entirely occupied by two large French windows, reaching three-parts of the way to the ceiling and opening upon the south terrace. Between these two windows was another, and narrower, book-case containing a number of handsomely bound volumes—which I afterwards discovered to be dummies—which effectually concealed a massive iron safe, or strong-box, deeply set in the solid masonry of the outer wall, the existence of which would scarcely have been suspected by even the most experienced of metropolitan cracksmen, so excellent was the imitation.

At the end of the room, facing the fireplace, stood a large writing-table with curiously carved legs, covered with dark maroon-coloured leather stamped with gold, while comfortable, deep-seated arm-chairs of similar colour and material were distributed here and there. In each of the four corners was a copy of some well-known work of art beautifully executed by an Italian sculptor, the somewhat severe and sombre tone of the room being partially relieved by several spirited bronzes and a few Parisian knick-knacks, but what struck me most at the time was a curious piece of tapestry of a faded greeny-yellowy colour, representing the meeting of King Solomon and the Queen of Sheba, which hung immediately above the mantel-piece.

The figures were the size of life and included a number of slaves bearing presents, but my attention was irresistibly attracted by a negro boy with a metal collar round his neck, who crouched in one corner holding a huge ape by a chain. Now my experience of monkeys and their ways—chiefly in connection with barrel-organs and Italians—had been more varied than agreeable, and I had arrived at the conclusion that the majority of them, notwithstanding their insinuating, not to say hypocritical, grimaces, are of uncertain temper. It at once occurred to me that the calf of Solomon's leg—the shin of which was protected by a sort of cricket-pad, the monarch being depicted in the costume of a Roman general, with helmet, breast-plate, short skirts and sandals—was in perilous contiguity to the ape. I had once been severely bitten in the thumb by one of them while attempting to abstract a nut from its paw under pretence of shaking hands, and my knowledge of the beasts inclined me to the belief that were Solomon to take a step backward, and inadvertently to tread upon the monkey's toes, regardless of the divinity which is said to hedge around a king, it would have its dominoes into the royal calf before you could say 'knife.' The opulent charms of the Queen appealed to me in vain, fascinated as I was by anticipation of the possible catastrophe, which had the effect of altogether diverting my thoughts from the more important matters in hand.

It may, perhaps, be supposed that I have been needlessly particular in describing what may appear to have been—and, indeed, was—a very commonplace, old-fashioned sort of room, but my reason for so doing is that it was destined, many years later, to be the scene of a rather important incident.

At the writing-table, seated in a high, circular-backed arm-chair, was Sir George, and near him sat the Rev. Mark Sealy. Lady L'Estrange was nestling in a low wickerwork garden-chair placed at one of the open windows, half in and half out of the room, apparently enjoying to the full the genial warmth of the Indian summer and engaged upon an intricate piece of crotchet-work, while a brace of long-backed Clumber spaniels, who were dozing upon the deer-skins in front of the hearth, grunted in a decidedly hostile manner as we entered the room, but beyond continuing to eye us suspiciously during the remainder of the interview, they continued to observe a strict neutrality.

Sir George, himself, was a tall, aristocratic-looking man of about five or six and thirty, with blackish-brown hair curling crisply over a broad forehead, and a complexion which was very dark without being actually sallow. His eyes were brown, his eyebrows arched and of a darker shade than the hair, and his face clean-shaven with the exception of a pair of carefully trimmed whiskers and a small imperial. The well-starched collar was encircled by a light buff-coloured silk neckcloth which cascaded over his shirt-front, and was tied with the utmost precision and secured by two minute turquoise-headed pins connected by a tiny chain of gold filagree. He wore a buff-coloured double-breasted waistcoat of a darker shade than the neckcloth, and a black velveteen shooting-coat with a high collar, fastened across the chest with a pair of onyx links, while a silver dog-whistle hung from a button-hole by a plain black ribbon. His well-shaped legs were encased in close-fitting nankeen breeches, and a pair of long gaiters, or overalls, reached three parts of the way up the thighs.

There was never anything the least bit rough or provincial about Sir George, and whether equipped for shooting—as on the present occasion—riding, or walking, he always presented the appearance of having just stepped out of a book of plates representing the latest development of the sartorial art, but although, perhaps, a trifle over-dressed and dandified according to our insular notions, he could never by any possibility have been mistaken for anything but what he was—a refined and cultivated gentleman.

Perhaps a young lady's confidential opinion of him—which I chanced to overhear while waiting at table—may serve to give a better notion of Sir George than a merely formal description.

"You see, my dear"—she remarked to her friend, "he's just one of those men who, whenever they come into a room full of people, manage to make everybody else look and feel a bit dowdy and commonplace, and put you on your best behaviour at once. It isn't that he's so particularly good-looking, and I don't suppose his clothes are different to other people's, but whatever the reason may be, the effect is exasperating in the extreme, and I always feel an insane desire to jump up, rumple his hair, crumple his neck-cloth, and make him waltz round and round the room until he's ready to drop. Oh, yes. He's always most polite and agreeable, but he never seems to thaw for a moment in society, and you'd certainly never think that he'd ever been wild as a young man, although you know, my dear, that people *do* say all sorts of funny things about him. A bit of a wet-blanket? Well, perhaps he is, but he's awfully nice all the same." The description must be taken for what it is worth, but as the young lady afterwards became Sir George's daughter-in-law, it is probably not very far from the mark.

Mounted upon one of his perfect-mannered, well-bitted horses, he would sometimes ride out to the meets, but his heart was not in the sport, and as soon as the hounds had thrown-off, he would turn his horse's head homewards, and, under the circumstances, it can scarcely be wondered at if the plain-spoken country-gentlemen called him 'Frenchy' and bestowed other equally opprobrious epithets upon him under the impression that he was wanting in nerve and pluck.

This, however, was very far from the case, the fact being that the society of the illiterate, port-wine-drinking Devonshire squires possessed no attraction for him, and although he had taken his degree at Camford and had learned to ride to hounds, he had never been properly entered to field-sports as a boy, most of his time having been spent on the Continent. Those of his neighbours who were inclined to doubt his courage or underrate his horsemanship, would have been the first to acknowledge their mistake had they seen him— as I frequently have at an hour when most of them were snoring between the sheets—mounted on a madly-plunging four-year-old, thoroughbred as Eclipse, that he was breaking-in for her ladyship's riding. At the back of the courtyard there was a circular, covered tan-ride, where, in wet weather, he would amuse himself for hours together, making the young horses wear, flex, and bend themselves, obedient to the lightest touch of hand or heel, leading right or left alternately, changing without breaking, and passaging, volting, and caracoling through all the intricate manœuvres of the *haute école*.

It would have been scarcely possible to have conceived a greater contrast to the speckless garments and fastidious get-up of the master of Netherleigh, than was presented by the rough-and-ready costume of the clergyman who was dancing Master Geoffrey on his knee. Passon Mark was dressed pretty much as when we first made his acquaintance by the river-side, except that he had exchanged the rusty black continuations for a pair of stout cord breeches and leather gaiters which bore abundant evidence of desperate encounters with blackthorn, gorse, and bramble. His shot-belt hung from his left shoulder and the lash of a formidable dog-whip protruded from one of his capacious pockets. The rest of the house-party had already started for the roots and stubbles, and Sir George and the Parson were only waiting to despatch my little business before joining them.

When the friendly Adams closed the door behind him, after favouring us with an encouraging wink, leaving us planted on the edge of the carpet, for the first time in my life I felt inclined to sink into the ground, and took refuge behind my uncle's coat-tails. Neptune, on the contrary, who had not neglected the opportunity afforded him of refreshing the inner man, was as bold as brass, for the frequent fishing and shooting expeditions during which he was accustomed to act as guide and henchman to gentlemen from a distance, had brought him into contact with sportsmen of every grade of society. Advancing without hesitation towards the table at which the baronet was seated, he pulled his forelock, and standing very much at his ease, assumed an attitude of polite attention—holding the broad-brimmed beaver in his left hand, the while he mechanically smoothed it's ruffled nap with the right.

"I am given to understand, Loveridge"—began Sir George, "that this lad is your nephew, and that you are his late father's eldest brother. You are aware, I presume, that his mother became entitled to a considerable sum of money under the will of my younger brother, the interest of which I have always paid her myself. This sum naturally reverts to your nephew upon the death of his mother, and it is with a view to consulting you as to his future career that I have summoned you here to-day."

As each sentence, uttered in a calm, dispassionate tone, fell upon his attentive ears, my worthy relative nodded his head assentingly, and with a turn of the wrist caused his rather disreputable headpiece to revolve slowly, in time with the words.

"Ever since my brother's premature death"—Sir George resumed, "I have continued to take an interest in the lad and his mother, and I have no doubt that you will agree with me that the life he is now leading is scarcely calculated to afford him any opportunity of future advancement, but rather the reverse. In making this statement you will, I am sure, acquit me of any intentional reflection upon your personal character or that of your family. On the contrary, I have always heard my friend here"—indicating the Parson—"speak of you as a steady and trustworthy person"—here my uncle smiled approval of the sentiment—"my remarks being only intended, therefore, to apply to the taint of moral depravity which seems to pervade the very atmosphere you breathe, and which is not peculiar to your people, but appears to be one of the inseparable concomitants of a nomadic life when pursued under unfavourable conditions."

The long, 'dictionary' words appeared to please Neptune hugely, and evidently assuming that they were intended to convey a direct personal compliment, the self-satisfied smile beamed out into a broad grin of approval, the while he caused his castor to revolve at an accelerated rate.

"I am also given to understand"—continued Sir George, "that in addition to the money which I have invested in reliable securities, your nephew, by the death of his mother, comes into possession of a trading-van which, with its furniture, stock, horses, etc., is valued by Mr. Sealy—who understands these matters better than I do—at about one hundred pounds. In consideration of the loss which he has sustained by his mother's death, I am prepared—in conjunction with my friend here—to act as the lad's guardian"—here my uncle's jaw dropped about three inches, but quickly recovering himself, he resumed his customary air of urbanity—"and it is proposed that, for the next few years, at all events, he shall take up his residence beneath Mr. Sealy's roof, where he will be well looked after, and I hope that he will endeavour to repay by his general good behaviour the time and trouble which will be expended upon his education. The van with its stock of baskets, horses, etc., will be sold, and the proceeds invested with the rest of the lad's small capital."

So far I had been listening with the utmost indifference to the foregoing conversation, never imagining for a moment that it related to myself until the meaning of the concluding sentences burst upon me with hideous distinctness, effectually interrupting my contemplation of the grinning ape and King Solomon's massive calves.

I was to be ruthlessly snatched from my hero-worship of my cousin Vester: from the companionship of pretty Lementina: from my dear old Granny, who spoiled me: from the horses, donkeys, dogs, and pets of every description: and last, but not least, from the wild, free life which I had learned so passionately to love during the past five years, and which involved that entire absence of every restraining influence for good which—as Sir George, after his slightly pedantic fashion, had put it—was one of the inseparable concomitants of the vagabond life I had been leading. I was to be compelled to live once more in a house—like a nasty Gorgio—to sleep in a close, stuffy room—I felt a choking sensation at the very idea—and—horrible thought!—to work. The prospect proved too much for me, and I burst out sobbing. To add to my discomfiture, as I turned away to hide my face, my hobnails struck up upon the treacherous boards and I subsided with unpleasant rapidity into a limp, dejected heap upon the polished floor—absolutely declining to resume the perpendicular despite the Parson's commands and a surreptitious but forcible reminder from my uncle's boot-toe. My introduction to polite society had proved a lamentable failure, and I hated everybody and everything.

In the meanwhile Lady L'Estrange, who had been watching the whole scene with a good deal of interest—and whom, I feel sure, the fear of hurting his feelings had alone prevented from laughing outright at the *prononcé* costume and assured bearing of my worthy relative—upon the importation into the little comedy of the tragic element, bore down to the rescue, and taking me gingerly by the sleeve, led me through the open window on to the terrace, and endeavoured by kind words and the exhibition of that unfailing specific, a piece of silver, to soothe my bitterly aggrieved feelings—an attempt in which she was not altogether unsuccessful.

The interview with my uncle proved a protracted one, and it was nearly an hour before I was recalled, during which interval the preliminaries had been settled and my fate sealed. As Neptune and I passed along the passages which led to the servants' department, in charge of an own brother to the supercilious one, my uncle appeared to be in the highest possible spirits, chaffing the haughty and outraged menial with even more than his wonted vigour, until I almost expected to see the powder rise in a halo from his indignant head, and at the one o'clock dinner in the servants'-hall—to which we had received a special invitation—he managed by dint of his charming freedom of manner and ready courtesy to insinuate himself into the good graces of every female at our end of the table, from the stately upper-housemaid to the grinning scullery-wench.

As we walked down the steep hill leading to the bridge, I noticed that his hand seemed loth to leave his trouser pocket, from the innermost recesses of which proceeded an unwonted metallic sound as of coins jingling together. All at once the truth flashed across me. The venal old reprobate had been bribed into giving his consent—I had been bought and sold into bondage, and for the time being I absolutely loathed my venerable relative.

*   *   *   *   *   *

A great change was indeed in store for me, and could I have foreseen the advantages which I might have derived from it, I should certainly not have moped and pined—as I did—at the idea of leaving the Combe. During the next few days I must have presented an edifying spectacle, for I treated, not only my relations, but the horses, donkeys, and live-stock generally, with a considerate kindness and openly displayed affection, which, to say the least of it, was rather a contrast to my usual behaviour.

I no longer drummed with my heels, or leathered with my stick, the hollow-sounding ribs of poor old Billy Button, Charlotte's patriarchal white *myla*,* when, mounted on his back, I drove the horses in from grass in the morning, but leaning against him, with my arms round his ragged neck, I confided my sorrows to his sympathetic ears.

I no longer hunted for the fresh-laid eggs of the speckled hens at break of day, sucking the appetising contents and allowing the blame to fall on night-wandering hedgehog or musky stoat, but brought them straight to my Granny, whose private property they were. The old lady was quite overcome by the sudden change in my behaviour, and evidently attributed it to quite another cause, for, catching me to her bosom in a close embrace, she warned me of the sad fate that had overtaken another of her grandchildren, who 'was tookt of a suddent just the very same way,' and who, after behaving more like an angel of light than the imp of darkness he probably was, '*moollered* less than a *dood pauli*.'†

Then, entering the van, she rummaged about in the

---

* Donkey.   † 'Died less than a month after.'

locker where she kept her store of charms and simples, finally returning with a small oilskin bag in her hand. With this she presented me, adding a few impressive words of advice and warning, and assuring me that, as long as I kept it about my person, my good luck would never forsake me. Needless to say that I went on my way rejoicing, for I felt that I possessed a talisman which raised me far above the level of the other boys, and for several years I attributed every change for the better in my fortunes to the influence of this little bag. One day, tempted by curiosity, amidst the deepest recesses of Hawk's Wood I ripped open the oilskin covering, and found inside a curious object enough. It was about three or four inches in length, and resembled the dried-up remains of a miniature horse's head attached to a bony, comma-shaped body which terminated in a curly whip-tail like that of a lizard.* Round it was rolled a scrap of yellow, time-stained parchment upon which were inscribed some caballistic characters which, no doubt, added considerably to the potency of the charm. I kept the little bag about me for many years, but it was stolen from me on the expedition up the Pomaroon River in Demerara by some nigger probably even more superstitious, and certainly no less unobservant of the laws of *meum* and *tuum*, than the denizens of Fernleigh Combe.

Passon Mark rode over to the camp on the day following our visit to the Court, and went into my mother's affairs with Charlotte. He found that she had in her possession at the time of her death a sum amounting to upwards of eighty pounds, the proceeds of my father's savings and of her own industry. This money old Charlotte—to her credit be it told—had religiously guarded and now handed over to Mr. Sealy, who arranged that the trading-van with its furniture, stock, horses, etc., together with the light cart and all my mother's goods and chattels, should be sold by auction at Exeter, where they were most of them purchased by Neptune and his brother, and partner, Sylvester, for the sum of seventy-eight guineas—less than half their value.

According to the compact which the venal Neptune had entered into with Sir George, I found that I was not to be

* Probably a *hippocampus* or *caballo di mare* purchased from some foreign sailor by the superstitious old Gipsy.

allowed to visit my relations except at stated periods, and then not without Mr. Sealy's express permission, but I did not allow the restriction to weigh very heavily on my mind, as I had determined that my stay at the Parsonage should not be a protracted one.

After taking an affecting farewell of all my relations, especially of old Charlotte—who was visibly affected—and pretty Lementina—who, I grieve to confess, exhibited a self-possession more creditable to her head than to her heart—I left the camp on foot with my cousin Vester, who had volunteered to see the last of me and who helped to carry my scanty belongings, while I, myself, was fully employed in dragging by a cord a refractory lurcher-pup which old Charlotte had insisted upon sending as a present with a view to propitiating the Rev. Mark Sealy.

CHAPTER XIII.

The Story of a Blighted Career.

BEFORE proceeding further, it might, perhaps, be as well were I to give a somewhat more detailed account of the life and antecedents of my future guardian, the Parson of Netherleigh, and for that purpose I can scarcely do better than quote the words of his most intimate friend, Sir George L'Estrange, in whose service I subsequently passed many years, and whom I have often heard relate the story at the dinner-table.

"My old friend, Mark Sealy, is the only son of the late George Sealy, who held the living of Netherleigh before him, and who enjoyed the reputation of being one of the most accomplished scholars of the day, in which respect alone—with the exception of his utter disregard for conventionalities—his son resembles him. Mr. Sealy himself superintended Mark's education, with a view to his taking a scholarship at

Camford, which he easily accomplished. The old gentleman was devoted to his books, of which he possessed a valuable collection and in the acquisition of which he spent the greater part of his narrow income, but Mark, the moment he could effect his escape from the study, rushed off to the moor or river, by the banks of which he loved to spend the long summer days, while in the winter he followed the hounds whenever he could secure a mount, and as my father was very fond of him, this was pretty often."

"In due course Mark went up to Camford, and having gained the scholarship for which his father had so carefully coached him, he resided the usual number of terms, and notwithstanding his devotion to field-sports of every description, terminated his undergraduate career by taking the highest honours."

"He then undertook the post of bear-leader to the son of one of our local magnates, in which capacity he visited nearly every quarter of the habitable globe. Upon their return to England, Lord Braunton not only made him a handsome present in addition to his salary, but offered him a living as soon as it should become vacant, as he had announced his intention of going into the Church. Mark accepted the present but declined the living, as his father was an old man and not likely to live long, and he had set his heart upon succeeding to the living of Netherleigh, which was in my father's gift. Sending most of his money to his father, with his usual recklessness he picked up a couple of hunters at Tattersall's, and went into the Shires for a month or two's hunting, but before very long he had lamed both his horses, and finding that hiring came rather expensive, he sold the cripples for what they would fetch and returned to Netherleigh."

"His next step was to get himself ordained, and having accomplished this, he went back to the 'Varsity—where he had made himself very popular—and accepted a tutorship. He now devoted himself to his College work, which must have been very distasteful to him, since his sympathies were naturally with those who shirked lectures, and mounting their hacks, galloped off as hard as they could lay legs to the ground to meet the hounds. During his afternoon rides —mounted on one of Sitwell's horses—he often managed to nick in with hounds, knowing from experience the likeliest places to come across them, and when these expeditions resulted—as they frequently did—in a dirty coat or a crushed hat, he was obliged to wait for the shades of evening before entering the town, passing the College gates in a long greatcoat which he kept for the purpose at the dealer's office."

"On one occasion, while hounds were running, he had the misfortune to jump into a road almost on top of the Dean of his own College, causing the old gentleman's cob to shy wildly, but the pace was too good to stop and apologise —for Mark was in front at the time—so, putting his hack-hunter at the opposite fence, he was out of sight in a twinkling. The worthy Dean who, for the moment, had assumed a slightly undiaconal posture across his cob's shoulder, scrambled back into his saddle, and being a thorough gentleman of the old school—God bless him, here's his health!—he never alluded to the chance encounter beyond remarking dryly the next time they chanced to meet: —'I had always given you credit for being a good scholar, Mr. Sealy, and the impression was confirmed by seeing you take that *double first* the other day.' Needless to say that the offender laughed heartily at the joke—as in duty bound—and that his apologies were graciously accepted."

"Shortly after his appointment as College tutor I went up to the 'Varsity, and in addition to his other duties, Mark became my private coach, and it was through me that he got into a scrape which nearly terminated his career at Camford. Having one day agreed to accompany me for a drive, we started together in one of Sitwell's dogcarts, between the shafts of which was a powerful and rather fractious horse. As soon as we got into the Stockwell Road, we were met by a stable-helper in charge of a high-couraged chestnut mare that I had ordered as leader, without saying a word to my companion. Mark remonstrated strongly at first, but, like a good-natured fellow, ended by giving way, so the chestnut was hitched on. All went well on the outward journey, but as soon as their heads were turned towards home, the horses began to pull a good deal more than was exactly pleasant, and I soon made the unwelcome discovery that I could not hold them. We then divided the work, Mark steering the leader, while I drove the wheeler, but after some narrow shaves my companion—who was a far better whip than I—was obliged to change seats with me and take the reins altogether."

"As bad luck would have it, on turning a sharp corner rather quickly, we almost bowled over the Senior Proctor, who was taking a constitutional, compelling the outraged dignitary to take shelter in a ditch. Instead of profiting by experience, Mark pulled up to apologise, and endeavoured to restore harmony by a joking allusion to Prince Charlie's Glenfinnan motto '*tandem triumphans*,' but the Proctor, who was a strict disciplinarian and deservedly unpopular—being the originator of the 'Spy-system,' which still flourishes at Camford as many an unwary undergraduate has discovered to his cost—obstinately declined to see the point of it or to accept the proffered apology, and making a personal matter of it on his return home, proceeded to lodge a formal complaint with the Dean of St. Saviour's, who, to make matters worse, was Vice-Chancellor at the time."

"Although, for aught I know to the contrary, there may be nothing in the statutes of the University to prevent a tutor from driving tandem or four-in-hand if it so please him, it required all the influence of some powerful friends, added to his personal popularity, to save Mark from losing his tutorship, but during the remainder of his Camford career he managed to avoid collision with the authorities."

"Possessing, as he did, considerably more than the average share of intellectual ability, he occupied his spare time in writing reviews for some of the leading journals and magazines, and having been introduced to a certain distinguished statesman as a first-class classical scholar, he materially assisted him in bringing out a translation of the works of some of the minor Greek poets. Soon after this he accepted a fellowship, and would in all probability have settled down into the regular groove of University life, had he not chanced at one of the College festivities to make the acquaintance of a young lady whom he shortly afterwards married."

"I ought, perhaps, to mention that he had previously been engaged to the eldest daughter of a country squire who lives not a hundred miles from here, but that her father refused to give his consent, and the young lady dutifully accepted a more eligible suitor. To a man of Sealy's highly sensitive nature, the period immediately succeeding a disappointment in love is a very dangerous one. For the time being all is vanity and vexation of spirit—the rose has lost its perfume, the wine its *bouquet*, and life is not worth the living. Then some pretty and, apparently, sympathetic girl comes along, the heart is caught at the rebound, and, according to the theory of averages, the odds—to say the least of it—are not altogether in favour of the match turning out a happy one."

"And so it proved in poor Mark's case. As far as outward appearance went Miss C—— certainly left very little to be desired. Formed upon the purest classical model, her beauty was of that faultlessly statuesque type which of all others is most apt to cause its admirers to attribute to its possessor a variety of intellectual endowments of a correspondingly high order. Unfortunately for himself, a tendency towards idealisation had always been one of Mark's most prominent characteristics. Enthusiastic and unsuspicious to a fault, he exaggerated every accomplishment, minimised every defect, and credited the object of his adoration with qualities which were not only altogether foreign to her shallow nature, but which—to do her justice—she never made any pretence of possessing. To say that she had broken as many hearts as she had worn out satin shoes on ball-room floors, might be to exaggerate, but to say that she was a bit of a flirt is to put it very mildly. Some of us did our best to dissuade him, but Mark could be obstinate when he liked, and, as usual on such occasions, our well-meant advice only did more harm than good."

"So they were married, and I was best-man, as in duty bound. Being compelled to give up his fellowship in consequence, he started with his wife for a tour on the Continent, from which he was recalled by the news of his father's death. Returning at once to England, he was instituted to the living of Netherleigh, and settled down steadily to his parish duties. But, needless to say, the inevitable disenchantment came all too soon. Stripped of the fanciful embellishments with which his ardent imagination had invested it, his idol lay shattered at his feet, and his disappointment was bitter in proportion to the height of the pedestal to which his loving hands had raised it, for, within two years of his marriage, the prospect of an active and useful career had been blighted by the heartless conduct of his wife, who eloped with a young cavalry officer who had been staying with my neighbour, Mr. Blount of Stowe. The event naturally caused a considerable sensation throughout the county, where all the parties were well known, and from that day the whole nature of the man underwent an entire change. From being cheerful and fond of society, he became depressed and reserved, and for more than a year after he was seldom to be met with beyond the limits of the moorland glebe-lands to which he had succeeded on his father's death."

"Suddenly, and apparently without rhyme or reason, he started upon an entirely new tack. For months he had resolutely declined to see anyone, either working like a labourer on his small farm, or passing his time in the library amongst his books, but one fine day the squires and farmers who hunt with Lord Braunton's hounds were electrified by the apparition of 'Passon Mark,' mounted upon a clever-shaped chestnut mare with a wicked eye, and turned out quite respectably in black coat and well-fitting boots and breeches. His old friend the master rode up and welcomed him back with a few well-chosen words, and Mark mingled with the field and chatted freely and cheerfully with his acquaintances. But those who knew him best noticed that, although there was a smile on his lips, there was but little mirth in his voice, and that about his eyes there lurked that hard, defiant expression which they have never altogether lost."

"The hounds were thrown into Sutcombe—a small hanging wood on a steep hill-side, and a sure find—the field being posted on the moor above, so as to force the fox to break across the vale. As usual, he broke at the lower corner of the covert, and Braunton's horn soon told the field that they were away. Skirting the lower side of the wood was a rushy pasture in which some oxen were feeding, and through which the hounds were now streaming in full cry, while, bounding the pasture, was a narrow, deep-sunk lane."

"The Water-Lane—as it is called—is, indeed, a typical Devonshire lane. Sunk some ten or twelve feet below the level of the meadows on either side, during the driest summer weather the wheel-ruts are flooded to the depth of two or three inches, while after heavy rain it becomes impassible for foot-passengers. Winter and summer, alike, its steep banks are clothed with a luxuriant growth of ferns, moss, and plants, and owing to its narrowness the tenants of the adjoining farms are in the habit of attaching bells to their harness, so as to give each other timely warning of their approach."

"The rest of the field came clattering, slipping, poaching, and sliding down the steep hill-side, and on reaching the bottom turned sharp to the right through the farm-yard which forms the only outlet into the lane—but Mark kept his mare's head straight with the line of the flying pack. The hounds had scrambled through the fence, and sinking the lane, had climbed the opposite bank, and were now streaming across the vale beyond. The fence which divides the pasture-field from the lane was plashed and strengthened at the weak places with stakes and thorns, and it was towards the lowest of these that the Parson made, and sitting down in his saddle as though he were riding at water, drove the high-couraged mare at them with voice and heels, like a second Quintus Curtius. The ground sloped towards the fence, and as she neared it the mare must have seen that there was something more than an ordinary hedge in front of her, for pricking her ears and measuring her distance, she got her hind-legs well under her, and rising at the fence, flew the yawning gulf like a bird on the wing, landing with her fore-legs well into the opposite field—but the crumbly soil breaking away from under her, she clung with her hind legs to the steep bank like a swallow to a house-wall. It was a toss-up whether they went backward or forward, but Mark, allowing himself to slip over her shoulder, had her by the head in a moment, and with a violent struggle she scrambled to her feet—then, climbing into the saddle without further loss of time, the gentleman in black had the hounds to himself."

"The majority of the field had pulled up to witness the reckless leap, and farmer Martin of Sutcombe, who rents the land, afterwards caused a stout post to be driven in to mark the exact spot where the mare's hind-feet left the ground, and another where her fore-feet had landed on the opposite bank—I should be afraid to say the exact distance, but you can measure it for yourself. The place has gone by the name of 'Passon Mark's Leap' ever since, and what has made it more memorable is the fact that an officer, to win a bet, tried to jump it in cold blood, but only succeeded in breaking his horse's back. After the hounds had broken up their fox, Braunton asked Mark to put his own price on the mare, but he refused to part with her, and her progeny have always realised good sums."

"His purchase of the chestnut and appearance in the hunting-field proved to be the last effort of a naturally sociable disposition to assert itself, for when the good mare met with an accident, the only link which connected him with his equals was broken, and he relapsed into his former habits, becoming not only careless of his dress and appearance, but deaf to the claims of social intercourse and utterly indifferent to the opinion of his neighbours. He will shoulder his gun and start off for long rambles across the moor with his spaniels for his sole companions, and his abrupt manners, combined with his disregard for boundary-fences and notice-boards, have frequently brought him into collision with keepers and others to whom his personal appearance was unknown—some curious encounters being the result."

"I could tell you any amount of anecdotes illustrative of his queer ways, but one is as good for the purpose as a dozen. On one occasion, during the month of April, he was sitting by the river side, smoking a short black pipe and busily engaged in mending his casting-line which had just been smashed by a fresh-run fish—I need scarcely add, not in the very best of tempers."

"While thus employed he became aware that a stranger on the opposite bank was endeavouring to attract his attention. The stranger proved to be none other than a certain French nobleman who rented some shooting in the neighbourhood and who, not content with killing and maiming—not through ignorance, but of malice prepense—every fox that showed its nose in his coverts, defied public opinion by openly bragging of his iniquities."

"'*Hé, la bas!*'—shouted the Gallic vulpecide, 'Say you?

I can come ovère dere, *hein?*'—but Mark went on with his work without taking the slightest notice."

"'Oh-hé, le gars! Cré nom de Dieu, es tu donc sourd?'—roared the Count, evidently mistaking the Parson for a yokel, '*Mort de ma vie, je te ferai entendre!*'—and taking up a large stone, he pitched it into the stream close to where Mark was sitting, sending a shower of spray over him."

"This had the desired effect of effectually rousing our friend. With difficulty controlling his temper, he looked up with a bland smile and replied:—'Pray excuse my inattention. You want to know whether you can come across here? Certainly, my dear sir, certainly.'"

"The Count, who wore thigh-boots and was carrying a trout-rod and basket, waded in without hesitation, but—as Mark was perfectly aware—he could scarcely have chosen a worse place for the experiment. All went well for three parts of the distance, but beneath the further bank the bed of the river shelved abruptly away in a succession of ledges, and suddenly, without the slightest warning, he stepped into eight feet of water, and was carried off his legs and rolled over and over by the rough stream. As spluttering, choking, and *sacré*-ing he was swept past, the Parson, fearing lest the consequences of his practical joke might prove disastrous, hurried down the bank and hooking his gaff into the strap of the Frenchman's creel, succeeded in arresting his downward career. As soon as his feet touched *terra firma*, the Count's bellicose temperament asserted itself, and shaking himself free, he struck an attitude of defiance and proceeded to overwhelm his preserver with a torrent of abuse. But the sight of a middle-aged Frenchman personating the tutelary deity of the Cran on a raw April day, his hat gone, the top-joint of his rod snapped in two, the line twisted round his body like a spirit-medium during a dark *séance*, and the minnow securely anchored somewhere in the small of his back, proved more provocative of mirth than awe-inspiring, and Mark had the greatest difficulty in preserving his gravity."

"'And now, M. le Comte'—said he, in his very best French, 'permit me to remind you that politeness costs nothing, and to hope that the next time you have occasion to ask a question of a man in a shabby coat, you will not commence by swearing at your informant. *Je vous souhaite le*

THE STORY OF A BLIGHTED CAREER.

bonjour!'—and raising his cap, he started off to look for another fish, leaving the irate Frenchman to scramble up the bank as best he might."

* * * * *

"I believe I am correct in saying that I am his only intimate friend, and this is certainly the only house where he calls and dines. He is, nevertheless, a great favourite with the labouring classes, amongst whom his plain, straightforward manner and reckless courage have earned for him a popularity to gain which many a more orthodox divine has striven in vain. He is always most kind and considerate to the poor, and will start at any hour of the day or night, and ride any distance to attend a sick-bed. It sometimes happens that he will be sitting in his study on a wild winter's night, occupied in dissecting some obscure classical author with the aid of his meerschaum and a lexicon. Suddenly the front-door bell jingles, and a small moor-farmer is shown in, hat and whip in hand, his coat and whiskers white and powdery with the drifting snow."

"'If yeu deu plaaze, Passon, mai pore missus be tookt mortial bad, and Doctor he deu sai as she wi' not last the naight threu.'"

"Ringing the bell and ordering his horse to be saddled, Mark lays his pipe across the open book, and with a few kind words of condolence, accompanies the poor fellow to the stable. Then, pulling his old weather-beaten hat well down over his eyes, turning up his collar, and buttoning his coat across his chest, he rides off through the snow and darkness without waiting to make the least change in his dress. Arrived at the small moorland homestead, he remains beside the sufferer until all is over, and then with a hearty grip of the hand and a few well-chosen words of sympathy to the bereaved husband, remounts his horse and retraces his way across the moor, frequently not reaching home until the following evening."

Such was the man who had undertaken the thankless task of educating me. How I repaid him for his trouble, my story will show.

CHAPTER XIV.

Life at the Parsonage.

MERGING from the sheltered Combe as the sun was sinking in the west, Vester and I crossed the common, alternately following the road which leads from Blackstow to Netherton, and taking short-cuts across the sandy waste—sending the grey-coated *shoshois* scuttling to their holes, where they lay, panting but secure, deep down beneath the roots of the now rapidly bronzing fern and stunted heather. Leaving the Netherton Road to our right at Netherleigh Bridge, we turned sharp to the left and crossed the river, lingering for a few minutes to peer over the parapet—urged by that irresistable something which compels every true-born fisherman, when crossing running water, to pause and endeavour with speculative eye to fathom the hidden depths.

As we leaned over the parapet, Vester flipped a fragment of stale bread-crust which he had unearthed from the innermost recesses of his pocket, towards the wary old trout who was taking his siesta in the shadow of the further arch—his nose almost touching the cutwater as he balanced himself against the pulsations of the stream by an almost imperceptible motion of tail and fins. As the pellet, overshooting its mark, rebounded from the masonry and dropped into the water about a yard above his lurking-place, the *genius loci* rose towards the surface to inspect the votive offering—then, catching sight of our heads projecting above the parapet, with a quick stroke of his propeller he scurried beneath the sheltering arch and was lost to our admiring gaze.

Resuming our journey we breasted the steep hill on the further bank of the river, and leaving to our left the lodge which guards the entrance to Netherleigh Park, after a long pull reached the comparatively level open country beyond. Skirting the park-palings for about a mile, we came in sight of the tiny hamlet of Netherleigh, which consists of about a dozen white-washed, straw-thatched cottages. The village only boasted one shop, the enterprising proprietor of which combined the avocations of grocer, tobacconist, linen-draper, baker, and post-master.

Passing through the village we pursued our way along the high-road until we came to the church, opposite which a rusty iron gate depended in a limp, disjointed sort of fashion from a single hinge, and marked the entrance to the Parsonage grounds. This antiquated piece of ironwork was propped back with a boulder from off the moor, so, passing through without let or hindrance, we entered a small thicket of larch and silver-firs which had evidently been planted with a view to sheltering the house from the blustering north-westerly gales which swept the high table-land. Emerging from the thick belt of trees, the carriage-road led through a couple of rushy paddocks in which gamboled and frisked a long-legged, rough-coated two-year-old, accompanied by his three-year-old brother. As we intruded upon their domain the inquisitive animals trotted round us with outstretched necks and flowing tails, making the best of their shoeless, shambling action.

"*Vafodu peero se les*"*—remarked Vester, whose practised eye had detected a sand-crack which adorned the off forefoot of the elder-born. "If Passon Mark don't keep his pigs fatter nor his horses, you'd better have *jalled* to the *chuvveni-ker* † to once. It's *ferreder* to *besh 'lagatus* the *bor a' poggerin'* the blessed *bars* and *a' shoonin'* the blessed *chiriclos a' gillyin'* and *a' shellin'* ‡ than"—but the remainder of the sentence can best be rendered by a series of blanks and dashes. Now this characteristic outburst on the part of my cousin was all the more inexcusable since I had borne up bravely so far, and by his emphatic denunciation of my prospective respectability, he was doing his best to throw cold water on my good resolutions.

The Parsonage was a low, rambling, two-storied building

---

* "His foot is unsound." † "Gone to the workhouse."

‡ "It's better to sit beside the hedge breaking the blessed stones and listening to the blessed birds singing and whistling."

in an advanced stage of dilapidation. The yellow, weather-stained plaster was dropping off in great mouldy patches and appeared to be only kept in place by the free growth of the Banksia roses which covered the front of the house. On either side of the hall-door was a sun-blistered, earwig-haunted wooden verandah painted a dingy blueish-green, while, from the eaves, beneath which the swallows' nests clustered thickly, there hung a length of broken gutter-piping —suspended in mid-air like the sword of Damocles—which involuntarily compelled the chance visitor to keep an eye aloft while he tugged at the rusty bell-pull. A number of long-legged game-pullets were pecking about and dusting themselves on the moss-grown gravel in front of the porch, and a litter of terrier-puppies were carrying on gardening operations with considerable energy in the one flower-bed, where a few scarlet geraniums and calceolarias were struggling for dear life with an invading army of convolvulus and couch-grass, and apparently getting none the better of the encounter. To the left of the house were the stables, half hidden by the shrubbery, and behind these again the farm-buildings, offices, and kennels.

Approaching the front-door of the deserted-looking building, we were about to pull the bell-handle, when, without any warning, a couple of long-backed, slate-coloured, wire-haired terriers tore through the open hall-door like a small tornado and precipitated themselves upon us, circling round us with white, snapping teeth, bristling hackles, and snarling, back-drawn lips, and it required all our agility and familiarity with canine tactics to keep the heels of our trousers intact without seriously injuring the little furies. At length, in response to our repeated applications, the bell was answered by a round-faced, slipshod handmaiden, who drove the dogs off and informed us that her master was out, so I agreed to walk part of the way back with Vester, whose temper—always rather uncertain—was ruffled at having to part with me, for, during the last five years, notwithstanding the disparity in our ages, we had become almost inseparables. The maid-servant had assured us that 'the master would not keep a nasty, dirty little mongrel like that'—alluding, not, as might have been supposed, to me, but to the brindled lurcher pup—so, burdened with the rejected quadruped and a long string of messages, Vester returned to the Combe, while I sorrowfully retraced my steps in the direction of the Parsonage.

My future pastor and master turned up about ten o'clock the same evening. He had been having a couple of days' shooting with a farmer at a distance, and marched into the house dusty and travel-stained as any *peerdo*,* with his gun over his shoulder, four brace of birds in his capacious pockets, an old retriever at his heels, and without even the traditional *impedimenta* of a tooth-brush and clean collar. Then the study bell rang, the flat-footed handmaiden trotted off with her master's slippers, and I was told to step upstairs and report my arrival.

The study was a dark, low-ceilinged room with two French windows opening on to the verandah. These were kept open all the summer and most of the winter, and afforded a most convenient short-cut for the dogs, whose well-worn 'runs' from door to window attested their thorough appreciation of the arrangement. As a living-room it was chiefly remarkable for an almost entire absence of furniture and for the presence of a very valuable and, I may as well add, a very dingy and disreputable-looking collection of books, which completely covered three of the walls and littered every available space—in fact, if you came into the room in the dark, you were safe to step on a dog if you didn't stumble over a pile of books, or *vice versâ*. In one of the corners stood a couple of gaffs, a landing-net, and a salmon-rod in its canvas cover. The top-joint of a trout-rod, very much warped, with casting-line and flies attached, projected from the top of one of the book-cases, the remainder of the furniture consisting of a table, a leather-covered arm-chair, a large earthenware tobacco-jar, and two or three well-worn deer-skins which did duty for hearth-rug and door-mats. A fine coating of dust and cobwebs overlaid everything, while the atmosphere was highly suggestive of coarse-cut cavendish. The Parson was seated in the arm-chair, one shooting-boot off, and engaged in a violent struggle with the other.

"Ha, Samson"—he began, "so you have turned up safe and sound, and the sooner you learn to make yourself useful,

* Tramp.

the better. Attention! Three paces to the front. Quick march. That's right. Right-about face and stoop down as if you were going to give a back at leap-frog. Now then, catch hold"—the refractory blucher was inserted between my knees, the other foot was applied to that portion of my anatomy which offered the most convenient leverage, I felt myself irresistibly propelled forward, and off came the boot with a 'plop'—'Camford-fashion' as the Parson called it.

"I daresay, my lad"—he continued, as I handed him his slippers, "you will find a good deal of difference at first between the confinement of a house and the outdoor life you have been used to, but I hope you will soon learn to fall in with the ways of the establishment, and then you will find things go pleasantly enough——." I hardly required to be told that if I didn't do so, I should find things very much the reverse, for I knew that Passon Mark wasn't the man to stand any nonsense. "And now I have no doubt that you will be ready for your supper, and I will tell Mrs. Grey to take charge of you, and to-morrow I will drive you into Netherton and get you some more suitable clothes"—and ringing the bell, he handed me over to Mrs. Grey the housekeeper, and after supper I was shown to my room, and notwithstanding my gloomy forebodings, was soon fast asleep.

The following morning I was up and about by daybreak, and having made friends with the terriers, I found my way to the kitchen, where I managed to ingratiate myself with old Alice, the hard-featured cook, by chopping firewood and performing a few trifling services of a similar nature—and in an establishment where the housekeeping is conducted upon rather a frugal scale, I can assure you that it is by no means a bad plan to be friends with the cook.

I soon, however, made the discovery that Mrs. Grey was a very different person to deal with, and that my proffered services and artless blandishments were alike thrown away upon her—she had, probably, at some time or another, had a considerable experience of them, and knew how to appraise them at their proper value. She appeared to have taken an instinctive dislike to me from the moment I entered the house, and as long as I remained in it she made the worst of everything I did or said, and if it had depended upon her, my sojourn at the Parsonage would have been as limited as even I could possibly have desired. She was a tall, good-looking woman of seven-and-thirty—according to her own account—but she certainly did not look her full age, and with her well-proportioned figure, erect carriage, and smooth brown hair neatly arranged beneath a becoming cap, to do her justice she looked the very model of a bachelor's housekeeper.

Now I must tell you that the Parson's housekeepers were at once the admiration of the neighbouring squires and the pet aversion of their worthy spouses. These comely but exasperating females, who caused the minds of the matrons to be exercised and harassed by the restless pangs of unsatisfied curiosity, never—as was reluctantly admitted—either by their conduct or deportment afforded the least ground for the shaft of scandal to light upon. They came, remained two or three years, some a longer and some a shorter period, and then departed as they came, quietly and without making any sign—possibly finding the view which was to be obtained from the window of the housekeeper's room just a trifle monotonous. So the gossips went on as before.

"Why"—they argued, "should the Parson, who never knows or cares whether he is eating cold pork or truffled turkey, require an expensive housekeeper to look after Alice, the one-eyed cook, and Jane the parlour-maid?"

"But why on earth shouldn't he, if he likes to?"—retorted their husbands, who not only appreciated the Parson's good taste, but envied his independence—and then at it they would go, tooth and nail, after the good old fashion. But they knew better than to apply to Mr. Sealy for information, for although the most careless and good-tempered of men, he was perfectly capable of asserting himself when occasion required.

Next morning, after breakfast, he drove me into Netherton, introducing me first of all to a barber, who sheared off my long locks close to my head—an indignity which, like my celebrated namesake, I very much resented, since amongst our people a closely clipped head is generally accepted as the surest possible indication of an enforced submission to the indignity figuratively and alliteratively termed a 'county crop.' We then went to a ready-made clothier's where I was fitted out with a couple of suits—one of stable-clothes and the other for best. I was also provided with the necessary linen, boots, cap, etc., and when, next morning I appeared in a brand new rig-out from top to toe, my hair neatly brushed and parted, and my hands as white as soap and water could make them, even Mrs. Grey congratulated me upon my improved appearance. "*O pooro Beng simmens a fino Ress, kun yuv tovella lescro mooi*" *—as Charlotte used to say, and when I looked at myself in the glass and noticed to what an extent my personal appearance had been improved by the garb of civilization, I insensibly became more reconciled to my position.

The Parson's establishment consisted, as I have told you, of Mrs. Grey the housekeeper, old Alice the cook, and Jane the parlour-maid, but besides these there was a handy-man called Joe Body, who worked in the kitchen-garden, milked the cows, and looked after the live-stock, in addition to a lad of sixteen called Mike, with red hair and pugilistic tendencies, the son of an Irishman who worked on the glebe-lands. The aforsaid Michael divided his time pretty equally between hindering Joe Body in the performance of his manifold duties, throwing stones at any moving object, and teasing every living thing that had the misfortune to come in his way. In the morning he was supposed to break and carry coals, chop firewood, clean the knives and boots, and sweep out the kennels, but I soon found that most of the work devolved upon me, and as a matter of fact he spent the greater part of the day in 'running ar'nds,' as he called it, to and from the village, where he amused himself by carving his initials on the newly-painted shutters of the general-dealer's store, or trying to make himself sick by colouring a fancy clay after a surfeit of bullseyes and toffee—an endeavour in which it is only fair to say that he was uniformly succesful. He was, nevertheless, a strong, wiry lad, with long arms and bony knuckles which could cut like a knife, as I very soon discovered.

It came about in this way. In spite of my poor mother's strongly-expressed disapproval, I had taken regularly to smoking after my arrival at the Combe, and was seldom to

* "The old Devil looks like a fine gentleman when he washes his face."

be seen without a short, black pipe between my lips. My mother, who was about the only woman in camp who did not smoke, used to beg me to remember what I had promised my father, but I was a self-willed young monkey and was, moreover, afraid that Vester—who had cut his teeth on an old pipe-stem—would make fun of me and call me *Gorgio* or *pauno-mooi*. During the sharp fit of sorrow and genuine contrition which immediately succeeded my dear mother's death, I made several virtuous resolutions, one of which, at all events, I kept. Taking with me my whole stock of dirty, well-beloved clays, I made my way to the moor above—so as to be out of the reach of temptation—and then and there I solemnly broke every one of them to pieces and trampled them deep into the black, yielding soil, swearing that to my dying day I would never smoke again. This resolve I kept in spite of temptation, and, curiously enough, it was my adherence to it which brought my head into contact with Mike's bony knuckles.*

Within a day or two of my arrival at the Parsonage I caught him indulging his taste for the forbidden weed in the woodhouse, and upon his offering to teach me to smoke, I replied that I had been a smoker for years—for I began when I was nine years old—but had lately given it up. This proved just a trifle more than he could swallow, and thinking that I was trying to come it over him, he gave me the lie direct, to which I retorted by making his nose bleed. It being then just one o'clock, some of the farm-labourers were coming in from the fields—amongst them Mike's respected progenitor—and a ring having been formed in the straw-yard, at it we went, hammer and tongs, like a pair of young bantams. Before we had fought a couple of rounds, the Parson himself rode into the barton, and we all dispersed in a hurry, but coming up to us, he enquired what it was all about, and having been made acquainted with the origin of the dispute, he insisted upon our fighting it out, as he didn't want any bad blood between us.

So the ring was quickly reformed, and with Passon Mark as referee, you may be sure that we both did our level best.

* In so doing young Loveridge was only acting in accordance with a well-known custom amongst Gipsies, in obedience to which the sorrowing survivor destroys some favourite article, or gives up some cherished taste or indulgence, out of respect for, and in memory of, the departed.—ED.

Although my antagonist was taller, older, and heavier than me, I was in much better condition for the job, and was, moreover, young Vester's favourite pupil, and consequently up to most of the dodges of the prize-ring. No doubt it amused the sporting Parson to see Mike rushing in, making his long arms and bony fists whistle round my ears like a thresher's flail, while I kept *bongerin'* my *sherro* and *tarderin'** until he overreached himself, when I would time him neatly on the dial. When you know something about the game, it gives you confidence and prevents you from losing your head. The first three or four rounds are generally spent in finding out exactly how much the other chap knows, and there is nothing pleasanter than to discover that you have got just a little bit up your sleeve. I soon found that I could do pretty much as I liked with my opponent in spite of an occasional *tatto-yek oprey the nok* or *mooi*,† which started the paint and cut my lips, and having made the discovery, I forthwith proceeded to treat the spectators to an exhibition of scientific out-fighting which should have delighted my master and guardian. As long as Mike was strong on his pins, I allowed him to cut out the work, guarding with my right and propping and countering with my left, but as soon as ever he began to tire, I assumed the offensive, circling round him and hitting him just where I liked, finally bringing the encounter to an end by feinting with my left—which caused him to raise his hands—when I let him have the right in the victualling department, curling him up like a hedgehog and knocking him completely out of time.

If by any chance a schoolboy should get hold of these reprehensible memoirs, let him try the effect of this manœuvre the next time he tackles a boy taller than himself. Pretend to hit at his head with your left, and as soon as your adversary raises his hands to guard, hit him in the wind as hard as ever you know how with your right, and it is ten to one that he won't want any more unless he is a very good plucked 'un.

Beyond a black-eye and a cut lip, I was not much the worse for the turn-up, but Mike looked very sorry for himself. As soon as it was over we shook hands and repaired to the pump to wash ourselves, pumping each for the other, and

* Dodging my head and drawing him on.   † Hot-'un on the nose or mouth.

LIFE AT THE PARSONAGE.

we never afterwards had as much as a word between us, but were always on the best of terms.

Having improved my outward appearance by the purchase of an outfit suitable to a lad in my position, my guardian proceeded to gauge my mental capabilities preparatory to taking my education seriously in hand. Mr. Sealy began by placing a copy of *Bell's Weekly Messenger* before me and requesting me to read aloud the account of the race for the St. Leger—which, if I remember rightly, had been won by a horse called Jerry. During the last few years I had had but little leisure or inclination for reading, but when living near Camford I had attended a dame's school, while my mother possessed a few well-thumbed books which had belonged to my father, amongst which was a copy of the *Pilgrim's Progress*, the *Life of Jonathan Wild the Thieftaker*, and the *History of Jack Sheppard*. There were also a few cheaply-bound books of a highly sensational character, such as *The Pirate's Revenge: or the Sixteen Stark Cold Corpses of the Caspian Sea*, in which the ruthless but gentlemanly pirate—who had been driven to adopt this rather irregular mode of life by a series of misfortunes of which he was the innocent victim—alternately waded up to his knees in gore, and then proceeded to pour forth page after page of the most moral and edifying sentiments. In *The Romany's Curse: or the Moaning Mountain Maniac*, the romantic Gipsy in his traditional costume of slouched sombrero, scarlet sash, and long mysterious mantle, avenged with ready *churi** the insults offered by the licentious nobleman to his dark-eyed *pirreni*,† the while the wrinkled beldame snatched the youthful heir from his nurse's arms, devoting the hated race to perdition, and uttering the most blood-curdling maledictions in that strange mixture of thieves' Latin and mumpers' talk which has so often done duty for genuine Romnimus.

These volumes I used laboriously to spell through during the long winter evenings by the light of a farthing dip, and I was therefore able to give a garbled version of the exciting contest so graphically described by the sporting correspondent of the *Weekly Messenger*. I made a much poorer show, however, when tried with a piece of easy dictation, for my handwriting would have puzzled an expert, while my spelling

* Knife. † Sweetheart.

was conducted upon a strictly phonetic system which possessed the somewhat questionable recommendation of being intelligible to its inventor alone. Passon Mark—for so I prefer to call him—appeared to take the same interest in my mental development as he always evinced when superintending the breaking of the colts which trotted about the paddocks. With all the power and resources of his highly-cultivated intellect he endeavoured to make the pursuit of knowledge both pleasant and easy for me, for having once taken a thing in hand, he was the last man in the world to abandon it until he had either demonstrated its impracticability to his entire satisfaction, or brought it to a successful issue.

As a subject for dictation—for instance—he would select some popular work on Natural History, from which he would read the passages most likely to interest me and which had especial reference to the birds, beasts, and fishes with which I was acquainted. These studies soon became a pleasure to me, and during the dictation I would often interrupt my tutor by expressions of surprise or corroboration.

"So elastic and strong is his covering"—he would read out, "that the hedgehog can sustain a fall from a height on to the hardest ground, without receiving the slightest injury."

"*Auvo*"*—I would eagerly exclaim, "I mind how me and Matty Orchard found a couple jest above Blackrocks, and throwed 'em down forty feet and more, and when we clim down and come to look for 'em, we couldn't find 'em nowhere. And it come on dark and we had to go back without 'em. And Charlotte she jest did take on about it, for she were terrible fond o' *hotchis*."

Or again—"The animal is easily tamed and even becomes familiar, feeding on soaked bread, meat or vegetables, which it will take from the hand."

"*Tatcho, Rye*"—I would interrupt, "that's jest like the *hotchi* as I sold to old Miss Lovegrove down to Bere. She use to pet it and feed it—although it were alive with fleas—but one night her little nephew took and hid it in her bed, and she never didn't buy no more off of me—she said as they was too familiar."

* "Yes."

The Parson never checked one of these outbursts, only interrupting me in order to make me pronounce my words correctly—so the lessons went on swimmingly, and before long I could read well and write a clear, legible hand, and I think I knew as much geography as most boys of my age, and a little history. After thoroughly grounding me in English, Mr. Sealy attempted to introduce me to his favourite classics, but although I managed to stumble through the Latin grammar—which I never could make head or tail of —the *Commentaries of Julius Cæsar*, and a book or two of *Virgil*—which I liked much better—I never took kindly to the dead languages, and he eventually gave up the attempt with reluctance, being forced to confess that they would probably be of very little use to me in any career that I was likely to adopt. Although such a subject may appear rather out of place in a story like mine, I feel that I should be doing my kind old master a great injustice were I to allow it to be supposed that, while the other branches of knowledge were cultivated, my religious education was neglected—on the contrary, Mr. Sealy never lost an opportunity of instilling into my neglected mind the broad principles of the simple creed which he professed.*

That Passon Mark was no stickler for formality, either in theory or practice, the following anecdote may serve to illustrate. It was about ten o'clock one stormy winter's night, and Mr. Sealy had been teaching me to tie a salmon-fly, and I was just putting the feathers, silk, and cobbler's

* "In endeavouring to arrive at something like a correct estimate of his character"—writes Mr. Blount, alluding to the Rev. Mark Sealy—"the fact must be taken into consideration that if he had followed up the career for which he was so pre-eminently qualified, his attainments as a classical scholar and his devotion to scientific research would have entitled him to a prominent place amongst the eminent men of the day. In an age when learned Professors glibly dispose of the Deity as a 'superfluous hypothesis,' old-fashioned folk—like myself—are perhaps somewhat apt to underestimate the temptation which science offers to a man of Sealy's temperament to stray into the devious paths of Agnosticism and systematic materialism, but all who knew and loved him — and who could do the one without the other?—will bear me out in asserting that, in spite of his somewhat cynical manner and intolerance of the dogmas, ceremonials, and mysticisms with which the exponents of various creeds have contrived to hedge in and obscure the great, central truth, it would have been a hard matter to have found amongst the ranks of the most orthodox divines a more liberal-minded, practical, or sincere Christian—albeit of the muscular school—than 'Passon Mark' of Netherleigh. Peace be to his ashes!"—ED.

vax, and all the rest of it, back into their tin box before going to bed, when the terriers began to growl, and in the lulls between the gusts we heard somebody at the hall-door, evidently trying to get the rusty bell-pull to work.

"Run out and see who it is"—said the Parson, and I went into the passage and opened the front-door a few inches and looked out, and there I saw a tall figure, and a gruff voice said in what was meant to be a confidence-inspiring tone—"You needn't be afeard. Jest tell t' Passon, will 'ee, that I wants to see un most pertic'lar—I do. If he arsts who 'tis, say as it be old Marster Pinfold—'Curly' Pinfold, that is—he'll know."

"Tell him to come in"—said Mr. Sealy, when I had repeated the message, and having scraped his boots and deposited his hat and the old horse-rug which he wore over his shoulders, in the hall, the mysterious visitor followed me into the study—and a queer-looking customer he was, and no mistake. As the light of the lamp fell upon him, I saw that he was a very tall, very thin old Gipsy, with nothing remarkable about him except his hair which, although rather scanty on top, hung down over his shoulders in thick, snaky locks which curled a little, corkscrew fashion, at the points. His strongly-marked features were cadaverous and seamed with deep lines, and a long, dirty white smock of coarse twill, such as drovers wear, which reached almost to his heels, gave him rather the appearance of a galvanised corpse attired in a winding-sheet, while tucked under his right arm was a parcel which, to judge by its outlines, resembled a big cigar-box wrapped up in a piece of coarse sacking.

Mr. Sealy began by asking him his business, but for a long time he could get nothing out of the old chap, although it was evident that he had something on his mind from the way in which he shuffled and beat about the bush, changing his leg, scratching his poll, and shifting the parcel from one arm to the other, so, at last, the Parson produced some whiskey, and having received permission to light his pipe, Mr. Pinfold's tongue began to wag more freely.

It appeared that his youngest daughter—who had lately been married and was travelling with them—had just lost her baby, which had died suddenly on the road between Bideford and Barnstaple. The poor little thing had not

LIFE AT THE PARSONAGE. 165

been baptised, and as there was some difficulty about getting it buried, they had come some thirty or forty miles out of their road to consult Passon Mark. Old Master Pinfold had chosen this late hour for his visit in order to keep the matter dark, the *vardos* being drawn up on the common until the Parson's decision should be known, when they intended to start at once without anybody being the wiser.

Mr. Sealy was evidently in a quandary—he puffed away at his pipe like a steam-engine and marched up and down the study, as was his habit when perplexed.

"That's all very well, Master Pinfold"—he began, "but you know that if the child died suddenly there ought to have been an inquest or a certificate and all the rest of it, and if I were to bury it, and it was found out, and the Bishop came to hear of it, there would be a pretty to-do."

"*Auvo, Rashai*"—said the old chap, "that's werry true, and I wanted to take and *chiv lis tooley poov*,* same as I most in general does, but my darter, as had 'tended Sunday school and been in sarvice, she took on so at thinking the babby wouldn't be buried in consetrated groun', that *mande kaired a mookto, ta chivved* the *tawni-yeck adrey lis, ta annered lis to tute, Rashai,* for to *poosh lis*" †—and it ended, as usual, by Mr. Sealy giving way, and old Master Pinfold took his departure—leaving the parcel behind him—evidently much relieved at the success of his mission.

That same night, just as the old church-clock was wheezing out its equivalent for midnight—it was never particular to a stroke or two—a couple of dark figures carrying a suspicious-looking burden, a lantern, and some tools, might have been observed—as the story-books say—climbing over the wall which separates the churchyard from the moor. The rain had stopped, but the heavy night-clouds, driving across the face of the moon, necessitated the lighting of the lantern.

"Just the very night for the body-snatchers to be at work"—as the Parson remarked. "We may think ourselves lucky if we don't get a charge of swan-shot in our legs"—for the country was up in arms against the Resur-

---

* "Put it under ground."

† "That I made a box, and put the little one in it, and brought it to you, Parson, for to bury it."

rectionists, and John Strong, the sexton, always kept a loaded gun handy. But, to tell you the truth, I was *trashado ajaw* without that, for I wouldn't, for the life of me, have crossed the churchyard by myself in the dark for fear of *bavolengros*, and when we came to the yew-tree under which my mother was lying buried, my hand shook so that I could hardly light the lantern.

The turf was then carefully spitted off, a hole dug with the spade, and the little box lowered into it. Then Mr. Sealy bent his head and I guessed from the motion of his lips that he was saying a prayer, and that put me in remembrance of my poor, dear mother's death and the solemn words of the funeral service—and what with thinking of her lying close to us, and what with seeing the little baby laid there beside her, I began to choke, and sob, and snuffle a good one, and the lantern blew out, and the matches were damp or something, and I couldn't get them to light, so we had to fill in the mould and put back the turf by what moonlight there was. Then we hid all the soil and stones that wouldn't go back in the hole, behind the yew-tree, and smoothed down the turf so that John Strong shouldn't suspect anything.

Then Passon Mark shouldered the tools, while I carried the lantern, and we set off home, and as we were crossing the paddock I said to him :—" Will that little baby ever go to heaven, Sir ? "—and he answered shortly :—" I'd be glad to exchange my chances for hers "—and told me not to say a word to anybody about the night's work, and I never didn't, from that day to this—not even to my own wife—for fear of doing the Parson a mischief.

CHAPTER XV.

A Scramble with a Scratch Pack.

LUCKILY for me the Parson was not one of those who endeavour to cram Greek and Latin, dry facts and drier figures, into the youthful system after much the same mechanical fashion as a groom forces hay into the chaff-cutter—to be caught up and rapidly digested by the busy brain, and then to drift away like chaff before the wind. On the contrary, he was of opinion that 'all work and no play makes Jack a dull boy,' and I had very little cause to complain of my treatment.

And here let me remark that as I look, sometimes, at the pale faces and spectacled eyes of an unduly large proportion of the young folk of both sexes on their way to and from their Colleges and High Schools nowadays, I can't help fancying that the little extra knowledge which they may acquire, must be dearly purchased at the expense of weakened eyesight and enfeebled health—the inevitable result of long hours of confinement in rooms lighted with hot, flickering gas, and of the curtailment of the hours of recreation consequent upon the high-pressure system now in vogue—and it has often occurred to me that, fifty years ago, the unexpected appearance of a boy of fourteen wearing gig-lamps, would have created much the same stir and excitement amongst his schoolfellows, as that of a big, yellow owl, who has incautiously ventured forth into the garish light of day, is wont to arouse amongst the tribes of small birds who mob and persecute him until he gains the sanctuary of some friendly ivy-bush.

However, as I have said, I had little cause to complain on the score of overwork. My outdoor duties consisted in exercising the horses and assisting the servants in any job that might be on hand—especially stable-work, of which I was very fond. Mr. Sealy was in the habit of breeding two or three colts every year, being able to work the half-bred brood-mares on the light soil of the moorland farm, and he used always to break the youngsters to saddle and harness himself—a congenial occupation in which it was my delight to assist him. As soon as their muscles were sufficiently set to stand the strain of jumping, he used to lunge the awkward young things over the banks, putting me on their backs when they could be trusted to negotiate a jump, and when they were strong enough to carry him, he would ride them out with the hounds, and generally sold them as four-year-olds to some of the neighbouring squires.

There was a good bit of chaff and fun amongst the field the first time he made his appearance at the meet with his second horseman—as they were pleased to call me—mounted on a useful-looking youngster and dressed in my neat stable-suit, cap, and clean neckcloth. It was my first mount with hounds, and I wished that my uncle Plato could have been there to see me. In a lively twenty-minutes over the straggling banks and partially cultivated enclosures which fringe the moorland, my light weight enabled the breedy four-year-old to show in front, and when the fox saved himself beneath a clitter of stones, my guardian came in for plenty of congratulations upon the performance of his young-'un and its rider.

I very soon became reconciled to life at the Parsonage, with its intervals of study and comparatively regular hours. I say 'comparatively,' advisedly—for Mr. Sealy did not conform to the hours which, by universal consent, are set apart for meals, which in his case were indeed movable feasts. There was not such a thing as a clock in the house, the time being regulated by the Parson's antiquated silver hunting-watch which, as often as not, he forgot to wind up, and which, owing to the countless contusions and immersions it had sustained, was no more to be relied upon than was the old Church clock, with its single hand and venerable sun-blistered face, which from time to time, during his intervals of comparative sobriety, was tinkered up and set going by John Strong, who did odd jobs about the village and combined the avocations of sexton, carpenter, and pig-killer.

My guardian would start off for one of his long, solitary

rambles across the moor or along the banks of the Cran at all times of the day, and the approximate hour of his return would have afforded a very legitimate subject for speculation. If he found himself too far from home towards nightfall, he would drop in at the nearest farm-house, and presenting the farmer's wife with the contents of his bag or basket, would ask for a shake-down for himself and dogs—a request with which they were generally delighted to comply, for, when he had a mind, no man could be better company than Mr. Sealy, and when amongst his inferiors he threw aside the barrier which his morbidly sensitive nature had raised between himself and society, chatting freely with the people of the house, and seeming to enjoy his pipe and glass of cider.

The following morning some pack of hounds might very likely be within reach, and if, as frequently happened, the friendly farmer volunteered a mount on some stale old hunter or raw young-'un that wanted schooling, Passon Mark would make his appearance at the meet in his weather-stained shooting-coat, thorn-worn breeches and gaiters, and heavy shooting-boots, and as long as the youngster's condition would allow of it or the old horse could boil up a gallop, he was sure to be there or thereabouts. For if as a fisherman he had few equals in Devonshire—managing, as he did, by dint of deep wading and throwing up-stream to attain the same results with the artificial fly as did my uncle Neptune with the natural bait—as a bruising rider he stood alone. Even tough Jim Baily the colt-breaker—a man altogether without fear, if not without reproach—who did most of the rough-riding in the neighbourhood, reluctantly admitted that for crossing a country there was nobody to equal the Parson. "Oh yes"—he would say, "I deu give Passon Mark best. He may break his blamed neck if he deu plaaze, but I've got a missus and fower kids to whoame, and that deu make a differ."

He was not one of those men whose 'going well' depends, to a great extent, upon that mysterious conjunction of favourable circumstances which combine to produce what is popularly known as 'their day out'—the immediate result, amongst other, and more occult, combinations, of an unimpaired digestion, a mount that inspires confidence, and a good start—but was always ready to go first, taking a line of his own, riding for falls, and shoving his nag over, under, or through, with a determination which his masterly horsemanship alone redeemed from the charge of recklessness, but which when combined—as in his case—with a perfect seat and hands, a quick eye for turns, and an intuitive knowledge of country, forms the principal factor in the composition of a really first-class man to hounds.

I think I have mentioned that my uncle Neptune was in the habit of trapping the otters which frequented the numerous rivers and streams throughout the district—collecting and preserving their skins, which he sold to the furriers at Bristol. About a year previous to my arrival, the Parson had come to the conclusion that fishing did not afford sufficient scope for satisfying the demands of his restless and energetic temperament during the summer months, and he determined to start a pack of otter-hounds. In order to carry out this idea two things were necessary—first, to collect the hounds, and, secondly, to propitiate my uncle Neptune, who had always been accustomed to regard the slippery *matchinesko-jookos* as his peculiar prey and perquisite. But having once conceived the notion, he lost no time in putting it into execution, and hunting up the addresses of some of his old college friends who had subsequently developed into M.F.H.'s, he wrote and asked them whether they could spare a hound or two that might be likely to answer his purpose. The result more than justified his anticipations, for in the course of the next few months a most miscellaneous assortment of dog-flesh arrived at the Parsonage, filling the kennels, barns, and outhouses to overflowing.

Amongst these were a couple and a half of old-fashioned, rough-coated otter-hounds, a present from a friend in Wales, and a couple of smooth-coated foxhounds that had been entered to otter in the North of England; and with these for a nucleus, Passon Mark proceeded to draft the ill-assorted pack. For there were some of all sorts, good, bad, and indifferent—the two latter strongly predominating. Some were too slow, and some too fast. Some were skirters, and some ran mute. Determined offenders who would run riot on anything from a badger to a butcher's boy. Splay-footed, blear-eyed sages who could do nothing but eat, and whom an indulgent master had despatched with a view to finding them a pleasant home for their old age in the far West. If such were their expectations, they were destined to prove fallacious, for a short shrift and two penn'orth of rope was the measure served out to the majority, and of the remainder he retained the three rough-coated otter-hounds, Hector, Hecate, and Harmony: Chorister and Careless, the smooth-coated fox-hounds from the North: two couple of valuable blue-mottled harriers from Wales: Rocket and Random, a couple of high-crowned, rough-sterned badger-pies from Badminton: and the pick of the foxhound puppies with which his friends Lord Braunton and Mr. Clithero had presented him.

His next step was to hold a solemn council of war with Neptune, whom he had previously propitiated by liberal gifts of tobacco and some hanks of particularly fine gut, upon which my uncle's affections had long been centred. A covenant was then duly drawn up, signed, sealed, and delivered by the high contracting parties, by virtue of which agreement the Parson was to hunt the valleys of the Cran, Braun, Lyd, Nym, and Black, with their tributary streams, and to capture and kill, to the best of his ability, any otters which might be foolish enough to allow themselves to be found by his very rudimentary pack. On his part my worthy relative bound himself and the members of his family to abstain from setting traps for, or otherwise molesting or destroying, the otters in the aforesaid rivers and their tributaries. He was, however, to receive as indemnity for the surrender of those prerogatives which he and his kinsmen had exercised from time immemorial, a royalty of three shillings *per* head, in consideration of which sum he guaranteed to give all the information in his power as to the habits and whereabouts of the otters aforesaid—which information, by reason of his frequent wanderings beside the river at all hours of the day and night, he was preeminently qualified to afford.

This covenant—none the less solemn because unwritten —having been duly ratified, Mr. Sealy's next step was to endeavour to interest Sir George in the sport, but in this— beyond eliciting an offer of pecuniary support—he completely failed, nor could the country gentry or farmers be induced to take the slightest interest in the matter, and although they gave the Parson permission to take the hounds through their meadows, they laughed in his face when he began to talk about the otters he expected to find—evidently looking upon his new venture as merely a fresh development of the latent insanity of which, in their heart of hearts, they suspected him.

Neptune and I could have enlightened them upon the subject, as, again and again, we had seen the otters fishing the big salmon-pool below Netherleigh Falls. Just on the edge of night, if you kept perfectly still, you might see their small, dark heads rising and sinking, as, in swift and graceful circles, they searched the swirling eddies of the pool, but at the least sound or movement they would disappear without leaving as much as a ring or ripple to break the smooth surface of the moonlit stream. Of a summer morning, just about daylight, we had often seen the old dog-otter returning through the shallows to his hover amongst the rocks and heavy water at the junction of the Cran and Black. Late in the spring, just before dusk, I have often watched the old ones emerge from the rocks and fish the junction-pool together, coming to the surface every few minutes with a fish in their mouths, which they would carry to their cubs, who lay, deep-hidden, in a fissure of the rocky bank. They would come to the surface at regular intervals—sometimes snapping at, and rolling over, each other in play or anger—and continue fishing until it became too dark to watch them. It is very easy to imitate their whistling call with a key or a piece of tobacco-pipe, and in this way the cubs are often drawn to the entrance of the fissure in which they are laid-up, and shot by the keepers. Otters breed at almost any time of the year—at all events from the spring to the late autumn—and the period of gestation is about the same as with the dog. If much disturbed by hounds or terriers they would take their cubs—which are born blind like puppies, and which they carry in their mouths as a water-spaniel does a duck—with them, and drop down with the tide to the rocks and caves on the coast below Blackstow.

With the very heterogeneous materials at his command, Mr. Sealy made his first start as a master of otter-hounds, and with the assistance of Mike and a farm-labourer of sporting, not to say poaching, proclivities, he began by exercising the pack on the roads and moorlands until they became a bit handy and would turn to his voice and horn. After a few preliminary but unsuccessful trials, the Parson started out one fine summer morning to make his public *début* by the riverside, with no one to help him but the son of a neighbouring squire, who had volunteered to act as whip, and the volatile Michael. I well remember the opening day, for Neptune had sent me up to the Parsonage the evening before to say that two old otters were working the upper waters of the Cran between Westford and Putford. The field consisted of three or four sporting farmers who had come out to enjoy a laugh at Passon Mark's expense: a strong contingent of the poaching fraternity from Cranford, headed by the blacksmith, a notorious character: Neptune, appropriately armed with a spear in place of a trident: and several of our people, including young Vester, Charley Klism, Frank, Perin, and your humble servant.

True to time, we found Passon Mark waiting for us at Westford toll-bar with a short but business-like pack. He was dressed with even less than his usual regard for appearances in an old flannel cap and boating-jacket—a relic of Camford days—which had once, presumably, been blue, but from which the colour had almost entirely disappeared, while the sleeves were shrunk up to the elbows: the before-mentioned black cloth trousers, shiny with wear and rolled up to the knees: and the rusty, white-seamed blucher-boots. Young Mr. Badderley was acting as first whip, seconded by Michael of the fiery crest, who was endeavouring, with but indifferent success, to imitate the language and deportment of old Tom Tarr, who hunted Lord Braunton's foxhounds.

"Yar, git to him, ye skulkin' thafe!"—he yelled at a foxhound puppy that had lingered behind for a roll on a flattened-out and enticingly odoriferous field-mouse, cutting at him viciously with a hunting-whip, and as the heavy thong curled back and nearly took a piece out of his own ear—for it is not the easiest thing in the world to hit a hound on foot —he whimpered out:—"Faix thin, 'tis wishin' I was lyin' in me warrum bid I am this minnit"—and rubbing the injured part amidst the unsympathetic laughter of the field, he shambled along after his master, meditating dire schemes of vengeance against the unconscious author of his mishap.

Although a few minutes law had been allowed for late comers, it was barely six o'clock when we turned off the road into the rush-grown meadows where the spiders had been busy weaving their delicate dew-bespangled webs of silvery filagree, which shone and sparkled like diamonds in the morning light. Obedient to a wave of the Parson's hand the veterans Careless, Hector, Harmony, and Hecate, a couple of the blue-mottled harriers, and old badger-pied Rocket— who, strange to say, had owned to the novel scent from the first—cantered gaily down to the river, followed at a more sober pace by the remainder of the pack, whom no inducements could as yet persuade to own to the strongest scent. With a short pack containing only a few couple that have been properly entered to otter, the earlier a start is made, the better, as the night-trail is still hot and strong and there is, consequently, a better chance of the young hounds and novices entering themselves and owning to the scent.

As they quested about and topped the bank at the end of the second meadow, the leading hounds hit on a drag, and Hector throwing up his sagacious head, proclaimed in deep, bell-like tones that the otter had lately passed that way, while Hecate, Harmony, and Careless endorsed his opinion, and the musical notes of the harriers helped to swell the chorus. Chorister, on the contrary,—a pure-bred foxhound who had been drafted from a well-known pack of north-country otter-hounds—would never own to the scent or leave Mr. Sealy's heels until the quarry was fairly afoot, but at the first 'gaze' he would dash into the strongest current, quartering and requartering the stream with the sagacity of a well-trained pointer, marking every turn and twist, and never relaxing his efforts until, with a final plunge, he made his strong teeth fairly meet in the tough jacket of his slippery foe. As they carried it steadily up-stream, the hounds seemed literally to revel in the steaming night-trail, while Rocket and Careless flashed ahead, returning, however, as the slower-going otter-hounds hung and stooped over the scent, yowling with delight and refusing to advance until they had made good every inch of the ground.

The otter was travelling up-stream, and when so doing

he generally keeps as much as possible to the bank, cutting off the corners from bend to bend to shorten the distance and avoid the stream, but when on the return journey, he seldom lands, but sticks to the water and takes advantage of the full force of the current.

At length we reached the deep pool below Putford mill—a deserted building which spans one branch of the river—and here all trace of the otter was lost. Before trying the mill itself, the Parson made a cast up-stream, to make assurance doubly sure, then, returning to the mill, he let the hounds work through the disused mill-leat and outbuildings, while with the terriers he explored the drains and culverts—but not a hound could mark him, and it seemed as if he must have doubled back through the mill-pool below.

Neptune alone is confident that he must be somewhere handy, and taking little Fury—one of the terriers—in his arms, he wades up the shallow mill-leat, probing every crevice and cranny with the shaft of his spear. At last he discovers an opening in the masonry which, unlike the others, is not covered with cobwebs, and into this he introduces the terrier, who gives herself just one shake and then disappears from sight. The rest of the field sit down on the parapet to watch the course of events and smoke an early pipe, while Neptune applies his ear to the cavity and listens intently, like a terrier at a rat-hole.

Suddenly his face lights up. "Sh—sh!" he whispers, "I hear 'em a'scrappin.' Stan' back. Here they *vels*"—and with a rush and a rattle a dark object shoots headlong from the hole and splashes and shoals down the shallow leat at a tremendous pace. The whole thing only occupies a few seconds, and in a moment all is bustle and excitement. The hounds race frantically along the parapet, and Chorister makes a dash at the otter as he glides into the deeper water, but missing him by the skin of his teeth, takes an involutary header into the mill-pool, while a din arises which makes the hanging woods of Putcombe echo again.

"Heu gaze! Heu gaze him! Heu bubble-a-vent!"—cries Passon Mark.

"Tally-ho! Forrard, for-rard!"—screams the sporting first whip, unversed in the orthodox language of the chace.

"See-ho!"—yell the poaching contingent from Cranford.

"Git to him thin, ye schamin' blaygart!"—shrieks Mike, cutting at his enemy the foxhound puppy—who, dazed by the tumult, is staring blankly about him—causing the poor brute to set up a dismal howl and then make off with his tail between his legs in the direction of the Kennels as hard as he can gallop.

But in the meanwhile the otter, scared by the din, heads straight down the pool, leaving a long chain of bubbles to mark his course, and passes the shallows below—which have been left unguarded—with the hounds close in his wake. Leaving the river unperceived, he makes his way up a deep water-furrow, but the master gazes him as he crosses a narrow strip of open, and, cutting off the angle, makes for another deep pool below. Fording the stickle with the excited pack at his heels, the Parson caps them on the line, and Chorister, hitting it off at once, goes away at score across the marshy bottom, closely followed by Careless and Rocket. The otter-hounds, true to their hereditary instinct, stoop and linger over the rich scent, as if they grudged a single whiff of it, throwing their tongues in ecstacy, and yowling and towling with delight, while the unentered hounds and puppies trot soberly along the bank, occasionally stopping to sniff at a rat-hole or stare at a moorhen, and evidently wondering what in nature is up.

Entering the long weir-pool below, some slow hunting takes place, as the wily beast turns and doubles: now taking advantage of an over-hanging bank or alder-stump: now sinking deep beneath the surface as his eager foes swim or scramble in close pursuit. Luckily there is no breeze, for with a curl on the water and a short pack, it is almost impossible to do anything with an otter in a long deep weir-pool, owing to the difficulty of gazing him—just as a wounded grebe or shag will keep under water an incredible time, coming up at long intervals to breathe and then only just showing the very tip of its bill above the surface. Here, for upwards of an hour, they work him backwards and forwards, and nothing but the marvellous instinct of the older hounds enable them to mark him, for the water, quickly fouling, prevents the field from rendering much assistance.

At last it gets too hot for him, and Neptune—who has stationed himself upon the weiring at the point where it juts out furthest into the stream—strikes at him with his spear as he dives past, but the water is rapid and discoloured, and shooting the lasher unharmed, he disappears amongst the tumbling waves of the rocky pool below. But the hounds are almost on top of him, and make the narrow gorge and hanging woods resound with their melody as they swim and plunge through the deep eddies and brawling stickles in their downward course, while the field scrambles and stumbles over the loose boulders which strew the shingly bank.

This time the shallows below have been properly manned, and it is clear that the end is not far off. The otter is evidently distressed, and comes to the surface more frequently, floating for a moment or two until, at last, Chorister makes a dash at him. The others join in, and hounds and otter come swimming, splashing, and worrying down-stream in a confused mass, and ground on the shallow, when Vester rushes in and tails him, flinging him high and dry on to the bank, where some of the unentered hounds, who have been listlessly surveying the proceedings, are with difficulty induced to join in the worry.

It is very difficult to get hounds to enter to otter, but once entered, they will run heel with the same fire and eagerness as the fresh scent, and only by the skill and experience of the huntsman—who notices the direction of the 'seal' and the position of the 'wedging'—can the difference be detected. When the peal enter the rivers about the end of June, the otters follow them in their progress up-stream, remaining during the autumn in the upper waters, where they hunt the salmon on the spawning-beds—their gliding, fish-like mode of progression enabling them to take the poor fish unawares while intent upon domestic affairs, just as a cat pounces upon a sparrow. But as the season advances and the spring floods wash the kelts down-stream towards the sea, they make for their breeding quarters amongst the rocks and heavy water near the mouth of the river. As the twilight deepens into night, the otter leaves his rocky fastness and works up-stream, travelling considerable distances and returning with the daylight—for unless he possesses some very strong 'hovers' there, he rarely passes the day on the upper waters. This is especially the case when the rivers are low, and when hunting the shallow moorland streams of the Kenn and Lyd, we always lay out overnight at some farm-house handy to the scene of operations. Kennelling the pack in an out-house, and starting at daybreak next morning, we threw off near the mouth of the river and worked up-stream, in order to intercept the otters on their return from their nocturnal rambles.

Not long after my installation at the Parsonage, I was promoted to the post of second whip—Irish Mike being relegated to the Kennels. Nothing succeeds like success, and the sport soon became popular, nor were there many who agreed with the dictum of crusty old Tom Tarr. That worthy having hacked out one day from the Kennels at Braunton Tracey to have a look at the novel sport, and being more at home in the pigskin than on foot, had managed to tumble head over heels into a deep hole. Out of sheer mischief someone had driven a spear through the roof of his hat, pretending to mistake it for the otter as it floated down-stream, and as they hauled the old huntsman out and made believe to stand him on his head to allow the water to drain out of his boots and pockets, he spluttered out:—
" It's just a d——d feulish spoort, that's what it is, neither meat nor mustard—summat atween a rat-hunt and a papper-chaase and only fit for a passel o' school-boys "—and snatching his hack's bridle from an attendant rustic, and jamming his well-ventilated head-piece over his dripping locks, he hoisted himself into the saddle and trotted off in high dudgeon, leaving a track behind him on the dusty road like that of a leaky water-cart.

CHAPTER XVI.

The Shingles below Brent Head.

ONE fine Sunday afternoon I had strolled down to Netherleigh Bridge, where I had arranged to meet my cousin Vester Loveridge. Spring had come with a burst, and the sun was shining in a cloudless sky. The blackbirds and thrushes were singing in chorus amongst the masses of rhododendrons which sloped down to the river from the terraced gardens of Netherleigh Court, the catkins were hanging in loose clusters from the hazels and willows which fringed the long, still pool above the bridge, and the elder-bushes were bursting into leaf. Every now and again the oily surface of the stream was broken by the rush of some great flat-sided kelt, whose white, glistening belly flashed for a moment in the glancing rays—then disappeared with a heavy splash beneath the smoothly gliding waters of the pool.

Dressed in a neat suit of West of England cloth, I lay extended at full length along the broad parapet of the bridge, my knees and elbows in the air and the back of my head resting upon my upturned palms. And as I lay there the mellow sunbeams beat full upon my face, and the cheerful notes of the water-ousel came to me, clear and mellow, above the rippling of the stickle below the bridge and the drowsy murmurs of the distant falls. All Nature seemed peaceful and contented, but my thoughts were out of harmony with the surroundings, and I waited impatiently for the sound of my cousin's footsteps. Upon the occasion of my last authorised visit to my relatives in the Combe, I had found old George Beer—who kept the Raven Inn at Blackstow—in close confab with my uncle Sylvester, and I knew from experience that his presence there portended the running of a cargo somewhere in the neighbourhood, and that the preliminaries were being discussed and the necessary arrangements made. I had been forced to return to the Parsonage without hearing the result, but Vester had promised to meet me here on the following Sunday, and I was consequently awaiting his arrival with impatience.

For the last year or two, matters had gone on smoothly enough—too smoothly by far to please me—the prevailing monotony being only occasionally varied by passages of arms with Mrs. Grey, in which, as I need hardly tell you, that experienced matron had generally managed to get the best of me. My restless nature longed for a little change and excitement, and the knowledge that a cargo was about to be run within ten miles of the Parsonage door was simply maddening. I was well aware that the housekeeper was only waiting for an opportunity of reporting me to her master, but the warm sunshine and the fresh breath of spring had set my pulses beating and sent the blood dancing through my veins like quicksilver, and I had made up my mind to chance it.

I had not long to wait, for my ear soon caught the sound of Vester's footsteps, which were easily distinguishable on the darkest night from the slouching gait of the country-folk or the measured tread of the *gav-moosh*. His handsome, hard-set features soon rose above the crown of the roadway, and lightly seating himself upon the parapet, he thus sarcastically addressed me:—

"*Sar shon mi rinkeno pal? Rawtfelo ryescro-dickin' geero shon tu tatchipé, too boot of a kral, man 'pausavel, to rokker a pauvero, chuvveno moosh si' mande.*"*

"There, there, Vester"—I replied conciliatingly, "*por mi Doovel's kaum mook dovo dinnelepenes, ta pooker mande chomani nevipenes. Shom moolo kinyo a'kerrin' posh o Rashimescrotan, ta shoondom chichi troostal o cuvva-prasterben.*"†

Anybody would have thought that Vester might have spoken kindly to me, but it wouldn't have been Vester if he had. My stern-visaged cousin was really fond of me, and with the exception of pretty Lementina Boswell—to whom

* "How are you, my pretty brother? A very gentlemanly-looking sort of chap yon are in truth, too much of a swell, I suppose, to speak to a poor, ragged fellow like me."

† "For God's sake drop that nonsense, and tell me the news. I'm dead tired of living at the Parsonage, and have heard nothing about running the cargo."

he was engaged—I don't think he cared much for anybody else, but his jealous nature took offence at my living amongst strangers, while the sight of my brand-new clothes and well-blacked boots—which to his distempered imagination made me appear the very embodiment of prosperous Philistinism—had, no doubt, upset him.

Calming down by degrees, he proceeded to inform me that the run had been fixed for the night of the first of April, when the tide would begin to ebb about ten o'clock. The place selected was a small cove—scarcely more than a fissure in the precipitous rocks—immediately below Brent Head. The landing-place was covered at high water, but as the tide began to ebb a tiny shingle beach was exposed to view, where the strong current had forced the pebbles into a series of shelving ridges, which varied according to the height of the tide, the force of the wind, and the action of the waves.

The cove was regularly used during the summer months as a bathing-place by the neighbouring farmers' sons and labourers, and a little above high-water mark a small spring of perfectly fresh water trickled from the rocks and filtered away through the shingles. A series of rough, flagged steps had formerly led from the old monastery of Brent—of which the foundation-stones alone mark the site—which formerly crowned the hill, to the spring. About two hundred of these steps still remained, but towards the foot of the cliff some convulsion of Nature had effaced the handiwork of the patient monks, and for the last few yards of the descent the intending bather was obliged to lower himself carefully down over the rocks, whose deeply indented outlines afforded plenty of resting-places for the hands and feet. The Beers had never attempted to run a cargo at this spot before, since it entailed a considerable amount of extra labour, but all the more convenient landing-places were watched by the Preventive men, and it was for this reason that the shingles below Brent Head had been chosen.

The night of Wednesday, April 1st, had been fixed upon because it was the first day of the annual Mop Fair and cattle-market at Norton—which lasted over two days—and also because most of the farmers and all of the Preventive men who happened to be off duty were certain to be there.

Passon Mark made a point of attending it, putting up at the Chichester Arms, for there was always plenty of sport going on in the way of wrestling, boxing, and single-stick, besides the chance of disposing of one of his young horses.

While living in Fernleigh Combe I had more than once been employed as scout and messenger when cargoes had been run, but it had always been my ambition to take part in the actual night work. Vester, however, was for once on the side of prudence, and advised me strongly to have nothing to do with it; but such an opportunity was not likely to occur again, and having once made up my mind, I was too headstrong to be easily turned from my purpose.

But, in the meantime, a strange thing happened, which served to fix the date in my memory beyond the possibility of mistake. As I have said, the spring had come with a burst and the weather was more like the middle of May than the end of March. On the night of the twentieth the wind, which had been in the West, suddenly backed to the N.E. and just on the edge of night a soft, fine snow began to fall. By six o'clock the following morning there was close on two feet of snow on the ground, and by ten o'clock that evening there was nearer three than two. The farmers on the high grounds lost nearly the whole of their lambs, the postmen were unable to deliver their letters, and the big Fair at Netherton —which was always held on March 25th—had to be postponed. The Exeter coach was overturned—luckily without injuring the passengers—but with the assistance of two additional pair of horses it managed to reach the first change, after which the coachman gave it up as a bad job, and the letters were sent back by the guard on horseback. The Falmouth and Plymouth coach and its passengers were obliged to remain at St. Austells, and several people lost their lives on the moors.

On the morning of April 1st I was up before daybreak and made my way to the stable. Having treated the chestnut colt to a double allowance of old beans, I proceeded to give him a final doing over, removing the superfluous hairs from his head, legs, and heels, pulling his mane and forelock to a proper length, and squaring his tail as short as the dock would permit, and at eight precisely he was led round to the front door in all the glory of a highly-polished bit and stirrup-irons, new girths, and well-cleaned saddle. The greater part of the snow had by this time disappeared and the carriage-road had been swept, but it still lingered in drifts and patches wherever the sun failed to penetrate.

Passon Mark was got up with extra care for the occasion—thanks to the provident forethought of Mrs. Grey—and in his dark-coloured suit and neatly-tied white choker secured by a gold-mounted fox-tooth pin, might well have passed for a model country clergyman of orthodox views and sporting proclivities, about to set out upon a round of parochial visits. As he placed his foot in the stirrup, the stable-proud beast set up his back like a tom-cat, plunging away from the door-step with a squeal and airing his hind shoes, but the Parson was in the saddle in a brace of shakes and cantered off down the drive, catching at the off-iron with his toe as he went.

For once in my life I was glad to see his back, and returned thoughtfully to the house, revolving in my mind plan after plan for administering the contents of a small phial containing a decoction prepared from the roots of the white poppy—which I had coaxed my Granny into giving me—and which, if dropped into the housekeeper's private teapot, would have the effect of rendering her harmless for twelve hours at all events. But luckily, perhaps, for both of us, I was spared the necessity of administering the opiate by the welcome announcement that Mrs. Grey was going to spend the evening with her one friend and confidante, the wife of a farmer living at Stuckley—a small village about two miles from the Parsonage across the moor. The coast now seemed to be perfectly clear if only I could manage to get back in time for breakfast next morning, and my spirits rose in proportion as the chances of discovery diminished.

The housekeeper took her departure in the course of the afternoon, and at tea-time I shammed a sick-headache and retired to my room at eight o'clock, telling Jane that I shouldn't be able to eat any supper, and asking her not to call me the first thing in the morning as the master was away. Then, carefully locking my door on the inside and plugging up the keyhole, I slipped between the window-bars, slid down the roof of the knife-house, and dropped noiselessly onto the heap of half-melted snow which still lingered in the shadow of the eaves. Carefully avoiding the village for fear of recognition, I took a short-cut to Netherleigh Bridge, and then made the best of my way towards the cross-roads on the moor above Fernleigh Combe, where I had privately arranged with Vester to meet him and the rest of the party.

On reaching the open moor above the camp, I found that a fresh north-westerly breeze was blowing, accompanied by occasional showers of sleet, which I knew would have the effect of raising a nasty, chopping sea in the Channel directly the tide turned, and as I crouched, wet to skin, to leeward of a clitter of big stones half buried in snow, and listened to the wind whistling through the stalks of the heather, I almost began to wish, like Mike, that I was back again 'in me warrum bid.'

It was only within the last two or three years that the Government had begun to realise the enormous proportions which the illicit trade between the Continent and England had assumed, and quite recently a coastguard station had been established between Buckland Point and Blackstow, while a revenue-cutter was permanently stationed in the Channel. The Beers of Blackstow owned a fast-sailing, sea-going yawl of close on 90 tons called the *Sarah*, and whenever farm work was slack, they were in the habit of running down the Cornish coast and across the Channel to Havre, Cherbourg, Granville, or St. Malo, returning with a mixed cargo of brandy—the high duty on which rendered it a most profitable article for importation—tea, silk goods, and tobacco.

The history of the *Sarah*—late *Seionara*—was a curious one. One summer, a military-looking gentleman of decidedly eccentric habits, who was supposed to have spent most of his time in foreign parts, had found his way down to Blackstow, and being struck by the quaint beauty of the place and the unsophisticated manners of the inhabitants, had purchased from old Squire Bamfylde—the still more eccentric lord of the manor—a plot of land of about four acres in extent, upon which he proceeded to erect a bungalow, ranche, or some such outlandish habitation, which combined the maximum of discomfort with the minimum of architectural beauty. In front of the bungalow, on a bank overlooking the harbour, was placed a small cannon with which the Colonel was in the habit of firing salutes on days of public rejoicing and other festive occasions—his black servant acting as master-gunner.

A beautiful yawl-rigged yacht called the *Seionara*—which, as I have been given to understand, is Japanese for 'Farewell'—took up her moorings in Blackstow Pill, and during the summer months her owner would cruise about in her, accompanied by a golden-haired lady and a black poodle of Satanic beauty aud abnormal intelligence. But, alas, the peaceful tenor of this Arcadian existence was one day rudely interrupted by the unexpected appearance of the bailiffs, who proceeded to annex the poodle and whatever they could lay hands on, and it being, unfortunately, low tide, and the bar only just awash, "the yacht"—as Mr. Thomas Moore might have said, "was still there, but the waters"—together with the yacht's owner—"were gone." So the *Seionara* was seized and sold by public auction, and was purchased by the Beers, who changed her name to the more familiar, if less romantic, one of *Sarah*, and having heightened her bulwarks, lightened her top-hamper, and cut away her after-deck to make room for cargo—thereby destroying the whole of her beautifully-fitted saloon and cabin accommodation—turned her into a coaster.

Upon their return from a trip to France, they would beat about the mouth of the Channel until nightfall, and then make for some landing-place which had previously been agreed upon, and where their friends were keeping a sharp look-out. The goods were packed in oilskin-covered bales weighing from ten to twenty-five pounds apiece, and in kegs which were headed up and caulked with a waterproof solution, which admitted of their being sunk and buoyed if necessary. Our part of the business consisted in keeping a look-out along the coast, and in supplying horses to transport the goods to some farm-house or other hiding-place in the interior, from whence they were again removed and eventually deposited with a cousin of old George Beer's, who kept a public-house at Netherton. The neighbouring gentry and farmers winked at what went on, if they did not openly encourage it, and strangers coming to look at some country-house which might happen to be for sale, were often struck by the size of the cellar-accommodation, which appeared out of all proportion to the rest of the premises.

I had not dared to show my nose in camp for fear of being sent back by Neptune—who was far too clever to take an active part in these expeditions—with a flea in my ear, but shivering with cold and wet through, I crouched under the lee of the boulders. At last the welcome tramp of men and horses fell on my ear. They came toiling up the steep, stony track in Indian file, the advance-guard consisting of the two Sylvesters and Pharoah Burton with three pack-horses tied nose to tail. These were followed by old Wisdom Boswell, Noah Burton, and Ned Stokes the *poshrawt*—each leading a horse. Then came Charley Klism and the two tall brothers William and Henry Orchard—*Lullobengris*, as we called them on account of their predilection for red-waistcoats—with three or four more horses tied nose to tail, while the rear was brought up by my cousins Frank and Perin—the latter mounted on old Whistling Jenny.

Crossing the closely-cropped uplands of Brent Downs diagonally, we bore away to the westward and began to descend the steep hill-side which overlooked the Channel. It was high-tide and a dirty night, and as the wind beat in our faces, bringing with it the roar of the breakers on the rocks below, we guessed that it would be a wet job as well as a heavy one. Leaving the horses in charge of Frank and old Wisdom under shelter of the turf bank which ran along the edge of the cliffs, the rest of us made our way down the steep hill-side, taking advantage—as far as they went—of the foot-hold afforded by the rough steps which formerly led to the spring. As we neared the rocks we were able to distinguish some figures standing out, shadowy and indistinct, against the white line of the breakers, and these proved to be two of the young Beers—John and 'Ginger'—with a couple of their men, who were keeping a sharp look-out seawards.

The men of our party lit their pipes, and all hands having taken a pull at a keg of brandy which John Beer produced, we proceeded to make ourselves as comfortable as circumstances permitted under shelter of the rocks, for although the tide had begun to ebb, the shingles were still covered, and it would be half-an-hour at least before it would be possible to run a boat ashore.

With the turn of the tide the wind lulled by degrees and

the rain cleared off, as is so often the case in the Channel, while inch by inch the shingles began to rise above the snap and snarl of the retreating waves—black at first but gradually whitening as they dried. The Beers had a dark-lantern with them, which, every now and again, they flashed across the cove for the boat to steer by—the light being invisible to anybody on the downs above by reason of the over-hanging cliff—and at length the muffled sound of oars creaking in the rowlocks was borne down the breeze, and a low whistle, three times repeated, told us that the long-expected boat was approaching. Having returned the signal, the Blackstow men—who wore long fishermen's boots—clambered down the rocks and dropped on to the beach, where they stood, knee-deep in water, on the sloping pebble-ridge, holding up the lantern for the boat to steer by, and steadying themselves as best they could against the wash and roll of the shingles and the strong undertow of the receding waves.

A minute or two later a heavily-laden four-oared boat, steered by old George himself, ran into the narrow inlet. The two men in the bow shipped their oars, and jumping overboard as she took the shingles, with the help of those on shore ran her up the shelving beach—but not sufficiently high to prevent the waves from breaking over her stern. No time was wasted in words, but the work of unlading was quickly proceeded with, and in less than twenty minutes the whole of the kegs and bales were piled on the beach, and the men —drenched to the skin by the short, chopping waves—ran the boat out stern first, and tumbling in over her sides, rowed off to the yawl, which was anchored about a quarter of a mile from shore.

So far we had taken no active part in the proceedings, but now John Beer threw a coil of rope up to us, and attaching the other end to one of the bales, it was hauled by us across the shingles and hoisted up to where we were standing —two of our men having climbed half-way down the rocks to fend the rope off the sharp points—and in this manner the kegs and bales were deposited one by one at our feet. Then our work began in real earnest, for we were obliged to carry the lighter packages on our backs up the rough steps, some of the heavier bales being hauled up with ropes to where the horses were waiting above. It was a tough job and no mistake, but the keg of spirits was kept going and we worked with a will.

We had scarcely finished before the sound of oars was again heard, and the boat having been beached as before, but with less difficulty, the same scene was reenacted. We all *bootied* like *grys*,* and those who fancy that Gipsies are a lazy, good-for-nothing race, should have seen us toiling under our heavy burdens up that everlasting staircase—as Tenny Klism said, it was 'ever so much worse than 'the stepper,' for they don't *kair tute rikker a posh-shell oprey tute's dumo, adoi.*' †

By the time I had carried my fair share to the top of the cliff, I had had about enough of it, but although the boat made a third and fourth trip, we were not required to do any more hauling, for the horses had as much as they could carry. Having landed the last boat-load the men set to work to scoop out a deep hole in the beach at the foot of the cliffs, just above high-water mark, using the stretchers as shovels, and having deposited the remainder of the cargo in it, they covered it over with shingles and left it to be called for on the first convenient opportunity. The yawl then got her anchor aboard and ran out into the tideway, while the boat made her way back to Blackstow, but Jack and 'Ginger' Beer waited to help us *pand* the *cuvvas oprey* the *trushni-boshtos*,‡ the heavier bales being made up as nearly as possible of equal weight, so that one balanced the other across a horse's back.

The young Beers accompanied us as far as the cross-roads, and after a parting pull at the spirit-keg, wished us 'Goodnight' and left us. As we skirted the edge of the moor and turned into the narrow bridle-path which led down to the Cran valley—down which, some four years previously, Dr. Lyons had galloped at breakneck speed upon a certain memorable October evening—the wind dropped altogether and the moon shone out bright and clear, bringing the figures of men and horses into strong relief against the deep drifts of snow which still lingered in the hollows. Our people were all provided with long sticks in case of attack—

---

* Worked like horses.
† 'Make you carry half a hundredweight on your back, there.'
‡ Make fast the goods to the pack-saddles.

for we were too heavily laden to run—and we had all of us passed our handkerchiefs over the crown of our soft felt hats or caps, poacher-fashion, tying them tightly below the chin and leaving nothing but the eyes and mouth exposed—thereby rendering the task of identification difficult if not impossible.

As the long line wound slowly down the valley, we were all of us in the highest spirits, chattering and jabbering away like a lot of schoolboys on a Saturday afternoon—for the hard work was over and the Hollands had loosened our tongues. As we entered the deep shadow of Hawk's Wood, the branches of which completely overhung the right-hand side of the lane, three figures suddenly sprang over the low boundary-wall, and at a whistle from old Vester which sent the wood-quests clattering from their roost in the fir-trees overhead, the men in the rear closed up to the front, leaving the horses in charge of Frank and myself. For the moment things looked ugly, but it proved a false alarm, the men turning out to be James Luttrell, the head-keeper at Netherleigh, and two of the under-keepers, who had been out watching for poachers, and hearing our voices, had laid in wait for us after the manner of their kind.

There was no fear of their rounding on us, for they liked the Revenue men as little as we did, and the knowledge that a small keg of brandy would be left at the head-keeper's cottage made things straight and pleasant. They accompanied us down the Combe as far as the camp, where I left the others and walked on with the keepers across the common and over the bridge, as far as the Park Lodges. Here I said 'Good-night,' and leaving them, pursued my way alone to the Parsonage, and creeping up the tiled roof like a belated tom-cat just as the cocks began to crow, was soon in bed and fast asleep, thoroughly tired out with the long night's work.

CHAPTER XVII.

The Affray in Hawk's Wood.

SO far, things had turned out even better than I could have anticipated, and I awaited the Parson's return on Thursday night without any misgivings. He proved to be in high good humour, having sold the colt well, so after listening to his account of the deal, I retired to bed and slept the sleep of the innocent. But early on Friday morning news reached the Parsonage which caused affairs to assume a very different complexion, and from sheer bad luck, rather than from any want of precaution on my part, I at length fell an easy prey to my ever-vigilant enemy the housekeeper.

The news was brought by the village postman, who informed Mr. Sealy that the dead body of Superintendent Lougher had been found early that morning in Hawk's Wood. It transpired that the Superintendent, who was a very smart officer, had received intelligence on Thursday evening while attending Norton Fair, that a cargo had either been, or was about to be, run somewhere on the coast between Buckland Point and Blackstow, and that having ordered his raw-boned chestnut mare—whose blaze face, lop-ears, and Roman nose, were as well known throughout the district as the Superintendent himself—to be saddled, he had started off to put the Revenue-officers on their guard. It was ascertained that he had left Norton—which was twenty-two miles from the spot where the body was found—shortly before ten o'clock on Thursday night, and allowing ten miles an hour as the utmost speed at which the old mare was capable of travelling with sixteen stone on her back, it seemed probable that the outrage had been committed shortly after midnight. The body had been found early the following morning by George Tudball, the woodcutter, as he was going to his work, and the old chap had started off at once to fetch Dr. Lyons from Blackstow.

The Superintendent was one of the best-known characters throughout the country-side. He was a massively-framed man of close on sixty years of age, with grey hair, dark eyebrows, a swarthy skin, and a determined expression. As a young man he had been celebrated for feats of strength, and had lately been specially appointed to the Netherton district with a view to suppressing the extensive smuggling operations which prevailed. About two years previously, a high Government official had paid a visit to North Devon incognito, in order to get up some of the details of the case, and he had made certain discoveries—especially as regarded the efficiency of the constables and Preventive-men themselves—which rather opened his eyes. The result was that Superintendent Lougher had been transferred from Deal, where he had hitherto been stationed, and where his vigilance had attracted the attention of his superiors. For the rest, when off duty he was as convivial and popular a man as you would wish to meet, could sing a good song and take his glass with the best, and when he happened to nick in with the hounds, the way the old chestnut used to hoist and lower his sixteen stone over the banks was a caution to weak nerves.

As may easily be imagined, the postman's intelligence caused my heart to sink into the very soles of my boots, and I went about my work feeling as if I had myself committed the murder, for I knew that the story of the successful run of Wednesday night would be sure to get about, and I was afraid lest, during the excitement which prevailed, one of the keepers might open his mouth.

As soon, therefore, as I had finished my morning's work, I started off to Netherleigh Chase to look for Luttrell, the head-keeper, and found him just sitting down to his dinner. Of middle height, broad-chested and powerfully built, rough as a badger and tenacious as a bull-dog, he stood, firm as a rock, on sturdy, slightly-bowed legs, while the clear grey eyes—equally ready to flash with anger or twinkle at a joke —the resolute mouth, and the firmly-moulded outline of the lower jaw, might well have convinced even the least observant that he was not a man to be trifled with. He was, in fact, an independent old fellow and curried favour with no man—a quality which is seldom appreciated as it deserves to be—but when you can find him, the services of a man of this stamp are well worth the wages of two ordinary keepers, for his reputation soon gets established, and poachers will religiously avoid a beat where they are not likely to have things quite their own way or get anything without fighting for it. The best of men have their faults, and Luttrell had his. He could neither read or write, and was as obstinate as a mule. His language to the beaters when they assumed Indian file instead of forcing their way in line through a piece of thick covert, was neither 'Yea' or 'Nay,' and towards the end of the season, if, in his opinion, his stock of hens had been unduly punished, the birds had a wonderful knack of finding their way back between the aforesaid beaters, instead of facing the guns at the 'point.' Still, the proof of the pudding is in the eating, and year after year, good seasons and bad, he would turn out from fifteen hundred to two thousand pheasants on his beat, and what he turned out, he kept—at all events the poachers had very few of them.

Old James had four or five men under him, and when the gentlemen came to shoot the coverts in November, each man turned out with his retriever in a slip and a good velveteen coat on his back, like a gentleman's servant. "Tom"—he would say to one—"just slip off to that knoll as quick as you can"—or, "Jack, you know where to go, and look sharp about it."—"Yes, sir"—they would answer, touching their hats, and off they would trot without another word, and if a pheasant was winged, or a covey of partridges fired at, there was safe to be a man just in the right place to retrieve the one or mark the other. This may seem a small matter, but let me tell you that it is the best possible indication that things are going on straight. As long as the underlings obey the head-keeper without a word and treat him with respect, you may be pretty sure that he isn't sending your game to market behind your back, for he couldn't do it without their knowing it, but when you see them grumbling and sulking and inclined to take a liberty with him and answer him back—then look out.

A couple of anecdotes will go further towards illustrating the character of the man, than pages of formal description. One day, while crossing some cultivated land on the skirts of Blackmoor, Luttrell heard a double shot at no great distance, and hurrying off in the direction whence it proceeded, he came upon a gentleman standing in the middle of a potato-field—in the act of recapping his gun after reloading. Walking up to him, he was about to ask him what business he had there, when the sportsman brought the gun to his shoulder, and pointing the muzzle straight between the keeper's eyes, shouted out excitedly:—"Stand back. If you come one step nearer I'll blow your brains out, you scoundrel!"

There was something about the man's eyes which struck Luttrell as being rather queer, and it providentially flashed across him that it might possibly be one of the inmates of Dr. Peters' private Lunatic Asylum near Blackstow, who had managed to elude the vigilance of his keepers, and getting hold of a gun by some means or other, had started off for an afternoon's sport. This impression was confirmed by the fact that while reloading his gun, the gentleman had poured the powder and shot in without measuring it, and that his fingers were cut and bleeding from contact with the trigger-guard. Without moving a muscle the keeper touched his hat respectfully, and said:—

"If you please, sir, Sir George desired me to give you his compliments and to say that you were welcome to go wherever you had a mind, and he hoped you would have good sport. I've just marked a nice covey down in a turnip-field close by, and if you'll come along o' me, I'll show you where they be."

The gentleman dropped the muzzle of his gun, and off they started for the turnip-field, where, sure enough, up got a covey of partridges.

"Mark!"—cried Luttrell.

"Bang! bang!" went both barrels, and in a moment the keeper's sinewy arms encircled the madman in a vice-like grip, and tripping him up, he threw him heavily to the ground. He had cunningly brought him to a field near which he had observed some farm-labourers at work, and blowing his whistle and shouting for assistance, the unfortunate gentleman—who fought and bit like a wild-cat—was eventually secured. Nothing but his self-possession saved Luttrell on this occasion, for Dr. Peters told him afterwards that if he had either advanced a step or turned his head, the lunatic would have blown his brains out to the deadest of dead certainties.

And now for an anecdote of a different kind. The property immediately adjoining the Netherleigh estate, on the Cranford side of the river, belonged to Squire Beaumont of Upcote, and after Ludlow left him, he had taken on a big, black-whiskered Devonshire man named Davis, between whom and Luttrell—who hailed from Somersetshire—there was not much love lost.

Now it so happened that an old hen-pheasant took it into her head to lay her eggs on the double bank which formed a portion of the boundary between the two estates, and, as may easily be imagined, each keeper considered that the nest belonged to him and kept a pretty keen eye on it—only waiting until she should have laid the full complement of eggs, before taking it. One morning the two keepers happened to meet on the boundary, not very far from the nest, and the following conversation ensued.

"Good mornen', Mister Luttrell"—begins Davis.

"Marnin', Jarge, marnin'"—replies Luttrell, "I d' reckon thee be 'st came to look arter thick there nesty."

"Raight yeu be"—says Davis, "I doant want to do nothen but what's fair and proper, but that hen were bred over teu our plaace, and you d' know 't 's well as I deu."

"Well, well, Jarge"—replies old James, conciliatingly, "she be nesting our side the bank anyways, but if so be as thee d'st reckon as she d' belong to thee, just walk solid* down to her, and put her off the nesty, and whichever side she d' wing to, shall have her."

The proposition sounded plausible enough, so Davis climbs up the bank, and walking quietly down to her, flushes her in the most impartial manner, then, jumping off the bank, he runs out into the field, the better to watch her flight. The bird, as if to verify his statement, flies for some distance straight along the bank towards the Combe below, then, spreading her pinions, sails away to the right in the direction of Upcote—finally dropping in a stubble-field on the outskirts of one of Squire Beaumont's coverts.

"Look-see!" cries Davis exultingly, "be ee satisfied?

* Slowly and steadily.

I can see her now, runnen up the harrish unner Monk 'ood."

But in the meanwhile the perfidious Luttrell, taking advantage of his rival's temporary absence, stoops down and proceeds to transfer the contents of the nest to his capacious inside pocket.

"Yes, sure-ly"—he chuckles, as he carefully stows away the last of the eggs, "t' hen be thine, right enough, and thee sh'lt keep her, but I'll take t' eggs. Fair does, ye know, fair does. Marnin', Jarge, marnin'"—and straightening his back and squaring his broad shoulders, old James marches off with his ill-gotten spoils, leaving his rival staring disconsolately at the empty nest—his belief in the efficacy of augury by the flight of birds having experienced a rude shock.

We very soon found out what an imposter Davis was, but, strange to say, the Squire, although shrewd enough in most matters, took a couple of years to make the same discovery, and by that time there was scarcely a head of game left on the estate.

To return to my story, Luttrell, like the good-natured old fellow he really was in spite of his surly exterior, readily promised to keep the fact of his having met me on Thursday morning a secret, but said that he could not possibly answer for the under-keepers. What made my position so uncomfortable, was the recollection that the two Vesters and Harry Orchard had fixed to return on Thursday night for the purpose of removing the remainder of the goods from the beach below Brent Head, with the assistance of the Beers. They were then to follow the rest of our people, who by that time would have struck camp and started off inland with the bulk of the cargo. It had been arranged that a light cart should be left behind at the *yoggin' tan* * in charge of Perin, into which the *cuvvas* † were to be transferred from the pack-horses, and having been covered up with tent-cloths, were to be rapidly driven off before daylight to the 'Nag's Head' —John Beer's house at Netherton—while the men followed with the horses. Having received their pay for the two nights' work, they were then to separate, the Orchards and Burtons making for Somersetshire, while our people started

* Camping-place.   † Goods.

on one of their regular rounds through South Devon and Cornwall.

On hearing the postman's story, I at once guessed that an accident must have happened, and I anxiously awaited the return of Mr. Sealy, who had ridden off to make inquiries near the scene of the reported murder. He returned late in the evening, and we then learned that the Superintendent was still alive, but had sustained concussion of the brain and other serious injuries from which he was not expected to recover.

To make a long story short, I was soon put out of my misery, for, within twelve hours, Mrs. Grey had heard from her intimate friend and gossip, the farmer's wife, that I had been seen by one of the under-keepers—a psalm-singing rascal named Ball, who was only fit to keep the birds off the corn, and always had his nose in the agent's pocket—in the company of several of my kinsmen at about three o'clock on Thursday morning. This was quite enough for the housekeeper who, meeting me in the hall and mixing up the dates, openly accused me of having been present at the attack on the Superintendent. In vain I denied the charge, and swore that I had never left my bed on that eventful night—which was true enough. My ever-vigilant enemy marched me round to the back of the house, and pointed triumphantly to the holes punched by my boots in the heap of accumulated snow which had slid off the roof and obstinately refused to melt. Then, flushed with victory, she betook herself to her master's study, and lost no time in repeating her precious bit of gossip, with a result which shall be related in the next chapter.

In the meanwhile I will give the exact particulars of the affray, as I afterwards heard them from my cousin Vester himself. To use his own words, as near as may be :—

"*Pooro*,* Harry and me, left the camp with five horses about eight o'clock on Thursday night. The rest of 'em had started with the stuff for Netherton before daylight that same morning, and we had 'greed to meet the Beers at the *chingerdromior*† soon after nine, to bring away the *cuvvas poosheni tuley* the *lon-pawni bars*,‡ afore the tide were up. As

* "The old 'un."   † "Cross-roads."
‡ "Goods buried under the shingles."

you mind, it come on close and muggy Thursday, for the wind had dropped and the Channel were full o' fog."

"We met the Beers soon after nine 'cordin' to 'greement, and it *lelled mende a kushto dui oras to rikker the cuvvas pral the choomba, ta pand lende oprey the gryor. We penned 'kooshto bok' to the Levinengros, ta hektered sig atoot the kekno-moosh's poov.** Just as we got to the cross-roads above Hawk's Wood, *posh adoi kai the veshenengros hoktered oprey mende rarde anpauli,*† old Jenny wickered, and, directly arter, we hears a horse comin' full sling up the Combe, and as it comes nearer and nearer, I *pens* to *Pooro:—'Dovo se o Sherro-dickimengro, tatchipé. Mande'd jin yuv's grasni's bavol amen deshell.'*"‡

"So we turns the horses sharp round and *jals* 'em up the *choomba* till we comes to the yew-trees *tuley* the *kauli-bars, ta 'doi men hatched akonyo drey de lok o' de moolo-rookies,*§ on the chance of his passin' us by in the dark. We knew it was him as soon as ever we saw the mare's white face through the mist. She was *a'shellin', a'goorin', and a'hooterin', sims a pooro gruveno,*‖ for the fog made her worser'n ever."

"'T was odds he passed us, for, as you d'know, he's not *flick* of his *yakkors*, but one of the horses stamped his foot agen a stone, *ta yuv bongered yuv's sherro atoot lescro pikko ta dickdas mende.*¶ Then he wheels the mare round and come straight at us as we was stood there still as mice in the shadow of the trees, and says he:—'So I've got you at last, have I? Here, come out of that, and let's see who it is.'"

"The rocks is too steep to climb, as you *jins* and if we'd done our push, he'd ha' been atop of up directly, so we never answers a word, but stands there crouched behind the horses."

"Then he touches the mare with the *busnis*,** and as soon as he gets under the shadow of the trees, he sees who it

* "It took us a good two hours to carry the goods up to the hill and load the horses. We wished 'good-luck' to the Beers, and hurried across the Downs."

† "Near where the keepers jumped out upon us the night before."

‡ "I says to the old 'un, 'That's the Superintendent, for certain, I'd recognise his mare's roaring among a thousand.'"

§ "Below Black-rock, and there we waited in silence in the shadow of the yew-trees."

‖ "She was whistling, roaring, and bellowing like an old bull."

¶ "And he turned his head over his shoulder and saw us." ** "Spurs."

were directly, and says he to *dad**:—'You old, smuggling horse-thief, you've put the double on me often enough, but I'll stretch you for this job'—and he whips the bracelets out of his pocket, and grabs at Pooro's collar."

"Now, as you d'know, it don't take not a very great deal to upset the old 'un, 'specially when he's got a drop in him, and says he:—'Stan' back, or *s'op mi Doovel* I'll hit the brains out of you'—and he ups with his *koshter*.† Then the head-police—bein' a Welshman and quick-tempered like the main on 'em—he ups with his huntin'-crop to strike at *dad*, and the old 'un he lands him *oprey* the *kor* ‡ with the *kosh*, and knocks him clean and cliver right out 'er the saddle, and as the mare jumped away from the stick, she must ha' trampled him, for his forehead were laid open, and I heer'd arter as how two of his ribs were broke. There he lays in the road, and never stirs hand nor foot, and we makes sure he were dead."

"Then we concerts what we was to do with the *truppo*,§ and *dad* was all for carrying of him down to the cart and driving of him off till we come to a quiet place by the river, and dropping of him in with a stone round his neck. Then I thinks on another plan. We catches the mare, and the other two carries him about a hundred yards further down the lane, and lays him on the turf by the side of the roadway with his head up agin a big stone, and smears it with blood so as to make believe he'd been throwd off his horse, accidental-like. Then I brings the mare up alongside, and makes her back and plunge across the road—to make the tracks look as if she'd shied at summat—and then I lets go her head and brings my stick down across her quarters, and sends her gallopin' up the lane *sims o pooro Beng sus dellin' lauki*.‖ Then we takes another look at him, to make sure he were dead, and goes back and fetches the horses and hurries on down the lane to where the cart were waitin', and just as we'd done loadin' it, who should come along but that there Joe Ball. He told us he'd been out *a'moskeyin'*¶ and asked us for a drop of French, and we gives it him, and then he has another, and off he goes without as much as

---

* "Father."   † "Stick."   ‡ "On the forehead."   § "Body."
‖ "As if the old Devil himself was kicking her."
¶ "Watching."

'Thank 'ee.' But when they *latchers* the *truppo drey* the *sala*,* what does the——do, but go straight to the magistrates and round on us. *Rawtfelo jooko, Beng te tasser leste!*"

The three men, fully believing that the Superintendent was dead, started at full speed with the cart and pack-horses for the 'Nag's Head' at Netherton, where they left the goods with John Beer, and received their share of the pay, then, guessing rightly that suspicion would ultimately fall on them, they separated from the rest of the tribe, and harnessing a fast-trotting horse to a light cart, drove off in the direction of Taunton. They remained for several weeks in hiding on the Quantocks, and then crossed into Dorsetshire, keeping close by day and travelling by night—working backwards between Blandford, Sherborne, and Crewkerne. As the Government were determined to put a stop to smuggling at all costs, and as the Superintendent's case had been pronounced hopeless, a heavy reward was at once offered for their apprehension, and it says very little for the pluck and enterprise of the rural constables that although their appearance was well known, as also the locality in which they were hiding, the men were never arrested, but being looked upon as desperate characters, were allowed to wander at large about the country for seven months.

At length, hearing that the Superintendent was recovering from his injuries, and feeling that anything was preferable to being hunted like wolves and half starved, old Vester arranged with his brother Plato—who lived at Bridgewater—for their surrender to the authorities. Plato performed his part of the business very cleverly and pocketed the reward—which was afterwards equally divided amongst the four of them—the men being taken to Exeter, where they were tried at the Assizes and sentenced, my uncle Sylvester Loveridge to five years penal servitude, and my cousin Vester Loveridge and Henry Orchard to two years imprisonment.

* "Find the body in the morning."

CHAPTER XVIII.

I Leave the Parsonage.

THE immediate result of Mrs. Grey's interview with her master — in the course of which my misdeeds were paraded in all their heinousness — was a summons to the study, where I found the Parson pacing up and down at full speed — his usual method of working off the steam when anything had occurred to upset his mental equilibrium. As soon as I had closed the door behind me, he brought himself to an anchor in in the arm-chair, and assuming a severity which was all the more impressive when contrasted with his usual free and easy manner, he first of all summed up the evidence for the prosecution, and then proceeded to pass sentence in due form.

He said that he had done his best to fulfil the self-imposed duties of tutor and guardian, and he believed that, to a certain extent, he had succeeded. He reminded me — rather unnecessarily, as I thought — that when I had arrived at the Parsonage some four years before, I was nothing but a ragged outcast with scarcely a shirt to my back or boots to my feet — my mental condition being precisely on a par with my outward appearance. He was willing to admit that the experiment of converting a homeless young vagabond into a respectable member of the community had not been unattended with interest, and that as he watched the gradual progress of my mental development, he was not without hopes that, some day or other, I might attain a position which would at all events be superior to anything which my birth and antecedents could have warranted me in aspiring to. That the progress I had made in my studies and the interest I had evinced in them, more than equalled his expectations and went far towards confirming his theory that the human mind, at a comparatively advanced age, could more easily be brought to a high pitch of intellectual culture if the brain had never previously been stimulated by study, etc., etc. Once fairly mounted on his hobby, he appeared to be entirely oblivious of the connection between certain recent events and my presence in the Library, and lighting his pipe, branched off into a disquisition upon the advantages which his system of education possessed—which, however, I will not inflict upon you.

Returning to the matter in hand, just as I had begun to think that he intended to say no more about it and let me off with a caution, he informed me that he did not believe that there was anything exceptionally vicious about me, but that the love of change and the craving for excitement which had been engendered and fostered by the wandering life I had been accustomed to lead, seemed to unfit me for the career which he had sketched out for me. He was of opinion that, as long as I remained in Devonshire, I should be continually exposed to temptations which must necessarily have the effect of unsettling me,* and he had come to the conclusion that the best thing I could do was to leave the neighbourhood for good. He would at once consult Sir George upon the subject and would acquaint me with the result of their joint deliberations.

Then suddenly exchanging his judicial manner for his usual kind way of speaking, he told me that I had been of considerable use to him in looking after the outdoor work and superintending the stable and kennel arrangements, and finished up by assuring me that he should be very sorry to lose me, and that if ever I got into difficulties I might rely upon finding a firm friend and a warm welcome at the Parsonage—and, as the sequel will show, he proved as good as his word, and better.

As I left the study I experienced an unwonted choking sensation in my throat and a burning about the eyes—for I was strongly attached to Passon Mark, whose fearless nature commanded my respect, while his unvarying kindness had touched a chord in my heart which had hitherto been silent— but I was determined not to show any symptoms of weakness

* This, it should be explained, was by no means the first time that young Loveridge had got himself into trouble, and upon a previous occasion he had been plainly told that his next escapade would be his last.—ED.

before the enemy, and gulping down my emotion and assuming an air of stolid indifference, I went about my work as usual. At the same time I began to realise what a golden opportunity I had thrown away, and I loathed the headstrong folly which had caused me to run counter to Mr. Sealy's views for my advancement. Recognising the full extent of the mischief which my restless disposition had dragged me into, I cursed the bad luck which always seemed to stick to me, and if I had happened to come across the housekeeper in a lonely spot, I am afraid I should have been tempted to settle our accounts after a rough and ready fashion which would have left a considerable balance in my favour, for, to tell the truth, it was just as much as ever I could do to keep the devil inside me from breaking loose.

As the result of his interview with Sir George, Mr. Sealy informed me that it had been decided to apprentice me to a certain Mr. Sellars, who owned a large carriage manufactory in Westport, a large seaport town on the south-coast, and who was under some obligation to the baronet. He told me that Sir George would continue to administer my small patrimony, and hoped that when I ceased to be exposed to the deleterious influence which my relatives appeared to exercise over me, I should settle down and endeavour to make the most of the opportunity that had been given me. Anybody who really understood my character would scarcely have taken such a sanguine view of the case, and I could not help wondering that the Parson—who ought by this time to have known me better—could have thought me capable of resisting the temptations of a large town, when I had been unable to keep out of mischief in such an out-of-the-way place as Netherleigh.

Since her ladyship's death, Sir George had led a most secluded life, and in proposing to place me under the supervision of Mr. Sellars, he had at all events done the best he could for me. It would, indeed, have required a second Solomon to have discovered any situation which I was really qualified to retain, and I have sometimes thought that it was a mistaken kindness to attempt to reclaim and civilize such an out-and-out young scamp as I was.

Before I left Netherleigh the Parson had me measured for some dark-coloured clothes suitable for town wear, which, with the rest of my small belongings, were packed up in an old travel-worn trunk with which he presented me. The leave-taking was quite an affecting one, for I had always been on the best of terms with all the members of the establishment with the exception of the housekeeper, to whom I took an opportunity of revealing the tragic and blood-curdling *dook* * which, after consulting the cards, my venerable grandam had predicted for her. The whole thing was a pure effort of imagination on my part, but I knew that comely Mrs. Grey was a firm believer in the supernatural and went in mortal terror of old Charlotte who, on being warned off the premises one day during the Parson's absence, had turned round, and with much wrinkling of brows and shaking of skinny and prophetic forefinger, had poured forth the vials of her wrath upon the amiable housekeeper, volubly devoting her body to temporal distinction and her soul to eternal perdition.

The Parson, himself, drove me as far as Netherton—from which place I should be able to get a lift into Exeter—and as I crossed the moor for the last time and cast a longing, lingering look at the range of woods which hid the valley where the camp had so lately been pitched, it needed all my companion's cheery talk to prevent me from sinking to the lowest depths of despondency. I parted from Mr. Sealy at the L'Estrange Arms, where I took a seat on the lumbering old Diligence which started every Monday, Wednesday, and Friday morning at 8 a.m. meeting the Royal Mail at the Half Moon, Exeter, and returning on Tuesdays, Thursdays, and Saturdays.

A six hours drive brought us to Exeter, where I was just in time to secure a seat on the "Flying Times," which started for Westport the following day. It was a glorious spring morning, and as the coachman gave the leaders their heads and sprang them up the gentle incline of the Westport Road, my low spirits seemed to vanish, as if by magic, at the touch of the life-stirring breeze. As the horses' shoes rang out merrily on the hard road, the novelty and excitement of being whirled along at the top speed of four well-bred nags sent the blood coursing through my veins, and caused that delightful feeling of hope and confidence in the future, which

* Destiny.

is never long absent from the youthful breast, to resume its wonted sway. I travelled by the Royal Mail instead of by any of the local coaches in order to be, as it were, under the wing of Tom Padley, the sporting guard, who seemed to me quite like an old friend, since he had put up his hands in former days against my uncle Sylvester and other members of the family. He was, moreover, a great ally of Plato's, and when I introduced myself as a nephew of the latter's, and told him that I was about to make a start in life in Westport, the good-natured guard opened out at once and proceeded to give me all the news of the road.

It appeared that he knew my future employer quite well, in fact, as he informed me, the very coach upon which we were then sitting had been built by that highly respectable firm. Padley had heard something about the reported murder of Superintendent Lougher, and by the proffer of sundry insidious beverages—which I felt ashamed to decline—he managed to worm most of the details out of me. The strong spiced ale was as brandy to me after the thin cider I had been in the habit of drinking at the Parsonage—the immediate effect of this method of obtaining information being to cause my head to fall forward on my breast, while the novelty of the situation lost all its charms before we had completed more than half of our journey.

As we rattled down the steep pitches which form the last stage into Westport, Padley shook me roughly and woke me up, and had he not done so I should most probably have rolled off the coach. The road ran along the shoulder of a steep range of hills, and as we at length came in sight of the old town slumbering peacefully beneath a dense haze of smoke, I felt that I had entered in earnest upon a new phase of existence, and shaking off with an effort the effect of my unaccustomed potations, I succeeded in collecting my scattered faculties. As the coach bumped and jolted over the roughly-pitched stones amidst the noise and bustle of a populous city, cowed and bewildered by the surge and hum of the crowded streets, it began to dawn upon me for the first time what an insignificant unit in the sum-total of humanity I represented.

As I was shaking hands with my new friend the guard in the yard of the Marlborough, I was accosted by an undersized and rather wizened-looking youth attired in a startling suit of checks, a low-crowned, broad-brimmed hat, and parsimonious trousers, who announced himself as Mr. Richard Sellars junior, and proved to be the second son of my future employer.

Catching up my small portmanteau, I followed my guide through the crowded streets, and after crossing two or three bridges and threading our way through an apparently interminable labyrinth of tortuous alleys, we emerged upon a spacious grass-grown square, where, high above our heads, the rooks had built their untidy nests in the lofty elms which surrounded it on all four sides.

As my conductor pulled up short and rang the bell of a large, gloomy-looking house, my thoughts involuntarily travelled back to the Parsonage and Fernleigh Combe, and as the servant girl ushered us into a dark, close-smelling passage and the street-door closed behind me with a bang, the old feeling of despondency took full possession of me again.

The dingy and uninviting exterior of Mr. Sellar's house was amply atoned for by the spacious apartments and by the air of solid comfort—so dear to the heart of the prosperous citizen—which pervaded the whole of the interior arrangements. The house, as I have said, formed part of a large square which enclosed a plot of grass some two acres in extent, in the centre of which a score of smoke-begrimed sheep were nibbling the scanty herbage round the base of a mouldy-looking bronze statue representing a verdegris-covered gentleman, in short petticoats and a laurel wreath, sitting a plunging horse with a grace and composure which spoke volumes for his nerve and horsemanship, more especially when we take into consideration the fact that the sculptor—who was presumably working by contract—when suiting him with a horse, had neglected to provide him with reins, stirrups, or any of the usual appliances for controlling the noble quadruped he bestrode.

Regent Square had formerly been the very hub and centre around which the most exclusive circles of Westport society revolved, but the fickle tide of fashion had long since ebbed away, leaving it stranded, high and dry, upon the barren shore of respectable mediocrity. My employer—a heavily-built, pompous-looking man of middle age and height, with iron-grey hair and a florid complexion—was a fair sample of the inhabitants of the quarter. His hair was brushed well back from his shining forehead, while his whiskers, of a darker shade than the hair, fringed a smug, self-complacent face, the skin of which was of an oily texture highly suggestive of the habitual application of glycerine, and which, in his case, was but the outward and visible indication of an oleaginousness which pervaded his entire being.

For a heavy man his execution of the really difficult Terpsichorean feat of advancing or retiring upon tip-toe with all the grace and agility of a professor of calisthenics, when ushering an influential customer into his sanctum, was little short of marvellous, while his lavish expenditure of invisible soap, combined with the air of insinuating urbanity, at once courteous and deprecatory, which he was wont to assume on these occasions, must have been as impressive to a stranger as it was edifying to the initiated, and even now I tremble to think what the consequences might have been, had he chanced to enter the office, unexpectedly, while his youngest son—his comical face puckered up into life-like imitation of his respected progenitor's—was preparing, with much shrugging of shoulders and washing of hands, to book my order for a slap-up four-in-hand.

For some reason or other, the explanation of which has never occurred to me, Dick is generally the scapegrace of the family, and young Sellars was no exception to the rule. He was an undersized and prematurely aged-looking specimen of humanity, with a gammy leg and a limp, but the humourous twinkle of his bright eyes went far to redeem the plainness of his wizened features, and within his narrow chest and attenuated frame there lurked enough of pluck and 'devil' to have completely equipped a couple of the longest troopers in the Household Cavalry. Mr. William, the eldest son, was a steady-going young fellow and a partner in the business, but the volatile Dick was at once the idol and the torment of his strait-laced parents. He had always been a delicate lad, but as soon as he succeeded in emancipating himself from the thraldom of his mother's apron-strings, he had developed the most pronounced sporting tastes, in direct opposition to his father's views. He may possibly have 'thrown-back' to some ancestor of Bohemian proclivities — although this is unlikely — but I believe that the real explanation of the matter was that somebody had once made the unfortuate remark in his hearing that he bore a strong personal resemblance to a certain popular jockey, who was then the idol of the sporting public—and upon this model Master Dick proceeded to form himself. He wore a hat the brim of which varied, according to the prevailing fashion in sporting head-gear, from the pretentious roll and curl of an archdeacon's, to the uncompromising severity of a carpenter's straight-edge, while his exiguous trousers were only persuaded to pass over his club-foot by a mechanical contrivance which remained a secret between himself and his tailor.

Nothing but a strong effort of will over nature could ever have induced him, in the first instance, to bestride the corky and heavily-gingered screws which he hired from Goodman, and mounted upon which, and attired in a suit of prismatic checks, he was wont to parade the streets of Westport and witch the hearts of the milliner's young ladies in Fore Street with very indifferent horsemanship. In the winter he used to attend most of the meets within distance, and favoured by his light weight he would charge fence after fence, just as they came, with a recklessness born of sheer ignorance and a total immunity from severe falls.

The manufactory in Regent Square employed upwards of a hundred and fifty hands, and was divided into various departments consisting of body-makers, smiths, wheelers, carriage-makers, painters, trimmers, etc. Mr. Sellars, himself, took two apprentices, of which I was one, and being apprenticed to the whole business of coach-building, we were obliged to learn the work of each department. The foreman of each department was also allowed to take an apprentice, who confined himself to learning the work of that particular branch of the business. Only a comparatively small portion of the carriage was actually manufactured upon the premises. The springs, axles, lamps, and most of the iron-work came from Birmingham, and the spokes from America; while the shafts, rails, and a good deal of the woodwork were supplied by a firm of bent-wood manufacturers in Westport. In many cases, especially when there was a press of business, nearly the whole of the carriage was sent down ready-made in sections from the Manufacturers to the Trade in London, and having been put together and painted in Regent Square, it was then stamped with the name of Sellars and Son and sent out in due course. However, as I always disliked the head of the firm, and never took any interest in the business, perhaps the less I say about it the better.

For the next four years I kept steadily to my work. Life at the Parsonage was indeed a paradise compared with my present employment, with its regular hours and dull routine, and had it not been for my desire of reinstating myself in Mr. Sealy's good opinion, and for the companionship of Dick Sellars—whose high spirits and quaint sayings always put me on good terms with myself when inclined to mope—I should have run away to my uncle Plato at Bridgewater, who would have found me some work better suited to my capabilities. I slept in a tiny attic under the slates, and was alternately roasted in summer and frozen in winter. I rose at daybreak, and after a frugal breakfast in the kitchen, went off to my work which—with the exception of an hour for dinner—lasted until 5.30 p.m., after which I was my own master until 9 p.m. at which hour Mr. Sellars expected all the members of the household to assemble for devotions.

Like most men of his type, my employer was inordinately fond of the sound of his own voice, and the function which he termed family devotions afforded him a fine opportunity for gratifying his weakness. After the regular prayers, he was in the habit of improving the occasion by favouring us with a more or less prolonged extemporary discourse of a semi-religious character, in the course of which it was his custom to animadvert severely upon any little shortcomings which he might have detected amongst his audience during the preceding twenty-four hours. It was a truly edifying spectacle to watch this worthy man walking down Fore Street on his way to Church on a fine Sunday morning, arm-in-arm with his better-half. His whole being seemed to be permeated by a moral and physical gloss, while the beams of the morning sun, as they radiated from his well-brushed hat, glittering shirt-studs, and heavy gold chain, were reduplicated and refracted by the shining black satin dress and sparkling bugles of his spouse.

He did not, however, make the mistake of allowing his religious convictions or conscientious scruples to interfere with the conduct of his business, and his was the master-hand which put the finishing touches to those elaborate specimens of the art of simple addition with which he favoured his customers about Christmas time. The head of the firm very properly reserved to himself the task of receiving his clients and of drawing up their little accounts —in both of which branches of the business he was unrivalled—and the misguided folk who sent in their carriages for repairs without even taking the precaution of asking for an estimate, must have been more surprised than delighted when they came to tot up the long columns of items, with their attendant figures, set forth in that beautifully distinct Italian handwriting. For, in his case, the velvet glove of effusive geniality fitted but loosely, and should a customer prove recalcitrant and flatly refuse to comply with his extortionate demands, the iron hand beneath was at once revealed in the shape of a lawyer's letter, and in nine cases out of ten, rather than go into court, the money was paid and the victim went his way a sadder but a wiser man.

By the end of four years I had acquired a fair knowledge of the mysteries of the trade, but I very much doubt whether I should ever have been able to settle down to the humdrum life of a respectable citizen, and a little unpleasantness with the head of the firm decided me to go out of a business to which I was altogether unsuited.

As I have said, Dicky Sellars was devoted to sport of every description, and his partiality for horse-flesh had long been a source of anxiety and vexation to his ultra-respectable parents, who appeared to regard the habitual bestriding of the noble quadruped as the surest indication of a moral depravity of the most malignant type. On Saturday afternoons I used sometimes to go for a ride with him, and Dick had introduced me to Goodman, the proprietor of the 'Westport Horse Emporium and Commission Stables.' When I had been short of money he had once or twice insisted upon paying for my mount, but as soon as Goodman found that I was capable of giving his horses a good show and could be trusted not to knock them about, he was always glad to mount me for nothing. The arrangement suited us both, for horse-dealing is as a second nature to one of my blood, and I helped to sell several of his horses for him, receiving a small commission upon each transaction.

At the end of two or three seasons Master Dick found himself rather deep in Goodman's books, and when the latter pressed for payment, rather than ask his father for the money, he preferred to go to one of the tribe of small usurers who represented themselves as 'willing to advance large or small sums, in town or country, at the shortest notice, on personal security.' Somehow or other the matter reached the ears of Sellars senior, and when the worthy man came to investigate the transaction and overhaul Goodman's little account—which, with the exception of the caligraphy, was almost on a par with the best of his own productions in that particular line—his rage knew no bounds, and noticing a couple of items to which my name was appended, he straightway summoned me to his presence, and after a furious harangue, in the course of which he accused me of leading his innocent offspring into all sorts of extravagance and profligacy, politely presented me with the key of the street. As soon, however, as he found that I had written a full account of the affair to Mr. Sealy, he changed his tone and retracted his notice of dismissal, but I had already arrived at the conclusion that building carriages for other people to ride in was but a poor game at best, and was only too glad of an excuse for cutting the business.

While riding Goodman's horses I had more than once been accosted by a certain Mr. Shice, a well-known character in the neighbourhood of Westport, who ostensibly exercised the profession of Veterinary Surgeon, probably finding the letters V.S. a very useful cloak to his rather extensive operations in the horse-dealing line. Like many other good judges of horse-flesh, he was himself but an indifferent performer in the pigskin, and as his nerve was scarcely on a par with his astuteness, he had been for some time on the lookout for somebody who could show off his horses and at the same time be trusted to keep his mouth shut. Now I was by no means a talkative individual—although, on occasions, I could rattle away fast enough—and as Mr. Shice had had plenty of opportunities of seeing me in the saddle, he may possibly have arrived at the conclusion that I might prove a useful addition to his establishment. Be that as it may, on hearing that I was about to leave my present employer, he came to me and made me certain proposals which, after consulting Mr. Sealy, I decided to accept.

In the meantime Passon Mark had invited me to spend a few days at my old quarters, from which I had now been absent a little over four years. It was with a light heart, therefore, that I packed up the battered old portmanteau, and after a final interview with the pompous head of the firm, made my way one fine summer morning to the Marlborough, accompanied by my staunch ally Dick Sellars, who came to see me off. We had an excellent though hurried breakfast together—for we were expecting the mail every minute—but after waiting till 10 a.m. for the bags, we gave her up, and started for Exeter all the lighter for her non-arrival.

The horses must have appreciated the difference, for the first stage out was all against the collar, and the roads ran heavy. There had been a tremendous thunderstorm in the night, but the sun now shone out bright and warm, and through the film of smoke which overhung the town and drifted slowly before the light westerly breeze, finally merging itself in the shimmering golden haze which obscured the horizon, it was easy to trace the position of the familiar squares and streets which, here and there, were intersected by sheets of glistening water, while a forest of masts appeared to be mixed up in inextricable confusion with branching elm-trees, church-spires, and warehouses. Beyond the town, again, the broad bosom of the channel was flecked with the foam of innumerable wavelets, which danced and sparkled beneath the glittering rays of the July sun.

We afterwards heard that the defaulting mail had been impeded in her progress by a wall which had been blown down across the road by the fearful gale of the preceding night. At Exeter I came across a friendly farmer who gave me a lift as far as Netherton, where I left my baggage to be brought on by the carrier's cart, and started on foot for the Parsonage.

Upon my arrival I found that Mr. Sealy had been away for the last two days with the otter-hounds, and was not expected back until late. Everything at Netherleigh was exactly the same as when I left it, with one notable exception.

I found that within a year of my departure Mrs. Grey had packed up her boxes one fine morning, and had been driven off to Netherton in the dog-cart by the auburn-haired Michael, 'leaving just as she come, without as much as a word, good or bad, to anybody'—as Jane informed me, and that within a fortnight the ramshackle fly from the L'Estrange Arms had deposited her successor at the door of the Parsonage. Mrs. Jones proved to be a brisk, cheery body with a word and a smile for everyone, and during my short visit I had no reason to complain of my treatment.

About nine o'clock the Parson arrived, wet through and not in the best of humours, for the heavy rain had flooded the streams and interrupted his sport, but he gave me a hearty welcome, nevertheless, and then retired to change his clothes, while I helped Mike to satisfy the requirements of the half-famished pack. I passed the evening in the study and, contrary to his wont, Passon Mark refilled his big German meerschaum several times before we separated, and it was not until the small hours that I made my way to my old bedroom, and soon dropped asleep in the blissful consciousness that I should not have to turn out at daybreak next morning.

CHAPTER XIX.

I Make the Acquaintance of Mantis Lovell.

THE following day being Sunday, I spent the interval between the services in renewing my acquaintance with the live-stock of the establishment, including the pack of otter-hounds which, thanks to judicious selection and drafting, could now boast twelve couple of working hounds besides some useful-looking puppies. Several of the neighbouring gentry had begun to take a keen interest in the sport, and offers of support and assistance came pouring in from all quarters—as not infrequently happens when a doubtful venture turns out an unqualified success.

The Parson was in the habit of spending Sunday evening at the Court, and on this occasion I accompanied him, and renewed my acquaintance with Neptune's patron, Mr. Adams. I picked up several items of local gossip in the butler's sanctum, amongst others that my relatives—with the exception of the two Sylvesters, the elder of whom was still doing time, while the younger had gone to try his luck in the metropolitan district—had spent the previous winter in the Combe, but had as usual left the neighbourhood in April. That pretty Lementina Boswell had refused to marry poor Vester when he came out of Exeter goal, and that the latter had left the camp for good and all, vowing vengeance upon his faithless sweetheart, but more especially upon whomsoever might aspire to usurp his place in her affections. That Sir George had offered to put Neptune into a small moor-farm, where old Charlotte might end her days in peace, but that the sturdy old people had respectfully declined the honour, declaring that they were got too old to learn new habits of life.

I presently received a summons to the library, where Sir George questioned me as to my doings during the last four years, and expressed himself as satisfied with my manners and appearance. I found him less changed than I expected, for although prematurely grey and aged, he had succeeded in throwing off, to a great extent, the effects of the severe shock which her ladyship's sudden death had occasioned him, and in the society of his old friend the Parson, and freed for the moment from the rather depressing influence of his spiritual advisers, he seemed more like his old self. As we were leaving the house, we met the two young gentlemen, Master Geoffrey and Master Francis, with their tutor, Father Dennis Massy. Master Geoffrey was a fine, well-grown lad, with curly brown hair and a fresh colour, but Master Francis was a slightly-built, delicate-looking child, with dark hair and his mother's eyes.

It had been arranged that we should start the following day for Bustle's farm at Three Tors—distant some fifteen miles from Netherleigh—and that after passing the night there, we should try the upper waters of the Kenn the next morning, sleeping at Blackford Inn and working the heavier streams of the Black on Wednesday. In accordance with this programme we left the Parsonage early on Monday afternoon, Passon Mark and myself riding two of the colts, while Mike, mounted on one of the brood mares, brought up the rear, and kept the pack from straggling.

As the result of an experience of several years, the Parson had almost entirely given up the old-fashioned rough-coated otter-hound, and relied mainly upon the foxhound strain. Being compelled to go long distances in search of sport, he soon found that the well-shaped feet of the latter enabled him to travel the rough country tracks with comparative impunity, while the splay-footed otter-hound returned to Kennel footsore, surly as a badger in a barrel, and quite unfit for work next day. He always took one or two couple of the old breed to find and start the otter, but, when once the quarry was afoot, the drive and fire of the pure-bred foxhound more than compensated for the wonderful marking powers and hereditary instinct of the slower-going otter-hound.

The following morning we started at daybreak. Throwing-off in the meadow in front of the farm-house and drawing up-stream, we succeeded in intercepting an otter on his way to the lower waters, but being short-handed and the river high —after the heavy thunderstorms of the previous week—we were unable to arrest his downward progress, and slipping past us, he saved himself amongst the rocks which border the deep pool opposite the ruins of Kenn Priory. By this time our field had been materially strengthened, and still working up-stream, we struck a hot drag at the withy-pool formed by the junction of the Kenn and Nene, and after about an hour's slow hunting we got on terms with the otter, and killed her within two fields of where we lost her consort. It was now two o'clock, and as we had ten miles to negotiate before we reached our sleeping-quarters, we made our way back to the farm, and having stitched up a nasty gash in old Fury's forearm, we left her in charge of Mrs. Bustle, and remounting our hacks, started off across the moor for Blackford.

It was a lovely evening, and after the hounds had been fed and bedded-down, we went out to look at the river. We lingered about the bridge for more than an hour, watching the small trout rising on the shallows and speculating upon the possibilities of to-morrow's sport, then, crossing the river, we strolled slowly up the further bank, our spirits being raised by the fresh 'seal' of an otter—easily distinguishable from the tracks of the dog, fox, or badger, by the absence of nail-marks, and by the fact that each foot leaves the distinct impress of five pads instead of four, as is the case with the above-mentioned animals.

Sauntering leisurely along the winding foot-path, on turning a bend in the river we came quite unexpectedly upon a Gipsy encampment sheltered from the wind by the steep slope of the valley, and screened from the prying eyes of wayfarers by the sharp *koonsus**—such a situation being always chosen, when available, by our people. The Parson's eyes sparkled at the prospect of a bit of fun, and producing a very disreputable clay-pipe, he placed it between his lips, and pulling his old hat well down over his eyes, advanced towards the tents. Mr. Sealy was a pretty fair Romany scholar, and like most gentlemen who have contrived by some means or other to pick up our *jib*,† nothing seemed to afford him greater amusement than to mystify any strange Gipsies whom he might chance to encounter by a display of his proficiency in their language. Our people are very averse, as a rule, to entering into conversation with strangers—unless, perhaps I ought to add, there seems a fair chance of getting something out of them—but experience had taught my companion that nothing more surely unlocks the lips of even the most surly and suspicious of 'travellers,' than the artless display of a well-filled tobacco-pouch. In the same way, if you want to draw out a Romany *chi*, pull out your watch as she passes and pretend to be looking at the time. There is something about the sight of a carelessly-displayed *ora* ‡ which acts as a potent spell—her attention is irresistibly attracted, and she can't, for the life of her, help saying "Please, my gentleman, can you tell me what o'clock it is?"

We found three or four grown men and about the same number of lads squatting round the fire, busily engaged in *chinnin' busahor* and *feeders*.§ While so employed, the lower

---

* A turning, corner, or bend. † Language: tongue. ‡ Watch.

§ Cutting skewers and clothes-pegs: the former are also called *koshters*, *skunyor*, and *pricklers*, and the latter *mashpeggi* and *tograms*.

part of the thigh is protected from the knife-blade by a thin strip of iron bound round the leg just above the knee-cap, and the tattered condition of the waistcoat—which soon becomes frayed and worn into a hole by repeated blows of the hand, or *koshter*, as it is drawn back in the act of cutting—reveals to the initiated the occupation of the wearer, as surely as the almost imperceptible drag of the leg betrays the identity of the *cheval de retour** to the practised eye of the *agent de la rousse*.†

I need scarcely say that the men had taken our measure before we had well turned the corner, and, stolid as Red Indians, betrayed no further curiosity in their visitors beyond bidding us a surly 'Good-evening.' We were certainly as enigmatical a pair as could well be imagined, and it would have taxed the wisdom of Solomon Lovell's illustrious namesake—for Lovells I knew them to be directly I set eyes on them—to have identified Passon Mark, at first sight, with a clergyman of the Church of England, while four years spent under the Parson's roof and four more of town life, had effected a considerable change in my appearance and bearing—and I was not sorry that such was the case, and for this reason.

It so happened that the Lovells were connections of ours, my Granny Charlotte's eldest sister having married old Matthias Lovell, who used to travel the district between Camford and Bristol, but dissentions had arisen among the two families, the members of which seldom met on racecourse or market-place without an interchange of civilities which usually resulted in a free fight and gratuitous accommodation in the local *stardo*.‡ Although our family was by far the weakest in point of numbers, in Vester, Charley Klism, and young Perin—who had already got his name up—we had three representatives, any one of whom could knock holes through the best Lovell that ever took a shirt off. And this reminded me that if my name should happen to leak out, I might look out for squalls, for rumour averred that although the males of the tribe were quick-tempered enough, they were mild as milk compared with fierce old Cinerella Lovell—mother of the men who were sitting round the fire, and of the two sisters, Mantis and Trainette, whose reputa-

* Ticket of leave-man.   † Police-spy.   ‡ Lock-up.

tion as the two handsomest Romany *chies* within the three counties was already firmly established.

As we neared the camp in full view of the party by the fire, in a few quick sentences I had informed my companion of the state of affairs, but the information evidently only served to heighten his appreciation of the situation, and he expressed his intention of having a look at the dark-eyed beauties at all hazards. Having passed the time of day, he gravely seated himself, Gipsy-fashion, beside the embers, and asked in Romninus for a light for his pipe. The men had probably taken him at first sight for a 'traveller' of some sort or another, but a glance at the otter-skin *toovalesko-gunno** at once dispelled the illusion, and despite the sunburnt skin and shabby, mud-stained clothes, the quick-witted Lovells had soon identified one, at least, of the strangers with the well-known Parson of Netherleigh.

As we sat chatting beside the fire, the figures of three women came into view round the bend below, and approached the camp with rapid steps. They were talking, laughing, and gesticulating as they walked, but one—a girl of about eighteen—was slightly in advance of the others, and as her face and figure gradually became more distinct, a low whistle expressive of surprise and admiration escaped the Parson's lips.

"Wh—ew! *vera incessu patuit dea*"—he whispered, rising to his feet preparatory to being introduced to the ladies of the family. "Walks like a thoroughbred, or, rather, like one of those Spanish *gitanas* I used to tell you about. Lucky we stopped, 'pon my word. Wouldn't have missed it for a good deal."

I had hitherto taken but little interest in the conversation, being fully alive to the awkwardness of my position and desirous of maintaining my *incognito*, but as my eyes took in the handsome face and perfect figure of Mantis Lovell, I felt that I would risk a good deal for a kindly glance from those dark eyes, and although I had sense enough to know that the present moment was unpropitious, I inwardly resolved that, come what might, it should be no fault of mine if the chance meeting on the banks of the Black did not ripen into a closer acquaintance.

* Tobacco-pouch.

After what I have told you, it may be imagined that I looked with some curiosity at old Cinerella Lovell, whose ungovernable temper had caused her name to pass into a byword amongst the Gipsies of the West-country—"*vafodi grasni sar Relli Kaumlo*"*—and, certainly, a greater contrast to the meek maiden of the fairy-tale than the wild-eyed, strong-limbed woman who now stood before us, it would be scarcely possible to imagine. Fortunately for us, she seemed, for the time being, in the best of tempers, and at once set about making the tea.

"*Hushta, Teerus*"—she cried to her youngest son, "*an a panli-gibben* for the *Rashi* to *besh-oprey*.† And what may be the *nav* of the dark-eyed young man as sits *bongo-herri*,‡ as if he was used to it? What! Loveridge?"—as the Parson, absent-minded as usual, inadvertently revealed my identity—"Never one of them mumping *churdos* from Netherleigh? Well, well, to be sure! Howsomedever, all Lovells isn't Kaumlos, and there's Loveridges and Loversedges, and the young man's welcome to a cup o' tea so long as he be'aves hisself."

It was evident that the old lady was in an unusually good temper, or my reception would have been more warm than cordial, but Solomon Lovell, the eldest son, and his brother Noah, were at no pains to conceal their animosity, and looked, if possible, blacker than Nature and the sun had already made them. However, I didn't care a button for their good opinion, and, regardless of their scowls, I took my place in the circle round the fire next to pretty Trainette, and chattered away with the best of them. The Parson was seated between Mantis and her mother, and was, as usual, endeavouring to elicit odd scraps of Romnimus from the elder woman. As soon as tea was over, the otter-skin pouch was handed round, and having filled her pipe, old Cinerella proceeded to relate the chief incidents of the day. The story was begun in English, but as the girls chimed in and the speakers grew excited, each trying to take the words out of the other's mouth, the conversation soon lapsed into the deeper Romnimus, a good deal of which was unintelligible

---

* "A vicious mare like Relli Kaumlo."
† "Hurry, Teerus, bring a wattled-hurdle for the Parson to sit upon."
‡ "Cross-legged."

to my companion, who sat nodding his head approvingly when occasion required, and taking mental notes, the while, for future reference.

"Well, as I telled you"—began Cinerella, "we started off to walk into Blackstow 'long the *tober*,* and there we sold the main of the *koshters*. Then we leaves the *bauro-drom* † and strikes *atut* the *bango poov* ‡ towards the *Tautoleero-tan*,§ and there we rings the bell and arsts to see the *pooro Ress*.‖ Presently the *pauno-sherro vels palal ta pookerdas mende* to *slom leste*.¶ So we walks right into the big hall with our *cushnees oprey* our *dumos*,** just as we was, and up the *puddemengros*†† all covered with fine carpets, into the *comaurus kai o pooro Ress sus a'lellin' o lescro hobben*." ‡‡

"'Good-day, Mrs. Lovell'—says the Squire, 'I hopes I sees you well'—and then he tells the *geero*, as were *hatched pauli yuv's skavven*,§§ to leave the room *ta peeavit* the *stiggur paul' leste*."‖‖

"'I do declare, to gracious, your darters is got more beautiful than ever, if such a thing is possible'—says he, and he winks at the girls and scratches his head, and goes on *pennin' dinnelepeues*¶¶ till we thought it was about time to be off."

"Then we arsts leaf to sell some of our *cuvvas* to the servants, and he arsts us what we'd a'got. Then Mantis she shows him her basket with a few laces and things, and he arsts her what they was worth."

"'A sovereign'—says she, as bold as brass, and he *lels* a *balanser* from his *putsi, ta dias lis a' lauki*,*** and makes her turn out all the *cuvvas oprey* the *salier*.††† The things wasn't worth *pange collor*,‡‡‡ and a pretty *dickomangri*§§§ they made. Trainette wants to sell him her nuts, but he wouldn't have Then 'em at no price, and *pooched* for a *chooma*‖‖‖ instead."

* "Road."   † "High-road."   ‡ "Across the meadows."
§ "The Rookery:" the residence of Squire Bamfylde, the eccentric lord-of-the-manor of Blackstow.   ‖ "Old Squire."
¶ "Flour-head—footman—comes back and told us to follow him."
** "Baskets on our backs."   †† "Stairs."
‡‡ "Room where the old Squire was eating his victuals."
§§ "Fellow as were stuck up behind his chair."
‖‖ "And shut the door after him."   ¶¶ "Talking nonsense."
*** "Takes a sovereign from his pocket, and gives it to her."
††† "Things upon the table."   ‡‡‡ "Five shillings."   §§§ "Show."
‖‖‖ "Asked for a kiss."

"Nasty old beast"—breaks in Trainette, who takes up the narrative at this point, but is at once silenced by her mother's angry '*Bosthrengi, chavvi. Hatch akonyo.*'*

"Then he turns to Mantis"—continues the old lady, "and says as how his fine housekeeper is a'goin' to leave, and offers her a *chinamangri a'moonti* † if she'll be his *kerriknee.*"‡

"A regular old *kovalo*,§ I call him"—interrupts Mantis indignantly, "he ought to have his *sherro morredo* and be *chivlo drey* the *diviou-ker.*‖ I do detest such silly old men" —a sentiment in which, needless to say, I heartily concur.

"By long and by last he offers to marry Mantis"—continues Trainette, taking up the running, "so we came away as quick as we could, and I sold my *poggramengros* to the *monishnec of the pannomengro* for her *paunishenengros,*¶ and we *velled kerri* with our *kipsis sor porder o' chichiben.*"**

It was now time for us to return to the inn for supper, so, taking leave of our new acquaintances, we hurried back to Blackford, the Parson declaring that old Cinerella was not half as black as she had been painted, while I walked beside him in a state of blissful preoccupation.

The following day a large field turned out from Blackstow —amongst others, three or four of the Lovells—and after fairly mobbing one otter to death and losing another in a strong drain from whence the terriers were unable to dislodge him, the Parson sent the hounds home in charge of Mike and the kennelman, while we returned to Blackford. From his experience of the previous evening my companion had been led to suppose that he would have but little difficulty in inducing the much-maligned Cinerella to disclose, for his benefit, the rich store of Gipsy lore with the possession of which she was popularly credited. You may be quite sure that I did my best to encourage the notion, but upon our arrival at the camp we found that matters wore a very different complexion, and had I not been, myself, an interested party, I should have enjoyed a hearty laugh at

* "Leave off, child. Keep quiet."
† "Five-pound note a month."   ‡ "Housekeeper."
§ "Lunatic."
‖ "Head shaved and be put in a mad-house."
¶ "Nuts to the wife of the turnpike-keeper for her flaxen-haired youngsters."
** "Came home with our baskets full of emptiness."

the Parson's discomfiture. The old woman was in a towering passion—although, unfortunately, anything but speechless with rage—and as Mr. Sealy politely greeted her, she poured forth a perfect torrent of imprecations upon his devoted head, and treated him to a few choice extracts from a private Commination Service of her own, the full purport of which—luckily for his peace of mind—he was unable to catch. Even the sight of the well-filled tobacco-pouch failed to mollify her, so, as the two girls were about to start to fetch some water from a neighbouring spring, I contrived to slip away with them unobserved, basely leaving my companion to bear the full brunt of the old lady's displeasure.

The girls told me that the reason of this outbreak was that Sol and Noah, with their uncle, old Juba Lovell, had started off early that morning to join the otter-hounds, instead of attending to their work, and that, upon returning to camp, they had been greeted with such a volley of abuse that uncle Juba had snatched up his fiddle and started off with his two eldest nephews for Blackstow, where, safe beneath the shelter of the Raven's wing, they were able to set their fierce old she-wolf of a relative at defiance. The girls did not dare to stay away any time from the tents, but I ascertained their movements for the next few days. On the Friday week they were to attend the market at Netherton, and as I was obliged to return on the following Monday to Westport, I determined, if possible, to leave the Parsonage on the Friday and remain in Netherton till Monday, when I could make an early start and catch the Mail at Exeter.

I do not propose to inflict upon you the ins and outs of that old, old story, the peculiarity of which is that, while it possesses scarcely any features of novelty for third parties, it is, nevertheless, of all-absorbing interest to the two principally concerned—let the scene and the actors vary as they will. My meetings with Mantis were necessarily secret, owing to her mother's ungovernable temper and the openly displayed hostility of her brothers, but stolen fruit is proverbially the sweetest, and during my stay at Netherton I was able to give my sweetheart a proof of my mettle, which, I think, went some way towards winning her heart—for in our line of life a chap who can't hold his own and a bit over, is not thought much of by the girls. During one of our long rambles, we came across a certain well-known character named Charley Hicks—Plymouth Charley, as we called him—who, being slightly the worse for liquor, proceeded to salute us with some of the obscene chaff for which he was notorious. But as I have already described our encounter*—the marks of which I shall carry to my grave—I need only say that I did not disgrace myself.

The branch of the Lovell tribe to which Mantis belonged, made their living, amongst other things, by attending the principal race-meetings, where the two sisters sold flowers to the gentry, and their male relatives set up the cocoa-nuts or sparred in the booths, while their fierce-tongued mother was content, for the nonce, to put a bridle upon that unruly member, and assuming an air of the deepest mystery—which her hawk-like features, swarthy skin, and glowing eyes, went far towards sustaining—consented, for a consideration, to reveal the future to the gaily-dressed occupants of the carriages.

I felt that it was indeed a black Monday for me as I left Netherton in the rumbling old Diligence on my way to catch the Mail at Exeter, and even the cheery talk and professional jokes of genial Tom Padley proved powerless to beguile the tedium of the long journey. Mantis had told me that we might very probably meet the following spring at Westport Races —which were held in May—but as we were then only in July, the intelligence did not afford me much consolation, and it was with a heavy heart that I returned to the old town and took up my quarters with my new employer, Mr. Shice, V.S.

* I should, perhaps, explain that, owing to want of space, quite one-third of the original manuscript has been omitted.—ED. See chap. II., p 16.

CHAPTER XX.

Mr. John Shice, M.R.C.V.S.

I HAD now reached the respectable age—as I then considered, of two and twenty—and had certainly gained as much experience of the ways of the wicked world as is usually acquired by a young fellow of my age and station. As I have hitherto omitted to give any description of my personal appearance, I suppose I may say now, without being suspected of vanity, that I was a rather smart-looking young chap, with a supple, well-knit figure, dark eyes and complexion, and regular features of the true Gipsy type. In face and figure I favoured my father and my uncle Vester—who were both of them medium-sized men and better adapted to the performance of feats of agility and endurance, than of those which necessitated the possession of exceptional muscular development—rather than my uncles Plato or Neptune, or the men of my mother's family, who were noted for their size and strength.

And now that I have given a rough sketch of myself, it is about time for me to tell you something about my new employer—Mr. John Shice, V.S. Up to the time of my entering his service I had always looked upon him as the model of a respectable veterinary practitioner, while his trimly-kept villa, with its shining brass door-plate and creeper-covered verandah, combined with his smart turn-out and general air of prosperity and good-fellowship, had greatly impressed me in his favour. I was, however, destined to pass the best part of three years in daily contact with him, during which period I had ampler opportunities of gauging his character than fell to the lot of the outside public, and it is by the light of subsequent experience that I must describe him.

Shice was a tall and rather good-looking man of about two and forty, with dark hair, face clean-shaven with the exception of a narrow fringe of whisker, and beady, restless eyes. The upper part of his body was broad and well-proportioned, but he fell away below, his legs being a trifle in at the knees and his feet large. When in company he affected an air of genial good-fellowship and noisy joviality, which the expression of the mouth—which was spoiled by the unusual development of the canine teeth—rather belied, giving him, as it did, somewhat the appearance of a well-disposed hyena. His manner invited confidence, being off-hand and hearty. In costume he affected the subduedly-sporting rather than the floridly-horsey style, always wearing a tall hat, dark-coloured, well-cut clothes, a scrupulously-tied twice-round white choker, and invariably making his appearance in public—like the great Sitwell—with a flower in his button-hole.

So much for his outward appearance, which was eminently respectable. But, as a matter of fact, Shice was a very fine specimen of the coping vet., a class of men of whom horse-owners in general would do well to beware, since it is next door to impossible for a member of the profession who is in the habit of lending himself to doubtful transactions in horse-flesh, or of identifying himself, however slightly, with the operations of the 'ring' of copers — amateur and professional—which exists in most large towns, to give an honest and unprejudiced opinion when, as continally happens, he has an interest—let it be ever so remote—in the sale or purchase of the animal in question.

In my time there were about five or six veterinary surgeons practicing in Westport and its immediate neighbourhood, and, of these, only two refrained from dealing altogether. One was an exceedingly clever and trustworthy man, and those who knew what they were about used to send for him from all parts of the West of England, whenever the amount of the purchase-money warranted the outlay. The other was equally straight and fairly clever, but rather too theoretical for practical purposes, having a constitutional aversion to getting on a horse's back. Neither of these mixed themselves up in any way with horse-dealing, and their opinion might consequently be relied on.

My employer was the third, and the remaining two were about on a par as regarded knowledge of their profession and honesty. Rough and ready, both of them, if they passed a screw for a small dealer they expected to receive a commission if it was sold, and with them a hand held up behind the would-be purchaser's back with all five fingers extended —when any previous intercommunication was impossible— accompanied by a look of interrogation and responded to by a furtive nod or wink, meant a five-pound note. Not that they often got as much, for if a nod is as good as a wink to a blind horse, a couple of fingers held up in accordance with the above-mentioned code of telegraphy would make the sorriest screw sound. Goodman of the Repository was also a veterinary practitioner, although not a member of the College. A clever man and an excellent judge of a horse, he would have been straight if he could have afforded it, but circumstances were sometimes just a bit too strong for him.

My employer was married to a woman considerably older than himself, who was supposed to have brought him money, and who certainly looked as if she should have possessed her fair share of that desirable commodity—since it might reasonably be presumed that neither her looks or her temper would have proved an attraction to such a consummate judge of woman-kind and horse-flesh as Mr. Shice was popularly credited with being. He occupied a pretty detached villa in the suburbs of Westport, fronting the sea, with some good stabling at the back, where he kept the horses which he used in the regular course of his business, but in addition to these hard-working slaves there were always three or four other animals of uncertain ownership and antecedents, that came and went, remaining a longer or shorter time according to his luck in 'placing' them.

These mysterious quadrupeds generally arrived at the stables after dark or early in the morning, when they were turned into the loose-boxes and kept under lock and key until they presented a more respectable appearance. An old canvas rug was thrown over them, and as soon as they had been littered down, their corn, boiled with some linseed, was given them soft and warm, and when they had finished it they would go down like so many fatting-pigs, and lie, quiet and comfortable, until they were disturbed.

Under this course of treatment they soon began to improve, and while kept in the rough their little ailments and blemishes were duly attended to. Enlargements from splints, curb, speedy-cut, spavin, etc., were temporarily reduced by the application of a vesico-sudorific which possessed the advantages of removing—for the time being, at all events—without leaving a blemish, those little lumps and bumps which are the bugbear of the dealer. Chipped knees and bare places were lightly blistered, windgalls reduced by the application of cabbage-leaf compresses, thickened sinews and filled legs fined down by a judicious alternation of blistering, douching, and bandaging, and the various affections of the respiratory organs attended to and palliated as far as possible.

Having been put through the sieve, the patients began to lay on flesh and fill the eye. Their long jackets were taken off, their manes and forelocks artistically pulled, water-brushed, or plaited and leaded, their feet trimmed and neatly shod, 'carty' legs clipped up to the knees or hocks, tails docked or squared, long hairs removed, shabby manes hogged, and the final polish—a praiseworthy but ephemeral imitation of the genuine 'bloom of youth'—applied.

They then only required to be put through the mill and sharpened up, made to stand out and show themselves, to bend their knees and necks by a severe course of ash-plant, spur, and dumb jockey, and be ready to spring to attention and prick their ears at the least tap of stick, flick of handkerchief, or rattle of corn-bin. The slugs were fed up to the collar, some sort of a mouth was put on the pullers—the most callous-mouthed can be made to go light in hand long enough to sell them, by previously lungeing them with a severe bit, but it only makes them twice as bad after—and those who evinced a disposition to 'nap the rust,' very soon discovered that they had come to the wrong shop. As soon as they were made up and fit to show, the harness-horses were transferred to the private-boxes at the Repository or to the stables of one of the confederacy, but the hunters were generally sent off to some coping farmer at a distance to avert suspicion. If a gentleman wanted a horse, Shice would tell him that he knew of a clinker that had never been out of the breeder's hands. It belonged to a farmer down the country, and if it could be bought at anything under such and such a price, it was dirt cheap at the money, etc., etc.

The outdoor education fell to my lot, while the stable operations were conducted under the supervision of Shice's head man, old Billy Mason, who was the sole repository of his master's secrets—and a queer jumble of villainy and incorruptibility I found him. On the whole, Shice had not much cause to grumble at his assistants, for Billy Mason, though a drunken old dog, was a first-class stableman and the handiest man—barring my uncle Vester—with the comb and scissors I ever came across, while I had been accustomed to ride big horses at exercise along with my father at an age when most children make the acquaintance of a rocking-horse for the first time. The year before my father's death, when I must have been about eight or nine years old, I well remember that old Mrs. Scott—father of John and Bill Scott, the famous trainer and jockey—who kept the Ship at Camford, gave me a shilling for sitting a bucking piebald pony called Beau-kicker at Cowingdon, where some of the college gentlemen were larking their hacks about, and for riding him backwards and forwards over a hurdle, with nothing on his back but a pad, with a sixpenny-bit under each knee, without dropping either of them.

Now most horses like to keep a bit in hand—either as regards pace, action, or both—and even the highest couraged animals won't always give it to you when you ask them for it—the old ones from craftiness and the young ones through greenness—and you will find, on an average, about one man in a thousand who can get that extra bit out of them when it's wanted, and that not by reason of any marked superiority of seat, nerve, head, or hands, but from a combination of these and fifty other nameless attributes which, like the gift of poetry, are innate and not easy of acquisition. Although I say it that shouldn't, I could do as much with horses as most men, and if it had been my fortune to have fallen into better hands I might have done well enough for myself, but Shice had not been slow to detect my latent capabilities, and being naturally fond of horses, I easily fell in with his views and became a willing slave of the local coping 'Ring.'

I have already alluded to Goodman as being the ostensible proprietor of the 'Westport Horse Emporium and Commission Stables,' but the concern was really owned and run by a confederacy consisting of Shice: Joe Barton, a flash, good-looking chap with a strong dash of Romany, who owned, trained, and rode a few leather-flappers at 'not under the rules' meetings: Mr. 'Cutty' Rayner, a sporting gentleman of the 'fly-flat' order: and a Gentile sixty-per-center named Ben Davis, who held a mortgage on the premises, pulled the strings, and absorbed the lion's share of the profits.

Each individual member of the firm had his private specs in horse-flesh, which were stabled, offered for sale free of commission, and passed by Shice, who did most of the dirty work for the confederacy and, in conjunction with the others, alternately 'crabbed' and 'chy-iked' as the case might require. Although he passed any horses belonging to Goodman and Barton, free of charge, he made a pretty good thing out of the amateur copers. If, for instance, one of the 'Fly-flats' sold an unsound horse that might have cost him five-and-thirty pounds, for eighty or a hundred through his instrumentality, he would not hesitate to send him in a bill of from eight to ten pounds for 'attendance.' Woe betide any unfortunate outsider who made a bid for any horse in which the fraternity were interested, for they would run him up ten or twenty before he could turn round, and if they happened to get shot, no great harm was done, for with Goodman in the 'pulpit,' the last bid could always be disputed. Goodman, himself, was the best of the lot, being a capital judge of a horse and a good fellow in the main, but he was not cut out by Nature for a sharp and consequently proved a failure at the business, being only kept on by Davis and Co. on account of his popularity and reputation for straightforward dealing.

Besides the above-mentioned, there were plenty of 'affiliated brethren' residing at a distance. Their *modus operandi* was as follows. Let us suppose that Joe Knight, the Exeter dealer, hears from Shice that there is a horse belonging to a neighbouring gentleman that is worth his buying. He travels up to Westport, calls on the owner, and having tried the animal in every possible way—and what Joe did not find out was not worth knowing, for there were few better judges or better buyers—finishes by offering less than half its real value and takes his departure.

A few days later a stranger—one of the 'Ring'—calls to look at the horse, does not know much about horses himself, but likes the look of him. Before purchasing would, however, prefer to have a professional opinion, and suggests Shice, V.S. That highly respectable gentleman then makes his appearance on the scene of action, examines the animal, and writes a certificate magnifying any little defects which the horse may possibly possess—finally declining, on technical grounds, to pass it sound. Stranger 'Regrets, etc., etc.,' and goes away without purchasing. The horse has now been effectually 'crabbed,' and the owner soon begins to hate the sight of the poor beast who is cheerfully eating his head off in blissful unconsciousness of the conspiracy of which he is the innocent victim, but a few days later Barton canters up on a thoroughbred screw, takes a cigar and a glass of sherry, and offers a pound or two more than Knight, 'on commission for a gentleman in London.' Owner, who by this time is heartily sick of the whole business, closes with his offer, the result being that Joe Knight—who stands a sovereign or two with Shice and Barton—gets the horse dirt cheap.

Joe Barton was always a puzzle to me. Nobody knew where he came from, how he was bred, or how he managed to live, but that he had Gipsy blood in him I was positive, for there was that unmistakable brazen-faced, black-and-tan sort of stamp about him which, like a dash of the tar-brush, no amount of civilisation, scrubbing, soaping, shaving, powdering, or brushing, is able to eradicate, and which, like the scent of the roses, will cling to you still, whether you like it or not. For the rest he was a most amusing, impudent, good-looking dog, always well dressed after a horsey fashion, with a neat figure and a pretty seat on a horse, while his careless, happy-go-lucky disposition made him generally popular in spite of his being a dead sharp. Always the very best of company, there never was such a chap for sport. His well-known face was invariably to be seen at the Ring-side, and his cheery "Time, lads! Seconds away!"—brought many a beaten man to the scratch for another round; in fact two dogs couldn't quarrel up a back street without Joe being there to set them by the ears.

He was reported to be married to a rich old lady—some

said to two—but, if he was, he managed to keep them out of the way and was, to all intents and purposes, a batchelor. As soon as he found out that I was pretty quick on my legs, he made great friends with me and trained me for the long-distance championship of the West of England, which I won two years in succession. Until he began to put on flesh, there were few prettier riders on the flat or over hurdles on the Western circuit, and I spent a good deal of my time in his company.

The reason that I mention him is that he gave me a bit of advice which, upon mature consideration, I elected to follow. It came about in this way. I had reason to suspect that he was not unconnected with the Burtons, and I was continually trying to catch him with traps artfully baited with scraps of Romnimus, which, however, he was far too wary a bird to walk into. One day, when I'd been at this game, he turned round to me as we were jogging home from hunting, and said:—"Now, look here, Sam. It ain't a morsel of good your going on caddling with your Burtons and your Romany, for I tell you I don't know anything about it. It don't pay, and that's the long and short of it, and the sooner you drop it and get people to forget how you're bred, the better you'll get on in the world. So take my tip and sink the Romany."

Well, when I came to think it all over, it struck me that there was a good deal of practical common sense in what he said, and I determined, henceforth, to imitate as closely as possible the habits, deportment, and manner of speaking of the Gorgios, and, as Joe advised, to 'sink the Romany.'

Such, then, were the characters with whom I was brought into daily contact, and it is hardly to be wondered at if my morals suffered in consequence. One day I would be on the back of one of Goodman's flatcatchers, which I would ride to the meet, and after getting a good start and showing in front for a few fields, would pull up behind a hay-stack and walk carefully home according to orders. Another time I might be showing a new purchase of Mr. Rayner's to a London dealer or riding it out into the country for a lady to look at, and now and then Joe Barton would put me up when he was unable to get the weight himself, while I had always plenty of work to do for my employer, which left me very little time for the study of the Veterinary Science, even if Shice had shown himself anxious to instruct me—which he did not.

I could easily fill a volume with descriptions of horse-dealing transactions in which I played a minor part—from the dead-cope of Joe Barton to the more delicate operations of Mr. 'Cutty' Rayner—but one horse-story is very like another. I saw a good deal of Barton and Dick Sellars in those days, and in their company I attended the local race-meetings, fights, running-grounds, and coursing-matches, while in the evenings we used to go to the theatre, or to other, and more questionable, places of amusement. But although fond of excitement and what is known as good company, it is only fair to myself to say that the recollection of Mantis Lovell —for in my case absence had made the heart grow fonder— had the effect of keeping me straighter than even my most intimate associates suspected, for if they had known that I remained true to the memory of a girl whom I had met but half-a-dozen times, and from whom I had neither asked or received any definite assurance of affection, I am certain that they would have regarded me as a possibly harmless, but undoubtedly hopeless, lunatic.

I am by no means anxious to dwell upon this chapter of my life, and luckily, perhaps, for me, my connection with my employer soon came to a natural termination. Although Shice was a pretty clever rascal, he possessed no education whatever beyond the mere technical knowledge of his profession which enabled him to carry on his business, and being naturally extravagant and fond of pleasure, his private affairs were in a shocking state of confusion. He never kept any books and seldom sent in a bill unless requested to do so, but every now and then, when pressed for ready money, he would send in some heavy outstanding account—without giving any items—always taking care to select for a victim some gentleman of a notoriously easy-going disposition with a good balance at his banker's, and charging just as much as he thought his customer would stand. His legitimate business would have been good enough if he had worked it properly, but his private expenses were heavy, and in addition to the pretty house in Westgate Parade, he was responsible for a second, and no less expensive, establishment in another quarter of the town. In order to meet the double expenditure he was compelled to lend himself to transactions with which, under more favourable circumstances, he might have declined to meddle, the result being that, as the end approached, nothing was too hot or too heavy for him to handle.

One of his best customers was a rich gentleman named Pelham, who was fond of keeping good-looking horses for which he gave long prices, and which he seldom mounted himself. Now it so happened that Shice had sold him a certain dark chestnut gelding called 'The Quaker' at a stiffish figure. He was nearly thoroughbred, though up to fourteen stone, showed any amount of quality, carried the saddle in the right place with plenty in front of it, and was as sharp as mustard and handsome as paint, with just the sort of action which goes down with the judges in the Show-ring. But he was no hunter, although he looked it all over, and a regular brute to ride. Although he would jump a made-up fence in cold blood well enough, no power on earth could get him over a country with hounds, and he came right over backwards with me four or five times the first morning I rode him.

Now, as Shice was perfectly well aware, Mr. Pelham always stood out for good manners, and was ready to pay for them. The horse would walk out of the stable as quiet as a lamb, with his ears nicely pricked, playing with the bit and stepping like a lady's hack, and would continue on his best behaviour until he happened to recollect an appointment in the immediate neighbourhood of his corn-bin. Selecting an opportunity when his rider, on the best of terms with his mount and the world in general, had allowed his suspicions to be lulled to rest, he would jump sideways across the road, and lowering his head, would proceed to revolve on his own axis like a tee-totum, winding up the performance with a series of kicks and bucks which might well have unshipped a stock-rider.

Having succeeded in getting rid of his new owner—who possessed the doubtful qualifications of a light seat and firm hands—at the first time of asking, and having repeated the performance as if to show that there was no fluke about it, Mr. Pelham sent 'The Quaker' to be sold with some other horses at Goodman's, where, by dint of unscrupulous 'crabbing,' Shice managed to secure him for about sixty guineas. My employer then sold him to a gentleman who lived in an out-of-the-way district in Wales, where the horse was not likely to attract the notice of the dealers.

By the end of the following summer his new owner was not sorry to part with him, and Shice bought him back again and put him under lock and key. 'The Quaker' was now six off and had furnished into a regular 'tip-topper,' and as soon as my employer had shortened his dock and got him up a bit, he showed him to Mr. Pelham in the rough—telling him that he had just bought him from a parish priest in Ireland—and ended by selling him to him again for close on four hundred guineas. The first or second time the unfortunate gentleman mounted him, 'Liberator'—as he was now called—not only served him the same old trick, but broke his collar-bone into the bargain. Unluckily, too, Mr. Pelham's stud-groom—whom my employer had foolishly neglected to square—recognised the horse by a peculiar trick he had of getting his tongue over the bit, and ended by letting the cat out of the bag. Shice consented to take the horse back again at a price, but although he afterwards sold him to a noble lord for a large sum, the story got about and it did him no good.

Transactions such as these soon brought my employer into disrepute, and as his practice began to decline, his creditors took alarm, and in order to meet their demands he instructed his solicitor to get in his outstanding accounts. Some of these had been running for years and were proportionately heavy, and as no items were furnished, there was much protestation and indignation amongst those who had employed him, many of whom altogether declined to settle their accounts, and it ended by his going through the Court.

As may be imagined, during these three and a half years I had plenty to occupy me, and little leisure remained for brooding over my love affairs. I occasionally received messages from Mantis through the Smiths, Boswells, or Bucklands, some of whom were always to be found in the Gipsy quarter—for every large town has its Gipsy quarter, though the fact be not patent to Gentile understanding—but my only chance of seeing her was at the annual race-meeting which was held on a high range of downs distant about a couple of miles from the town. The sisters were, as I have told you, acknowledged beauties, and were consequently enabled to obtain fancy prices for their bouquets—which cost them little—and for their smiles—which cost them even less. It was during the second of these meetings that I made the discovery that Mantis returned my affection with a warmth which equalled my own, and her heart once gained, I felt secure in the consciousness that I could trust her to remain true to me in face of the many temptations to which her good looks and the life that she led necessarily exposed her.

I had hitherto spent my money as quick as I earned it, but I determined for the future to turn over a new leaf, and to save up something against a rainy day. All my good resolutions and plans for the future were, however, scattered to the winds by my employer's bankruptcy, and without a word of warning, I found myself again thrown upon the world without any immediate prospect of obtaining employment. After spending several months in a vain endeavour to obtain some situation for which my previous experience qualified me, I found myself at the end of my tether, and after making a rather heavy inroad on my small capital, I was obliged to apply to the Parson of Netherleigh for counsel and assistance.

With the considerate kindness which invariably characterised his treatment of me, Mr. Sealy at once set to work to find me a situation, and after making enquiries in Westport as to my conduct, he sent me word that Sir George had consented to take me into his service. It appeared that the valet—a Maltese—who had been with the baronet for so many years, was just recovering from a sharp attack of rheumatic fever, and that Sir George had offered to send him back to Italy to recruit his health, with the option of returning to Netherleigh in the autumn if he felt equal to facing the English climate, In the meanwhile I was offered the situation on trial, and, as it seemed a good opening, I did not hesitate to accept it.

CHAPTER XXI.

The L'Estranges of Netherleigh Court.

THE reader has already been placed in possession of the circumstances under which I was first introduced to the notice of Sir George L'Estrange, but on looking through the back pages of manuscript I find that I have forgotten to give even an outline sketch of Netherleigh Court, the beautiful seat of the L'Estrange family, and as the omission must be rectified before going any further, being at best but a poor hand at description and knowing nothing whatever about architecture, I prefer to quote *verbatim* a few excerpts from the pages of a well-known Guide-book, just as in giving an account of the life and antecedents of Mr. Sealy, I felt that I could not do better than use the *ipsissima verba* of his most intimate friend, Sir George L'Estrange.

"Netherleigh Court"—says Mr. White, "is built upon the site of the old Norman Abbey of the same name, of which only a small portion of the chapel and refectory remains intact. Its general outline resembles an irregular triangle, of which the two principal sides front, respectively, the south-east and south-west, the third side—which faces the north—being mainly occupied by the servants' department, laundry, dairy, offices, ect."

"The Court is noted as a wonderful example of mediæval domestic architecture, and its irregular outlines, fantastically-twisted chimneys, and broad terraces commanding the thickly-wooded valley of the Cran—which serpentines around the base of the steep and, in places, precipitous hill upon which the house is situated,—present a most picturesque appearance. The older portions of the house date back to the time of the Edwards, the comparatively modern part having been completed during the reign of the Virgin Queen.

The house contains an almost unrivalled collection of furniture—chiefly of the time of Elizabeth—and arms, besides a most interesting series of family portraits."

"From the roof of the Court a commanding view of the surrounding country may be obtained. To the south and south-west lie the barren, heather-clad wastes of Cranmoor and Nymmoor, backed up in the far blue distance by the loftier ranges of Dartmoor. Far away to the north the horizon is bounded by the waters of the Bristol Channel, which at this point widens out and merges its identity in the broad expanse of the Atlantic, while, between the Channel and the Court, extend the undulating ranges of Blackmoor and Brent Down, separated from each other by the deeply-indented and sharply-winding valley of the Cran. The river, rising far away to the south amongst the granite boulders of Cranhead, flows past the hanging woods of Westford and Putcombe, and rounding the base of the steep hill upon which the Court is built, leaps impetuously over the falls below—then, flowing almost due north, empties itself into the Channel at the little fishing port of Blackstow."

"The main entrance—above which frowns the grim portcullis which forms one of the principal attractions to visitors of antiquarian tastes—faces the south-east, and on that side the ground slopes gently away in a succession of broad, gravelled terraces and bright-hued *parterres*, while at the south-west angle a marble-paved terrace, protected by massive balustrades, overhangs the valley, whose precipitous sides are clothed with a dense growth of oak, birch, and silver-hazel. Standing on this terrace, it seems as if the spectator could easily pitch a stone on to the roadway of the bridge which spans the river some two hundred feet below."

"The east end of the house communicates with the chapel —beautifully restored in the time of Sir Eustace L'Estrange —which originally formed a portion of the Abbey. Towards the north the grounds, which are thickly planted with rhododendrons, present in early summer one mass of fragrant blooms varying from the deepest crimson to the most delicate lilac, and amidst these dense masses of luxuriant vegetation are to be found secluded nooks and sheltered walks which cross and recross each other, and eventually lead to a rustic summer-house overlooking the large salmon-pool below the falls."

"The whole extent of Netherleigh Chase, together with the adjoining lands owned by the L'Estrange family, comprise an area of upwards of thirty thousand acres, a considerable portion of which is moorland. On the further, or western, side of the river are included the hamlets of Washford and Cranmeet, together with the long line of woods which skirt Brent Down. On the eastern bank is included the greater portion of the parish of Netherleigh, while to the north the estate is bounded by the river Black, which joins the Cran about three miles above the picturesque little fishing village and harbour of Blackstow."

So far Mr. White—but now that I have defined the geographical position of the Netherleigh Court estate and supplied the topographical details, I should just like to say a few words about the old place as I knew it when I first went into service there; for I suspect that things are very different now, and I am told that a branch line has already been opened through the Cran valley, and that Blackstow is likely to develop into a fashionable autumnal resort.

Well, when first I went there, after leaving Westport, to valet Sir George, I thought it a very nice old place indeed, and I expect that most people would have been inclined to agree with me. As regards the house, I noticed that strangers seemed to be most struck by a queer-looking sort of a rusty iron harrow which worked in a groove over the south entrance, and which, as I have heard say—for I was always a terrible one for asking questions—used to be dropped down on to the toes of unwelcome visitors as a hint that the proprietor was 'not at home:' by the Banqueting Hall with its Minstrels' Gallery—a place like the organ-loft of a church, with two rows of benches, one above the other, and the front of the gallery all panelled in black oak, with the L'Estrange arms in the centre—and its Lady's Boudoir: and by the great staircase with its broad, shallow stone steps, massive walls, and stout oak barrier which could be closed in time of need: but, for pure enjoyment, give me the stables and the garrets, say I—what games we used to have there, to be sure, me and the young gentlemen!

The Banqueting Hall, which opened out of the Entrance

Hall, was—between ourselves—a cold, cheerless, draughty great barn of a place, with a black and white flagged floor and stone walls covered with dingy hangings which ran right up to the roof. On one side of the hall was a yawning fireplace, large enough to roast an ox whole, which consumed more coal than all the cottages in the village put together, and which was banked up night and morning like a furnace, but never made the place any warmer. Above this fireplace was a high carved oak mantelpiece, and immediately above this, again, was a large stained-glass window just where you would expect the flue of the chimney to be—and where on earth the smoke went to was always a mystery to me and Master Geoffrey and Master Frank.

The hangings which covered the walls were almost entirely hidden by pictures of queer-looking old ladies and gentlemen in black, wooden frames, and by suits of armour, moth-eaten flags, rusty swords, pikes, halberds, blunderbusses, horn powder-flasks, stags-heads, and suchlike rubbish, which harboured the dust and gave the housemaids a sight of trouble, and half-way up to the roof were a couple of little windows which opened out of what was called My Lady's Boudoir—not that her ladyship ever used it—from which the ladies could look down and see and hear all that was going on in the hall below, when the musicians were fiddling and tootling in the gallery opposite, and the gentlemen were hobnobbing over their wine and telling stories—at least I suppose they used to do so in the olden time, but as long as I was at Netherleigh the family always dined at a quarter to eight in the west dining room.

The strangers who came to look at the house, when the family were away, used to make a great fuss about the hall, but, as I said before, for real solid enjoyment give me the garrets. On a wet afternoon when the young gentlemen were a bit fractious and troublesome by reason of their being unable to get out, they would come to me and say:—"Samson, just go to Adams' pantry and see if you can't find the keys of the garrets"—for, you see, the keys were always hid away in a drawer in the butler's pantry for fear lest any of the servants should take a light there and drop a spark—for the floors were all rotten with age and as dry as tinder. Then we used to sneak off up the winding turret stairs, up and up and round and round, like flies crawling up a corkscrew, till Master Frank felt quite giddy and had to sit down in one of the little slits in the thick walls which served as windows; but having reached the top at last and having unlocked the little iron-studded oak door, we found ourselves in Tom Tiddler's ground.

The garrets extended, below the roof, the whole length and breadth of the house, and I should think that you might have stowed away a regiment of soldiers there without crowding them. If you weren't very careful you would hit your head against the great cross-beams which supported the roof, and if you looked up to save your head, it was about even betting that you put your foot through one of the numerous holes in the floor where the dry-rot or the rats had eaten the planks away. For the rats regularly swarmed all over the house. There was a standing reward of tuppence apiece for them, and the grooms used to cut off the tails of all they caught and take them to the head-gardener, who paid them and then buried the tails where they couldn't find and dig them up again—a canny chiel was Muster Muckenzie. I remember there was an old cradle which had once belonged to Master Frank, and which had been hung up, with some blankets in it, by a couple of ropes to a beam in the garrets, so as to be out of the rats' way. But the artful brutes managed to get into it somehow—I suppose by climbing along the beam and down the ropes—and having eaten up or carried away every scrap of the blankets except the four corners, lay there snug and warm and brought up successive generations of ratlets in it, and it was always a sure find when we brought the terriers with us. My bedroom was over the pantry and next to the laundry, and if I happened to lie awake at night I could hear the rats go 'flop—flop—flop,' one after the other down the laundry staircase and out into the drying-ground—not that they ever kept me awake much.

The garrets were full of queer nooks, corners, and rooms, of all shapes and sizes, some so dark that you could see nothing without a candle at mid-day, while you could only just manage to creep into others by squeezing through a narrow opening in the lath-and-plaster partition. Grimy cobwebs hung in heavy festoons from the beams and clustered in every corner, and such a collection of rubbish and odds and ends was never seen out of a curiosity-shop—old horse-hair-covered trunks, leather valises, travelling-boxes, postillions' jack-boots and knee-guards, pistol-holsters, a Sedan-chair, an enormous moth-eaten bear-skin rug with the grinning head and claws complete, oak chests full of books, papers, and music in manuscript—in fact the accumulated lumber of successive generations.

But although it was very pleasant to rout about amongst these treasures, and play at hide-and-seek, burglars, and suchlike games, the principal attraction, after all, was the Priest's Room. Some portions of the garrets had evidently been used as servants' living-rooms at some time or another, for here and there you would come across a fireplace with its carved stone mantel and, perhaps, a hole in the wall at the side, where they used to keep their tankard of egg-flip warm while they toasted their toes of a cold winter's night. Now, in one of the darkest of the many dark corners, was a trap-door which, upon being raised, disclosed a short flight of steps, and upon descending them you found yourself in a small room about twelve feet by ten, with a little fireplace in one corner and a window which had been bricked up from inside. It had evidently been fitted up with some regard for the comfort of its temporary occupant, for some shreds of tapestry which had once covered the nakedness of the plaster walls still clung to the wooden mouldings of the cornice to which they had been attached.

This snug little hiding-place—which was generally called the Priest's Room, and which had probably been used as a refuge in times of persecution—had been artfully contrived between the garret floor and the ceiling of the room below, but, try as we would, we never could make out its exact whereabouts from outside.

Then in fine weather the Chase was a delightful playground. According to tradition the oak-trees had all had their heads cut off by some Royalist ancestor when King Charles was beheaded. Whether or not the legend was founded on fact, I am unable to inform you, but certain it was that every single oak had been pollarded at some time or other, and that in their hollow limbs and gaping trunks the jackdaws built their untidy nests in hundreds, while all the ferrets in the county would not have succeeded in dislodging the thriving colony of rabbits from their fastnesses amongst the gnarled and branching roots. In the nesting season the keepers used to shoot and poison the Jacks and destroy their eggs wholesale, but do what they would they could never keep them in check—for they came in from the cliffs on the sea-coast—and during a backward spring, when there was but little cover for the pheasants' nests, the grey-headed rascals would carry off and suck the eggs almost as fast as the hens laid them.

*　　*　　*　　*　　*　　*

And now that I have told you something about the Court itself, I must proceed to say a few words about its owner, Sir George L'Estrange, and as it will be necessary for me at a later stage of my story to go more fully into his private affairs, I will confine myself at present to giving a bare outline of that portion of his life which had become public property.

Like their neighbours the Langrishes and Fazackerleys, the L'Estranges had been Roman Catholics for generations, and their united establishments formed quite a stronghold of Papacy in the heart of Devonshire. It had been the custom of these families to intermarry, and it was a piece of common gossip that Sir George had deeply offended old Mr. Langrishe of Morthoe—who, according to the same reliable authority, had fully intended that the youngest and prettiest of his two pretty daughters should become the future mistress of Netherleigh—by unexpectedly bringing home a wife from the Continent. Whether Sir George was to blame in the matter is more than I can say, but it undoubtedly constituted a bitter cause of offence, and had brought about a coolness between the two families.

Upon his return to Devonshire with his wife and Master Geoffrey—then an infant in arms—neither the Langrishes or the Fazackerleys had called at Netherleigh, and the county families had shown by the coolness of their reception that they altogether disapproved of the marriage—the fact being that something more than a rumour had reached the neighbourhood to the effect that the antecedents of the new Lady L'Estrange were not quite all that could be desired.

Perhaps nobody, with the single exception of Mr. Sealy, possesses a more intimate acquaintance with the events which preceded and followed this most unlucky marriage than myself, but for the present it will be sufficient for me to give the following particulars. Upon leaving the University Sir George—then Mr. L'Estrange—who, in spite of a liberal allowance, had managed to get into the hands of the Jews, had been sent abroad to enlarge his mind by making what it was then the fashion to term the Grand Tour, and finally settled down for a couple of seasons in Paris, where his grandfather—Sir Geoffrey—had succeeded in right of his wife to a valuable household property which for many years had been let to a foreign Embassy.

At length, having grown rather tired of the Continent, he determined to return to Devonshire by way of Bordeaux, and being compelled to pass a couple of days in the crescent-shaped capital of the Gironde, he happened to stroll into the principal theatre—which is situated at the corner where the Rue Chapeau Rouge joins the broad Allées de Tournay. A provincial company was playing there, and it was upon the boards of the rambling old theatre that he first saw the woman—or girl rather, for at that time she could not have been more than eighteen—who was destined to become the future mistress of Netherleigh.

The history of Mdlle. de Gonidec was, shortly, as follows. Her father had been an officer in the army of the first Napoleon, and after taking part in the abortive military demonstration at Boulogne, he gained his majority upon the frozen field of Austerlitz, where the Old Guard broke through the serried masses of the Russians, and then proceeded to rout them in detail—as the history-books tell us. Being severely wounded during the campaign, he was invalided home and retired from the service with the rank of Colonel. Having lost all his money in imprudent speculations, his family were left to support themselves, and it was his youngest daughter, Lucille, who made her *début* on the boards of the old theatre at Bordeaux. and who eventually became Lady L'Estrange. The exact date and locality where the marriage took place did not transpire—it must be remembered that there were no telegraphs or society journals in those days,—but it was known to have taken place in

France about the year 1816, and it was not until after the death of his father—which occurred shortly after—that Sir George brought his wife and infant son back to Netherleigh.

Boy though I was at the time, how well I remember her ladyship as she strolled along the terrace, chatting and laughing with the sturdy Norman *bonne* who had charge of Master Geoffrey. She wore the quaint, short-waisted dress of the period, and the luxuriant masses of her golden-brown hair were coiled up above the well-shaped head, showing off the graceful outline of the neck to perfection. She must have been lovely as a child, and when I saw her last, a few months only before her death, her slight, girlish figure and lustrous brown eyes with their heavy lashes and clearly-marked eyebrows, together with her ridiculously small hands and feet, made an impression upon my boyish memory which the finger of Time has been powerless to efface. She had been her father's favourite daughter, and was, by all accounts, of a most loving and lovable nature, but like most pretty women she was fond of gaiety and admiration, and her lively disposition, combined with her undeniable beauty and Parisian costumes, proved a constant source of offence to the female portion of the local aristocracy, of whom I have heard my master remark:—"When they have exhausted the subject of their poultry, and their children, and discussed the relative merits of all-wool clothing and red-flannel as a material for winter under-wear, you have seen them at their best."

Luckily, perhaps, for themselves, the young couple cared but little for the highly respectable but, truth to say, somewhat ponderous form of entertainment which prevailed throughout the neighbourhood. They could afford to be independent, if not of public opinion, at all events of county society, and it was generally admitted that there were few better country quarters than Netherleigh Court. During the spring and autumn the house was always full of pleasant people, and the rest of the year was spent in visiting the estate which Sir George owned on the west coast of Ireland, or amidst the gaieties of the French capital.

Everything went on as well at Netherleigh as could have been expected under the circumstances, until the birth of poor Master Francis, but within a few weeks of that event her ladyship caught a chill which resulted in inflammation of the lungs, and died after a very short illness. Master Frank was a very delicate child, and either on account of a physical malformation which threatened eventually to develope into a hump-back, or because, in his grief, he looked upon him as the indirect cause of his mother's death, Sir George—in all other matters the most impartial and kind-hearted of men— never took the same interest in his second son, and entrusted his education entirely to Father Massy, the household chaplain. Although I did not enter his service until some years later, I have always heard that the change for the worse in my master's health and spirits dated from her ladyship's death. His unusually erect figure contracted a premature stoop, his dark hair became streaked with grey, and he no longer took the horse-exercise in which he formerly delighted, but spent most of his time in the library, devoting himself to literary pursuits and the education of his eldest son, Master Geoffrey, to whom he was devotedly attached.

But, unless I am careful, I shall overrun the scent again, and must hark back to matters which more immediately concern myself.

CHAPTER XXII.

I Enter the Service of Sir George L'Estrange, and Accompany Mr. Geoffrey to Camford.

MY last recollections of Westport were embittered by the shockingly sudden death of my chief friend and companion, poor Dicky Sellars, who was killed by his horse rolling on him.

Poor Dick, his first bad fall proved his last! Towards the end of March, one bright, sunny day, he was riding a stale old hunter of Goodman's. The dust was flying from the fallows in clouds and the ground was as hard as a turnpike-road, and at the first drop-fence they came to the artful old brute, dreading the concussion to his fore-legs, came down all of a heap and rolled over on to his side, killing his rider on the spot. It is at this time of the year that serious accidents may reasonably be expected, for, when the ground gets hard, a stale hunter will not jump out or attempt to save himself on landing, and prudent people give their old slaves a chance and make their young horses do an extra turn instead.

This occurred only the day before that upon which I had arranged to leave the old town for good and all, and I delayed my departure in order to attend his funeral. It was a sad wind-up to my Westport experiences, but I had the melancholy satisfaction of seeing my ill-fated friend laid in his last resting-place beside the sad sea-waves, and after bidding 'Good-bye' to my small circle of acquaintances, I mounted the mail-coach with a heavy heart. Notwithstanding the bright sunshine it was bitterly cold, and the bundle of soiled horse-litter into which our feet was thrust was but a poor substitute for the luxurious foot-warmers of the present day. I reached Exeter more dead than alive—for I had managed to get a severe chill standing about at the funeral—and took the Diligence to Netherton, and so on to Netherleigh by carrier's-cart.

As might have been expected, I found a good many changes in the house which I had almost come to regard as a home. The door was opened by a new parlour-maid, and I found that Jane had united her fortunes to those of the fiery-headed Michael, and that the pair had started an opposition general shop in the village, where they retailed tooth and stomach-ache by the ounce to the unsophisticated youth of Netherleigh. Like her predecessors, cheery Mrs. Jones had found herself unable to support the tedium of existence at the Parsonage on the moor, and her place was now filled by a stately and austere-looking matron of the 'quite a superior person' type, who rejoiced in the familiar name of Smith and appeared to have got, not only the small household, but its master also, pretty well under her thumb.

Mr. Sealy had lately met with a severe accident whilst riding a young horse to hounds, having been laid up with a fractured thigh-bone—and that, as I have good reason to know, is no joke. The confinement appeared to have exercised a very depressing effect upon him, and in a moment of dejection he had consented to sell his now valuable pack of otter-hounds to a rich gentleman who had lately come to reside in the neighbourhood. This gentleman afterwards built spacious kennels near Cranford, and hunted the district regularly. Contrary to the Parson's advice, he gradually discarded the foxhounds which formed the backbone of the pack, and went to great expense to re-introduce the purebred otter-hound. These he was compelled to van about the country, and either in consequence of the difficulty of obtaining fresh strains of blood or from some defect in the sanitary arrangements, outbreaks of disease were of frequent occurrence—a thing unknown in the rough-and-ready, makeshift Kennels at Netherleigh—and a year or two afterwards the pack was decimated by rabies.

The Parson was just able to get about with the aid of a stick, and with characteristic pluck had driven fifteen miles to attend the last meet of the season, and with his injured thigh tightly strapped up, had ridden the same youngster that caused the accident until the hounds found their fox, when he reluctantly yielded to the persuasions of his friends and drove home. He informed me that it had been definitely arranged that I was to go to Netherleigh Court on a six months' trial as valet to Sir George, and that if I gave satisfaction, and the baronet's old servant did not return by September, I was to receive forty pounds a year, which, with perquisites in the shape of tips from visitors and left-off clothes, seemed to me to be a very enviable berth.

After procuring some respectable clothes in Netherton, I was driven to the Court and handed over to Mr. Adams, whose duty it was to initiate me into the mysteries of my new calling. The Netherleigh establishment was not only one of the largest in the county, but it was conducted upon a very liberal scale, while the household arrangements were always kept up to the highest pitch of perfection. The young gentlemen gave me very little trouble, and were inclined to treat me more as a companion than a servant, but it was a very different thing with Sir George, who was often irritable and peremptory and always most fastidious in his dress, and I am sure that he would rather have gone without his dinner altogether, than have been compelled to sit down to it without changing every stitch of clothes about him, from top to toe. I always called Sir George at nine, and he breakfasted upstairs, seldom appearing in public until luncheon-time. Lunch was at two o'clock, and at half-past three to the minute, one of the perfect-mannered hacks was brought round to the hall-door, and scrupulously attired and looking the picture of a high-bred gentleman of the old school, my master proceeded to take the daily horse-exercise which the doctors insisted on.

Now I had not served my apprenticeship under Shice and been in the company of flash Joe Barton and Co., without learning a thing or two, and as soon as I was fairly settled in, I sent to Westport for what I required, and then set to work to turn out my master's breeches, boots, etc., in a style to which they were unaccustomed down Netherleigh way. I was also able to give the old Irish stud-groom a hint or two which he was not above taking, and when Sir George noticed the difference in the way he was turned out, although he would never have dreamed of saying a word to me about it, he expressed his satisfaction to Mr. Sealy who, in turn, took an opportunity of repeating it to me.

I have no intention of repeating any of the gossip of the servants'-hall or back-stairs' scandal, for the simple reason that although often amusing enough and sometimes even exciting at the moment, it would necessarily lose a good deal in the telling, and was, moreover, only of passing interest. With the exception of Adams and myself all the servants—from Mr. Louis, the French cook, to the stable-helpers—were Roman Catholics, and came, most of them, from Sir George's Kilmore Castle estates in the Co. Kerry. The only meal which the upper and under servants took together was the one o'clock dinner in the servants'-hall, which was a very formidable affair, the greatest order and decorum prevailing. All the upper servants sat together at one end of the table, and as long as we remained, scarcely a word was spoken, but as soon as the cheese made its appearance, we all rose in a body and adjourned to the house-keeper's room—stalking out in single file, each with our glass in our hand, the procession being headed by Mrs. Barry, the housekeeper, and whipped in by Mr. Adams.

The services, which were held in the large and beautifully restored chapel at the east end of the house, were conducted by Father Dennis Massy, the household chaplain, who had been living at Netherleigh ever since Sir George's marriage, and had superintended the education of his two sons. Father Massy had his private suite of apartments in the west wing, where accommodation was always provided for any stray priest who might happen to be staying in the neighbourhood and who might come over to assist him with the chapel services. As I have already mentioned, two of the largest adjoining landed proprietors were Roman Catholics, and, with their households, were in the habit of attending the weekly services at the Court. Besides these there was quite a small colony of labourers and servants who had married and settled down in the district, and these, with the households from Erleigh and Morthoe, formed a far larger congregation than that over which Mr. Sealy presided.

Father Massy—a most benevolent-looking, silver-haired old gentleman, who spent most of the daytime in hunting for beetles and butterflies, and his nights poking about the plantation with a horn-lantern and a net, prospecting for moths—was very far from realising the popular conception of a Jesuit priest, to which society he belonged. His amiable disposition and gentle manners made him a general favourite, and whenever any member of the household was in trouble, he would go straight to Father Denny, well knowing that he could rely upon his advice or intercession.

Every year the family was in the habit of making an autumnal pilgrimage to a small watering-place on the East Coast, called Sandford-on-Sea, in order that the young gentlemen might enjoy the really fine air for which that rather dreary little place was celebrated.

The vicar of the parish had been a college friend of Sir George's, and when Passon Mark ran down for a fortnight—which he generally made a point of doing—many a quiet rubber was played, with the local Doctor for a fourth. A few miles inland there lived an eccentric old gentleman named L'Estrange—a distant relative of my master's—who still adhered to the traditional costume of a French nobleman of the last century, and who never drove beyond the park gates without a couple of *picqueurs*, or outriders, in green and gold uniforms, white breeches and gloves, and jack-boots.

The local gossips averred—but I must leave the compilation of the Chronicles, scandalous or otherwise, of Sandford-on-the-Sea to a more competent scribe, and get on with my own story without delay; and for the same reason—very much against my inclination, I can assure you, for although, as so often happens, I thought little enough of it at the time, it was, perhaps, the happiest period of my life—I must pass over the annual visit to Kilmore Castle in the Co. Kerry, with the shooting at seals from the cliffs as they popped their heads up to take breath at certain places along the coast—and just like the *pooro Beng* they looked, with their black, glistening, uncanny heads, deep-set eyes, and whiskered muzzles, as they rose and sank on the long Atlantic swell—the banging at rock-pigeons in the caves, or the salmon-fishing in the Kilmore River. And what a river it was, in spite of all the poaching, and how the water roared and eddied amongst the rocks till one's head became dizzy, as the boatmen poled the cot amongst the rapids, and the silvery peal leaped around in scores!

Ah me! Those were good times and no mistake. I have only to shut my eyes to see Master Geoffrey crouching in the bows, eagerly watching every cast of the 'three hooks' —the 'right yoke' as Patsy Ryan called it. Suddenly the rod would bend and the line would tighten as if the hooks were fast in a rock. "I'm in him! Tak the rad, yer anner! Tak the rad!"—Patsy would cry, trembling with excitement and as white as if he'd murdered a turnip and washed his face in the blood—for although the water-bailiff had been sent 'up the street' with half-a-crown to buy a box of matches, there was a heavy penalty for 'stroke-hauling'—and as he handed over the rod and seized the pole, the line would go screeching through the reel, and Master Geoffrey would hold on like grim death as they ran the cot down the rapids and I gaffed a twenty-pounder in the smooth water below, while Micky Doolan's "Whirroo-ho-hoo," as he gave it plenary absolution with 'the Praste,' might have been heard in Tralee.

Master, or Mr. Geoffrey L'Estrange, as I suppose I must

call him now, Sir George's eldest son and heir to the Netherleigh estate—the Irish property not being entailed—was a fine specimen of a young Englishman. Blessed with a superabundance of health and high animal spirits, devotedly attached to field-sports of every description, and inheriting none of the stiffness and formality which distinguished—and to a certain extent, alienated—his father from the easy-going Devonshire squires, he was as frank and fearless a young gentleman as you would wish to see, and as it had been for some time apparent that he was rather more than Father Massy could comfortably manage, it had been arranged that he should eventually accompany his great friend Mr. Cecil Blount to Camford.

Mr. Blount was nearly two years older than my young master, but with him it was a case of an old head on young shoulders, and for sound common-sense he would have compared favourably with the majority of men of double his age and experience. It was chiefly with the hope that he might act as a drag upon his rather too rapidly-inclined companion, that Sir George had persuaded his old friend, the Squire of Stowe, to allow his son to accompany Mr. Geoffrey to Camford. They both matriculated in due course, and entered St. Saviour's as gentlemen-commoners, and at the end of a couple of terms Mr. Geoffrey begged his father to let him take me back with him to Camford in the capacity of private servant. Sir George was by no means anxious to dispense with my services and to return to the ministrations of one of the Irish footmen—for during my residence at Netherleigh, although I say it who shouldn't, my manners had improved considerably, and, thanks to Adams' tuition and Joe Barton's advice, I had begun to acquire an air of sedateness and respectability which had hitherto been conspicuous by its absence—but he was unable to refuse his son anything, and at the end of the Long Vacation I accompanied my young master back to Camford.

Sir George allowed him to keep three horses, while Mr. Blount had a couple of hunters, so I was forthwith entrusted with the management of the small stud, and combined the duties of stud-groom with those of private servant. Those were the times for servants, for gentlemen were gentlemen in those days. None of your cheap tailors and shoddy reach-me-downs at three guineas the suit, shabby and bagged at the knee in a fortnight, and worth nothing when they do come to you; but cutaway coats, double-breasted fancy waistcoats, changed two or three times a day, cravats by the drawerful, trousers ordered by the dozen pair, and rows of tops, shooting, and walking-boots that did your heart good to look at—but of all the thieves I ever came across those scouts were the very worst.

For the next three years or so my masters—as I shall call them in future—remained in college, and led the pleasant life of rich gentlemen-commoners. They had plenty of money and were not afraid to spend it, and owing to the fact that the gold tassels on their caps secured them a comparative immunity from the attentions of the dons and censors, they shirked chapel and cut lectures with a persistence worthy of a better cause, while their energy and perseverance in surmounting such trivial obstacles as time and distance in order to attend the meets of the neighbouring packs, should have ensured their taking high honours had they been applied to the pursuit of knowledge instead of to that of the fox.

Sir George treated his son very liberally. When a young man he had, himself, managed to get pretty deeply into debt, and had acquired some practical experience of money-lenders and their little ways. I have heard it said that he kept several race-horses in training, but never owned one good enough to win a race, besides spending a good deal of money on jewellery, cards, and other pleasures—and, as we all know, there's nothing like a slow horse and a fast woman to make the money fly. Be this as it may, he allowed Mr. Geoffrey fifteen hundred a year and a couple of hunters, upon the understanding that if he exceeded his allowance, instead of leaving his debts unpaid or going to the Jews, he should borrow the money from his father, paying interest upon it at the rate of five per cent. This arrangement was found to work most satisfactorily, and although Sir George always insisted upon the interest being punctually paid, I fancy that Mr. Geoffrey found his father a very accommodating banker.

After the regulation number of failures my young gentlemen managed to scrape through the intermediate examinations, and finally went into lodgings with a view to reading for their degrees. Being emancipated almost entirely from the supervision of the dons, they were not long in making the discovery that there are few more convenient head-quarters than Camford for young men with liberal allowances or unexhausted credit, and they shot pigeons, drove, hunted, and attended race-meetings to their hearts' content, varying the monotony of existence by an occasional run up to town.

Amongst other things they invested in a couple of long-tails, which it was my privilege to school and train over the same track where, twenty years previously, old Mr. Scott used to gallop his horses. Of all the dangerous brutes to school, recommend me to a stale old steeple-chaser. A young horse will, at all events, do his best to jump, and if he makes a mistake, he tries to save a fall, and if he gets down, he is on his legs again as quick as he knows how—but there is no catch in schooling an artful old customer who has had all the gas taken out of him. He knows well enough that it is not the real thing, for his mane has not been plaited, there is no crowd to excite him, and he misses the roar of the ring, the flash of the silk jackets, and the shouting of the spring-captains—the consequence being that he hits everything as hard as he dares, takes the ground once or twice, and if he happens to get upsides of you in a ditch, he doesn't forget to stay there.

Besides the chasers we had a couple of useful hunters that could gallop a bit, with which we did pretty well at the college 'grinds,' and the freedom with which my masters backed their fancies at the small cross-country meetings they attended in the neighbourhood, must have caused the hearts of the local bookmakers to rejoice exceedingly.

However, their heads were screwed on the right way—Mr. Blount's especially—and I don't think they hurt themselves much at the game or purchased their experience above market-price, but without intending it, they managed to do me a good bit of harm—they and their friends between them. It used to be:—" Here, Samson, go round and see if you can get me a pony on this or that for such and such a race, and you can stand a couple of sovs. yourself "—or Mr. Standish of St. Jude's would send for me, and it would be:—" Come in Sam and take a glass of port. Do you think that horse of yours will stay the distance with his penalty in the Open Race at the St. Saviour's 'grinds'?"—And then in the vacation it was just the same—for Sir George encouraged Mr. Geoffrey to bring some of his Camford friends down to Netherleigh—"Samson this" or "Sam that" till it is scarcely to be wondered at if I got a bit above myself in consequence. Believe me, for every servant who is spoilt by harshness or overwork, a hundred are spoilt by over-kindness. The one *may* ruin a man, the other is pretty well certain to.

CHAPTER XXIII.

Life at Camford.

SITWELL had long since retired from business, his premises being occupied by a very well-known character named Bill Smith, who horsed the coaches running in and out of Camford, and let out hunters, hacks, and pony-traps to the gentlemen.

On one occasion a select party, consisting of my masters and about a dozen of their friends, had chartered a drag from Smith, and under the escort of that experienced Jehu, had started in high spirits for Bridgeford Races. Amongst those present —as the reporters say—we noticed the Earl of Raasay— better known as 'Susan'—a good-looking young nobleman and president of the 'Blazers'—to which select coterie my masters had the privilege of belonging. A sound cricketer and one of the best bats in the 'Varsity eleven, but too lazy to be of much use in the field, he was very popular despite his quick temper and a tendency to put on what his detractors called 'side.' Lord Cheltenham — otherwise 'Cherubim'—an hereditary legislator in embryo, all head and legs with no body, whose round, mottled face, absolutely devoid of expression, Jem H—— used always to compare to a plum-pudding atop of a pair of tongs, and who did his best to appear fast despite a secretly cherished predilection for white mice, snakes, squirrels, and other *feræ naturæ* of an equally objectionable character. Mr. Standish of St. Jude's Hall, a big, broad-shouldered, good-looking man in a coarse sort of way, an acknowledged authority upon wine, women, and horse-flesh, and an adept at all games of skill or chance, who played billiards and shot pigeons a bit above the average, trained and rode his own horses whenever he could get the weight, had already run through a fortune and *post-obited* the paternal Standish to the uttermost available farthing, and whose knowledge of the world, if somewhat dearly purchased, was already beginning to stand him in good stead amongst his less sophisticated juniors. The Honourable Percy Barker, a long-headed, hard-riding scion of a long-headed, hard-riding family, a good all-round man and unpleasantly strong—as you very soon found out if you happened to run against him in a football scrimmage or a Town-and-Gown row. Sir Granville Fazackerley—otherwise 'Granny'—of Erleigh, a fine property about ten miles from Netherleigh, one of the most perfectly proportioned young men I have ever seen, with regular features, blue eyes, auburn hair, and, notwithstanding the hard life he led, a complexion which a girl of seventeen might have envied. A good race-rider, a desperate young gambler, and a great favourite with the ladies, he was the cleverest and quickest two-handed boxer I ever remember to have seen, and Nat used to swear that if he had the handling of him for three months, he would back him to fight any man of his weight —amateur or professional—in the kingdom. Lord Findon, a puffy-faced young nobleman with a large property in Downshire and a mania for driving coaches, who modelled himself on poor George Nelson of the 'Flying Times,' affected many-caped, down-the-road coats with cheese-plate buttons, and who was never so thoroughly in his element as when drinking 'dogs-nose' out of a pewter pot and chaffing the barmaid at a road-side public. To these may be added my two young gentlemen and half-a-dozen of the Reggies, Dollies, Freds, and Charlies of the St. Saviour's set, whose ambitions did not soar above the wearing of stupendous checks, the cracking of hunting-whips about Quad, and the occasional post-vinous demolition of a few windows—and the coach-load is complete.

The rough element mustered pretty strong on the course, and towards the end of the day, as the contents of the hampers disappeared, the natural high-spirits of the party found vent in the usual chaff and horse-play, the result being that one of the crowd of cads and hangers-on who surrounded the drag managed to intercept the flight of an erratic champagne-bottle with his head, and got rather badly cut in consequence. Two or three unwary members of the party were mobbed on their return from the enclosure, and finally rescued after a sharp scrimmage, but before the saddling-bell rang for the last race it became apparent that the leader of the roughs had withdrawn his forces, and it was rumoured that they were lying in wait for the St. Saviour's drag just outside Bridgeford.

Unfortunately, there was no other road home, and here Bill Smith's ready wits came into play. Hastily going round the course he managed by copious libations of champagne and a liberal distribution of cigars, to persuade some half-dozen of the principal residents and tradesmen of Bridgeford to take a seat on the drag, and having distributed them judiciously amongst the undergraduates, he mounted the box and started on the return journey with a confident smile on his rubicund visage, a big cigar between his lips, and a knowing twinkle in his beady eyes.

As the drag neared the small market-town close to which the races had been held, it became evident that the enemy was in force, while the strong strategetical position which he occupied spoke volumes for the leader's practical acquaintance with the rudiments of 'Varsity *kriegspiel*. At a point about half-a-mile from Bridgeford the coach-road narrowed to a mere lane and dipped between high banks as it crossed a stream at one of the fords from which the town derived its name. But Bill Smith's practiced eye had taken in the situation at a glance, and waking up the wheelers with the double-thong, he gave the free-going leaders their heads and dashed through the ford at a hand-gallop which carried us half way up the opposite acclivity. Now came the critical moment. Armed with sticks, stones, and any other missiles which happened to come handy, the roughs lined both sides of the narrow, deep-sunk lane, and prepared to greet the coach-load with a murderous volley.

When, however, they recognised a popular landed-proprietor and M.F.H. on the box-seat, while two or three well-known town's-people occupied prominent positions on the roof, their rage knew no bounds, but although they vented their disappointment in derisive yells and savage execrations, they refrained from letting go at the passengers. I was inside with two other servants, and having drawn up the wooden blinds, we crouched down on the floor and prepared for ructions. And lucky it was that we did so, for as the coach rolled by, the baffled mob discharged a volley at the panels which reduced the blinds to splinters and played old Harry with the crockery.

In addition to their other pursuits my masters were regular patrons of the drama as represented at the shabby little temple of Thespis which dragged on a precarious, *semi-sub-rosâ* existence at Camford, and were, moreover, personally acquainted with some of the minor stars of the theatrical profession in London.

About nine o'clock one foggy night in November, a rather noisy supper-party was assembled in one of the University lodging-houses under the very shadow of St. Saviour's venerable, smoke-begrimed walls. The scene—I grieve to relate—was enlivened by the presence of ladies, Miss Tottie St. Claire and her amiable and accomplished lady-friend Miss Dottie de Vere, to wit, two ornaments of the theatrical profession who had been lionised about the town by an enterprising youth named Lumley, otherwise 'Slums'—whose cheek, to put it mildly, was as extensive as his credit—and finally introduced to the complaisant lodging-house keeper as his cousins from the country.

Mr. Geoffrey had been asked to join the party, but although a previous engagement had prevented his accepting the invitation, he determined, with Mr. Blount's assistance, to contribute his share towards the evening's enjoyment. Soon after dark I was despatched with a note to his tailor in the High, and brought back a parcel which proved to contain the flowing robes and spotless bands of a Proctor, and with the assistance of false whiskers, darkened eyebrows, a pair of gold spectacles, and a little judicious padding, Mr.

Blount—who was a tall, dark-complexioned gentleman and rowed seven in the St. Saviour's boat—was soon made up into an excellent imitation of that much-to-be avoided official the Senior Proctor. Mr. Geoffrey and I were then made up to represent the 'bulldogs,' and putting on thick top-coats with the lower part of our faces enveloped in woollen comforters, we emerged into the darkness of the night, and crossing the High at a rapid pace, and taking advantage of the narrow back-streets which abound in the old town, made our way by a circuitous route towards the scene of the festivities.

As we turned the corner of Frog Lane, a benighted undergraduate, emerging from a billiard-room, ran slap into the arms of the *pseudo* Proctor, who in solemn tones demanded his name and college, which he proceeded to enter in his betting-book, at the same time adjuring his victim to appear at his official residence at half-past nine the following morning. Then, being undesirous of playing Box to the Cox of the genuine article, we made the best of our way to Mr. Lumley's lodgings, and opening the street door, Mr. Geoffrey and I preceded Mr. Blount up the narrow staircase.

On reaching the landing we came full upon a white-waistcoated waiter—none other than the lodging-house proprietor himself—who was endeavouring to extract the last dregs from a bottle of champagne by the simple process of applying the neck to his capacious mouth, at the same time elevating the butt and tilting his head back. While in the very act of assimilating the gooseberry, our tall hats and great-coats obtruded themselves upon the retina of his dexter optic. For a moment he remained motionless, as if petrified with terror—then, dropping the bottle with a crash, he fell back against the wall, while his pasty face rivalled the dubious hue of his waistcoat.

Leaving the unhappy man limply supporting himself against the passage wall, Mr. Blount ordered me to knock at the door of Mr. Lumley's sitting-room, from whence proceeded the unmistakable sounds of revelry. The knock was succeeded by a dead silence, so, being the most professional-looking of the party, I threw the door wide open, and taking off my hat, stood at attention, while Mr. Blount, assuming the well-known manner of the burly Senior Proctor, entered the room closely followed by Mr. Geoffrey, who remained in the shadow of the door to prevent a retreat.

As the tall figure and flowing robes of the Proctor filled the doorway, you might have heard a pin drop, and consternation was depicted on every countenance, but more especially upon that of the host, whose washed-out face assumed a ghastly pallor, while the flush of excitement faded from the cheeks of the guests, with the notable exception of the two ladies, whose complexions—for reasons best known to themselves—remained unchanged amidst the universal panic. It must be remembered that the Proctor's visit meant rustication, at the very least, for all present: the proprietor of the lodgings would have lost his licence: while the actresses would have been afforded an opportunity for 'rest' and reflection in the enforced seclusion of the 'Spinning House.'

But suddenly, to the relief of all present, my masters threw off their disguises, and a yell arose which threatened to bring down the ceiling; Mesdames St. Claire and de Vere exhibited very little of the repose which the poet has led us to associate with the deportment of ladies of their aristocratic name and lofty lineage, and as the remains of the dessert began to fly about the room in all directions, I deemed it expedient to beat a retreat.

Although always to the front when any fun was going on, it must not be supposed that my masters belonged to the loafing brigade who haunted the billiard-rooms and hotels, and who after taking a turn or two up and down the High, finally retired to their rooms and played loo or hazard for high stakes—an amusement which generally resulted in the loss of all their available ready-money and the acquisition of a considerable amount of unnegotiable 'paper.' On the contrary, they were both keen sportsmen in the best sense of the word, and although welter weights, were generally to be found in the first flight when hounds really began to run.

During the last term of his residence Mr. Blount performed a feat—as any old St. Saviour's man will remember—the execution of which necessitated the possession of an unusual amount of combined nerve and horsemanship. In order to win a trifling after-dinner bet, mounted on his clever old hunter Gehazi—the original 'lepper' as white as snow—he jumped all the gates on the towing-path between Camford and Ouseley. I forget the exact number of gates—most of which would swing open at a touch—but there were a goodish few, while in several cases the horse had to take-off from, or land upon, the worn and gaping timbers of a foot-bridge.

Towards the end of the Long Vacation I generally accompanied Mr. Geoffrey upon a visit to Sir James Fergusson's—an old friend of Sir George's, and sleeping-partner in a well-known banking firm in the City—who rented a large estate in the Western highlands, where the deer-stalking and grouse-shooting were first-class, while Mr. Blount passed a good deal of his time with some friends in Touraine. Sir James was a kind-hearted but peppery Scotch gentleman of the old school, and although no sportsman himself, he was a staunch game-preserver and took a keen interest—amounting almost to a mania—in the habits of the birds and beasts which frequented the woods, lochs, and forest.

Lady Fergusson was a charming hostess, possessing, as she did, the rare knack of making everybody feel perfectly at home without any apparent effort. Upon the arrival of a visitor who was unused to the ways of the house, she would take him aside and say:—

"Now, Mr. So-and-so, our hours are as follows. Breakfast at nine: luncheon at two: dinner at a quarter to eight: but this is Liberty Hall and there is no reason why you should be present at any particular meal if you have anything else to do"—and although the guests seldom availed themselves of the privilege—for there was a man-cook and the wine was of the very best—it just made all the difference, and there was an absence of restraint and formality about the life at Strathdhu which contrasted agreeably with the regular hours and humdrum routine of the Netherleigh establishment.

Talking of Sir James and his hobbies puts me in mind of a story. As Mr. Geoffrey and I were coming back from stalking one evening—I always carried my master's rifle—we took a short-cut through the Castle Wood at the back of the house and flushed two or three woodcocks out of the bracken. Now, as it so happened, they were going to shoot the Castle Wood next day for rabbits, and my master was full of these woodcocks and talked of nothing else all dinner-time. Sir James chanced to overhear him, and turning to him, said:—" My dear boy, please to remember that the flight-birds are not in yet, and that those birds you saw to-day were all of them bred here, and I wouldn't have them killed on any account."

Then, of course, Mr. Geoffrey began to wish that he had kept his tongue quiet, but the mischief was done and there was nothing more to be said.

Next morning young Mr. Gilbert Fergusson, my master, and the other gentlemen, started off to beat the Wood, as arranged.

In any other part of the United Kingdom the Castle Wood might well have been reckoned a very respectable-sized estate, but up there it was merely a handy beat for an off day. And whether they drove it for roe with the chance of a stag, or beat it for rabbits and woodcock, it was more or less of a picnic, and the ladies always rode the ponies up to the luncheon-house. Roughly speaking it was an undulating tract of pine-forest between four and five miles in circumference, intersected by numerous goyles—or burns, as they called them there—where the peaty moor-water was churned into creamy foam as it leaped from ledge to ledge beneath the white-stemmed birches and crimson-berried rowans, and the roe-deer poked their impudent noses out of a tangled growth of bracken, fern, and bilberry. Here and there were open glades where the rabbits skipped and dodged amongst the tussocky grass, and across which the old hinds, closely followed by their calves, leisurely picked their way in Indian file towards the moor above—past the tiny loch where the ducks paddled amongst the rushes, and the frowning crags where the wild-cat reared her young and the white-tailed eagle was uncommonly fond of taking his noonday siesta.

Just as we came to the burn near which we had seen the birds the previous evening, up gets a woodcock, somebody fires and misses, and my master knocks it over without thinking what he was about.

"Confound it, Geoff"—cries young Mr. Fergusson, "there'll be the deuce and all of a row about this"—but before the words were well out of his mouth, up gets a couple of cock right and left. My master covers the first one—

whether he intended to fire or not I can't say—and Mr. Gilbert, being, I daresay, a bit keen and jealous, lets go at it and knocks it over with his right barrel but misses the other bird, and Mr. Geoffrey—who was a nailing good shot—wipes his eye. Then one or two more got up, and were either killed or missed, and after that we did not see another all day. At lunch a council of war was held.

"What on earth are we to do with these blessed birds, now we've got them?" says Mr. Fergusson. "We can't throw them away, and I'm hanged if I dare take them back to the house."

"I'll tell you what we'll do, Gillie"—replied my master, "my man can cook a bit in a rough sort of way. Let's have 'em for lunch."

No sooner said than done. Some dry sticks were collected, and one of the gillies fetched some clay, which I kneaded up into hollow cases. Then I put a woodcock into each of them—Gipsy fashion—feathers and all, covered them up, and baked them on a pine-wood fire. When they were ready, the clay was cracked and the feathers came away with it, the birds were cut open and cleaned, and the gillies having been sworn to secrecy, those sacred woodcocks were then and there solemnly devoured in broad daylight within a mile of the Castle. The secret was well kept, but when my master left, he went to Sir James and made a clean breast of it, and, as I need scarcely tell anyone who knew the old baronet, was freely forgiven.

And now let me ask you whether you have ever seen a conceited idiot of a chap, who fancied he could ride a bit, try to sit one of those Highland steers caught up out of a herd that was running wild on the hillside—a shaggy, snorting brute about fourteen hands high, with bloodshot eyes and a coat like a doormat, nothing in front of you but a pair of curly horns, and the concentrated evicting powers of twenty buck-jumpers? I have—once—but it would have taken an instantaneous shutter worked by electricity to record the experiment. One more question. Have you ever seen a Scotch gillie laughing heartily? I once saw about a dozen of them holding their sides, and some of them actually rolling on the heather in convulsions. It was upon the same occasion, and they evidently thought it very funny—I didn't.

The house—or Castle, as it was called—was a very ugly old building with pepper-box turrets and a coating of grey stucco, and like most mansions of the same date and architecture, extremely draughty and uncomfortable, but the excellence of the sport and the lavish hospitality which prevailed made ample amends for any shortcomings in the accommodation, while the surrounding scenery was wild and romantic enough to satisfy the most exacting admirer of the picturesque. I should like to tell you some of our stalking adventures, but all shooting stories are very much alike, and as, during one of our visits, an incident occurred which, in my humble opinion, bordered very closely upon the supernatural, and for which I have never been able to account in anything like a satisfactory manner, I will tell you about that instead.

Although the descendant of a race which popular superstition and ignorance has frequently accredited with the possession of occult, not to say supernatural, powers, I am a very matter-of-fact individual, and if anything happens for which I am at a loss to account, I always prefer to treat it as a coincidence and nothing more—and this appears to be the most obvious, if not the only possible, explanation of the incident which I am about to relate.

Captain Archibald Macdonald, the owner of Strathdhu, had lately succeeded to the estate upon the death of a distant relative. Beyond the rent of the place as a sporting residence, he derived scarcely any income from the property, and as his private means were limited, he was only too pleased to let the Castle and the shootings to such an eligible tenant as Sir James, and after a short visit to Strathdhu to put things straight, he accompanied his regiment to India.

I was sitting one sultry afternoon, towards the end of August, upon the river bank about a mile below the Castle, watching Mr. Geoffrey thrashing away at a long, sullen-looking pool which derived its name from a rock, the general outline of which bore some fanciful resemblance to a seal, and which, when the river was in order, was almost submerged, but now reared its slimy head and shoulders full three feet above the level of the water. On the further bank of the river was a pine-wood, and beyond that, again, a a precipitous mountain-side where a few sheep—tiny white specks in a wilderness of granite boulders and purple heather

—were cropping the scanty grass. Behind us the bank rose abruptly till it reached the level of the coach-road which, at this point, ran through a birch-wood, and beyond that, again, the forest stretched away towards the north in an interminable succession of sky-lines which 'flattered only to deceive.'

It was a blazing hot afternoon with thunder in the air and nothing to break the oppressive stillness save the occasional splash of a black-backed, copper-bellied salmon, the snap of a bursting broom-pod, the clucking chuckles of a couple of white-tailed *rookomengros** as they chased each other amongst the pine-boughs, or the faint tinkle of a distant sheep-bell from the moor above. It was clearly no use fishing, so at last my master laid down his rod in disgust, and throwing himself full-length amongst the bracken, proceeded to light a cigar for the benefit of the midges.

We might have been sitting there half-an-hour—maybe more, maybe less—watching the fish jumping in the eddy at the head of the pool, when all at once a curious sound—half wail, half whistle—came stealing up the valley from the eastward, and seemed to fill the air around us. It is many years ago now, and I have never heard anything quite like it before or since, so at this distance of time I scarcely know how to describe it. It seemed to proceed from no particular point, but to pervade the whole wood behind and around us, rising and falling like the sough of the wind through the heather on a bleak hillside—but shriller, more penetrating, and continuous.

At one moment I could have sworn that somebody was blowing a dog-whistle very softly and steadily within thirty yards of us, but as quick as I made up my mind where the sound proceeded from, it would travel away in the opposite direction, and although, as I have told you, I am neither imaginative or impressionable, and was, moreover, strictly sober and wide awake at the time, it gave me what they call the 'goose-creeps'—for no mortal being could have gone on whistling like that without stopping to take breath. I have since heard a very similar sound produced by the wind whistling through the telegraph-wires, but in those days the electric current had not invaded the Western highlands, and I was altogether at a loss to account for it.

* Squirrels.

My master, who was lying down about thirty yards from me, must have noticed it about the same time, for he sat up and called out:—

"Just climb up the bank, Samson, and see who it is making that infernal whistling row"—and, to tell the truth, I was not sorry to obey him, for there was something 'nae thet cannie' about it, to my mind.

As I climbed the bank, gaff in hand, and forced my way through the narrow belt of birch-wood until I reached the coach-road, the sound swelled louder and louder—then gradually died away to the west in the direction of the house. For some moments I remained perfectly still, listening intently, but no living thing was stirring and the sound was not repeated. A few minutes later an old shepherd came in sight, driving a score of sheep before him along the road, and followed by a very handsome collie. My master had joined me by this time.

"Hi, mon!"—he began in his chaffing way, addressing the shepherd. "Ded ye heer anybody whustlin' the noo?"

The old man stared at us with whiskey-sodden eyes:—"She's na spekin' the Engliss, whateffer"—he answered gently, with the soft accent which distinguishes the Highlander from the Lowlander, and passed on his way.

"I didn't say you were, you old idiot"—rejoined Mr. Geoffrey, who was always inclined to be quick-tempered and seemed to think that the old fellow was shamming ignorance. "Look here. What'll you take for that collie of yours?"—but the old shepherd vouchsafed no reply, and calling to his dog in Gaelic, went his way, shaking his head and muttering to himself until he turned a corner in the road and was lost to sight.

The following day being Saturday, Mr. Macdonald—the minister who officiated once a fortnight at the little church at Strathdhu—and his daughter—a tall, delicate-looking young lady with fair hair and complexion and a bright colour—dined and slept at the Castle as usual.

My master happened to sit next to Miss Macdonald at dinner, and as I was handing round the sherry I heard him telling her about our little adventure of the previous afternoon, which must have made a greater impression upon him than it had on me—for, to tell the truth, I had never given the matter a second thought. There were some twelve or fourteen to dinner that night, and as I worked my way round with the decanter, for some reason or other I happened to look across at Miss Macdonald, and noticed that she had turned deadly pale. The minister must have noticed it also, for he at once left his place and going round to his daughter's assistance, gave her his arm and led her from the room.

Upon his return he apologised to his host for his daughter's behaviour, adding that she was rather inclined to be delicate, having outgrown her strength, and had been foolish enough to allow herself to be upset by something that Mr. L'Estrange was telling her—" And, perhaps "—he continued, " in order that there may be no mystery about it and to absolve Mr. L'Estrange from any blame, I ought to give you some explanation. You are aware, Sir James, that my daughter is engaged to her cousin, Archie Macdonald, who is now with his regiment in India. Well, you must know that there are some old-wife's havers to the effect that previous to the death of the head of the clan a strange, whistling sound—the 'Death-whistle of Strathdhu,' as they are pleased to call it—is heard in the strath. I need hardly say that this is all rubbish, but my daughter is, or professes to be, a firm believer in the Highland traditions, and being, as you know, rather inclined to be delicate and over-strung, it may, perhaps, be understood that Mr. L'Estrange's story was something of a shock to her. However, I have no doubt that she will have forgotten all about it by to-morrow morning."

As far as I can recollect this was all that took place, and there the matter ended. At the close of the Long Vacation I accompanied my master back to Camford, and at the end of the term we went down to Devonshire, as usual, for Christmas. One morning, about December of the same year, Mr. Cecil Blount rode up to the hall-door at Netherleigh, and, contrary to his usual custom—being naturally of a cool temperament and deliberate in his movements, the very reverse of my master, who was hot-headed and impetuous—came bursting into the breakfast-room in a highly excited state.

"Hallo, Cis!"—cried Mr. Geoffrey, with his mouth full

of buttered-toast, "What's the matter with you this morning? You look as if you'd just met old George Beer's ghost."*

"Look here, Geoff"—replied Mr. Cecil, producing from his coat-pocket a crumpled newspaper which he proceeded to smooth out on the table with his hand, "you remember what you told me about that pretty Macdonald girl up at Strathdhu? Well, just listen to this"—and he read out:—"August 27th, at Nagpore, Central Provinces, India, of fever, Hugh Archibald Macdonald, Captain Royal Highland Fusileers."

* * * * * *

I take it that most people who have knocked about the world as much as I have, must have met with at least one strange experience, but although I have known several curious things happen, this is the only one which I am unable to explain to my satisfaction. I have told the story —to the best of my recollection—exactly as it occurred, and I must leave the reader to draw his own conclusions.

CHAPTER XXIV.

Matrimony and Green Seas.

IT must not be supposed that all this time I had lost sight of Mantis Lovell, for although our opportunities of meeting were necessarily few and far between, we had established a system of intercommunication, by means of which I was kept informed of her movements. During the last term of my master's residence I came across the Lovells at Ascot, where the two sisters, dressed exactly alike in neat black silk dresses, short red cloaks, and broad beaver hats, not only managed to dispose of the contents of their flower-baskets over and over again, but were even honoured with the patronage of Royalty.

---

* Father of the present 'old George Beer,' who, with his eldest son, was killed in an encounter with the Revenue officers on Brent Downs.

As I contrasted Mantis' erect form, darkly-flashing eyes, pearly teeth, and clear olive skin, with the made-up figures, pinched-in waists, and artificial complexions of some of the fashionable beauties in the enclosure, I came to the conclusion that my sweetheart did not lose much by the comparison; and such was evidently the opinion of Mr. Geoffrey and his companions, who, upon the sisters approaching the St. Saviour's drag, began to question me rather closely about them. But not feeling myself called upon to reveal the exact state of the case, I only told him as much as I—in my wisdom—thought good for him to know. As things turned out, it would have been far better if I had informed my master that Mantis and I had been engaged to each other for a long time, and that I had made up my mind to marry her on the first opportunity that presented itself, in which case a great deal of misunderstanding, misery, and—as some would term it—crime might have been avoided, and the one action of which, amongst many others perhaps equally bad, I have always felt genuinely ashamed, would have found no record in these Recollections.

Even as it was, things might have remained as they were for some time to come, had not my master been induced one night, after a large wine-party given to celebrate the success of the St. Saviour's boat, to take part in a riotous demonstration directed against the head of his college, which resulted in a general smashing of windows and the destruction of a good deal of valuable property which it was impossible to replace. Amongst other little pranks, the young gentlemen thought proper to tie an iron kettle, tightly packed with gunpowder, to the knocker of the Dean's hall-door, which they painted a bright vermilion, and to illuminate the pond in the centre of the quadrangle after a highly original fashion, but, luckily for all parties concerned, the hastily improvised fuse had declined to ignite, or the results might have been serious. The unpopular head of the college—anticipating the statesmen of the present day—had secured the services of one of the Proctor's satellites to act as private detective and keep watch and ward through a strongly-barred window which commanded a view of the quadrangle; but just after 'hall,' an undergraduate sent a bottle of soda-water—which he had concealed under his gown—whizzing through one of the panes with such deadly effect that the affrighted 'bull-dog' gave notice on the spot.

The following morning Mr. Geoffrey and three of the ringleaders were summoned to appear before the authorities, and this time his gold tassel proved powerless to avert the sentence of expulsion which was passed upon the whole party. This was all the more aggravating as my master had really been reading hard for his degree, which he would probably have taken in the course of the next few days. In the meanwhile he took rooms at an hotel to wait until Mr. Blount heard the result of his examination, and as soon as the name of the latter appeared in the lists, the two gentlemen started for Devonshire, while I was left behind to pack up everything and bring the horses down by road.

It was during this same term that I obtained leave to attend my cousin Vester's great fight with the second best man in England, which he won after a most sensational battle in fifty-eight minutes. I should very much like to give the details, but I am informed that, nowadays, prize-fighting is considered a brutal and degrading sport, so, for once, I will refrain.*

As may be imagined, the news of his son's expulsion from Camford was a severe blow to Sir George; but, like a sensible man, he endeavoured to make the best of it. He had always intended that his eldest son should go into Parliament, but his plans were upset for the present, and at a cabinet council consisting of the baronet, Father Massy, and Passon Mark —for the clergyman and the priest were the best of friends— it was determined that my young master should be sent on a prolonged foreign tour, in the course of which he would have an opportunity afforded him of seeing life outside the narrow limits of continental society.

It was arranged that Mr. Paul L'Estrange—a bachelor of wandering habits and the second son of Mr. Adrian L'Estrange of Georgetown, Demerara—should be asked to undertake the duties of bear-leader, a post for which his

* This reticence is highly characteristic of the author's modesty, the fact being that—*teste* Mr. Cecil Blount—having obtained two days leave of absence, Loveridge borrowed a suit of his master's best clothes and stayed away for a week, finally making his way back to Camford on foot in a very dilapidated condition, *plus* a black eye, and *minus* his watch and chain.—ED.

varied experience of travelling and comprehensive knowledge of foreign languages admirably qualified him. Mr. Geoffrey at first flatly refused to leave England, as he did not want to miss a season's hunting, and it was not until old Mr. Blount had been persuaded to allow his son to accompany him that the expedition was finally fixed for the autumn of the same year.

As my young master intimated to me pretty plainly that he should expect me to accompany him upon his travels, I felt that I could scarcely refuse to do so; but during the past few months I had been very busy with my day-dreams, and the new arrangements completely knocked all my little plans on the head. It must be remembered that time had not been standing still, and I was now thirty years of age, and as I was not likely to get any younger, I had determined to marry and settle down with the girl of my choice, cost what it might. With this object in view I had long had my eye upon the snug berth of stud-groom at Netherleigh—then occupied by old Dan Hurley, who was crippled with the rheumatics and would have been only too glad to retire with a small pension—with its comfortable cottage and liberal salary, and I knew that I could count on Mr. Sealy's influence to secure me the situation as soon as it should become vacant.

It may, therefore, be imagined how utterly my plans for the future were upset by the contemplated expedition, which was fixed for October. I at once wrote to Mantis, urging her to try for the last time to obtain her relatives' consent to our immediate marriage—for although we intended to dispense with it if necessary, I preferred to be on decent terms with my future brothers-in-law, with whom I had already had more than one passage-at-arms. In the affectionate but, truth to tell, somewhat unintelligible missive which I received in reply, she assured me that it would be worse than useless to mention the subject again to her mother or brothers, but added that she had an old aunt living in the suburbs of Plymouth who had always been very fond of her, and upon whose secrecy we might rely—finally suggesting that we should be privately married in that town. Under the circumstances it was exactly what I should have proposed myself, so, having applied for a fortnight's leave on pretext of saying 'Good-bye' to my relations near Bridgwater, I travelled down to Plymouth as fast as the mail could carry me, and was there introduced to her aunt, Genty Lovell, who, finding that although for years a *kerengro*,* I could still *rokker* the *pooro jib ferreder* † than most of her nephews, received me with open arms.

One fine morning, towards the middle of September, Mantis and I were quietly married before the registrar, and having obtained an extension of my leave on some pretext or another, we passed as happy a honeymoon by the peaceful waters of the land-locked harbour as often falls to the lot of sinful mortals—be they gentle or simple. But time and tide wait for no man, and as my leave expired on October 1st, I tore myself away from the arms of my young wife, and mounted the Exeter coach somewhat cheered by the reflection that if things turned out luckily, we should at all events meet once more before I sailed.

My master and Mr. Cecil Blount—both of whom knew the Continent by heart—were anxious to forsake the beaten track of the tourist. Now Sir George's cousin, Mr. Adrian L'Estrange, owned a large estate near Georgetown, Demerara, in which Sir George had formerly held a half share which, upon his accession to the Netherleigh property on the death of his father, Sir Pierre, he had made over to his cousin, who was a comparatively poor man. It was therefore arranged that the party—consisting of Mr. Paul L'Estrange, my young master, Mr. Cecil Blount, and your humble servant—should sail in one of the West Indian mail-boats, and that after visiting Barbardoes, British Guiana, and the West Indian Islands, we should make our way back *viâ* the United States and Canada.

Mr. Blount had just returned from a visit to Touraine, where he had enjoyed some fine sport with the boar and the wolf, and as Mr. Paul L'Estrange was to join us at Plymouth, Mantis had arranged to stay with her aunt in order to see the last of me at the old seaport.

It must have been about the third week in October that the Netherleigh drag started for Exeter with a full load, consisting of the baronet himself, old Mr. Blount of Stowe, his son Mr. Cecil, Passon Mark, Mr. Geoffrey, and myself,

---

* House-dweller.   † Talk the old language better.

together with some of the lighter luggage — the heavy baggage having been sent on by carrier. The parson had volunteered to accompany the travellers as far as Plymouth, but Sir George and old Mr. Blount were to return with the drag, after seeing us fairly started on the Plymouth coach at Exeter the next morning.

We slept that night at the New London Hotel, and as it had been blowing a tremendous hurricane and raining in torrents, in consequence of which the mails were sure to be several hours late, Ward determined to start without them. After a rather affecting farewell from the two old gentlemen, the rest of the party mounted the Plymouth coach. The coachmen nodded to the ostlers, who whisked the loin-cloths off the horses and sprang away from the leaders' heads, the guard sounded a few cheery notes on his horn, and off we started at a merry pace down the street and over the bridge at the bottom of the hill.

It was a lovely bright morning after the storm, and the sun shone out as hot as in July, causing the nags to lather profusely as they collared the ascent to Haldon racecourse. On either side of the road the steep fern-covered banks of ruddy sandstone were honeycombed with rabbit-burrows, and every now and again a pheasant who had been drying his plumage in the warm rays, would rise with a 'whirr' and sail away across the adjoining stubble. On reaching Cobbett's Oak Hill we were met by a couple of trace-horses, and most of the passengers got down to walk, for the almost perpendicular ascent was seamed and furrowed with a hundred tiny watercourses which raced merrily down; the flints and gravel had been washed up into ridges, and a regular torrent had overflowed the gutters on either side—crossing and recrossing the roadway at frequent intervals, and hollowing out for itself a deep channel where the white froth was still lying in glistening patches.

So far we had been sheltered by the wooded heights of Haldon, but on reaching the moor above we saw that the outlines of Dartmoor were veiled in cloud and mist, and the strong southerly gale took us full in the face, and gave us a foretaste of what was in store for us. As we emerged into the open country the effects of the heavy storm were very apparent—trees, hay-stacks, chimney-pots, and sign-boards lying in profusion throughout the whole length of our route. On reaching Plymouth we found that Mr. Paul L'Estrange had not turned up at the hotel, and pending his arrival my masters—as I shall still continue to call them—were lionised over the old seaport by some friends of theirs in the 29th Regiment—which was stationed at the St. George's Square Barracks—while I very soon found my way to the lodgings which Mantis had taken.

Mr. Paul L'Estrange arrived on the following day, and was soon on the best of terms with everybody. He was a tall, spare-built, dried-up-looking man of about five-and-thirty, with a bronzed skin and a long, drooping moustache, which, combined with his lively manner and slight French accent often caused him to be mistaken for a foreigner. He proved a great acquisition, and by his amusing conversation and anecdotes contrived to keep up the spirits of his companions—who were rather depressed at leaving England—and from the moment of his joining us at Plymouth, until he left us in Demerara, he was the life and soul of the party and a universal favourite on board ship.

Upon my telling Mr. Geoffrey—who was a most indulgent master, though apt to be short-tempered at times—that I had some relations living in Plymouth, he dispensed with my attendance until everything was ready for a start, and in the society of my wife I spent two happy days, the perfect enjoyment of which was only marred by the knowledge that I might be required to start at any moment. At last the dreaded summons arrived, so handing over to Mantis some money which I had drawn from my small deposit with Mr. Sealy, and which was more than sufficient for her requirements, I bade her a sorrowful 'farewell,' and left her to the care of kind-hearted old Genty Lovell, with whom I made arrangements for forwarding any letters from abroad.

Passon Mark and some of the officers of the 29th Regiment accompanied my masters to the office at Devonport, where we mounted the Falmouth coach and in less than ten minutes found ourselves crossing the steam-ferry. Our four blood-tits, all mettle at starting, entered the boat without the slightest fear or hesitation, and at the sound of "As you were" from Charley Symonds, they halted with military precision, never moving a muscle until we reached the Cornwall side of the stream—passing close under the stern of the Admiral's flagship, the *Adelaide*, which presented a beautiful picture, for the moon shining out from behind the heavy banks of night-clouds, caused every spar and shroud to stand out in high relief against the pitchy darkness of the background.

We put up at the Royal Hotel, Falmouth. Next day was very stormy, with a heavy gale from the west accompanied by a high sea and thunderstorms at intervals. The captain of H.M.S. *Skylark*—in which vessel our passages had been taken—sent in to inform my masters that he should start next morning, blow high or blow low—and start we did, worse luck, passing a rough night beating down Channel. It was my first experience of life on board ship, and during the agonies of sea-sickness I would have given my very soul to exchange my narrow, close-smelling berth for a bed of damp heather under the bleakest boulder on Cranmoor—for, like the majority of my people, I was but a *chuvveni berengro* and hated the *lun-pawni*.*

The following morning everybody was awakened by a loud crash overhead, which brought all the able-bodied passengers on deck in a trice. It appeared that we had shipped a very heavy sea, which broke fore and aft on the deck. It made a clean breach through our starboard quarter, knocking the helmsman down and breaking his head. Not content with this, it snapped several heavy timbers and the fly-wheel short off, and washed the binnacle and compass, log-lines, log-glass, lamp-shades, eight hammocks, and the *Skylark* signals, smack through the larboard quarter berthing.

It would have required a good deal more than this to have fetched me out of my berth, where I lay and felt like death; but the following day I managed to crawl on deck, and was surprised at the extent of the mischief—nearly the whole of our starboard bulwarks had been carried away, while the hole in the larboard quarter through which the binnacle had been driven looked exactly as if it had been done by a cannon-ball. The sea was running mountains high, and the wind began to blow a hurricane at midnight—in fact, I think those four days we spent in the Bay of Biscay were the very worst of my life.

* Poor sailor and hated the salt-water.

Owing to bad weather and variable winds it took us a fortnight to run 1,300 miles; but at last the sailors told us that we were within 80 miles of Teneriffe, and about noon we sighted the Grand Canary under a dense haze. Towards evening the haze began to clear away, and on our lee quarter we had a splendid view of the Grand Canary, while right ahead of us was the lofty peak of Teneriffe with a glorious sun setting behind it. The passengers continued to gaze at the beautiful scene until dark, and then returned to their wine and drank 'absent friends' in a bumper; but coffee was hardly served before their joy was turned to sorrow by the doctor, who reported the death of the lieutenant. Within forty-eight hours his remains had been consigned to the deep, upon which he had passed twenty-seven years of his life without promotion.

The next to fall ill was Mr. G——, a great friend of my masters', who was attacked with violent pains in the stomach. Having tried every sort of remedy without success, the doctor—who thought very badly of his case from the first—proceeded to take several ounces of blood from him and applied a strong blister, while I was told off to look after him.

An evening or two later the poor gentleman sent me to the captain and obtained his permission to bury him in Barbadoes if possible, and then remarked to me, as I was lighting a candle:—"Samson, I shall never live to see that candle burn out." As my master and Mr. Blount were going down the companion about one in the morning, he caught sight of them and called them in. "God bless you" —he said; "see what frail creatures we are—near death even in the midst of life. Wish everybody 'Good-bye' for me. We shall meet again, I hope." He continued in this pitiable state till daylight, when it pleased God to put an end to his sufferings. The captain called the passengers on deck to consult as to the disposal of the body, when it was ascertained that there was not sufficient rum on board to preserve it until we reached Barbadoes. There was no alternative, therefore, but to commit the remains to the deep, and his funeral was over within six hours of the breath leaving his body.

The captain, who had been very bad, seemed to grow

worse instead of better, and evidently entertained but little hope of his own recovery, for he ordered the master to throw him overboard in the event of his death, instead of taking him to Barbadoes. He came on deck for a few minutes, but although he bore his sufferings wonderfully well—being of tougher material than poor Mr. G—— was made of—his eyes looked like lead and he was obliged to turn in again, and, shortly after, the doctor reported him delirious.

At last, after a rather eventful and disastrous voyage of thirty-four days, we cast anchor off Bridgetown, Barbadoes, alongside H.M.S. *Seringpatam* and *Crocodile*, and were immediately surrounded by boats full of black ladies and gentlemen; but the only one allowed on board was Black Betty—according to report an old flame of the captain's—who took us ashore in the *Billy Ruffin* and showed us the way to Hannah Lewis'.

My masters, being well supplied with introductions, spent most of their time in visiting the different estates in the neighbourhood, and as I was anxious to see everything that was to be seen, they generally managed to find room for me in most of their expeditions during their stay in the West Indies.

I took an opportunity of visiting the celebrated Betsy Austin, the landlady of the Clarence Hotel, and one of the best known characters on the island—her description of the hurricane which had devasted the island a few years previously* was well worth listening to.

The officers of the 52nd Regiment were very hospitable, and my masters dined with them frequently, while the General fixed a day in order to enable them to witness a review of the Black Mutineers. These men had been captured just a year previously on board a slaver off the African coast by one of H.M. cruisers, and having been taken to Trinidad, were drilled into soldiers. No sooner had they been entrusted with arms, than they listened to the persuasions of one of their native princes—a gigantic negro, six foot six in height, named Dâaga—who disclosed a plan for capturing their officers, and promised to lead them back to their own land. Accordingly, they one night rose in a body,

* 1831.

seized upon some casks of ammunition—most of which was, luckily, blank—and proceeded to fire on their officers. The alarm was raised, and after a desperate struggle they were all captured. Three of the ringleaders were shot and the rest, by the General's orders, were brought to Barbadoes and formed into companies. A few months before the review, they did not even know their own names, but each man wore round his neck a metal label upon which his adopted name and number were marked in plain figures. They were all tattoed according to their rank in their own country, the big swells being scarred all over their faces, but their drill would not have discredited any British soldiers who had been the same time in the ranks.

Yellow Fever was very bad at the time, and although life was pleasant enough, a man might be eating a hearty dinner at 7 p.m. and in his grave within twelve hours. My master was very queer one day, but hot brandy and water and the usual remedies brought him round, but four of his friends died during our stay, including another of the passengers.

This was a Mr. B—— from G—nb—y, in Somerset, who had been sent out by his relations in a dying state without any introductions, and owing to his sickly appearance he had been refused admission to the hotels, and had been forced to take up his quarters at a very disreputable house. My master had visited him several times, but as Mr. Geoffrey was ill, he sent me down to look after his effects. Upon going up to his room, I found it in possession of half-a-dozen Yankee skippers, who were dancing the Kentucky reel—the great thing appearing to be for each man to give his partner as heavy a fall as possible, and either their heads must have been as hard as cocoa-nuts, or the floor uncommonly soft. The coffin containing Mr. B——'s body had been placed on a table and pushed into a corner, and on it there sat a hideous, white-haired old nigger, who was scraping away at a fiddle, and beating time with his foot, causing the grog-glasses to slop over. I was made to pledge the skippers in a glass of grog, and made my escape, thinking myself lucky to get off so easily.

One morning the packet from England was signalled, and having shipped all our traps, bedding, etc., we went on board the *Pluto*, bound for Demerara—the steam was up,

"All hands up anchor!" and as the shades of evening began to close in we rapidly left Barbadoes far astern.

Being Christmas Eve, the sailors had a flare-up in the galley and a regular spree—a fiddle and drum was mustered and dancing and singing kept up till a late hour, with "Three cheers for absent friends and a merry Christmas to them!"

We made a quick run to Demerara and anchored off Georgetown, the water changing from blue to yellow as we approached the land, until it finally attained the peasoup-like consistency of the Bristol Channel. We put up at the Victoria, and the following morning Mr. Adrian L'Estrange's manager arrived with carriages to take us out to Buonavista. Mr. Paul L'Estrange introduced his cousin and Mr. Blount to his father—a fine old gentleman with a ruddy complexion and flowing white locks—and a large party sat down to dinner, which was served in magnificent style, as I was bound to admit, and afterwards sat up to see the old year out.

We spent several days at Buonavista and then started for El Dorado—another estate which Mr. L'Estrange owned on the further side of the Essiquibo—as the manager was ill and Mr. Paul had to undertake his duties *pro tem*. As the gentlemen intended to make an expedition up the Pomaroon, they laid in a stock of provisions, seltzer-water, hammocks, etc., in Georgetown, and embarking on board the smart schooner *Maria*, Captain Jack, we ran quickly down to the Essiquibo, and having spent a couple of days at a fine estate on Leguan Island, crossed the broad estuary of the Essiquibo and landed at the El Dorado estate.

The gentlemen were longing to commence their expedition up the Pomaroon, where they expected to get some shooting, so a large *conial*, or canoe, was got ready, and the whole party started in her, propelled by twelve nigger paddlers, and followed by another canoe containing provisions, baggage, etc. Before proceeding far we met two *conials* full of Indians, perfectly naked and the wildest-looking lot of devils I ever set eyes upon—I should just have liked my old Granny to have seen them. The expedition lasted a week, and during it we visited several encampments of Buck Indians. They seemed a very idle and contented set of people, and were of middle height and a dark bronzy-red in colour, with glossy black hair, deep chests, and extremely small feet and hands. They possessed a great many *cassava* grounds, which they planted at different times of the year, thus ensuring a succession of crops.

CHAPTER XXV.

A Cruise among the Windward Islands.

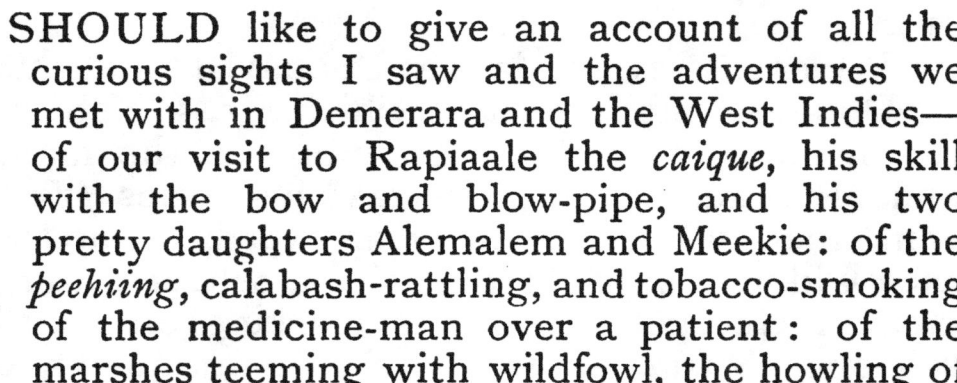

I SHOULD like to give an account of all the curious sights I saw and the adventures we met with in Demerara and the West Indies—of our visit to Rapiaale the *caique*, his skill with the bow and blow-pipe, and his two pretty daughters Alemalem and Meekie: of the *peehiing*, calabash-rattling, and tobacco-smoking of the medicine-man over a patient: of the marshes teeming with wildfowl, the howling of the baboons in the forest at night, and the splendid magnolias which bordered the lagoons and scented the air: of the queer sayings and doings of the plantation negroes, and their superstitious belief in the power of Obi. Of these and many other things I should like to tell you, but Dr. Carew says that it has all been done over and over again, so I must stick to my own story instead, merely relating one or two little incidents which I hope may prove of interest.

The negroes who paddled our *conial* were as sulky and lazy as possible on the outward journey, but as soon as their heads were turned towards their stable they became very lively, larking and singing in chorus all the way, and keeping time with their paddles.

The following may be taken as a sample of the verses:—

> Ginger-beer and brandy, oh!
> Brandy come from Lunnon, oh!
> Ginger-beer he berry good cheer,
> But brandy come from Lunnon, oh!

> De Cap'en he say I shan't go ashore,
>   I shan't go ashore for to spend my mon-ey.
> I don't care a d—n what de Cap'en say;
> I don't care a d—n what de Matey say;
>   But I will go ashore for to spend my mon-ey.
>   Hurrah, boys, hurrah!

> Rose, Rose, coal-black Rose,
> I wish I may be jiggered if I don't love Rose.
>   I went into de garden for to get some thyme,
>   De watchman he come an he strike me be-hine;
> Rosey, Rosey, Rosey, Sambo come,
> Listen to de banjo, tum tum, tum!

It didn't matter what the words were as long as they went with a swing, for they could do nothing without making a noise of some sort.

During the last day but one of our return voyage Mr. Geoffrey was attacked with fever, and appeared completely prostrated by the short walk from the boat up to the planter's house where we were to pass the night. Mr. Paul L'Estrange had been compelled to return earlier in the day to the El Dorado estate, and as Mr. Blount had accompanied him, I felt that I was placed in a very responsible position.

I sent off at once for the nearest doctor, who administered calomel and took several ounces of blood, but my master continued very ill all day and night. Next morning he was much worse, and as the doctor did not inspire me with confidence, I determined to get him back to El Dorado at all hazards, and with the assistance of five stout niggers I managed to get him down stairs and into a conveyance.

The responsibility of moving my master in his then exhausted condition was a very serious one for me to assume, but I felt that everything depended upon getting him back to the coast, where he would enjoy the advantages of good nursing and an experienced doctor. Nothing but strong salts kept him going during the drive, and upon our arrival at the manager's house all life and sensation appeared to have left his body. Rallying a little when we had got him to bed, he bade 'Good-bye' to all of us—as we thought, for ever—and immediately after he was seized with spasmodic convulsions of the limbs, the legs were drawn up towards the body, the hands were clenched, and the sight failed entirely.

He continued in this alarming condition for some time, when it pleased God to restore him to us, and to arrest the hand of Death in its descent. With the help of restoratives he gradually acquired bodily sensation, and the doctor—who gratified me by saying that if my master had remained by the river another twelve hours, no power on earth could have saved him—administered a strong dose of opium and calomel and applied a blister to the back. The fever continued for several days, but the crisis was passed and the attacks diminished in intensity, and aided by quinine his strength came back to him by degrees, but it was quite a fortnight before he was fit to be moved to Georgetown.

During his recovery the gentlemen amused themselves by making experiments with the deadly *woorali* and blow-pipes—which they procured from the Indians—upon fowls and pigs, and in nearly every instance a wound proved fatal within ten minutes of the poison entering the circulation.

At length we re-embarked on board the schooner *Maria*, bound for Georgetown, and on the return voyage Captain Jack as near as possible sent us to the bottom in the Parika Channel of the Essequibo. We had been sailing in company of two other schooners, and I was in the act of opening a bottle of Madeira in the cabin, when the little vessel suddenly heeled over and 'crash' went all the loose crockery—a white squall had struck the *Maria* and she was on her beam ends in a moment.

As the water came pouring down the hatchway, my masters rushed on deck and I was not far behind them, as I strongly objected to being drowned in the cabin like a rat in a drain-pipe. The little schooner was lying gunwale under with the waves pouring and racing over her decks. The crew were endeavouring to take in the foresail, and to make matters worse the chain-cable, which had been coiled amidships, had rolled into the lee-scuppers and prevented her from righting. The captain was entirely to blame, as he refused to take the hint, although he must have seen the two other schooners—who were racing with us—shorten sail. The squall was followed by a dense sea-fog accompanied by rain, and although it was quite impossible to see our course by the buoys placed to warn vessels off the numerous sand-banks, the pig-headed brute of a skipper refused to lay-to and drop anchor, and when the mist cleared away, the *Maria*—having twice missed stays—was not fifty yards from one of the banks which, as the wind was then blowing, would have reduced the little craft to lucifer matches in about two hours.

As soon as the next packet arrived from Barbadoes, my masters took leave of their host and his family—Mr. Paul having remained at El Dorado—and we went on board our old friend the *Pluto*, bound for Grenada, our course lying past the rugged outlines of the Tobagos. We anchored in St. George's Bay and had a run ashore, and then went on to Kingston Bay, St. Vincent, where we stayed for several days with a friend of Mr. Adrian L'Estrange's named McLeod. The chief event of our visit to St. Vincent was an expedition to a volcanic mountain called the Soufrière, some 4,000 feet high, and here Mr. Blount had rather a near squeak. As we were going along a narrow ledge on the face of a precipice, Mr. McLeod gave his horse—a valuable stallion—to his servant to lead behind him, when the animal happening to tread on the nigger's projecting heel, the latter gave him a job in the mouth with the bit to keep him back. The high-mettled beast instantly reared, the edge of the precipice crumbled away beneath his feet, and over he went. The nigger held on to the reins like grim death, while the poor beast clung to the ledge with his fore feet. His struggles were dreadful. when, suddenly, the bridle slipped over his ears and he disappeared into the abyss below. The path was too narrow to turn, and Mr. Blount was riding close behind. His horse becoming frightened, reared up and tried to turn, but Mr. Cecil, quickly shifting his whip into his left hand, struck him across the nose on the near side and just managed to keep him straight. He was in a very critical position for a moment or two, but, luckily for him, his nerve was pretty good. I should mention that during our stay the lady of the house, her son, a man-servant, and—before we left—Mr.

McLeod himself were all seized with yellow fever. The man-servant died and some of the other cases were very severe.

We left Kingstown in a small sloop bound for Martinique, and tripping our anchor, rounded Fort Charlotte in style, but were soon becalmed off a dangerous reef called the Bottle and Glass. Near this place is a precipitous cliff some four hundred feet high, crowned by a solitary white cedar. To this gruesome spot—so the story goes—a Carib chief enticed his wife, whom he had reason to suspect of infidelity, and attempted to push her over the cliff, but the good lady —mindful, possibly, of the impressive words of the Marriage Service—exhibited at this critical juncture an attachment which, to say the least of it, was both ill-timed and highly inconvenient, and clinging closely round her husband's neck, dragged him after her into the surf which boiled and leaped four hundred feet below—where they no doubt proved a very acceptable addition to the *menu* of the sharks with which the place abounds. We lay there becalmed several hours, watching the surf break against the base of the beetling cliff, and I remember that the story made a deep impression upon me at the time.

The calm changed to a gale, which soon raised a heavy sea, and the obstinate brute of a captain refused to put back, although the *Swallow* was a very crank craft, with a mainsail big enough for a ten-gun brig and a crew of four men and a boy, only one of whom knew a rope's end from a round of beef. We ran gunwale-under to St. Lucia, and then stretched across to Martinique, clearing the island of St. Lucia about dusk.

We anchored off St. Pierre, Martinique, and it was beautiful to witness the day breaking over this exquisite scene. The town was hushed in deepest repose, but soon the gentle 'tinkle, tinkle' of a bell stole across the slumbering waters, while, shortly after, from the distant hum of human voices, it was evident that the business of the day had commenced in earnest. Two or three boats containing fishermen crept out from beneath the shadow of the trees and proceeded to describe a large semi-circle, dropping their nets as they went. After presenting their letters of introduction, my masters hired a boat, and we visited the ruins of Port Royal, the late capital of Martinique, which had been destroyed by an earthquake the previous month.

We stayed several days at St. Pierre, and then went on board the schooner *Royal Adelaide*, bound for Dominica. As we were weighing anchor, Captain Kirk pointed out to my masters the American Consul rowing towards the *Astrée* frigate in the roadstead, and told them that he wanted to make him pay the wages of a Yankee sailor whom he had engaged for a certain period, but who now wanted to leave before serving his time—for this reason he wished to clear the Bay before the Consul reached the French frigate. We therefore crowded on all sail, but had not gone a couple of miles before we saw a wreath of white smoke, followed by a flash from the upper deck of the frigate, while an eighteen pounder came skimming along and ploughed up the water about a hundred yards astern. Johnny Crapaud no doubt thought that this would have the effect of bringing us to, but with the Union Jack at our peak and a light breeze off the land, we only laughed at him and sang out:—"Good shot, Johnny, but put in some straighter powder next time!"

It soon became apparent to him that we were cracking on without any intention of lying to, and 'Bang, bang!' came two more shots from the frigate, which both fell a long way astern on our larboard quarter, and Johnny, finding his long eighteens too short for us, sent the long-boat and pinnace in pursuit. On they came, with twelve rowers in each, but we had still good hopes of escaping. All went well for some miles, but off the Pearl Rock it fell a dead calm. In vain the skipper whistled for a breeze and put the ship about, but not a breath of wind could we catch, and the long-boat, straining every nerve, came up hand over hand.

The excitement was glorious, and reminded me of smuggling and poaching days, and I would have given a year's wages for just one shot at the officer in the long-boat. As soon as they got within range, two marines, one on each side of the mast, began peppering away at us with their muskets, and our skipper, seeing that escape was out of the question, put back the top-gallant sail and lay-to for them.

Directly they came alongside, two marines, armed with muskets and fixed bayonets, boarded us. The officer in command could not speak a word of English, or our skipper French, so Mr. Blount was called upon to act as interpreter. The officer said that his orders were to bring the schooner alongside the French frigate, to which Mr. Cecil replied that as we had no arms we surrendered, but that if the officer wanted to take the schooner back, he must work her with his own men. The officer agreeing to this, within three hours we were lying at anchor under the *Astrée's* guns. After a long palaver, in which it was decided that the captain should pay the Yankee seaman's wages and that the American Consul should settle the bill for powder and shot, we weighed anchor again, and once more stood out into the roadstead, bound for Roseau, Dominica.

We stayed there some days, visiting several estates and another sulphur mountain, and then left Dominica in the brig *Helen*, bound for Porto Rico. The brig had formerly been in the Guinea trade, and under the name of the *Don Francisco* had put many a guinea into her owner's pocket. But one fine day the *Don* had the misfortune to come across a cruiser named the *Griffin*, commanded by Lieutenant D'Urban. The slaver had four feet of water in her hold, in addition to five hundred negroes of the Onago tribe, which must have handicapped her considerably. The *Don*, however, possessed the knack of going and led the *Griffin* a regular stern chase, but, as the leak increased, the cruiser came up hand over hand and fired into her—upon which a terrible yell arose from the lower deck, plainly indicating the nature of her cargo. She was eventually captured and taken into Roseau, where the slaves were distributed amongst the neighbouring estates.

We made a splendid run from Dominica, and the gallant old slaver—she was by far the fastest vessel I ever set foot upon, and gave one the pleasant 'feel' of a seasoned hunter after riding a lot of green youngsters—cleared the ugly reefs to the north of St. Thomas before dark.

We made Porto Rico next morning, but were not allowed to set foot within the strongly fortified walls until the inquisitive Custom House officials had examined our papers and every single thing we possessed. The roofs of the houses were flat, with balconies to the first floors, where the dark-eyed *senoras* and *senoritas* sat in the evening, arrayed in full dress, to attract the admiration of the loungers on their way to the Promenade.

The gentlemen made several excursions into the interior, visiting different sugar plantations, and we witnessed some strange sights; amongst others a magnificent procession called the *Ecce Homo*, when the levity of the priests shocked even me, and evidently made a deep impression upon Mr. Geoffrey—Roman Catholic though he was—which his Protestant friend, Mr. Blount, did his best to confirm. Near the tail of the procession stalked a celebrated brown-skinned, bare-legged *padre*,* with flashing black eyes and a rope round his waist, who appeared to be the idol of the populace. His admirers—especially among the fair sex—had been in the habit of surreptitiously snipping off and appropriating portions of his skirt, after much the same fashion as I have seen the crowd endeavour to pull hairs out of the tail of a popular race-horse—the result being that his nether integument no longer served the purpose for which it was originally designed, and would most certainly have attracted the attention of the Lord Chamberlain at home.

At this point, either because I happened to grin, or because I did not feel called upon to go down on my marrow-bones, my enjoyment of the spectacle was somewhat marred by a burly Spaniard 'bonneting' me from behind, and by the time I had practically demonstrated the superiority of the Protestant layman militant, the procession had entered the Franciscan Church, and I was ignominiously dragged off, amidst the jeers of the populace, to the *stardo*—from which I was with difficulty rescued by the active intervention of the American Consul,† who was a friend of my masters'.

Having obtained the permission of the Commandant, our party visited the fortifications, and, following the ramparts, came to the city burial-ground—one of the most miserable places imaginable. The Spaniards lay their dead on the surface of the ground under brick arches, and as soon as the process of decomposition is complete, the head of the arch is knocked in and the corpse ejected, while the coffin, grave-clothes, etc., become the perquisite of the sexton—a plan which, although undoubtedly economical of space, has its objections, and would scarcely

* Castellar.   † John O. Bradford, Esq., U.S.A. Consul, Porto Rico.

recommend itself to the favourable consideration of the Sanitary Authorities at home.

Just inside the entrance-gates of the cemetery were several large heaps of skulls and other remnants of mortality, the flesh and portions of the grave-clothes still adhering to many of the bones, which had been summarily ejected from the coffin after a few weeks' sepulture in order to make room for fresh customers—the relatives of the deceased having failed to pay up the arrears of rent due for the vault. The grave-digger himself—a negro—exactly resembled a huge sexton-beetle, and dwelt in a tumble-down shanty constructed entirely of coffins and fitted up *en suite* with the same materials—one coffin serving for his bed, another for his wardrobe, and others for different purposes. We found him engaged in the apparently congenial occupation of routing out old coffins, sorting the contents, and making a bonfire of the cere-cloths, bones, etc., and as my master remarked to Mr. Blount, "He would have given the grave-digger in Hamlet two stone, and then have lost him." We did not stay long in that cemetery.

One morning I walked out to the ramparts before breakfast to witness the execution of a real, live buccaneer. The gentlemen would not go, as they thought it would spoil their appetite, and I should not recommend the spectacle to anybody with a weak stomach—especially so early in the day. The man was the captain of a desperate gang of pirates which infested these seas, and confessed to no less than fifty-two separate murders—which struck me as being a large order, even for a gentleman in the wholesale line of business. He had once set fire to the town of St. Thomas, and had twice been condemned to death—escaping both times by bribing the officer of the guard.

The Government then set a high price on his head and circulated descriptions of his person throughout the island, drawing especial attention to a white mark on his right hand, which had been caused by a musket-ball in some sea-fight. The crafty rascal, knowing that this conspicuous mark must sooner or later lead to his identification, went off to Paris, where he placed himself in the hands of a skilful practitioner, who performed an operation which effectually obliterated all traces of the scar. He then returned, like a giant refreshed, to the scene of his former exploits, and continued to carry on his rather irregular pursuits up to the time of his arrest.

The whole town made a holiday of it, and turned out *en gala* to witness the execution of this notorious Barabbas —a dark-skinned, dandified, devil-may-care sort of gentleman of the genuine penny-plain-twopence-coloured stamp. He had received a cutlass wound on the forehead, and a red bandana was knotted round his head to conceal the bandages, while the heavy gold earrings, the embroidered shirt of the finest possible linen—very open at the throat, so as to show the muscular, sunburnt neck and chest—the loose velveteen trousers with their rows of silver buttons from knee to ankle, the broad scarlet sash wound round the waist, and the small shoes with their heavy silver buckles, completed a costume which brought back to my mind the heroes of the penny-dreadfuls which I used to pore over in my mother's *vardo* by the light of a farthing dip. As, strongly guarded, he walked with a jaunty step from the castle to the ramparts, the priests who surrounded him kept holding up their crucifixes before his eyes, but, taking no notice of them whatever, he stopped every now and again to light a fresh cigarette or drink a glass of grog at the expense of his numerous admirers, and I noticed that more than one laced handkerchief was waved to him from the balconies as we passed beneath—a compliment which he returned by placing his hand on that portion of his anatomy were his heart should have been, and bowing, while he showed his white teeth in a self-satisfied grin.

Arrived at the place of execution, he sauntered round the fatal chair and examined the instrument with which he was about to be garroted with the air of a *connaisseur* —pushing aside the priests, who continued to hold up their crucifixes before his eyes. The scaffold, which was raised some four feet above the level of the ground, was about twelve feet square. The stool upon which the culprit is seated was placed at the base of a stout upright post, from which, at the level of the criminal's neck, an iron collar projected, while a sharp-pointed steel screw, propelled by a powerful lever, passed horizontally through the post, on a level with the collar.

Hitherto the bright-coloured, picturesque crowd of onlookers—consisting, for the most part, of women—had been laughing, chatting, smoking cigarettes, and eating fruit and sweetmeats in the best of tempers, just like the pit and gallery of a theatre at home; but already the national craving for blood was beginning to take possession of them, and as they surged round the scaffold the heat became intense, and the soldiers had the greatest difficulty in pushing them back with their muskets.

With the exception of the principal actor, everybody appeared to be in a great state of excitement, as a rumour had been industriously circulated to the effect that the soldiers had been bribed, and that a desperate attempt would be made to rescue the pirate at the last minute. Having obtained the permission of the officer in command—who, like everyone else, was puffing away at a cigar—he proceeded to make his last dying speech and confession, which ran as follows:—

"If I have injured any man here present, I hope he forgives me, as I forgive everybody. The man who betrayed me, I raised from beggary to affluence, and he was base enough to place me in the Morro, from whence I have twice escaped, and I should not be in this chair, about to end my life in such a cowardly manner, had I possessed more than three doubloons when arrested. Adieu!"

A very handsome quadroon girl, who was standing with some other women in the front rank of spectators, tried to force her way through the *cordon* of soldiers, but was thrust roughly back. At the word 'Adieu!' she uttered a piercing shriek, and fell back, apparently lifeless. He was a bloodthirsty monster, no doubt, but I could not help admiring the pirate's composure at that supreme moment. Deliberately seating himself upon the stool, he leaned calmly back, as if about to be shaved, and a moment later was securely bound to the post and his neck encircled by the fatal collar. In accordance with the traditions of his calling, the brawny ruffian who officiated as executioner leaned over him and begged his victim's forgiveness in a low tone, while the priests held up their crucifixes and continued to mutter prayers for the repose of his soul.

At this juncture a considerable disturbance, accompanied

by scuffling, jostling, and shouting, arose on the outskirts of the vast crowd; but I was unable to ascertain the cause of it. The soldiers on that side of the square faced right-about, and raising their muskets, prepared for action. The crowd surged to and fro: men cursed and women fainted: the officer in command, anticipating a rescue, threw away his cigar and waved his sword, which glittered in the bright morning sun: the executioner seized the lever-handle and gave it a couple of quick turns: the sharp-pointed screw pierced the spinal cord, and the pirate's career came to an abrupt conclusion.

The show was over and the crowd dispersed in the best of humours, the men smoking, the women chatting and laughing, and the children playing about, and half an hour later nothing remained to mark the scene of the recent tragedy, save the roughly-constructed scaffold and a small heap of blood-stained sawdust.

* * * * * *

My masters had secured passages on board the *Water-witch* for Baltimore, and having laid in a good stock of provisions, we went on board on April 1st, just as the anchor was catted. For more then a fortnight we made scarcely any progress on account of the variable winds and calms, but at length the monotony of the voyage was varied by a heavy gale from the S.W., which raised a tremendous sea and obliged us to lay-to under a close-reefed main-topsail, with the waves running as high as the yard-arms. For seven days—during which we were mostly hove-to in the Gulf of Florida—the gale continued and the sea ran mountains high, and to add to our misfortunes the brig sprang a leak which required continual labour at the pumps to keep under.

We were more than three weeks making the passage, but at length we heard the welcome sound of "Land oh!"—"Where away?"—"Two points on the weather bow!"—and were soon bowling up Chesapeake Bay to the tune of eight knots an hour. The alarm-bells were ringing from every steeple, and several houses in the West-end of Baltimore were blazing away merrily—but this, we were told, was an everyday occurrence in Yankee-land. Our game little brig made the best of her way up the Chesapeake, and by sunset we were off Annapolis, the capital of Maryland.

We only remained two days in Baltimore, starting for Washington from the Baltimore Railway Office. To prevent accidents, steam-engines were forbidden in the city, and each carriage was drawn by four splendid grey horses with flowing manes and tails. The team attached to our carriage was the finest I ever saw in any public conveyance in any country, each horse standing over sixteen hands, with plenty of blood and bone, and good action. About two miles outside the city the engines were attached, and in little more than two hours we found ourselves in Washington, where we put up at Gadsby's Hotel.

Next morning Mr. Blount paid a visit to the President,* and after a stay of two or three days we went on to Philadelphia, putting up at the Tremont House Hotel. We remained here for a fortnight or more, and a very pleasant place it was, and then travelled by river and railway to New York, stopping on the way at Bourdington, on the right bank of the Delaware, as Mr. Blount wanted to pay a visit to some nobleman whose acquaintance he had made while staying with his relations in France.

* * * * * *

"† Here the majority of the passengers take the train, and a one-horse car drops us at the small hamlet of Bourdington, in New Jersey. Leaving our baggage at the hotel, I take G—'s arm, and we follow the banks of the Delaware until we reach a large gate. No sooner do we enter, than I catch sight of two figures, one of which resembles the object of my search, but they are so hard at work that it seems scarcely credible, so, to make assurance doubly sure, I post myself behind a tree and take a quiet survey. The elder of the two appears to be about sixty-five years of age, has a florid complexion, and wears a suit of mourning and

* Mr. Van Buren.
† The remainder of the chapter consists of an extract from Mr. Blount's Diary—kindly placed at my disposal by the Squire of Stowe—describing a visit to Joseph Buonaparte, ex-King of Spain, then living at Point Breeze under the title of Comte de Survilliers.

stout shoes. Armed with a hatchet, he is now lopping away at a branch—now directing some workmen who are levelling a bank near the river. The other figure is that of a man of about five-and-forty, who is also of a florid complexion, wears a shooting-coat of English cut, and is chatting with his companion."

"I have no longer any doubt, for I have seen the well-known eye, and fearing to be caught skulking, I advance straight towards him reverently, hat in hand."

"For a moment or two he looks me over, evidently failing to recognise my face, and then advancing a couple of steps, he gives me his hand cordially, and says:—'*C'est bien Monsieur Blount?*'"

"I congratulate him sincerely upon his good looks, and assure him that the three years which have elapsed since we met have made him younger—and, as I speak, I retain his hand, which I would fain have kissed."

"You start? But I can tell you that better men than I have kissed this hand in byegone days on bended knee—for this man has been a king. 'Tis Joseph Buonaparte, who, with his hatchet in his hand, is far happier beneath his reverse of fortune than he was ever likely to have been whilst surrounded by the nobles and court of Spain. I inform him that I am not come to make a stay, and that I have only three hours in which to see him and his park, and with much difficulty insist upon not interrupting him. Seeing that I am determined, he makes us over to his secretary's son, saying:—'You have all the keys. Drive *ces Messieurs* round the park, and we will meet at the house.'"

"The park contains about 10,000 acres in a ring-fence, and is well laid out. The ex-King's farms look better than those of his neighbours', and there are decoys and plantations well stocked with game, which afford great amusement to the Count, who is a crack shot. I must not forget to mention a place already made famous by the pen of Cooper. Here, formerly, stood the Indian town of Delaware, and on this very spot those interesting characters, Hawk-Eye, Le Gros Serpent, and Le Cerf Agile, wandered in all the unconstrained freedom of nature."

"Time being short, we return to the house, and I regret

that my haste will not permit me thoroughly to enjoy the fine pictures and busts which fill the long suite of apartments. I pause, however, between two sea-pieces by Vernet, to steal a glance at the beautiful profile of a young lady seated upon a sofa, who is playing with a Blenheim spaniel. Who could view the face, the eyes, the expression, without tracing in his niece's features the lineaments of Napoleon?"

"Hurrying from the house, we run against the Count. '*Pas si vite!*' he exclaims, looking at his watch, 'you have not half seen my house yet. You shall, at least, drink a glass of wine with me, and my English coachman shall drive you back.'"

"This, of course, proved irresistible, and the kind-hearted ex-King showed us every room in the house. In an ante-room near his bedroom he paused before a bust, and pointing towards it, said:—'*Vous le connaissez, n'est ce pas? C'est O'M—r—a. Vous rappelez bien O'M—r—a, et vous voyez que je n'oublie pas mes amis Anglais en Amerique.*'"

"Descending to the north dining-room, we were introduced to the fair lady, and to those of the household with whom I was not previously acquainted. In this room is a full length of Napoleon in his imperial robes, by David. Under this picture we drank together a glass of excellent Madeira, and it was with feelings of the deepest respect that I bade the genial ex-King '*Adieu.*'"

"As we drove off in the well-appointed carriage, I watched him until we turned the corner, and then gave myself up to a train of thought, drawing a parallel between his brother's fate and his own, until we pulled up at Bourdington."*

* The party then travelled on to New York, where Loveridge resumes the thread of his story.

CHAPTER XXVI.

A Chapter of my Life which may very well be Skipped.

I HAVE now brought you to as far as New York, but in so doing I have unavoidably got rather ahead of my story, and before going any further I must ask you to return with me to the Tremont House, Philadelphia, where I will introduce you to two individuals—one of which was destined to exercise considerable influence over my future career: the other, in a lesser degree, over that of my master.

There are few better places for studying character than the public saloons of a large Transatlantic hotel, and had I been a lady novelist in search of a hero, I might have found one all ready-made to order—taking him at his own valuation—in the person of Bill Johnson, the Canadian rebel, who occupied the room next to Mr. Geoffrey. This gentleman modestly styled himself 'the Hero of a Thousand Isles,' and was a rather fine-looking man of about fifty years of age, with a sunburnt face, aquiline features, iron-grey hair, and short side-whiskers—and if his prowess in the field was in any way commensurate with his performance with his knife and fork, he must needs have proved a very formidable antagonist.

However, I had plenty to occupy me, now that we had got back to town life, without hunting about for possible heroes and heroines, although one of the individuals to whom I have alluded might, at a pinch, have been made to do duty for the latter. This was a certain Mrs. Guldenstein, the widow of a rich German Jew who had made his fortune on Wall Street. The late lamented—so report said—had managed to run up a pretty considerable pile, which—according to the same unimpeachable authority—his relict was endeavouring, with some success, to knock down. This, as I had afterwards ample opportunities of ascertaining, was very far from being correct, for the widow had a head on her pretty shoulders, and during her calmer moments must have been a fairly good match for her worthy spouse. When I first saw her at Tremont House, she was a remarkably handsome woman of close on thirty years of age. She wore her dark hair rather short and parted on one side, which, although it gave her a slightly masculine appearance, at the same time harmonised well with her rather defiant style of beauty—but her eyes were her strong point, being large and lustrous and full of expression.

Mrs. Guldenstein's father had belonged to one of the oldest and most respected families in Virginia, but, unfortunately for his daughter, he lost his life in one of those sanguinary encounters which were then of frequent occurrence in the Southern States. The landed-property went to the sons, and within two years of her father's death Louise Carson—then a schoolgirl of little more than sixteen—had eloped from her brother's house with a handsome but good-for-nothing gambler named Laroche, whose fascinating manners and reckless disposition appealed, all too strongly, to the young girl's wayward and romantic temperament.

Laroche belonged to the large and rapidly-increasing class of professional gamblers who were already beginning to acquire a questionable notoriety in the Western towns, and who infested the river-boats on the Mississippi and Missouri. Upon the death of her father Miss Carson came into a considerable sum of ready-money, and, as long as that lasted, her husband appears to have treated her fairly well. His marriage seemed to have changed the luck of the broken-down 'sport,' and during the three years of their wedded life Madame Laroche had comparatively little to complain of. But at length the spell was broken: her small fortune went the way of the rest, and her husband began to display his true colours, but before his indifference had time to degenerate into downright brutality, a stray bullet put an end to his career.

Feeling ashamed to return to her home in Virginia, the young widow went to stay with some friends at St. Louis, where she made the acquaintance of her second husband who was 'bossing' a Government contract in the neighbourhood. After a very brief and formal courtship, Louise Laroche exchanged her name for the more prosaic one of Guldenstein, and shortly afterwards returned to his sumptuous house in Maddison Square, New York.

Although her predilection for the romantic had received a rather severe check, her restless disposition prevented her from settling down quietly for any length of time, and feigning a desire to visit her husband's native land—old Guldenstein had started in life as a *dégraisseur*, or renovator of old hats, in the Juden-gasse, Frankfort—the lively lady dragged her spouse from New York to Paris, from Paris to Vienna, from Vienna to Berlin, and from Berlin to London. They took up their residence in the latter city for a couple of years, and it was here that she acquired the pronounced Anglomania which manifested itself in the tailor-made, London-cut habits, and the well-appointed turn-out with its English groom, which were the admiration of all beholders. After seven years of domestic felicity, old Guldenstein started in search of the Lost Tribes, and his place on Wall Street knew him no more, but previous to taking his departure from this world of sorrow, he made a will by which he left nearly the whole of his large fortune to his widow—taking care, however, to tie it up pretty tightly.

Mrs. Guldenstein was a wonderful woman for animals. She was in the habit of breaking her horses herself, and of making them go through all sorts of performances, after the manner of Mr. Rarey. Her house was always full of cats, dogs, and pets of every description, while the stables and outbuildings contained a collection of hopping, creeping, and climbing live-stock which, in my humble opinion, would have been much happier in their native wilds or a zoological-garden.

My masters had made her acquaintance at the Tremont House, and occasionally accompanied her for morning rides along the winding Wissahickon or for pleasant evening drives through what is now Fairmount Park, and on their departure for New York Mrs. Guldenstein had recommended them to a certain hotel in Fifth Avenue—adding that they might very possibly meet again before their departure for Canada.

I have been particular in giving a full account of the widow's antecedents, as it would have been necessary to do so sooner or later, and I will now proceed to give a short description of another, and less agreeable, character, who was also residing at the Tremont House. This was an individual of the name of Oscar Jansen, better known to his acquaintances—for friends he had none—as 'the Baron,' and described in the hotel-clerk's book as 'Baron Oscar Jansen, Two Services' Club, St. Jermyn's, London, England.' He was a stoutly-built, purple-cheeked, coarse-looking man of middle age and height, with a confident bearing and a self-satisfied air; small, restless eyes of a dark hazel, and dyed hair and moustaches—which latter were carefully waxed to a point *à la militaire*. A Cockney by birth and a town-dweller by predilection, he was always scrupulously dressed, and never appeared so much at his ease as when arrayed in a well-cut frock-coat and a glossy silk hat with the true Stock-Exchange polish, which fairly took the shine out of the Wall Street crowd—in fact, I should very much doubt if he possessed such a garment as a shooting-coat or had ever in his life put on a pair of breeches and gaiters.

Notwithstanding his foreign-sounding appellation, he was, as I have stated, an Englishman by birth, and had once held a commission in a line regiment, which he had been compelled to resign under circumstances not altogether creditable to himself. Nobody seemed to know whether he had any legitimate claim to the title of Baron, which was understood to have been acquired by him in return for certain services—the exact nature of which did not transpire—rendered to some petty Teutonic potentate, and in nine cases out of ten it was bestowed in jest rather than in earnest. Whenever, for purposes of his own, he wished to produce an impression, he was wont to sport a small green-and-yellow ribbon in his button-hole, which was said by the maliciously-inclined amongst his acquaintances—and there were plenty of them—to represent the most Honourable Order of the Sack and Boot, which the aforesaid potentate had been graciously pleased to confer upon him. To give the devil his due, I never knew him to lay serious claim to the title, nor was it engraved upon his visiting-cards, but it looked well in a prospectus, and was to be found amongst the list of directors of the Dead Sharp Claim—which speculation he was then engaged in financing—and of other undertakings of a similar nature nearer home.

Although there might be some doubt about his patent of nobility, there was none whatever as to his being an extremely shrewd man of the world, and as I suspected from the first —and had, afterwards, ample opportunities of verifying—he was one of the most plausible and finished scoundrels I ever came across in the course of a pretty varied experience, and his valet, George Wilson, ran him pretty close.

On the occasion of a lady—who was stopping in the hotel—laying claim to a little Spanish lap-dog which Mr. Blount had brought from Porto Rico, the Baron came forward and kindly offered to vouch for the respectability of his friends—as he was pleased to call them. Mr. Blount declined to avail himself of his good offices, leaving his defence entirely to Prudina who, seated on his knee, treated the advances of her *soi-disant* mistress with superlative contempt, and trotted out of the room after him to the confusion of the blushing fair one. Having managed to scrape acquaintance with my masters, he spared no pains to make himself agreeable, and ended by returning to England in the same boat. Mr. Geoffrey was of a most frank and unsuspicious disposition, but Mr. Blount—who was a year or two older—had seen more of the world, and advised my master, from the first, to have nothing to do with the plausible Baron.

We reached New York about the middle of May, and took up our residence at a fine hotel in that—to my mind— much overrated thoroughfare, Fifth Avenue, which, at that period, was paved with badly-pitched cobble-stones which rendered carriage exercise a torture rather than a pleasure. The thermometer averaged 90° in the shade, and most of the fashionable people had left the city and were disporting themselves at the seaside.

One of the things which struck me most was the primitive and unconstrained fashion in which the occupiers of some of the best houses lounged about the entrance in full evening costume, or sat upon the front-door steps, where they gossiped and chatted far into the night, enjoying the cool breeze. My masters were well provided with introductions, and although the season was practically over, there were still plenty of picnics and excursions, which, with occasional drives behind a pair of fast trotters, dinner-parties, and theatres, enabled them to get through the time pleasantly enough; but at last they grew tired of the heat and bustle, and we made a move to a certain favourite seaside resort, where we found the fashionable portion of New York society disporting itself on the long sandy beach and well-kept lawns.

So far, nothing more had been seen or heard of Mrs. Guldenstein; but we had scarcely settled down in the comfortable hotel, with its low, gabled roof and spacious, creeper-covered verandahs, before I saw her English groom drive in with a pair of trotting-horses, followed by a lad in charge of her hacks, and the following day the widow herself arrived with her pretty Creole maid, Virginie.

Before going any further, I should like it to be understood that it is altogether contrary to my wishes that the record of the events of the next twelve months finds a place in these pages. As yet I had done nothing that I need be ashamed to relate, and, if I had my own way, I should prefer to maintain the good character which I had hitherto borne, but Dr. Carew reminds me that as I have assumed the *rôle* of conscientious autobiographer, the evil must find place with the good.

I should mention that, since our arrival in America, my masters—who were very keen on sport in any shape or form—had taken a lively interest in the splendid trotting-horses which were to be seen to perfection on the various tracks in the neighbourhood of Baltimore, New York, and Philadelphia. While staying at the latter place they had made the acquaintance of most of the principal owners and breeders of trotting-stock, and at Baltimore they had seen the prince of American riders and trainers*—then a young man of about three-and-twenty—mounted on the grand old bay Dutchman, beat the well-known performer Harry Bluff, and the flying Lady Suffolk. Mrs. Guldenstein had accompanied them upon a visit to J. Hammil's establishment near Philadelphia, and it turned out that, after our departure, she purchased a couple of smartish trotters from him, that had made some fair records over the Hunting Park Course. She

---

* Hiram Woodruff

had ordered a light, hooded Boston waggon to be built for them, and harnessed to this racing-looking vehicle, the gallant browns, Rifleman and President, made their first appearance on Atlantic Avenue, which, at certain hours of the day, was thronged with smartly-dressed people and elegant equipages of every description.

That it was a pretty tony outfit was the general verdict, and a small crowd of idlers assembled opposite Acacia Cottage to witness the start. Mrs. Guldenstein, neatly dressed after our English fashion and wearing a pair of workmanlike dog-skin driving-gloves, climbed into the crank-looking vehicle and took the reins from the groom, and the horses, although evidently not much used to pole-work, started off quietly enough, and gradually settling into their stroke, went up the Avenue at something better than a 3.40 gait—but, as they warmed to their work, the pace increased, and the fair charioteer soon made the unpleasant discovery that she was powerless to check their onward career. Like most American horses who have trotted in public, they were fair pullers—especially President, who was a plucky customer—and the more you pulled at them, the more they took hold of you. The groom then assumed the ribbons, but with no better result. The horses, who seemed bent on beating the clock, sped past the hotel, where the loungers were smoking and sipping iced-drinks: past the picturesque frame-houses with their shady verandahs, where the ladies sat working, reading, and gossiping in their rocking-chairs: past the trimly-kept lawns, where the young people abandoned their games at the tramp of the flying hoofs and the rattle of the wheels: past the groups of well-dressed people on the Promenade, who, ostensibly listening to the band, were in reality getting through a very creditable amount of quiet flirtation.

They had, luckily, just cleared the Avenue, when Rifleman shied violently, carrying his companion off the track, and both horses, breaking badly, started off at a gallop along the sandy, shell-strewn beach. Under the circumstances this was just about the best thing that could have happened, but, unfortunately, they dashed into a soft place where a patch of yielding, sand-covered mud formed a sort of quagmire, and after two or three frantic plunges to regain their footing, the terrified animals landed on their heads, snapping the pole, upsetting the waggon, and causing the light spider-wheels and fancy ironwork to assume the appearance of a coil of lead-piping which has been carelessly thrown on one side by the plumber.

Mrs. Guldenstein was luckily pitched clear of the wreck, and, scrambling to her feet, she at once ran to the horses, who had succeeded in floundering out of the quicksand and stood, trembling and sweating, with the remains of the pole dangling between them—but the unfortunate groom had dropped into the thick of the scrimmage, and looked a pitiable object, as, pale and mud-bespattered, he picked himself up and hobbled off to his mistress, with the blood trickling from an ugly cut on the head, his wrist badly sprained, and all the starch taken out of his immaculate collar and choker.

I happened to be stolling along the Avenue at the time, and guessing that the breakaway would result in a smash, I jumped into a hack and drove along the Beach Road as fast as the surly, ill-conditioned brute of a driver could be persuaded to go. By the time I reached the scene of the accident a crowd of loafers had assembled, some of whom were staring at the groom as if he were some newly-discovered and highly interesting specimen of the *genus homo*, while others were holding an informal inquest on the body of the Boston waggon, whose mangled remains lay strewn about the beach.

I at once proceeded to place the hack at Mrs. Guldenstein's disposal, assisted the half-dazed groom to disentangle the horses from the broken harness, and made arrangements for having the remnants of the waggon conveyed to the livery-stables, and the widow—who was profuse in her thanks—started back to town in the hack, after requesting me to call at her villa on my way home to let her know whether either of the horses had sustained any serious injury.

Later on, I accompanied the horses back to their stable, and having stitched up a cut, which the impetuous President had received, with a piece of galvanized wire off a soda-water bottle, I made my way to Acacia Cottage, and was conducted by Virginie to the dining-room, where I found the widow—attired in a loose white wrapper of some airy-looking fabric, in which were twisted a few bows of yellow ribbon—smoking a cigarette after dinner surrounded by her pets, and looking as cool and collected as if she had just returned from a quiet stroll on the Avenue—the only trace of the recent accident being a bruise which, half hidden by the dark, closely-curling hair, discoloured the white skin of the forehead.

At each corner of the table, seated upon their respective mats of gaily-coloured worsted, were four large cats, two of which were white Angoras, and the others sleepy-eyed, long-coated Persians. A rose-crested cockatoo was whittling away at the top-rail of her chair and sidling restlesstly up and down after the manner of his kind, and a tiny marmoset—a sort of a cross between a squirrel, a lizard, and a monkey—nestled on her shoulder and made ugly faces at the intruder. A Persian greyhound, like a consumptive Scotch deerhound with a silky blue and white coat and a long, tufted tail, shared the hearth-rug with a brindled bull-dog of the most approved British pattern, whilst a number of Perso-Angoric kittens skirmished around and made things generally lively.

Mrs. Guldenstein insisted upon my taking a glass of wine, and appeared relieved when I told her that the horses had received no injuries beyond a few cuts, which only required a little dressing and attention. She kept me talking about twenty minutes, and although it may seem an unpardonable piece of presumption upon my part to take any notice of a lady's appearance, it must be remembered that neither the men or the women of my race are notorious for diffidence, and I must confess that I left the Cottage very much impressed by the personal charms and fascinating manners of the lively widow.

A few days afterwards Mrs. Guldenstein begged my master to give her some advice about ordering some new harness, bits, etc., and as the subject was one with which he had little practical acquaintance—never having been in the habit of troubling himself about stable details—he offered to send me down to the Cottage to give her the benefit of my experience. As soon as I had taken a good look round, I began by telling her that it was no use for her to keep her present groom—who was a drunken, incapable rascal—and, with her permission, I engaged a steady, respectable man, who had not served his apprenticeship under Peter Whelan without learning something about trotting-horses, to take his place as soon as disengaged. I took an opportunity of running up to New York to order the necessary harness, and at the same time succeeded in procuring some mouthing and curb bits, bearing and side reins, and breaking-tackle, and before long I managed to get some sort of a mouth on the young horses, who soon began to come nicely to hand. Like most American-bred animals, they were tractable enough if you took them the right way, and had been taught to slow-down at the word of command, and only needed a little bitting and pulling-about to make a very smart pair. In place of the ill-fated Boston waggon, I picked up a light, second-hand, English-built phaeton which, like Mr. Campbell's landau at Georgetown, was to be sold a bargain—and for the same reason—and as soon as the horses began to bend their necks a little and settle down quietly to their work, I used, in the absence of her groom, to accompany the widow in her drives, and under my tuition she soon began to recover her nerve, which had been a bit shaken by the accident.

One thing led to another, and during the next few weeks, without any premeditation on my part, I was brought into daily contact with Mrs. Guldenstein, and as our intimacy increased, it became impossible for me to shut my eyes to the fact that I was rapidly acquiring an influence over her wayward and impulsive nature, which the semi-confidential relations that accident had established between us afforded exceptional opportunities of establishing.

Things went on comfortably enough for some time—as long as I had plenty to eat and drink and not too much work to do, it was always good enough for me—until I made the discovery that my feelings for Mrs. Guldenstein were becoming a good deal warmer than my position warranted, even if I had not been a married man—but perhaps the less I say on this subject the better, as it can scarcely be any pleasanter for gentlefolk to read than for me to write. It is only fair to myself to state that, up to this time, the idea of endeavouring to gain the affections of the handsome widow had never seriously presented itself, and if, by degrees, I allowed my allegiance to my wife to waver, it must be taken into consideration that Mrs. Guldenstein possessed charms both of person and manner calculated to turn a cooler head and drown the voice of a better-regulated conscience than mine. Idleness is, indeed, a fruitful source of mischief both with men and horses, and if there had been plenty of work to keep me occupied, it is probable that I should have continued quietly in my master's service, but during the hot weather the gentlemen were continually 'excurting' about the country, visiting the different seaside resorts or attending trotting-matches on the Beacon, Centreville, and other courses—the result being that I was left with a good deal of spare time on my hands, and got a bit above myself in consequence.

One morning, as I was leaving Acacia Cottage, where I had been with a note from my master, I was joined by Virginie—Mrs. Guldenstein's maid—who informed me that she was going into the town to do some marketing, and it struck me at the time as rather odd that, instead of leaving the house by the back entrance, she walked with me boldly past the front-windows, from whence I knew that her mistress would have a full view of her proceedings. As we strolled along the broad Avenue, past the enclosures where the birds were singing merrily amongst the peach-orchards, the Creole began to banter me about my intimacy with her mistress, then, suddenly changing her tone, she turned and faced me:—

"*Dites donc, M'sieu Sanson*"—she began, "you will tell me, *hein*, that you are so *aveugle*—what you call it, blind ?—not to see that it only depends of yourself whether you return to that *triste pays de la brume éternelle*, or whether you remain in this glorious land of liberty—*riche, hereux, et comblé de bienfaits?*"—with a good deal more to the same effect. She went on to say that she had good reason to believe that her mistress was sick to death of the trammels and restrictions of fashionable society, and longed to exchange the oppressive atmosphere of the large towns for the free and unfettered life which she had led with her first husband.

Virginie, herself, had been born and bred near Savannah,

Georgia. Her vivid imagination drew a highly-coloured picture of life in the Southern States, and although I pretended, at the time, to treat the whole thing as a joke and passed it off with a bit of chaff, her words made a deep impression on me. I have no wish to make myself out any better than I am, but it should be remembered that I was still a comparatively young man, that my brain was heated and my pulses quickened by the glowing warmth of a semi-tropical sun, that for the last few months I had been leading a life which was fast unsuiting me for the dull routine of my regular employment—and last, but not least, that since the day I had taken leave of Mantis at Plymouth, I had not received a single line in reply to the many letters which I had sent her.

Had it not been for my cursed habit of keeping things dark, it would, no doubt, have transpired that I was a married man, and all the trouble would have been avoided. But however that might have been, Virginie's suggestions opened up an entirely new prospect to me—the seed had fallen upon fertile soil, and matters were shortly after brought to a crisis by the arrival of unexpected and unwelcome news from England.

My master was now, for the first time, really beginning to shake off the effects of his severe attack of fever, and it had been arranged that, as soon as his health had been thoroughly established, we should start for Montreal, and that after spending the autumn and winter in Canada, we should return to England in the spring by way of Quebec.

It was about the middle of July, and we had just returned from a trip to New York, after witnessing the wonderful performance of Dutchman over the Centreville Course, when that good horse, ably driven by Woodruff, travelled the three miles in the then unprecedented time of 7.41. Upon opening the letters which were waiting for him at the hotel, my master found that one of them contained an urgent summons to return to England. It was from Mr. Sealy, and stated that the health of his old friend, Sir George, which for some time had been giving cause for anxiety, had completely broken down. That he had more than once been found by the servants in a semi-unconscious state, and had repeatedly alluded to the absence of his eldest son.

That as soon as his health appeared to be restored for the time being, he had begged him—Mr. Sealy—not to interfere with his son's evident enjoyment of his travels by informing him of his condition, but that in view of what he considered to be the serious state of the case, he had, in defiance of his old friend's wishes, taken upon himself the responsibility of informing my master of the unsatisfactory state of affairs at Netherleigh.

Under the circumstances there remained, of course, only one thing to be done, and Mr. Blount decided to abandon his projected trip to Canada, and to return with my master by the next mail-boat—which started the following week. It may, therefore, be imagined how completely my half-formed schemes appeared to be nipped in the bud by this sudden change of plans. Since my conversation with Virginie I had endeavoured—and not unsuccessfully—to harden my heart to the voice of conscience and the promptings of my better nature, and it was in no very amiable frame of mind that I set about making the necessary preparations for our departure. But next morning, as luck would have it, on my way back from my swim before breakfast, who should I run against but Virginie, on her way to market with her basket on her arm. As I walked beside her, she lost no time in informing me that Mrs. Guldenstein was very much upset by the news, and that she had been sitting up with her mistress, who was in a highly nervous and excited state, which, she assured me, was entirely owing to my approaching departure, and, as if to confirm her statements, later in the day I received a note from her mistress requesting me to call at Acacia Cottage, as she wished to make me some acknowledgment for the trouble I had been put to, and required my advice upon different matters connected with her stables, etc., etc.

Now, whatever my faults may have been, slowness at taking a hint was never one of them, and as I made my way to the Cottage that evening, I determined that if matters were as I had reason to believe them to be, and the opportunity should present itself, I would not leave it save as its future master. It is not necessary, nor would it be expedient for me to give a detailed account of the interview which followed—suffice it to say that as Virginie let me out at the little wicket at the end of the trimly-kept lawn, I experienced no unpleasant qualms of conscience, and after thanking her for her good offices and receiving her congratulations, I returned to the hotel in a high state of elation, and proceeded to put the finishing touches to the packing in a very different frame of mind to that in which I had commenced it.

It had been arranged between us that I was to say nothing to Mr. Geoffrey until we reached New York, and it was with very mixed feelings that I made my way to his room on the following Monday, prepared to make a—comparatively—clean breast of it, and to ask him to dispense with my services in the future. I had always been blessed with a very average amount of assurance—or, as some might say, impudence—but I needed it all at this moment, and it was a long time before I could screw up my courage to knock at his door. My master's was one of those open, unsuspicious natures which to know is to love, and although I was prepared to brazen it out if he cut up rough, I must confess that for the first time since I entered his service, I felt regularly ashamed to look him in the face. I believe that if, instead of giving his consent to my remaining in the States, he had called me an impudent rascal and told me to pack up my traps and go aboard, I should have been thankful for an excuse for backing out at the last minute—although, at the same time, it is quite on the cards that I mightn't have obeyed him.

I need hardly say that he was completely taken aback at the news, but suppressing the astonishment which he was unable to conceal—probably out of deference to my feelings—he congratulated me heartily upon what he was pleased to term my good luck, and rushed off to Mr. Blount with the news. The latter gentlemen, as I have told you, had seen a good deal more of the world than my master, and, consequently, took a far less rose-coloured view of the situation. He proceeded to put the common-sense aspect of the case very plainly before me, warning me of the unhappiness which so frequently attends the union of two persons of unequal social status, and reminding me that although the widow possessed undoubted attractions both of purse and person, she had, nevertheless, a violent temper which showed itself on the slightest provocation. He put it all before me in the kindest possible manner and with a due regard for my feelings—which may very possibly appear, under the circumstances, to have been a work of supererogation—but finding that my mind was evidently made up, he wished me the best of luck and joined my master in making me a handsome present, in order to enable me, as far, at least, as outward appearance went, to meet the widow as much as possible on equal terms.

The following morning I accompanied my late master on board the steamboat—the accommodation being very different to that provided aboard the floating palaces which now make the trip in six days, so bad, in fact, that many people preferred to take their passages on board a sailing-vessel—and as I scrambled down the side of the liner and took my place in the pilot-boat in which I was to return from Sandy Hook, I felt that I had indeed cast off the last link which connected me with the old country. As the big vessel began to forge slowly ahead, I noticed the purple cheeks and dyed moustaches of 'Baron' Jansen amongst the crowd of faces which lined the taffrail, and I felt glad that Mr. Blount had decided to accompany my master back to England.

* * * * * *

The least said, the soonest mended. A few weeks later I went through the form of marriage with Mrs. Guldenstein in the quiet little town of Flemington, Huntingdon County, New Jersey, where some distant relations of the widow's were living.

CHAPTER XXVII.

Two Dreams and their Consequences.*

FROM New Orleans we worked northwards to Montgomery, by way of the Alabama River, and so on to Savannah, where I amused myself as best I could by riding about the country, shooting snipe in the rice-fields, and getting laid up with a sharp attack of feverish ague. The streets, many of which were bordered by rows of fine live-oak trees, were little better than sand-tracks, the only attempt at a roadway—of which the inhabitants were excessively proud—which led to the cemetery of Bonaventura, being composed entirely of oyster shells. Some of the houses, which were built of red sandstone, were handsome edifices, and the whole town, with its enclosed plots of grass and fine avenues of magnolias and live oaks, reminded me strongly of the old country.

I had by this time had some experience of the life for which, as a boy, I had so ardently longed, and I must confess that it had not altogether come up to my expectations. I could not help noticing that whenever we came across any of my countrymen or the better class of Americans, they seemed to regard me with a certain amount of suspicion, and although America is, of all countries, the one where a man who has risen from the ranks might reasonably expect to escape notice, I soon found out that any civilities which I might receive were purchased with Mrs. Guldenstein's

---

* In accordance with the author's desire, I have omitted his description of his life in the States. Suffice it to say, that after having what he terms a 'high old time' of it in New York, Saratoga, Boston, and other places, he passed several weeks on a plantation belonging to a relation of Mrs. Guldenstein's, near Baton Rouge, on the Mississippi, and then made his way to New Orleans with the intention of returning to New York.—ED.

money, and I had on more than one occasion been asked by my own countrymen whether I had not some Gipsy blood in my veins—which insinuation I had indignantly repudiated, accounting for my dark complexion by saying that my mother had been a Spaniard.

But besides being subjected to these and similar annoyances—the natural consequence of the false position I occupied—I had had my fling and was beginning to get home-sick. I contrasted the heat and glare and the ceaseless rush and struggle after the almighty dollar, with the cool grey skies, the rugged moorlands, and the green pastures of the old country, and I longed once more to hear the cry of the hounds and to see Passon Mark, mounted upon a rough-coated four-year-old, topping a razor-backed bank. I was bad enough—goodness knows!—and I experienced but little compunction at having deceived Mrs. Guldenstein, but the fact was that I had acted upon the impulse of the moment and was beginning to see the mistake I had made. Luckily for me, the three restraining influences which always exercised a more or less direct control over my life and actions, although for some time in abeyance, were beginning to re-assert themselves, and these were, firstly, a feeling of respect and affection for my kind friend the Parson of Netherleigh: secondly, one of gratitude to Sir George and his family: the third, and the strongest—believe it who may in the face of all that had passed—an overwhelming desire to see Mantis once more and, if possible, obtain her forgiveness.

These thoughts of the old country were awakened, in a great measure, by a vivid dream which I will attempt to describe. I dreamed that I was mounted on one of those high-priced hunters of Sitwell's upon which my poor father used to ride out to visit us at the cottage near Camford in the old days. In place of the sandy roads and the low-lying rice-swamps of Savannah, a large tract of undulating country, intersected by stone walls, extended in every direction as far as the eye could reach. A few isolated clumps of trees were dotted about, which, from the respectable distance apart at which they stood, looked as if they partook of the cold nature of the soil in which they grew, and had quarrelled with one another. Upon these trees not a leaf remained, and, with the exception of a patch of gorse of about three acres and a half, enclosed by a four-foot stone wall, scarcely a scrap of verdure was to be seen.

On one side of this enclosure was a roadway. On the further side of this, again, was a small homestead—which was occupied by numerous grooms with led-horses—and towards this roadway and homestead figures in red coats were converging from all points of the compass, and galloping as if their very lives depended on a minute. One line of road was so completely filled with pinks and bits of blood as to present the appearance of a line of Hussars on the march.

Where on earth could I be? Surely I was not at Old Farm—the hour 10.30 a.m. and the cavalry regiment nothing more or less than a strong contingent of Camfordians, who had done the twenty-two miles in something under an hour and a half. The riders arrived at the homestead quite out of breath, but in a brace of shakes they were on their fresh horses, and the smoking hacks and mud-bespattered overalls consigned to the tender mercies of the cads—who gave their charges two-penn'orth of beans apiece and then made out a bill of fifteen shillings for corn, hay, turnpikes, etc.

Outside the homestead is a snug paddock where gentlemen's servants are walking good-looking horses up and down, and amongst others I recognise Mr. Geoffrey, who is leading my second horse and touches his hat respectfully to me as I ride up, while old Gehazi—who is always as lively as a kitten at a meet—is doing his level best to unship Mr. Blount, having taken advantage of an unguarded moment when that gentleman is endeavouring to light a cigar.

Here are three stout gentlemen in black, with merry, round faces, and in that corner a thin, aristocratic-looking man in an old pink and high collar, is making over his hack to a well-fed groom in a chocolate-coloured coat with yellow facings. There is a business-like look about this individual—who is whistling 'A southerly wind and a cloudy sky,' while his groom places a pair of woollen gloves beneath the saddle-flaps in case of rain—which contrasts strongly with the flurry and excitement of the young bloods in the homestead. The latter mount and concentrate upon a piece of rising ground in the roadway, and amongst them are at least a hundred faces which appear to me just as distinct in this vision of the night as they were wont to do in the flesh.

Here sits the Flying Captain, and there, the centre of a group of country gentlemen, appears a florid, cheery face, always beaming with a smile. It is Lord C——l, mounted on a square-shaped bay well up to twenty stone. He is tapping his boot with his whip, and saying something pleasant to everybody—what a jovial scene!

> Here the covert-hacks smoke, while so joyous and gay
>   The shake of the hand goes around,
> And, the overalls off, Messrs. Martin and Day,
>   As usual, transparent are found.
>
> Here Jem H——, the huntsman, points Oppidan out,
>   For perfection of legs, feet, and head:
> While the rest of the puppies come crowding about,
>   And snatch at his "mossels o' bread."

At this moment a quiet-looking gentleman in a black coat—who, by the deference paid to him by the younger sportsmen, would appear to be the master of the pack—after casting a glance to windward, pulls out his watch and orders the hounds, who have been anxiously longing to jump the wall, to be put into the gorse. A gamekeeper, in orthodox velveteens and leather leggings, opens the gate and allows the huntsman and hounds to pass—then, leaning his gun against the wall, proceeds to seat himself upon the top rail. Three or four gentleman are exhausting all their powers of persuasion in a vain endeavour to keep the youthful Nimrods in their proper places, but, in spite of their efforts, some of the young bloods push on determined to see the fox break. A whip is stationed at the further corner of the covert, and his well-trained horse seems scarcely to breathe for fear of heading the fox—a silent but forcible protest against the unruly behaviour of the impetuous spirits behind.

In the meanwhile the gorse shakes again. A well-known note proclaims that Reynard is at home, and Jem, standing up in his stirrups, gives one 'tootle' on his horn and shouts out in musical tones:—"'Ave at 'im there! Yoi Hoppidan, good 'ound! 'Ave at 'im there!"

The hounds all respond to the cheer. The whip at the corner is seen to hold up his cap, and three or four minutes later he screws his thumb into his right ear, and with a scream which inspires terror in the heart of the flying varmint—who, by now, is nearly a mile ahead—sings out:—" Tally-ho! Tally-ho!"

As Jem tops the wall, he makes a piteous appeal to the better feelings of the young gents who are jostling and thrusting their way to the front:—

"For Gawd's sake, gentlemen, give 'em a fair start"—he implores, and then, seeing that by this time every hound has settled down to the scent, he turns round in his saddle and shouting derisively:—" Now ketch 'em and be d———d to ye"—assumes the lead, closely followed by some two hundred in red, whom he experiences but little difficulty in shaking off during the first fifteen minutes, and when the hounds throw-up at a sheep-pen after a sharp burst at best pace, he finds himself alone with the Flying Captain, two swells from Cheltenham, a spare-built gentleman on a well-bred bay with grey hairs in his mane and tail, two or three hard-riding squires, and an equal number of Camfordians—amongst whom the tall figure of Mr. Blount is conspicuous—who have ridden like good men and true throughout and were well placed when hounds checked.

My nag had been skimming over the stone walls like a bird on the wing, without ever putting a foot wrong—as horses have a knack of doing in dreams—but at the sudden check I woke up with a start, and, jumping out of bed, satisfied myself by a peep through the Venetians that it was nothing but a dream after all.

I can only suppose that my digestion—usually pretty good—must have been upset by the habit I had acquired of bolting my food in imitation of my neighbours in the dining-saloon, or, perhaps, by the ague from which I had been suffering, for, a day or two later, I had another dream, the horrors of which are still so vividly imprinted upon the tablets of my mental vision, that even now, when I instinctively feel that the first phases of that awful nightmare are about to recur, the very terror which it inspires enables my dormant faculties to free themselves from the bonds of sleep, and as I start into a sitting position and wipe away the beads which have begun to gather on my forehead, it is an unspeakable relief to see the dull, grey light of early morning stealing through the heavy bars, and to know that some thousands of miles separate me from that dread abyss where the everlasting surf is booming and leaping beneath the fierce rays of a tropical sun.

I dreamed that I was lying idly stretched upon the slippery, sunburnt turf, beneath the solitary cedar tree which overhangs the precipice near the Bottle and Glass reefs.* A thick sea-fog obscured everything, but dimly and dream-like through the drifting mist I could discern the forms of the Carib chief and his faithless wife struggling upon the verge. Hitherto I had taken no interest in the spectacle, but, suddenly, as the figures melted into space, I felt a clammy, vice-like grip upon my throat, which froze the very blood within my veins and caused my heart to stand still. Long, supple fingers twined themselves amongst the folds of my neckcloth, and the figure of a woman, resistless, but impalpable, seemed to force me towards the precipice.

I was determined to find out who my assailant was, and with a desperate effort I twisted myself free and threw my left arm around the trunk of the cedar tree, while with my right hand I clutched at the throat of my tormentor. Gradually the vague outlines assumed a definite form, and I knew that I was face to face with Louise Guldenstein—for the haze had drifted away and the sun shone full upon her face. The angry light which I knew so well flashed from her dark eyes, and as my grip tightened upon her throat I could trace the course of the full veins beneath the white skin.

At first I had fancied that it was someone altogether different—someone whom I had wronged, if possible, even more deeply—and a feeling of intense relief took possession of me, only to be succeeded by one of savage exultation. As I forced her backwards, inch by inch, until she hung suspended above the surf which boiled and roared four hundred feet below, I knew that the huge blue sharks were lazily swimming in circles amongst the jagged rocks at the base of the cliff. I felt that I had mastered her, and I was about to cast her from me, when, to my horror, the soil began to crumble beneath my feet, the rugged bark to which I clung broke away from the trunk, and in a moment we

* See Chap. xxv., page 282.

were whirling through space, while the boom of the surf sounded in my ears like the roar of heavy artillery. I struggled—and awoke in a profuse perspiration, and leaping out of bed, threw the shutters wide open and gazed with a feeling of intense relief across the sandy street, where a few negroes were already astir.

It was nothing, of course, but a touch of the feverish ague from which I had been suffering, or indigestion, and being fully aware that a dream is generally but the reflection or continuation of our waking thoughts, I should not have considered the incident worthy of mention, had not the two dreams, following so closely one upon the other, had the effect of making me seriously consider whether the time had not arrived for breaking the fetters which my own hands had so willingly forged.

Only the previous day Mrs. Guldenstein had treated me to one of those violent scenes which had lately become of more and more frequent occurrence, and which were beginning to render domestic life almost insupportable.

I had persuaded her to part with some of the more objectionable zoological specimens, and I got on very well with the horses and dogs and even with some of the cats. The birds were all right enough—with the exception of the cockatoo, who had evinced a decided antipathy to me from the first, and who, after punching a piece out of my lip with one of his Judas-like kisses, had met with an accident which necessitated his consignment to the hands of a local taxidermist—but I made up my mind to draw the line at live-stock in the bedrooms. It appeared that the widow had been in the habit of allowing the progeny of her long-haired Oriental favourites to share her pillow, and the little brutes—who had just entered upon the hobbledehoy stage of their existence, and had begun to develop most of the vices of the mature mouser without having acquired the thin veneer of decorum and morality which alone causes them to be tolerated in polite society—rendered night hideous and put sleep completely out of the question by their riotous gambols.

My time was continually occupied in serving ejectment summonses upon strong contingents of feline followers from the adjoining premises, who were in the habit of organising 'surprise-parties' on the landing—the doors and windows being all left wide open—and as it was impossible on these occasions to discriminate between my wife's pets and their visitors, if one of them was ever 'lost, stolen, or strayed,' I was always accused of having made away with it.

The vague notion of returning to the old country had lately begun to assume a more definite shape, while my wife's unreasonable jealousy and violent temper, coupled with the close watch which she kept over my actions and private expenditure, culminating in the scene of the previous day and followed by the dreams which I have attempted to describe, all tended to confirm my half-formed resolution.

To make a long and unpleasant story short, it ended by my deciding to return to England, and having once made up my mind to a certain course of action, I was not long in maturing my plans. Our supply of ready-money happened, unfortunately, to be at a very low ebb, but on the pretext of wishing to attend an important sale of blood-stock which was shortly to be held at Augusta, I managed to obtain bills to the amount of $3000. One fine morning, having packed up a few necessaries, I drove down to the wharf with Mrs. Guldenstein, and having given her to understand that I should be back from Augusta in the course of a day or two, I said 'Good-bye' and went on board one of the river-boats bound for that town, but getting out at the third or fourth landing-place up-stream, I took the next boat back to Savannah, and driving to the railway depôt—which had not long been opened—took a ticket to Charlestown, which I reached without any adventures.

As I walked down to the docks next morning, I felt like a boy who has run away from school. The sun was shining brightly on the cheerful-looking houses with their gaily-painted balconies and verandahs, a fresh breeze was ruffling the broad expanse of water which is sheltered from the Atlantic gales by Folly and Sullivan Islands, and, moreover, I had a good supply of ready-money in my pocket—the best possible antidote against low spirits.

No wonder then that my heart felt lighter than it had done for some time past as I hurried along the straight line of streets which run parallel with the course of the two rivers, in spite of the blinding clouds of dust and sand which came driving along from the direction of the harbour. I had made enquiries at the hotel as to the best means of procuring a passage on board one of the fast-sailing clippers engaged in the rice and cotton trade between Charleston and England, and had been directed to apply to the agents of Messrs. Baird and McGuckin of Baltimore. I ascertained at their office that a vessel was to sail that very day for Liverpool, but that by waiting a couple of days I could secure a berth upon the clipper ship *Altamaha*, which would deliver a consignment of tobacco at Westport before proceeding to discharge the bulk of her cargo at the London Docks. Thought I to myself, 'I'll wait for the *Altamaha* and chance the delay,' and as this was to be the last occasion upon which I was likely to appear in the character of a gentleman at large, I made the most of the opportunity—I can tell you. I never was much of a one at saving money, it was always 'light come, light go' with me, and I treated the crowd and lived like a fighting cock, and besides the hotel-bill—which was pretty stiff—I was flat enough to drop the best part $1,500 to a euchre-sharp, and in the muss which followed I should probably have lost the number of my mess into the bargain, had it not been for the timely assistance of a Frenchman named St. Croix, who was stopping at the same hotel and waiting for the same vessel.

I went on board the racing-looking *Altamaha* somewhere about the middle of January—as near as I can recollect—but before sailing I wrote a long letter to Mrs. Guldenstein acquainting her with my previous history, and begging her to look as leniently upon my conduct as she could—which letter, I believe, never reached its destination. Tripping our anchor, we slowly worked our way through the intricate channel in charge of a pilot-boat, passing the low-lying shores of the famous Sea Islands, which supply a large proportion of the cotton which Charleston exports. Immediately in our wake came another pilot-boat in charge of a well-known Baltimore clipper called the *Titus D. Pollardine*, which was noted for some surprisingly quick runs across the Atlantic. As we cleared the land and stood out to sea upon the same tack, I had a good opportunity of admiring the graceful lines of the rival clipper, and for nearly three days we kept close company. As she ripped through the black water with every stitch of creamy canvas drawing, a broad, curling roll of seething, milk-white foam rose before her stem—now casting a strong reflected light upon every seam and rivet of her burnished copper as she topped a roller: now pouring in a cascade from the counterfeit presentment of *Titus D. P.* as she buried her nose in the following sea. During the war, when the commerce of other ports was entirely cut off by our cruisers, these daring craft ran the blockade successfully, fought as privateers, and, once fairly to windward, could set the combined fleets of Europe at defiance.

I was the only passenger on board, with the exception of the Frenchman, St. Croix, who was just recovering from a severe attack of yellow-fever and was making the voyage to England for the benefit of his health. It has been my lot to come across some queerish characters in my time, but I am unable to recall anyone who impressed me so forcibly as did this man. Frightfully emaciated from the effects of the fever, his broad, muscular shoulders, deep chest, and long, sinewy arms, plainly indicated that in his best days he must have been a roughish handful—as we say—while his handsome features, tanned to the colour of mahogany by long exposure to a tropical sun, showed traces of the hard life he had lived for the last twenty years.

He informed me—and I have no reason to disbelieve him—that he was the youngest son of a noble family in Brittany, and had been sent out to the West Indies to make his fortune, which he had succeeded in doing, although not precisely in the manner contemplated by his aristocratic relations. After spending a few years in Martinique he had embarked in the slave-trade—which was then in full swing—and after commanding a brig which traded in ebony between the Gulf of Guinea and the Caribbean Sea, he had become the principal agent of King Apogée of Dahomée, and resided for several years at Wieder.

Until we neared the English coast we experienced exceptionally fine weather, varied by occasional gales from the west, and during the long evenings I had plenty of time to listen to St. Croix's stories of life and adventure in the slave-trade. It appeared that it formed part of his duties to accompany King Apogée upon his slave-hunting expeditions into the exterior, and he gave me many interesting particulars respecting that dusky potentate and his subjects—which, however, scarcely come within the scope of the present narrative. He told me that the people are principally herdsmen and worship the Snake and the Goat, and that the King always received him on state occasions in a large house built of mud, the principal apartment of which was panelled and corniced with human skulls—trophies of war. He stated that King Apogée was so confident that the British government would revive the slave-trade, that he still keeps up all his forts, record-offices, etc.

"The English"—said St. Croix, "have paid twenty millions to abolish the slave-trade, and, verily, it was a noble act. But have they succeeded? Your members of Parliament will say 'Yes,' but I say 'No'—and I say, moreover, that the present system of enticing negroes from one island to another is every bit as bad, and sometimes worse, than the old slave-trade. Small craft are at this moment running from island to island to *purchase* negroes, and upon arriving at their destination the captains receive twelve dollars *per* head—to be afterwards deducted from the negro's wages—for each man's passage, and six dollars premium *per* head—in Demerara it is twenty—from the colony for the importation. Does not this smack of dealing in human flesh and blood? Very few of these vessels are seaworthy and all of them are very badly found in water and provisions. In the event of a week's calm or a few days of bad weather, what becomes of the cargo? I could tell you, but you might not believe me. John Bull has expended his twenty millions, and his conscience is satisfied, so *vogue la galère*. However, as you very truly remark, it will be all the same a hundred hence. *Nous n'avons qu'un temps a vivre*, so pass the bottle."

Notwithstanding the debilitating nature of his complaint the Frenchman was always the best of company, smoking endless cigars and consuming an amount of brandy which made even the well-seasoned skipper shake his head. We always spent the evening in the cabin, and the worthy captain would reel off fish, snake, and alligator yarns calculated to bring the blush of conscious shame to the cheek of Ananias, while St. Croix and I related our experiences and compared notes. To a person of a well-regulated turn of mind he would, no doubt, have appeared a scoundrel of the deepest dye, but I must confess that I found him a pleasant fellow enough and a capital companion.

We made a wonderfully quick run across the Atlantic, but on nearing the English coast we were driven out of our course and severely damaged by a south-easterly gale. The gale was succeeded by a dense fog, but the skipper carried on just the same, as he had a bet with the captain of the *T. D. Pollardine*—the result being that the *Altamaha* as nearly as possible ran her bows against the Land's End. We made the remainder of the passage to Westport in a heavy westerly gale, and my heart leaped within me as we sighted the familiar coast, and sailing up the smooth waters of the harbour, were soon lying, safely moored, alongside North Quay.

CHAPTER XXVIII.

I find Myself once more in Westport.

THE day of our arrival proved to be Sunday, and it was quite like old times to hear the church-bells pealing from the numerous towers and steeples and to see the streets swarming with sober citizens, soldiers, dapper clerks, and tawdrily-dressed factory-girls, all out for their evening walk, while the lumpers and idlers loafed about the quays smoking their pipes and watching the vessels drifting in with the tide, and the foreign seamen lounged against the doorposts of the lodging-houses.

Yes, it was Sunday at Westport and no mistake, and

as I strolled with St. Croix along the narrow, ill-paved streets of the old seaport and listened to the Cathedral chimes, my thoughts reverted to the day—just about seventeen years ago—when I, a friendless and inexperienced lad, had first set foot in it, and had been taken under the kindly protection of poor Dicky Sellars.

I guessed that I should find but few of my former associates to the fore, and was agreeably surprised to hear that Joe Barton was still living at his old diggings over the tobacconist's shop at the corner of Fore Street. Thither I accordingly made my way, accompanied by St. Croix, and having ascertained that the object of my search was at home, I crept noiselessly up the stairs, and opening the door quietly, peeped into the well-known snuggery, which contained a miscellaneous assortment of sporting-gear, including racing-saddles, weight-cloths, patent bits, four-in-hand, hunting, and cut-and-thrust whips, spurs, canes, boxing-gloves, greyhound slips, couples, etc., while the walls were adorned with moth-eaten foxes' brushes, masks, and pads, pipe and stick racks, and cheap coloured prints representing the shining lights of the Ring and the pets of the Ballet.

Stealing on tiptoe across the room, I tapped its occupant upon the shoulder—but it was no use trying to take Joe by surprise.

During my residence in the States I had allowed my moustache to grow, and dressed in a light suit of fashionable cut, my naturally swarthy skin burnt almost black from exposure to sun and wind, it would have been small wonder if my old crony had failed to identify me with Mr. Sellars' whilom apprentice, while the decidedly piratical appearance of St. Croix—who would have needed very little making-up to have passed on the boards of a Transpontine Theatre for Paul Jones or the original Captain Kidd—might well have induced a less case-hardened individual to assume a strategetical position half-way between the open window and the bell-pull. But as I held out my hand his quick eye caught the small, white scars on my knuckles—which, like the bullet-wound on the pirate's hand at Porto Rico, it would have required a surgical operation to efface—and grasping it and the situation at the same instant, he gave me a hearty welcome and proceeded to tell me all the news of the day—

the greater portion of which, although interesting enough to me at the time, has nothing whatever to do with my story. I managed, however, to elicit the important fact that Mantis and her sister had attended the principal race-meetings the previous year, as usual, and cheered by this scrap of information I took my departure, having arranged that we should all three dine together later on.

I was obliged to remain in the old town for a few days in order to settle upon some course of action, and to procure a rig-out better suited to the climate than the flimsy but fashionably-cut garments—the handiwork of an eminent New York artist—which I was then wearing. Although my principal object in returning to England was to seek out the woman I had so heartlessly deserted, and to attempt by my future conduct to make some reparation for the wrongs I had inflicted, I had hitherto formed no definite plans, since my course of action would necessarily have to be guided, to a great extent, by circumstances. I had no means of ascertaining the present whereabouts of the Lovell family, nor was I even aware, for certain, whether Mantis had heard of my escapade in America—although I took it for granted that she had. I knew, well enough, that I had no reason to doubt the constancy of her affection during my absence, provided only that she had remained in ignorance of the true state of affairs, but I was at the same time well aware that if the story of my faithlessness had reached her ears, I might expect the worst from her high spirit and passionate nature, while if I happened to come across my amiable brothers-in-law, I knew that my blood alone would satisfy them for the insult offered to their sister.

Altogether, it will readily be understood that my position was not a pleasant one, and, to tell the truth, I almost began to regret that I had not stayed in the States, where I was well off, for after deceiving Mr. Geoffrey—in the matter of my two marriages—I did not dare to show my face at Netherleigh or even consult my kind friend the parson.

My first step was to pay a visit to the Gipsy quarter, and hunt up any stray Coopers, Smiths, Bucklands, or Boswells, who might be found *hatchin' drey* the *gav* at this time of year. With this object in view I made my way—accompanied by St. Croix, who was to sail for London the following day—

to a delectable locality in the suburbs popularly known as Fiddler's Rents, where the tumble-down shanties and open spaces formed a congenial habitation for three or four Gipsy families during the winter and early spring. Here, sure enough, I found three Boswell brothers with their wives and families, but being regular *kerengroes* *—seldom travelling further from Westport than their legs would carry them in the twenty-four hours—they were unable to give me much information. We then made our way to a piece of waste ground, about four acres in extent, which was surrounded by a six-foot wall of solid masonry and went by the name of Tanner's Yard, but which was, to all intents and purposes, one of those 'travellers'' paradises, a regular *kekno-moosh's-poov*, or no-man's-land.

The frosty February day was drawing to its close, and the shades of evening were settling down apace over the gloomy neighbourhood as we entered the yard, where a sort of bastard fair was being held. Some fifteen or twenty show-vans were *lagered* together and roofed-in with canvas, forming a couple of irregular amphitheatres where wild-beasts and waxworks were being exhibited. Upon the entrance platform in front of each of the rival shows, a small but leather-lunged brass-band was braying and drumming for dear life. A mechanical organ of twenty-donkey power, worked by a crank attached to a merry-go-round, was grinding out a series of popular discords in opposition to the bands, while the harsh creaking of the boat-swings, the muffled 'Bang! bang!' of the rifle-galleries, and the shouts, shrieks, and laughter of the populace, combined to form a very Pandemonium, with which the lurid glare from the naphtha 'flare-ups' was strictly in keeping.

Bless my soul, how like old times it was, to be sure! Here were the broadsman and the 'bonnets': the thimble-*engro*: the vendor of cigars and blood-oranges: the itinerant artist who, with dextrous scissors, cut out your likeness from a sheet of black paper, and then proceeded to transfer it to a piece of cardboard by a singularly expeditious and primitive process: the stone-breaker: the one-legged sailor, and the rest of the canting crew.

"Here y'are, capting! Roll, bowl, or pitch! You puts

* House-dwellers.

down one penny and you takes up three! 'Ave a shot?"—yells a stubbly-chinned ruffian, thrusting a wooden ball into my hand and pointing to a couple of nine-pins roughly fashioned out of an old mop-handle, and set up, just the width of the ball apart, on a bit of level ground. Dear me, how funny it all seemed! I had run after the ball and helped to set up the pins hundreds of times, and here I was playing the gentleman among them. The little 'fakement,' by the way, in setting up the pins, is to advance the left-hand pin—facing the player—about half an inch, which makes it almost impossible for a right-handed man to bowl them both down when set up the full width of the ball apart—and *vice-versâ* for a left-handed player.

St. Croix put down a shilling—incautiously displaying a handful of gold and silver as he did so—and insisted upon my having a shot.

"'T aint the fust time as you 've been at that game"—growled the man, as, leaning well forward, I pitched the ball against the top inside edge of the left-hand pin, causing it to cannon off onto the other and knocking them both down, "I must run and git change for a sufferin'"—and suiting the action to the word he disappeared amongst the crowd.

"Hi-diddle-diddle! Hi-diddle-diddle! the right 'un goes hup the middle"—bawls a spotty-faced man attired in a long, greasy great-coat and very little else, at the same time protruding a dirt-begrimed palm upon which a doubled strip of list is artfully coiled up in the shape of a Catherine-wheel, "The hold, hancient game of Prick-in-the-Garter, as played by the Hemperor of Rooshia and Queen Mary Anne Toinetty. Ha, sold again!"—as St. Croix fails to find the end of the loop with a small wooden skewer. "That's the honly chance the hold man's got. Now I'll show yer 'ow it's done——"

As I did not require any instruction upon this point, I left my companion—who appeared immensely amused with the novelty of the situation and entered thoroughly into the fun of the fair—and crossed the ground to where two or three genuine Gipsy *vardos* were drawn up alongside the wall. Here I found a large party of the Bucklands gathered round the camp-fire, and from them I ascertained that the Lovells had been passing the winter on the Hampshire coast, and that some of them were certain to attend the great horse and cattle fair which is held at Bristol on the first Thursday in March.

Returning to the show-ground with John Buckland—a short, thick-set young fellow whose brothers were busy with the *koshters* and cocoa-nuts—in search of my companion, our attention was arrested by a surging crowd collected round one of the caravans at the back of the travelling menagerie. The centre of interest proved to be St. Croix who, with his left hand, had pinned the 'roll, bowl, and pitch' man by the throat, and was holding him jammed against the tyre of a van-wheel in a decidedly uncomfortable and Ixion-like posture, while, with his right, he was defending himself from the onslaught of three or four more of the gang. Just as we arrived upon the scene of action, he launched out backwards with his leg like a mule, catching one of the ruffians full on the breast-bone with his sharp-pointed heel and sending him staggering back into the arms of the mob, amidst cries of "Brayvo, Frenchy!" from a small minority who appeared anxious to see fair play.

Knowing that my companion had a considerable sum in notes and gold about him, I was about to elbow my way to his assistance, when young Jack Buckland stopped me.

"*Hatch a vongish*"*—said he, "there's more of 'em there than them four"—and darting away, he quickly returned with two of his brothers armed with *vusserin'-koshters* †—then, pushing our way through the rabble, with a few blows distributed right and left we soon dispersed the Frenchman's cowardly assailants, who, it appeared, had hustled and tried to rob him.

"*Kanau, meero pal* ‡"—said Jack Buckland, "you'd best clear out of this before the barney rises. There's a dozen or more of 'em here to-night as 'd *chin* your *gurlo ta chiv tute drey* the *pawni* for *pange collor*" §—so we concluded to take his advice. St. Croix insisted upon giving our body-guard a couple of sovereigns for their trouble, and having seen us clear of the worst part of the town, they wished us "*Kooshto-rarde!*" ‖ and turned back, while we made the best of our

---

* "Wait a moment."   † Sticks for throwing at the cocoa-nuts.
‡ "And now, my brother."
§ "Cut your throat and throw you into the water for five shillings.
‖ "Good-night!"

way to the Marlborough, where we found Joe Barton impatiently awaiting our arrival—and a right merry evening we spent.

As time was getting on and I wanted to find out what had become of my relations during my absence, I determined to pay my uncle Plato a visit, and a few days later I took my seat on the coach and travelled up to Bridgewater. Both the coachman and guard were strangers to me, and I found that the sinister predictions of poor Tom Padley were in a fair way of being realised. The days of stage-coaching in the West of England were indeed numbered, and as we entered upon the dead levels near the uninteresting little town of Bridgewater, we were compelled to cross the bridges lately erected by the Bristol and Exeter Railway Company, while large gangs of navvies and platelayers were busy putting the finishing touches to the embankments and laying the rails of the broad-guage line which was opened to the public the following year.

Arrived at Bridgewater, I gave my small portmanteau to a boy to carry, and walked out to the farm on the outskirts of the town, where I found my uncle employed, with the assistance of his two sons, in driving some newly-purchased cart-colts and mares into their respective paddocks.

I had not seen my uncle for more than ten years, and it was some time before he could realise that it was indeed his nephew Samson, but as soon as his mind once grasped the fact, I found that both he and my cousins had heard of my having married a *barveli peevli-gueri drey* the *Nevvi Tem*,* but, curiously enough, were quite in the dark as to my previous marriage with Mantis Lovell. It appeared that gossiping old Neptune had learned all the particulars of my escapade from his patron Mr. Adams, the Netherleigh butler, and it was, of course, impossible to say how far the news might have spread.

As soon as uncle Plato found out how the land lay, he began to pitch into me right and left, not, as might reasonably have been supposed, for having deserted my lawful wife, but for having been such an unmentionable fool—only my uncle put it a good deal more forcibly—as to come back to England with only a beggarly hundred or so in my pocket,

* Rich widow in America.

when the widow was worth thousands and thousands—with a good deal more to the same effect. Now, this was a bit rough on me, for I was trying, once in a way, to do the right thing, and I stood in need of a little help and encouragement.

So, as I very soon found that it was useless to look for any assistance from my uncle, I was reluctantly obliged to take my cousin Jasper into my confidence. I knew that he would be starting in a few days to attend Bristol March Fair, and he promised that if the Lovells were there, he would deliver a letter—which I gave him—to my wife, or else arrange for its safe delivery.

Upon my cousin's return after an absence of several days, I found that the only members of the Lovell family who had attended the fair had been the two eldest brothers—Solomon the Surly and Noah. Jasper—according to his account—had cautiously refrained from entrusting my missive to their charge, and had given it to a young Gipsy of his acquaintance, who had promised to deliver it with his own hands. I had taken the greatest pains to impress upon my cousin the necessity of keeping my return from America a secret from the Lovells—with the exception of Mantis and her sister—but upon cross-questioning him I found, to my disgust, that he had been having a glass with Solomon, and knowing Jasper's easy-going, communicative disposition, I didn't require to be told that my wily brother-in-law had pumped him pretty dry—in fact, he admitted as much. It was, therefore, with a good deal of anxiety that I waited for a reply to my letter.

In the course of a few days an answer came, sure enough, in the shape of an almost illegible scrawl in an unknown handwriting—the wrapper in which it was enclosed bearing the Southampton post-mark—beginning "My dare *pal*,"* and concluding with "yure loveing *pen Tranet Kamlo*."†

Now, although my wife's handwriting was, to put it mildly, far from being a model of caligraphy, it was at least intelligible, while the blurred and blotted scrawl which I held in my hand would have required an expert to decipher. I was just able to gather that Mantis had met with a slight

---

* "Brother."
† "Sister, Trainette Lovell"—*Kaumlo* being Romnimus for Lovell.

accident which prevented her from writing, and that they were travelling the South-coast district and would be in the neighbourhood of Exeter in about three weeks time—the letter concluding by making an appointment for a certain day and hour at a convenient trysting-place in the suburbs of Netherton, known to us as the *Pirrenos' Dromyia*, and to the world at large as the Lovers' Walk.

After reading as much of it as I was able to spell out, I remained in precisely the same state of uncertainty as before, since, beyond the assignation, the letter contained no message from my wife, nor was there anything in the wording of it which afforded me the slightest clue to the state of her feelings towards me. Still, on the principle that 'no news is good news,' there was nothing to discourage me. The very fact of my having received an answer of some sort seemed to augur well for the future, and being naturally of a sanguine temperament, I looked forward with impatience to the moment which was to bring me face to face with Mantis.

CHAPTER XXIX.

The Lovers' Walk.

IN the meantime I earned my keep by lending a hand with the horses, and two days previous to the date appointed, I took the coach to Exeter and made my way to Netherton, where I put up at a small roadside inn, just out of the town, kept by a widow and known to the travelling fraternity as MacAlister's. I was aware that I might very possibly come across some of the Netherleigh Court household in the town, but my moustache so altered my appearance that after Joe Barton and my uncle had failed to recognise me, I felt that I need hardly fear detection even if I should chance to meet Passon Mark himself.

The time appointed for the meeting was seven o'clock, and although I had hardly given it a thought hitherto, it now struck me that it was rather a curious hour for a wife to select for an interview with her husband, although I knew that Mantis might have some difficulty in getting away by herself. When I left MacAlister's the sun had already sunk behind the distant range of Brent Downs, dyeing the western heavens with richly glowing tints, which gradually faded from a vivid carmine into a yellowish haze as the evening drew on apace, and finally gave place to a clear steely grey—a sure indication of a frosty night. A few benighted rooks were hurrying back to their roosting-places among the elms of Netherleigh Chase, while the half-dozen pedestrians I met upon the high-road seemed little disposed to loiter by the wayside, but hurried onwards in the direction of the town with heads bowed down to avoid the searching blast of the keen March winds.

As a rule, I felt the changes of weather little enough, being of a hardy nature, but I suppose that my residence in the tropics had rendered me somewhat susceptible to the difference of temperature, for, although warmly clad in a pea-jacket which I had bought at Westport, I caught myself shivering as I crossed the wooden footbridge and took the path which led through the fields. It was certainly not an evening which even the most ardent of lovers would have selected for a meeting with the object of his affections, and as I climbed over the stile and crossed the water-meadows where the mist hung like a pall and marked the course of the river, my thoughts went back to the long summer evenings when the dew lay heavy on the mowing-grass, and Mantis and I had lingered by the selfsame stile to listen to the long-drawn, oft repeated 'churr-r-r' of the night-jar, which came to us, clear and distinct, from the recesses of a neighbouring coppice.

Alas for those long summer evenings of our youth!—when the big sedge-flies and fluffy-winged moths came floating down the narrow runlets between the weeds, and the heavy trout rose confidingly in the shadow of the further bank. Alas for those long summer evenings of our youth!

—when the air was laden with the scent of the new-made hay, and the girl of our heart required a little gentle persuasion before she would venture to cross the meadow where the sleek-coated, wild-eyed Devons were lazily cropping the rich herbage, and nestled closer to our side as we skirted the high wall of Tracey Park, where, according to tradition, a solitary wayfarer had been robbed and murdered by tramps, and his body sunk in the deep pool below the clump of alders.

Again I say, 'Alas, for those long summer evenings!' Since then the trout have been educated in accordance with the higher standards, the mist from the river strikes damp and chill, and the night-jar seems, if possible, hoarser than usual, while as for the girl of our heart—well, thank God, though stone-walls and iron-bars may separate us, she is the girl of our heart still, and will remain so until the bitter end.

Once more I have wandered from the proscribed track, and once more I must apologise and retrace my steps. The Lovers' Walk was a broad, gravelled path about three hundred yards in length, which skirted the wall of Tracey Park, and was approached at either end through a light iron turnstile. The wall which separated the Walk from the Park was about ten feet high, and crowned a steep bank from which the ivy drooped in long festoons, and between it and the Walk was a narrow belt of thick scrub and underwood. On either side of the gravelled path was a row of pollard sycamores, whose shapeless limbs, disfigured by fantastic warts and huge excrescences and gnarled and warped by the storms and sunshine of centuries, seemed to clutch at each other overhead like the long, bony fingers of some gouty giant. At intervals, along the Walk, were placed a few rustic seats, upon which the young couples from Netherton were never tired of carving their initials, while on the side furthest away from the Park-wall a steep, fern-covered bank—the loose boulders of which it was principally composed being supported in places by masonry—sloped abruptly down to the river, which foamed and brawled some twenty feet below.

It was a clear, frosty night, and as I passed through the turnstile and entered the avenue, the cold, pale light of the rising moon filtered through the interlacing branches overhead, exaggerating every deformity of knot and bole and tracing weird shadows on the gravel beneath my feet. As I hurried along the Walk with all my senses on the alert, expecting every moment to see Mantis step from behind a tree, I caught sight of a figure seated upon one of the rustic benches at the further end, and my heart beat quicker at the thought that within a few seconds I should find myself face to face with the woman I had so passionately loved and so cruelly deserted. As I approached, the figure rose to meet me, and throwing back the shawl which partly concealed the head and shoulders, disclosed—to my intense disgust and disappointment—the grizzled locks and dark, angry countenance of fierce old Cinerella Lovell—a pretty wind-up to a fool's errand.

As she advanced towards me, stretching out her arm to bar my passage, I could see that her features were working with suppressed rage and excitement, and the moonlight, falling full upon her face, caused her swarthy skin to assume a livid hue.

"Ho! Ho!"—she began in a croaking, taunting tone, and I could tell by the way her fingers clutched at her shawl that it was with difficulty that she kept her hands off me, "so my fine gentleman Loveridge has come all the way from the *Nevvi Tem* a' purpose to meet the silly lamb, and has run agen the old fox. But my Mantis is miles away with her *pirreno*,* and my gorgeous Samson has got to settle with old Relli instead"—then, throwing aside all restraint, my vindicative mother-in-law poured forth the pent-up torrent of her wrath upon my devoted head, and after exhausting her by no means limited vocabulary of complimentary epithets, she proceeded to curse me in the orthodox manner, both sleeping and waking, by land and by water, in life and in death—winding up her peroration with the following cheerful *dook* † :—

"*Shoonta tu! Chicklo bengesko sap! Pau mi deari Doovel's rawt, agal tu shon koorickni poorodearer, juckalesti maus velessa, soomgarenna te i tuki zeeiaw. Kanau, 'Kooshto bok' mi fino Ress!*" ‡—and turning away with a gesture which, although

---

* "Sweetheart." † Prediction.

‡ "Hark ye! Filthy devil's spawn! By my dear Lord's blood, before you are a week older, you shall be meat for the dogs, and your entrails shall rot. And now 'Good-bye,' my fine gentleman!"

expressive of supreme contempt, at the same time detracted considerably from the solemnity of her anathemas, the fierce old woman was soon lost to sight amongst the shadows of the over-arching sycamores.

Now, I was quite the last person to be frightened by the curses of a half-crazy hag, for during my childhood I had had some experience of old Charlotte's talents in that particular line and congratulated myself at having got off so cheaply, but knowing the vindictive disposition of my wife's relations, I was not disposed to underrate the threat contained in the last part of Cinerella's sinister prediction, and determined to keep clear of my amiable brothers-in-law—little imagining, however, how soon the threat was to be put into execution.

Feeling that it would be useless to attempt to extract any information from Cinerella in her present excited state, and knowing that she wouldn't leave the Walk until she had watched me out of sight, I slowly retraced my steps along the avenue in the direction of Netherton, intending, however, to put the double on her and follow her as soon as she should have satisfied herself that I was well on my way back. I calculated that I could afford to give her a good start, as, for nearly two miles, the path followed the river bank, and she could not well leave it until she reached the highroad. As I sauntered along, revolving many things in my mind and trying to hit upon some expedient for ascertaining the truth about Mantis, I was startled by the sound of gravel crunching beneath a stealthy footstep, and as I swung sharply round, I received a blow across the head from a heavy stick, which, had it not been for the quilted flaps of the fur cap—a remnant of my brief prosperity—which I had worn on the voyage and which I had happened to put on as the night was cold and frosty, would most probably have terminated my earthly career on the spot.

As it was, I staggered back two or three paces, half dazed by the force of the blow, and instinctively threw up my arms and ducked my head to avoid another, which I guessed would follow the first. 'Thud' it came, sure enough, but glanced off my elbow, half paralysing my arm, and as the dancing sparks caused by the concussion of the first blow faded away from my brain and the sight returned to my eyes, I could just make out that I was beset by three men, two of whom I had no difficulty in identifying as my brothers-in-law, Solomon and Noah, but the third was unknown to me. The suddenness of the attack and the violence of the blow had thrown me off my balance—no less mentally than physically—for the moment, but it was no time for star-gazing, as the men were closing in on me with their sticks raised ready to strike, so, lowering my head, I dashed between Noah and the stranger, and plunging through the thick underwood, set my back against the ivy-covered park-wall and waited for the next move.

If I could have got a clear start, I should have made a bolt for it, but they were too close to me, and, for a short distance, were as fast as I was—besides, I had on a heavy pea-jacket and was a bit above myself in condition. As I turned and faced my assailants I thought of the plucky fight St. Croix had made against similar odds at the fair in Tanner's Yard, and I determined to sell my life dearly. I had the advantage of being in the deep shadow, and if I could only have laid my hands on a weapon of some sort and they'd given me a fair show, I'd have made things lively for some of them, but I'd nothing in my hand but a light bamboo cane which I knew would fly to pieces at the first blow, and as for a fair show—well, it wasn't exactly their game. Providentially, however, my foot struck against some loose stones which had probably fallen from the coping of the park-wall, and hastily stooping down and groping among the brambles and ivy, I picked up the first that came to hand.

In the meanwhile the Lovells had divided their forces and were pushing their way towards me through the brushwood—Sol on my left, the stranger in the middle, and Noah on my right. As they closed in on me, the thick bushes and overhanging branches prevented them from using their sticks, and guessing that they meant to rush in and drag me out into the open Walk, I determined to put my mark on one of them at all events.

As the man in the centre raised his stick, as if to strike, Sol made a spring at me and I saw something glitter in the moonlight—but knowing that he was the leader of the party and the most dangerous of the three, I had kept my eye on him, and turning round, with the full swing of my right arm

I brought the sharp-edged stone against his head, catching him on the ear and dropping him like a log. Unfortunately, the impetus of the blow caused the stone to fly out of my hand, and I was simultaneously tackled by the other two, who seized me by the arms and collar and endeavoured to drag me back to the path—but feeling that my safety depended upon keeping amongst the trees, I stuck to the stranger like grim death, while Noah struck at me as we whirled round in a desperate rough and tumble.

We were 'circling some'—as they say in the States—now up, now down, and letting go at each other whenever we had a chance, when a fourth party appeared on the scene in the person of Cinerella, who had evidently been keeping a look-out, and now hovered round us like an old carrion-crow, encouraging my assailants by word and gesture.

"*Bostramenga, mi chavvies!*" she croaked. "*Bostramenga! Kosher yuv tuley. Siklo, siklo, pau mi Doovel's kaum! Komeni vellela shian. Kooshto, mi chavvies, kooshto!*"—as, in spite of my struggles, they succeeded in dragging me into the pathway: "*Chin de rawtfelo jooko's gurlo, ta vust leste aley de kor. Kai se o churi?*" *—but we were too busy to listen to her chatter.

My monkey was fairly up, and if I'd happened to have had a knife handy, I shouldn't have scrupled to use it—for I could see that they meant murder and nothing else. Backwards and forwards we swayed, now in the light, now in the shadow, striking, kicking, and wrestling, but we were at too close quarters for the blows to take full effect, and for every one I gave, I received a couple. As long as Sol kept out of the way I wasn't afraid, for I could feel that my man was getting beat, and at last I tripped him up and fell on him.

So far I have attempted to tell you the story of the encounter in the Lovers' Walk in strictly conventional language, but, by so doing, I'm likely to make a mess of it—it sounds too much as if it happened on the stage or in a story-book. A prize-fight with ropes and stakes, referee and seconds, is all very well, but when it comes to a rough-and-tumble of a dark night in a lonesome place with a couple of heavy chaps

---

* "Look alive, my sons, look alive! Strike him down. Quick, quick, for the Lord's sake! Perhaps somebody will come along. Well done, my sons, well done! Cut the dog's throat, and pitch him over the bank. Where's the knife?"

atop of one, you might just as well try to describe a dog-fight—with its munching and mouthing and tearing and growling—in poetry.

Let me tell you about it after my own fashion. You see, I weighed about twelve-stone-nine—I never varied three pounds for thirty years till I came here—and Shandros—that's the man who tackled me, who's name I didn't know then, but I found it out afterwards, as I shall tell you presently—weighed about a stone over me, maybe more, maybe less. A tall, big-made chap he was, with muscles like iron from strapping horses—he'd been employed in a livery-stable in Southampton—and a head clipped as close as a cocoa-nut and just about as soft, but a terrible one for the drink, and that doesn't do a man any good when it comes to a long tussle with nobody to call 'time.' My clothes were all stiff and new, so that he could grup me by them, while his were so rotten that I couldn't get a proper holt of him, and by the time I *did* get upsides of him, he was as near naked as makes no difference—his coat was torn pretty nigh off his back, and if he'd put on a shirt that morning there wasn't more than enough of it left to make a *pongdishler*.*

When I fell atop of him—it was the lush that beat him—I put my knee into him . . . . he gave a sort of grunt and loosed his holt of me. Then I got him by the *menpangooshi*,† which went twice round his neck and was tied in a knot, and twisted it tight till he was dark in the face; but Noah put the toe of his boot into my ribs till I heard them crack, and that old devil of a Relli kept hitting me over the knuckles with a stone to make me leave go—and that's as much as I remember rightly, for just then Noah got a chance at my head with his *koshter* and sent me spinning. Dazed by the blow and sick and sore from the hammering they had given me, I struggled to my feet—only to receive a crashing blow right across the forehead.

Have you ever chanced to be struck over the eyes with a heavy stick? If not, I'll tell you what it feels like. It feels exactly as if a large wine-bottle, filled with a million dancing sparks, has been shattered to atoms on your temple. Then something soft, and warm, and sticky gets into your eyes and nearly blinds you—that's blood—and then you probably don't recollect a great lot more—at least, I didn't.

* Pocket-handkerchief.   † Neckcloth.

A red mist swam before my eyes, and throwing up my arms, I staggered backwards across the Walk. My legs caught in something or other and tripped me up: I heard a noise like the snapping of rotten wood, and I felt that I was falling, falling—then a shock and the gurgling of water, and I became unconscious.

* * * * *

Between eleven and twelve o'clock that same night, Mr. Bolitho, the veterinary surgeon from Netherton, was driving back from Exeter with his son. He was as kind-hearted an old fellow as ever lived, although an uneducated man and more of a cow-doctor than a V.S. Many a time, when I was a bare-footed youngster, had I run after his shandrydan and hung onto the back-rail of the dickey along with the other *chavvies*. The old gentleman would make-believe to frown at us through his great horn-rimmed spectacles like a benevolent owl, at the same time threatening us with the thong of his hunting-whip with which he occasionally tickled up the lazy, broad-backed cob—but he was fond of children, and we youngsters knew it, and seldom parted company with him until we had succeeded in extracting whatever stray coppers he might happen to have about him.

Well, upon this particular night, about a mile from the town, the Bolithos overtook and all but ran over a man who was keeping as nearly as possible in the middle of the road, and who, from his unsteady gait, appeared to be under the influence of drink. As the occupants of the chaise turned round to remonstrate with the supposed reveller, the moonlight fell full upon him, and young Bolitho noticed that he was deadly pale and bareheaded, that his features were disfigured by a dark stain which, commencing at the temple, discoloured the left side of the face, neck, and collar, and that with his right hand he appeared to be supporting his left arm, which hung awkwardly from the shoulder.

The cob was at once pulled up and the Bolithos proceeded to examine the man, who, from the dark colour of his skin and heavy moustache, appeared to be a foreigner. Although perfectly conscious, he seemed to be in a bad way —his left shoulder was evidently dislocated, and his clothes, besides being torn and covered with dirt, were dripping wet as far as the waist. He answered all the questions put to him in good English, giving them to understand that he had been set upon and roughly used by some persons unknown, invariably concluding with the same sentence, " I fell over the bank and rolled into the water—fell over the bank and rolled into the water "—which he kept repeating over and over again like a parrot.

He appeared to feel no pain and to be quite unconscious that there was anything at all unusual about his appearance, but seeing that he was not in a fit state to be left by himself, the kind-hearted old Samaritan induced him, with some difficulty, to get into the chaise, and having propped him up with cushions as well as they could, they started again for Netherton.

Mr. Bolitho drove straight to Dr. Martin's, and the man —who by this time had relapsed into unconsciousness and was breathing heavily—was carried into the surgery and the police communicated with. With the assistance of the Bolithos the doctor succeeded in forcing the shoulder back into the socket, and having stitched up the wound on the temple and bandaged and plastered the head, which was badly cut and bruised, the patient was placed on a stretcher and—his address having in the meanwhile been ascertained —carried back to MacAlister's. He was then put to bed and carefully examined by Dr. Martin, who found that in addition to the dislocation of the shoulder and the injuries to the head, two of his ribs on the left side were broken. He appeared to be sleeping peacefully enough, but besides having lost a good deal of blood he was evidently suffering from concussion of the brain, and, as the doctor informed the landlady, it was quite possible that he might never rally from his present comatose condition. Having made some further enquiries about the wounded man, Dr. Martin promised to send someone to watch beside him and took his departure, having given instructions that the patient was to be kept warm.

I need hardly inform you that the patient was none other than my poor self, and I may add that I continued in this drowsy, semi-conscious condition for four or five weeks, during which time the brain was slowly recovering from the injuries it had received. And as I lay in the Valley of the shadow of death, the voice of the woman I had loved and lost seemed to come to me at intervals, muffled and indistinct, as from a great distance, and once I fancied that my old friend and master, the Parson of Netherleigh, was standing beside my bed, but when I made an effort to shake off the stupor which oppressed me and to stretch out my hand towards him, a mist came over me and I wandered off again to the dark boundary-land of dreams and shadows, where the restless spirit lingers about the cross-roads of Life and Death, as if hesitating which path to choose.

At length, one morning, a weight seemed to have been removed from my brain and I awoke with my senses in their normal condition. I felt wretchedly weak and my eyes—which were shaded by the surgical bandages with which my head was cris-crossed—were unable to bear even the soft grey light of morning which came creeping in through the chinks of the shutters. Like a child who has just awoke from some horrid nightmare, I made an effort to sit up in bed and rub my eyes, but found that my left arm was strapped to my body, while the whole of my left side, from waist to shoulder, was one large bruise, which caused me such intense agony that I sank back upon my pillow in a state of utter collapse.

As I lay there very still and quiet, scarcely knowing or caring whether I was asleep or awake, alive or dead, I heard the door-handle turn, followed by the creaking of a board, and became aware that I was no longer alone. From the lightness of the step and the faint rustling of a dress, I guessed that it was a woman who had entered the room, and I became dimly conscious that someone was bending over me and that a skilful hand was rearranging the pillows which my movement had displaced.

I was afraid to look up lest it should prove to be only another of those illusions which had so often tormented me, but in spite of my efforts to restrain myself, a wild hope had taken possession of me, and as the footfall died away again I opened my eyes, and pushing back the bandages which shaded them, was just in time to catch sight of the figure of a woman noiselessly leaving the room. As she was in the act of closing the door after her, she looked back for a moment and all my doubts were dispelled—it was Mantis. For the second time, in spite of my previous experiences, I started up and uttered her name, but I was so weak that the excitement proved too much for me and I fainted dead away.

When I came to myself the fresh spring breeze was blowing in at the open windows, the sun was shining brightly, the young starlings were whistling and chattering under the thatch, and, best of all, my dear wife was kneeling beside my bed, my right hand tightly clasped between both of hers!

* * * * * * * *

There are certain moments in the lives of all of us—ill-regulated and obscure though they be—which may well be regarded as sacred, and I will not attempt to describe the scene of confession, forgiveness, and reconciliation, which ensued—indeed, for the matter of that, there is little enough to tell. Suffice it to say that for the first time for nearly two years I felt strangely happy and contented. In my feeble condition I took everything as a matter of course, and never even thought of enquiring how it came to pass that my wife —who, but a few weeks previously, I scarcely expected to see again—was sitting beside my bed as if we had never been separated. My brain was still too weak to allow of serious thought or reflection: I knew that she was there and that my long journey had not been in vain—and that was enough for me.

CHAPTER XXX.

I Re-enter Sir George's Service.

FROM that day my health began to improve rapidly, and thanks to my having led an active and fairly temperate life, I experienced none of those complications, in the shape of fever and inflammation, which Dr. Martin had anticipated.

Every incident of the fierce struggle for life, up to the moment of receiving the final blow, was clearly stamped upon my memory, but to this day I have not the remotest conception how I found my way back to the high-road, and with regard to my meeting with Mr. Bolitho, and all subsequent events, my mind was a complete blank. Owing to the severe nature of the injuries I had received, my progress was necessarily slow, and many days elapsed before I was able to sit up in bed or take solid food, but when, at length, I was able with my wife's assistance to hobble across the room and take my seat at the window, even Dr. Martin—who was an inveterate old croaker—was forced to acknowledge that I was out of danger and in a fair way towards recovery.

In proportion as my body gradually acquired strength, my mind resumed its activity, and I obtained from Mantis a detailed account of the events of the last few weeks.

Needless to say, she had never received my letter, which, thanks to the carelessness of Jasper's messenger, had fallen after all into the hands of her brother Solomon who, with the assistance of his mother, had prepared the nice little trap into which I had been flat enough to fall.

It appeared that the Lovells had travelled through Dorsetshire, and keeping to the line of what is known as the Salisbury road, had approached Exeter by way of Lyme Regis and Colyford—finally pitching their tents at a *yoggin' tan*, well known to the travelling fraternity, upon Beggar's Bush Common, close to Brympton, a small village half-way between Exeter and Netherton.

Upon the day appointed by the letter for the interview, Sol and Noah, accompanied by a cousin of theirs named Shandros Kaumlo—who had been hanging about after Mantis for some time—left the camp at sunrise, and, as it afterwards transpired, spent the greater part of the day at a little roadside public called the Nag's Head—a noted house-of-call for poachers—where they were joined towards evening by their amiable parent. They were all pretty well primed by this time, and a council of war was held, at which it was finally settled that I should be quietly put out of the way, the plan of campaign being that Shandros and Noah were to attack me with their sticks, while Sol—who carried no stick, as I had at once remarked—was to watch for an opportunity of *chivvin' lescro churi drey mande's buckko**—as they elegantly phrased it—and that I was then to be dropped into the river. The spot had been selected with a good deal of cleverness, for although a favourite walk in summer-time, scarcely a soul passed that way at this time of year, and it was the only place for miles, on that side of Netherton, where the river ran close to a public footpath.

The two girls, with their young brother Teerus, had been left in charge of the camp, and were under the impression that the others had gone 'creeping' for pheasants—which always command a ready sale at this time of year—in Tracey Park. It was past midnight when Noah and Shandros returned with their clothes torn and bearing evident marks of a struggle, but there was nothing very uncommon about that, and they told the girls that they had come across the *yogengros*, that Sol had got his *sherro poggado* and was lying *gaverdo*,† and that they had come for the light cart to bring him away before daylight.

The fact was—and the circumstance probably saved my life—that when I had fallen backwards over the steep bank, pitching amongst the rough stones and brambles and rolling down to the river, where I lay half in and half out of the water, Noah and Shandros, who were peering down into the

* Slipping his knife into my liver.
† Keepers, that Sol had got his head broken and was lying hidden.

obscurity to see whether I stirred—and who would otherwise have finished the job by pushing me into the stream—had been recalled by old Cinerella, who had gone to look after Solomon and had found her favourite son in a very much worse condition than she had anticipated. He proved to be quite insensible, and, being a heavy man, they had the greatest difficulty in getting him through the iron entrance-wicket and in carrying him into the open fields beyond, but having got him as far as the nearest pond, they bathed and bandaged up his head—finally leaving him under a haystack in charge of his old *chovahauni**** of a mother.

It was some days, however, before he was sufficiently recovered to take the road, when the Lovells started for Cornwall, travelling by easy stages. It was not until they had reached Moreton Hampstead that, from certain hints which Shandros Kaumlo let drop in the course of conversation, Mantis began to have some suspicions as to what had really taken place, and immediately set her youngest brother Teerus to work to find out the truth. The news of my having contracted a bigamous marriage with a rich widow in America had reached the Lovells through Neptune—who had made matters worse by chaffing my brothers-in-law about it—and Mantis had determined to hold no further communication with me in the event of my returning to England. But when she heard how I had been served and that I had been left for dead by the river in the Lovers' Walk, her woman's heart obtained the mastery over her wounded pride, and confiding her destination to her sister Trainette, she left the camp and set out on her long, solitary tramp back to Netherton.

Arrived at that town, she commenced making enquiries, and finally ascertained at the constable's house that a man answering to her description had been taken to MacAlister's. She then went straight to the inn, and after a good deal of difficulty succeeded in convincing the cautious old landlady—to whose safe-keeping Dr. Martin had entrusted my watch, loose cash, and the note-book containing all that remained of the $3000—that she had a right to take up her quarters by my sick bed, and undertake the duties of nurse.

* Witch.

Dr. Martin had succeeded in alarming Mantis to such an extent by his despondent view of the case, that she determined to make an expedition to Netherleigh Parsonage, in the hope of persuading my old friend the Parson to come and see me. Mr. Sealy now heard for the first time the whole story of my marriage at Plymouth from the lips of the woman I had deserted, and his indignation at my conduct knew no bounds. I must have altogether failed to convey a correct impression of the Parson's character, if I have not made it abundantly evident that anything in the shape of deceit or treachery would be certain to meet with his severest condemnation, and the very fact that the guilty party had been a pupil of his only tended to make matters worse. At first he flatly refused to stir a step in my direction, but, like many other equally determined men, he was not proof against the pleading of a handsome woman, and ordering the dog-cart to be put to, he drove my wife back to Netherton.

It must have been his voice that I fancied I heard during an interval of semi-consciousness, but finding that nothing could be done and that my recovery was very doubtful, he took his departure, promising, however, to return if he should receive intelligence of any change in my condition.

During my convalescence I forbade Mantis to go near the Parsonage again, as, in my weak and nervous state, I was morbidly anxious to avoid an interview with a man who, I knew, must heartily despise me. My one object now was to regain the use of my limbs and to clear out of Netherton as quickly as possible, for I shrank from meeting the contemptuous glance of those calm grey eyes, and had already determined that, as soon as I was strong enough to move, we would travel up to London, where I had little doubt of being able to obtain employment.

One afternoon, as I was sitting at the open window imbibing copious draughts of the invigorating breath of spring, and happy in the consciousness that while the strength was slowly returning to my limbs, the aches and pains were gradually leaving my poor, battered body, I saw, to my horror, the well-known form of Passon Mark ride slowly up the dusty street, and, soon after, I heard his voice in the bar-parlour below. I knew, then, that I was caught like a rat in a trap, and to make matters worse my wife had gone out for a walk.

A guilty conscience is the worst possible of companions for a sick room—as elsewhere—but I need not have alarmed myself, for as the door opened I saw that there was a kindly look in the Parson's eyes, although the mouth was set firm and resolute as ever. As he crossed the room I noticed that his step had lost much of its former elasticity, and that he limped slightly as he leaned upon a stout stick which had taken the place of the old, hammer-headed hunting-crop. His hair, too, was very grey and his slight habitual stoop had become more pronounced, but there was the same light in the dark eyes and the same cheery ring in the voice which, in former days, had caused old one-eyed Melody to throw up her sagacious head and yowl with delight, and had encouraged the hesitating fox-hound puppies to make their experimental plunge into the troubled waters of the Cran.

For the first time, perhaps, in my life, my composure forsook me, and I broke out into a perspiration from sheer nervousness as I placed a chair for my visitor. Seating himself, he looked me carefully over and then began:—

"There, there, my lad"—for although a rather dilapidated specimen of a man of one or two and thirty, I suppose I was still a lad in the Parson's eyes—"sit ye down and don't excite yourself, for I haven't come here to inflict a long jobation upon you, and as your wife—who, by the way, is just such another as your poor mother and a long way too good for you—has told me that she has forgiven you, I have no intention of raking up the past, especially as you seem to have been pretty severely punished already. You appear to inherit two fatal defects of character—one, an instability of purpose which prevents you from profiting by any opportunities of advancement which may be placed in your way: the other, a fatal habit of concealment which seems to be inherent among the people of your race. Depend upon it, Samson, the straightforward course is the one which pays best in the long run, and that the man who is clever enough to play the part of a successful scoundrel must, necessarily, possess abilities which, in nine cases out of ten, if applied to any legitimate pursuit, would not only enable him to distance his competitors, but would ensure him the respect of admiration of his fellow men."

"Now I should like you to give me a plain, unvarnished account of your proceedings from the time you left Mr. Geoffrey L'Estrange's service in New York, up to the present day, and, in asking you to do so, you may rely upon it that I am not influenced by any motives of idle curiosity."

In all probability it was a precisely similar condition of mental and physical prostration to that which I was now experiencing, which, once upon a time—as the old rhyme tells us—prompted a certain distinguished historical character to express a desire to be received as a member of a religious fraternity. Without any attempt at concealment or prevarication, I gave Mr. Sealy a circumstantial account of my proceedings, from the commencement of my acquaintance with Mrs. Guldenstein up to date, concluding my narrative by producing, in a fit of candour which, to tell the truth, I afterwards bitterly regretted, the note-case which contained all that remained of the money that—to use a euphemistic term—I had borrowed from the widow to defray the expenses of my journey to England.

"Well, well, Samson"—said the Parson at the conclusion of my story, "you certainly appear to have made the most of your brief experience of fortune's favours, and to have driven, literally, at full speed along the broad track which terminates in the well-graded descent of the old Latin poet. I have reason, however, to believe that everything you have told me is substantially correct, and I hope that you will have no occasion in the end to regret your frankness."

He then told me that, only a day or two previously, Mr. Geoffrey had received a letter from Mrs. Guldenstein, in which she informed him of my desertion of her and enquired whether anything had been heard of me in England. He added that she had spoken of me in much kinder terms than I had any right to expect, and seemed disposed to blame herself for the misunderstandings which had resulted in our separation.

"And now"—continued the kind old gentleman, "I may tell you that, in the first place, nothing but your wife's urgent entreaties could have induced me to hold any communication with you, but having heard your story and believing, as I do,

I RE-ENTER SIR GEORGE'S SERVICE.

that you are sincerely anxious to atone for your past misconduct, I intend once more to exert my influence in your behalf with Sir George, who is always complaining that he has never been properly looked after since his son took Loveridge away. But, before I move in the matter, you must restore the remainder of the money which you obtained from Mrs. Guldenstein to its rightful owner, and if you will entrust it to my charge, I will see that it reaches its destination."

From the bottom of my heart I thanked the best friend a man ever had for his good offices, and, as will be seen, I gave him no further cause for regretting his kindness; but I must confess that it struck me very forcibly, at the time, that the Parson was not one to do things by halves, and as I saw the crisp bank-notes—which I had obtained in exchange for the American bills—disappear into his capacious pocket, I began to reflect that, in spite of his recommendation to candour and honesty, even these virtues might possibly be carried to an extreme. You see, I was beginning to feel a bit better again.

A few days after his visit, I received a note from Mr. Sealy informing me that Sir George seemed disposed to take me back into his service, as his old Maltese valet Terelli—who had taken my place when I left England with Mr. Geoffrey—had not proved equal to the really hard work of a sick room. The Parson advised me to take a run down to the seaside to recruit my health before making a personal application for the situation, as I seemed at present scarcely strong enough to undertake the rather arduous duties of looking after a confirmed invalid, and concluded by saying that as he had relieved me of my spare cash, he would advance me some money to defray the expenses of my visit, and settle with Mrs. MacAlister and Dr. Martin.

I need hardly say that I gladly availed myself of his kind offer, and after spending a week at Plymouth, we returned to Netherton and put up at MacAlister's, where I prepared myself for my interview with Sir George—an ordeal which I dreaded more than I can describe.

For the first time for nearly twelve months I indulged in the luxury of a clean shave, and as my moustache disappeared beneath the keen blade, I felt that I had dropped the last of the borrowed plumes under which I had lately been masquerading. My wife congratulated me upon my improved appearance, and as I passed through the bar-parlour, kind-hearted Mrs. Mac emerged from her sanctum with a black bottle in her hand, and thus addressed me:—

"Saftly noo, Mister Loveridge, mon, saftly. I'm thenkin' ye'd best tak joost a wee, wee drappie to warrum yere whame afore ye tak the road. My gudemon, Dooncan, when he wass wi' the Maister, wad never pit a fute upon the hull 'ithout his 'mornen,' an' to the last he'd never stir abraid till he'd souped his gill o' Marmasoull." Now, my personal recollection of the late lamented MacAlister's habits, inclined me to credit the generally-received report that he had eventually fallen a victim to his patriotic devotion to the dew of his native mountains, for when, one morning, his pony came back to the stable alone, and he was found lying, face-downwards, on Putcombe ford in six inches of water, there were plenty of uncharitable people ready to make affidavit that death had resulted from the shock occasioned by the water to his system, rather than from suffocation.

However that might have been, having swallowed 'just a toothful' of the potent spirit to please the good lady, I made my way up the street, and following the Blackstow road for about a mile, struck across the moor for Netherleigh. As I breasted the steep hill and toiled wearily along the rough path, I could not help contrasting my present enfeebled condition with my return to Netherleigh upon a previous occasion, when, full of health and spirits, my difficulty had been to refrain from breaking into a run.

When, at last, I reached the lodge-gates, I felt dead beat, and as Mrs. Luttrell let me in, she stared at me as if I had been a visitor from another world.

"Lawk a'mussy me!"—cried the stout Somersetshire dame, "if it beant Samson Loveridge as went to the Hingies along of the young Squire, and looking for all the world like a mawken. Now do'ee set'ee down inside and bide awhile till I draas 'ee a drap a' zider. They did a'tell I as so-be as thee 'dst marr'd a foreigneer or summat"— but the steep hill and the hot sun had been too much for me altogether, and as I leaned back against the wall, her words seemed to hum in my ears like the musquitoes on the Pomaroon.

However, a long draught of the cool cider soon pulled me together again, and having enquired after old James, I thanked the good-natured keeper's wife and resumed my way. Soon after entering the Park my ears caught the quick, measured stroke of hoofs upon the turf, and turning a corner I saw two horses coming at full speed along the broad strip of greensward which bordered the gravel drive, and in the riders I recognised my late master, Mr. Geoffrey, and Miss Winifred Blount—Mr. Cecil Blount's youngest sister—while, cantering more sedately behind them, came Miss Blount, escorted by a stout cavalier mounted upon a rough-actioned shooting-cob. As he leaned forward, blobbing awkwardly up and down in his endeavours to keep pace with his fair companion's well-trained hack, the face of the last-mentioned rider was invisible to me. I noticed that his trousers had worked nearly up to the knees, disclosing a pair of magenta-coloured socks and highly-varnished boots, and, as he drew nearer, I recognised to my surprise the purple cheeks and waxed moustache of 'Baron' Oscar Jansen.

As soon as he caught sight of me, Mr. Geoffrey pulled his horse up, allowing Miss Winifred to shoot ahead, but the Baron trotted by without noticing me—his small, beady eyes twinkling with satisfaction at the progress which he evidently flattered himself he was making, while his uneven teeth protruded from beneath his dyed moustaches in a stereotyped grin.

My young master addressed me in his usual frank, off-hand manner, for all the world as if nothing had happened, and as I stammered out some broken words of apology, he stopped me at once.

"There, there, Samson"—he said, "I don't want to hear anything more about it now. I haven't forgotten what you did for me when I was down with yellow-fever, so we'll let bygones be bygones. Another time you shall tell me how you came to get so knocked about, but at present you'd better go on quietly to the house and get something to eat and drink before you see my father"—and touching his horse with his heel, he was off again like a shot.

I suppose that my brain could scarcely have entirely recovered from the effects of the injury it had received, for, as I turned away, the blue eyes and golden hair of Miss Winifred, her sister's grave, handsome face, the grinning Baron, and my master, all seemed to be whirling round in a confused reel, and I was obliged to sit down on the turf by the roadside under an elm-tree to collect myself. I think I must have dozed off to sleep, for, when I came to, the red-deer were staring at me with solemn, inquisitive eyes. Their horns had begun to sprout in great mossy knobs from their heads, while their rough, grey winter jackets were hanging in tatters, allowing the ruddier garb of summer to appear beneath.

The rooks were wheeling high above their nests in the elms overhead, keeping up an incessant cawing the while: the rattle of the lesser-spotted woodpecker sounded at regular intervals from the direction of the Avenue, and the wood-quests flitted with lazy, drooping flight from clump to clump, paying but little heed to the intruder. Three cuckoos were chasing each other in and out of the hawthorn-bushes, pausing, now and again, upon some outstretched branch to reiterate their mellow note, while overhead the glorious sun was shining through a shimmering golden haze. It was, in fact, one of those splendid spring mornings which are to be enjoyed to perfection in no place better than in the sleepy West Country, far away from the busy hum of cities, and as I sat and sunned myself, revelling in the genial warmth, I fell into one of those day-dreams, which are so far preferable to their congeners of the night, inasmuch as the forms which they are wont to assume are more directly under the control of our desires.

I daresay the whisky and cider had something to do with it, but I was at length effectually aroused from my reverie by the sound of footsteps on the gravel, and turning round I beheld the portly form of Mr. Adams, clad in a suit of tweeds, and carrying a double-barrelled gun under his arm. He was evidently taking a turn round to see whether there were any young rooks out, for the butler was a privileged individual, and in his character of naturalist was allowed the free range of the Chase. I had always been upon the best of terms with the sport-loving old Yorkshireman, who seemed

I RE-ENTER SIR GEORGE'S SERVICE.

delighted to see me again and gave me a hearty greeting, and we walked slowly back to the Court together.

The big stable-clock was striking one as we hurried round to the back entrance, and I was just in time to give myself a brush up before the dinner-bell rang. A good many visitors were staying in the house for the Netherton Races and the annual Hunt Ball—amongst others Mr. Cecil Blount, his two sisters, Oscar Jansen, and some old College friends of Mr. Geoffrey's. The party below-stairs included Mrs. Barry, the housekeeper: Terelli, Sir George's old valet who, unable to sustain the monotony of existence at Netherleigh—which, however, he had contrived to vary with two severe bouts of D. T.—was about to return once more to his native land: two gentlemen from London who appeared to be recognised authorities upon all topics appertaining to society and the Turf, and who spoke of Robinson, Scott, and Marson, respectively, as Jem, Bill, and Job: hatchet-faced James Wilson, the Baron's confidential servant, whom I had met in Philadelphia and cordially detested: two or three ladies'-maids: Adams, and myself.

As may be imagined, upon returning to the housekeeper's-room after leaving the servants'-hall, I at once became the centre of the general interest and the pump-handle was set going with a vengeance, but I had not spent twelve months under the shadow of the star-spangled banner without learning the advisability of holding one's tongue in mixed company, and the conversation soon drifted into ordinary channels. Amongst other topics the state of Sir George's health was discussed, the general opinion being that it had grown steadily worse since the installation, as household chaplain, of Father Considine, who had succeeded Father Dennis Massy, and upon this subject Terelli—who was a professed atheist, smoked countless cigarettes, and, according to Adams, slept with a yellow-covered novel under his pillow and a dozen of the best French brandy under the bed—waxed very eloquent, while the butler and the housekeeper exchanged significant glances. Whether there was anything serious in Mr. Geoffrey's attentions to the youngest Miss Blount was a moot point. The chances of Lord George's flying filly—who, with her dam, just three years previously had been knocked down to his lordship at Tattersall's for fifty odd guineas—for the Oaks, the impending fight for the championship, and the price of Great Westerns, formed the principal topics of conversation, and finally James Wilson left the room in a white rage on my proceeding to draw him on the old subject of his master's title and military achievements.

In the course of the afternoon I had an interview with Sir George in the study, and was shocked at the alteration which the last two years had effected in my old master's appearance. He was scrupulously dressed, as of yore, but the well-cut clothes hung in wrinkles from the wasted figure, his hair had turned quite white, and I fancied that I detected an uneasy, harassed look about the eyes, and a nervousness of manner, which I at once put down to the effects of his illness, and which contrasted strangely with his former reserved and rather haughty bearing.

But, to tell the truth, I didn't pay very much attention to Sir George's appearance at the time, for I was too much taken up with my own affairs. I was greatly relieved to find that, beyond asking me some questions about Mr. Geoffrey's illness, my old master made no allusion to the events of the past twelve months, and the result of our interview proved highly satisfactory to me, for within a fortnight I had resumed my old place in the household, while Mantis was installed in one of the model cottages which had lately been built just outside the Park gates.

CHAPTER XXXI.

Life at Netherleigh Court.

DURING the next four or five years which I spent in Sir George's service, few incidents occurred worthy of special notice. But, like the calm which so often preludes a storm, this tranquil state of things was not destined to last for long. To a social weather-prophet, the rather strained nature of the relations between Mr. Geoffrey and Father Considine—who, as I have mentioned, had succeeded Father Dennis Massy as household chaplain—might possibly have indicated the quarter from which the gale might be expected; but we were a contented, well-fed household down at Netherleigh, and, beyond the ordinary gossip and chatter of the servants'-hall and housekeeper's-room, did not trouble our heads overmuch about what went on above-stairs, and, for my part, I had my hands full—what with looking after Sir George, and valeting Mr. Geoffrey.

Before I had been many hours in the house I found that Father Considine was an individual of a very different stamp to easy-going Father Denny, and came much nearer to realising, both in character and appearance, the popular conception of a Jesuit priest. He was a very intellectual but delicate-looking man of about eight or nine and thirty, with a singularly noble head, well-chiselled features, a dark, sallow complexion, and a figure which was tall and erect but spare to the verge of emaciation. If it had not been for his haggard, half-starved appearance—the result of a constitutional infirmity—he would have been a decidedly handsome man, but there was something about him which prevented him from becoming a favourite with the household. Why this should have been the case, I can't exactly explain, for it is much easier to give one's reasons for liking a person than for disliking him. It wasn't that there was anything particularly offensive in his manner or address, on the contrary, he was always most gracious and conciliatory, but there was an air of conscious superiority about him which, to say the least of it, was extremely irritating to inferior beings like myself, and he gave me the idea of being continually on his guard to repress the half-contemptuous smile which lurked about the corners of the well-cut mouth.

Educated in Paris, he had afterwards accepted a professorship of Natural Philosophy at the Jesuit Seminary for the sons of the Irish nobility and gentry at Clongowes, near Clare, in the Co. Kildare. Forced to relinquish this appointment on account of asthma—from which he suffered terribly, and which often prevented him from lying down or taking rest at night—his naturally energetic temperament was compelled to succumb to his bodily infirmity, and his life henceforth became a continual struggle in which the ambitious spirit mastered, and in turn was mastered by, the weakness of the flesh. Although obliged to retire from the active career which he had mapped out for himself, he was in constant communication with the centres of religion and science in Paris and Dublin—the only relaxation which he permitted himself being that of music. He was a perfect master of that most difficult of instruments the violin, and often, when retiring to my room after being detained late in attendance upon Sir George, have I paused outside his study door to listen to the harmonious strains of the muted strings which came floating down the silent corridor, and being able—like many of our people—to *kil* the *bosh a bitti mi kokero**—I was the better able to appreciate the excellence of the performance, and to admire the musician, little as I liked the man.

My duties kept me up late and I used often to meet him rambling about the house at night, for when his malady prevented him from lying down or taking rest, he would wander off to the library and spend the long watches leaning against the mantelpiece, absorbed in the perusal of some abstruse philosophical or theological treatise which he had routed out from the well-filled book-shelves. I never liked the man myself and I think he returned the compliment, for I had

* Play the fiddle a little myself.

nick-named him 'the Bat'—from his nocturnal habit of flitting noiselessly about the house attired in a sombre-coloured dressing-gown and list slippers—and he very soon found out who had given him the name, for precious little went on in the house without his knowing it.

The history of his appointment as household chaplain was, shortly, as follows. Mr. Francis, the second son, had always been a delicate lad and for the last five or six years had been compelled to winter abroad. As Sir George's ill-health prevented him from accompanying his son, he had been obliged to procure a travelling-companion for him, and Father Considine—who was glad of an opportunity of spending his winters in a warmer climate and had received the highest recommendations from influential quarters—had consented to accompany him as bear-leader and spiritual adviser, in the performance of which duties he had displayed an unusual amount of discretion and ability. Upon Mr. Frank's return in the spring, his tutor had generally been invited to spend a few weeks at the Court, and in course of time he succeeded in acquiring a complete ascendancy over his pupil, and managed to make himself not only acceptable, but almost indispensable, to Sir George. During our absence in the West Indies Father Massy had received an unexpected summons to Ireland, where he had been appointed Vice-President of St. Patrick's College, Maynooth, and in the natural course of events Father Considine slipped quietly into the berth which the kind-hearted old priest had so long occupied in the Netherleigh household.

Within a twelvemonth of his appointment as chaplain, he had the whole establishment completely under his thumb. Large sums were spent in redecorating and beautifying the chapel, a splendid organ was purchased, and the Catholic portion of the household—including, as it did, all the servants with the exception of Adams and myself—was daily paraded for early service, and, under the energetic supervision of the new-comer, the discipline of the Seminary was substituted for the easy-going routine which had characterised the rather lax sway of simple-minded Father Denny.

And now, in order to make the situation a little more intelligible, it becomes necessary for me to say a word or two about Mr. Geoffrey. Hitherto, as far as this story is concerned, he might just as well have been Mr. Tom, Mr. Dick, or Mr. Harry, but because I have been too busy with my own affairs to devote any space to a description of my young master's character, it must not on that account be supposed that he was a nonentity. On the contrary, he possessed a very marked individuality which was beginning to manifest itself in a variety of ways.

Since his return from the West Indies, he had sobered down a good deal, and, very much to Sir George's delight, had lately shown an inclination to take the position in the county to which, as heir to the Netherleigh estates and fifty thousand a year, he was entitled. Although fond of field sports and country life, he managed to spend a good deal of his time in London—where he was a member of two or three of the best Clubs—and it was probably there that he first acquired a taste for politics. Squire Beaumont of Upcote, who had represented Netherton in Parliament for the last five and twenty years, was about to retire, and, as the recognised candidate in the Conservative interest, Mr. Geoffrey now made a point of attending the meetings of the various Agricultural Associations and Farmers' Clubs in the neighbourhood, and possessing, as he did, plenty of shrewd common-sense, a fair share of wit, an excellent delivery, and a natural aptitude for public speaking, his speeches soon came to be regarded as the feature of the evening at the local political gatherings.

So much, then, for Mr. Geoffrey L'Estrange in his public capacity; but it is with his private life and domestic relations that we are more especially concerned. Although, as a boy, he had been brought up according to the tenets of the Catholic faith, owing to his fondness for field-sports Passon Mark had become more of a father-confessor to him than Father Massy, and Mr. Frank less of a companion than Mr. Cecil Blount; while the four years he had spent at Camford, the society of his clear-headed Protestant friend, and his subsequent travels, had the effect of considerably enlarging his views on the subject of religion. Without professing any very strong convictions one way or the other, he had been shocked at the openly displayed profanity and mockery which characterised the processions and ceremonials of the Roman Catholic Church in the West Indies, and upon his return to Netherleigh he absented himself more and more from the services in the chapel—either passing his Sundays with his old friend the Parson or with the Blounts of Stowe—and set himself steadily to work to counteract the influence which Father Considine had succeeded in establishing over his younger brother.

The Squire of Stowe was the next largest landed proprietor to Sir George, and Netherleigh being the nearest church, from time immemorial the Blounts had occupied a huge pew like a spacious loose-box enclosed by wooden panelling about five foot high, and furnished with a table, a stove, and several roomy arm-chairs. The pew was in a sort of recess or private chapel off the side aisle, just behind the carved oak screen which separated the chancel from the nave, and nothing but the heads of the occupants were visible to the rest of the congregation. Just outside the pew was a stone tomb with the life-sized figures of a lady and gentleman reposing peacefully, side by side, with their hands crossed upon their breasts, and a queer little dog at their feet; but what always interested me most, when I was living at the Parsonage, were the inscriptions deeply cut into the panels which formed the inside of the pew. For generations and generations it had been the custom for every male member of the Blount family to carve the date of his birth, marriage, and any important event of his life, upon the panels, and some kindly hand had invariably put the finishing touch to the story of his career by adding the date of his death.

If a visitor was staying at Stowe, he was generally reminded to provide himself with a pocket-knife, wherewithal to commemorate the date of his visit during the sermon, and these inscriptions not only formed a valuable record of the family history from the earliest times, but proved a great attraction to tourists, who frequently drove out from Netherton to inspect them.

It was a four-mile drive from Stowe to Netherleigh, and the Blounts generally put up at Mr. Sealy's stables, and latterly Mr. Geoffrey had sometimes accompanied them to church, sitting in the family pew. Perhaps that he had so little in common with Mr. Frank—who was of a studious and retiring disposition—may have made the laughing eyes of Miss Winifred Blount appear all the more attractive after the monotony of the home circle, for it was about this time that his engagement to Mr. Cecil's youngest sister was given out.

Without entering into unnecessary details, I think I have shown that the elements of discord lay ready to hand, and that it only needed a bit of a breeze to fan the smouldering embers into active flame. In narrating the events which followed I cannot do better than adhere to the exact sequence in which they came to my knowledge, and in order to do so I must reintroduce that remarkably astute individual, 'Baron' Oscar Jansen.

Notwithstanding his decidedly coarse and chairman-of-a-Metropolitan-Music-Hall-like appearance, the Baron belonged to the select number of those who pull the strings, and possessed abilities of no mean order, which enabled him to turn the follies and weaknesses of his fellow-men to his own peculiar and pecuniary advantage. He was always to be seen at the principal race-meetings, theatres, and other gatherings of a similar nature, where, by means of a nicely-calculated prodigality, he managed to cultivate the acquaintance of young men of fortune, amongst whom his undoubted knowledge of the world caused him to be held in some respect. On these occasions he affected an air of reckless *bonhomie*, and being gifted by nature with a remarkably thick epidermis, was always prepared to play the part of butt or buffoon—that is to say, just as long as it suited his book to do so. He must have possessed some private means, for he was invariably well-dressed and went everywhere, and, in conjunction with two or three more of the same kidney, owned a leg in some horses trained in a small South-country stable. The little confederacy to which he belonged was notorious for the patience and long-suffering with which it conducted its operations, and if, every three or four years, one of its long-bottled-up candidates brought off some carefully-planned *coup* and placed a Steward's or Royal Hunt Cup to its credit, it appeared perfectly content, while a few useful leather-flappers paid the hay and corn bill and kept the wolf from the door in the interim.

The versatile nature of the Baron's genius and avocations may best be inferred from the fact that whereas, on weekdays—or, to speak correctly, on week-nights—he was generally to be found behind the scenes or in the manager's box at the Boudoir—of which cosy but unlucky little theatre he was part proprietor—on the Sabbath, in his *rôle* of churchwarden, and in praiseworthy, if unconscious, imitation of his Semitic prototype, he carried the bag at the dingy but fashionable place of worship affected by the religiously disposed amongst the upper ten of St. Jermyn's. In addition to being a promoter of bubble-companies and holding a third share in the Cohens' hell in Earl Street, he was a fraudulent trustee, and more than one man is now holding horses or walking the streets without a shirt to his back, who can trace his ruin more or less directly to his acquaintance with the too plausible Baron, while the curious part of it all, and what speaks volumes for his acuteness, was the fact that he still continued to be a member of a first-class London Club.

For some months after Mr. Geoffrey's return from America the house had to be kept pretty quiet, but latterly Sir George's health had ceased to give cause for any immediate anxiety, and although unable, himself, to play the part of host or participate in their amusements, the kind-hearted old baronet encouraged his son to invite as many of his friends to Netherleigh as he chose. My young master, who was of a sociable disposition, availed himself to the utmost of the privilege, and two or three times a year a large and, truth to say, rather noisy party—consisting, for the most part, of old Camford friends—was in the habit of assembling for the Spring and Autumn Races, and for the covert-shooting later on. Amongst others, Jansen—who had made himself very agreeable to Mr. Geoffrey during the return voyage and had managed to obtain an invitation—was a regular visitor. He had laid himself out from the first to ingratiate himself with Sir George, and had succeeded in so doing, but the younger members of the party—including Lord Findon, Mr. Standish, Sir Granville Fazackerley, and two or three more of the old St. Saviour's set—amongst whom Jansen was most unpopular, used to make him the object of all sorts of practical jokes which, as a rule, he took in very good part; being quite satisfied to have his revenge later on in the day when the card-tables were laid out and the candles lit in the smoking-room.

To do them justice the young gentlemen were ripe for anything, from pitch-and-toss to manslaughter—as the saying is—and warmed by the fine old port for which the Netherleigh cellars were justly celebrated, their high spirits sometimes led them to exceed the strict limits of order and decorum. When there was no hunting, shooting, or racing going on, they would start off for a day's badger-digging in Brockley Wood, and as there was always plenty of beer going on these occasions, half the idle blackguards in the district would assemble, and the proceedings were usually enlivened by a series of dog-fights and a turn-up or two among the bipeds—of which Sir Granville and Lord Findon were the chief promoters.

'Granny' Fazackerley—as the owner of Erleigh had been nicknamed at Camford—was a frequent visitor and a great friend of Mr. Geoffrey's. On hearing that my cousin Perin was the recognised local champion, he induced me to entice my unsuspecting relative up to Netherleigh one Sunday afternoon by specious promises, and having inveigled him into a loose-box, the young baronet and the Gipsy fought half-a-dozen rounds just for the pure love of the thing, in which Perin got decidedly the worst of the encounter, as closing was not allowed, and he refrained from using his right once or twice when he might have done so with effect—but Sir Granville was by far the cleverer boxer of the two, and a five-pound note helped to salve my cousin's bruises, while the gift of an old suit of clothes sent him away as happy and contented as a dog with a meaty bone.

And here, while upon the subject of high spirits and practical jokes, let me record my impression of the youthful aristocracy. Before I went into service I always fancied that the tip-top swells—Dukes, Lords, and such like—were a dull, stuck-up lot, as stiff and starched as their shirt-collars, and it wasn't until I had stayed with my master for the shooting and the hunting at two or three large houses in Norfolk and Northamptonshire, that I found out my mistake. What you may term the upper-middle classes may be sedate and decorous, but for regular mad skylarking and high jinks, I never came across any section of the community to equal the youthful members—ladies, Lord bless 'em, as well as gentlemen — of the so-called 'hupper sukkles' of society.

Bless my dear heart, yes, they were as lively a set of boys as ever I wish to see, and as for their practical jokes, there was no end to them. One morning they were strolling round the kitchen-garden after breakfast, smoking their cigars and picking fruit. An old beaver-hat happened to be stuck on a stick to keep the birds off some seeds.

"Tell you what, Baron"—says Mr. Standish, "you shall stand within five yards of me and I'll bet you half-a-crown that you don't hit that hat chucked straight up into the air. I'll stand on one side of that wall"—pointing to a brick wall about seven or eight feet high—"and you shall stand on the other, as close as you like to me, and I'll sky the castor quite slowly any time within five minutes, and bet you half-a-crown you don't touch it with either barrel."

"If you'll toss it straight up, not less than eight or ten feet above the wall, just opposite to where I'm standing, I'll take you"—replies the wary Baron.

"Done!"—says the other, and off goes Jansen to the gun-room to borrow a shooting-iron, which he carefully loads with a small handful of snipe-shot and a fair charge of powder—he wasn't going to miss, bet your life.

Half-an-hour later Mr. Standish and the Baron take up their respective positions on either side of the wall.

"Time!"—sings out Mr. Geoffrey—who was referee—with his watch in his hand.

"Ready!"—says the Baron, and shortly after up goes the tile, revolving slowly in the air and presenting a mark which the veriest tyro could scarcely have missed.

"Bang!"—went the first barrel, and the hat jumped as if somebody had kicked it.

"Bang!"—went the second barrel as it descended almost on top of the muzzle of the gun—and what was left of it would have made an excellent wine-strainer. But when the Baron went to pick it up, he reluctantly arrived at the conclusion that half-a-crown would scarcely compensate him for the damage sustained by his best Sunday-go-to-meeting bell-topper, which, I regret to say, had been feloniously abstracted from his bedroom while he was unconsciously charging the petard wherewithal to hoist it.

One day, after dinner, during the September race-week, Mr. Geoffrey had been relating some of his deer-stalking experiences in Scotland, and the Baron—like many town-dwellers a good rifle and pistol shot—whose notions on the subject of sport were hazy in the extreme, innocently inquired whether there was not some good deer-stalking on Cranmoor—possibly confusing deer-stalking with stag-hunting.

"Some of the very best in the United Kingdom"—gravely replied Sir Granville, "you ought to have a turn at it before you leave, as you are such a good performer with the rifle"—and on this hint they acted.

As usual, I was taken into their confidence, and entrusted with the execution of their nefarious designs. A day or two later, when the whole party was assembled at breakfast, Adams entered the room, and going up to Mr. Geoffrey, said:—

"If you please, sir, Luttrell has sent word to say that a fine stag and two hinds were in Putcombe Wood last night, and were seen crossing the river at Westford this morning, going towards High Tor."

This was the signal agreed upon, and with one accord all the conspirators began to clamour for permission to go after the big stag.

"I'm game to go"—begins Mr. Standish, "if nobody else wants to."

"So am I"—says Sir Granville. "I'll tell you what we'll do. We'll toss up."

"No you don't"—cries his lordship, with well-simulated indignation, "it's my turn. Granny went last time"—and so on, but at last, with a ready courtesy and forbearance with which their most intimate friends would scarcely have credited them, they one and all waived their claims in favour of the Baron.

"Tell Sandy to fetch my double-barrelled Purdey from the gun-room, and to meet us at the front-door in an hour's time"—says Mr. Geoffrey to Adams, "and you'd better look sharp and get ready, Baron, if you really mean to go"—and an hour later the whole party assembled on the gravel in front of the hall-door to see their victim off.

Sandy Fraser was a tall, full-bearded young Highlander,

who had formerly occupied the post of 'tod-hunter,' or trapper, and assistant deer-stalker at Strathdhu. Mr. Geoffrey had taken a fancy to the lad, and as he had rather outgrown his strength—having sprouted in a twelvemonth or so, after the manner of his race, from an angular hobbledehoy to a bearded man of six-foot-one—he had found him a place as under-keeper at Netherleigh, and—cannie Scot that he was!—Sandy had hitherto evinced no disposition to return to Rossshire, probably finding the Netherleigh mutton and Adams' home-brewed, very passable substitutes for the whisky and oatmeal of his native glen. For the first few months after his arrival he had been like a fish out of water, for he spoke but very little English, and whenever he happened to come suddenly across any of the red-deer he would drop, instinctively, like a well-trained setter, and then sneak away through the tall fern on his hands and knees until he succeeded in putting the wind between himself and their nobility, and it was a long time before he could realise the fact that the lordly denizens of the Chase were utterly indifferent to the presence of the inferior animal.

On the morning in question, neatly dressed in stalking-cap, jacket, and knickerbockers of Strathdhu mixture, his telescope slung over his shoulder, the rifle snugly reposing in its waterproof case in the hollow of the left arm, and a stout shepherd's stick in his hand, Sandy looked quite the gentleman, and as his keen grey eyes took in the Baron's adipose proportions and rather startling costume, his face assumed for a moment an expression which might well have taxed the powers of a Leech to catch and reproduce.

"Now, Sandy"—said Mr. Geoffrey, "you quite understand that you're to take Baron Jansen by the Netherton road as far as Westford. Cross the river there, and make good the ground round High Tor. Then, if you don't find them, you'd better spy the small corries round Black Tor and Three Barrows, and work your way home across the moor."

"Andeet, then, an' I'll do me fery best"—replied Sandy, "but a'm joost thenken we'll note get near them wi' the foreign shentlemans dressed thet fushion, whateffer!"

The fact was that, like most men of his type, the Baron was fond of a bit of colour, and the cravat of a vivid crimson slipped through a cat's-eye ring, the delicate pink and white-striped shirt, the creamy freshness of the ample waistcoat, and the dark navy-blue of the serge lounging-jacket, while doubtless possessing their merits from an æsthetic point of view, were of rather too pronounced a tone to recommend themselves favourably to the critical eye of a deer-stalker, while the shepherd's-plaid trousers and the neat town-made boots, were better adapted to strolling about the terraces and conservatories, than for coping with the asperities of a Devonshire moor even in summer-time. His hands were encased in a pair of slightly-soiled lavender kid-gloves, and a Glengarry forage-cap, bearing the badge of his old regiment surmounted by a black-cock's tail, was jauntily cocked very much on one side of his shining forehead, round which the scanty threads of his purple-black hair had been artfully coiled and coaxed into a delusive semblance of juvenility.

"Here, this will never do"—cried my master. "Somebody lend Jansen a light-coloured shooting-coat and a pair of leggings. Don't all speak at once. Standish, one of yours would about fit him."

"Delighted, I'm sure"—growled Mr. Standish, who had been reluctantly compelled to admit the Baron's superiority at all games of chance and skill from pitch-and-toss to picquet, and hated him accordingly—so the coat was sent for, a pair of leather gaiters borrowed from Adams, and at last everything was pronounced ready for a start.

"Just a small one before you go, Baron?"

"*Pullia skene dhu!* Here's blood on the black knife!"

"Here's luck, Jansen, and more power to your elbow!"—chimed in the conspirators, and we were off—for I had been deputed to carry the whisky-flask and sandwiches and to see that everything went right.

It was a sultry morning, and as we crossed the old bridge at the bottom of the hill and tramped along the Netherton road, the dust rose in blinding clouds, nearly smothering us. Arrived at Westford, we crossed the Cran by a trestle-bridge and struck across the moor—following the line which the deer were reported to have taken.

At length Sandy sat himself down with his back against a big stone, pulled out his telescope, breathed on the glasses and polished them with his handkerchief, stuck his stick firmly into the ground, and proceeded to spy out the nakedness of the land. The Baron, gasping and panting like an apoplectic lap-dog, threw himself at full length upon the heather and set to work to sample the luncheon which the ever-thoughtful Adams had provided, and I was by no means sorry to follow his example, for at each step our feet sank deep into the coarse, rushy grass and scrubby heather. At last Sandy closed the glasses with a disappointed snap, and having loaded the rifle, put the stops on, and returned it to its waterproof cover, we resumed our tramp. To one who, from a child, had been accustomed to the precipitous hill-sides and rugged corries of Strathdhu, the rough broken ground and undulating ridges of Cranmoor must have seemed but molehills, but although I could beat him on the road, it was heart-breaking work to keep up with that long-legged, spring-heeled-Jack of a Highlander across the heather. At every step he went off the ball of the foot with an elastic spring which lifted his heel three or four inches clear of the ground, while his stride was as untiring as a wolf's, and, as Mr. Blount used to sing:—

"The wolf is a beast, though I ne'er knew one did,
Can run without stopping from Tours to Madrid."

The Baron was soon reduced to a pitiable condition, and in vain tried to handicap the too energetic stalker by the gift of a couple of his biggest regalias, which, however, only appeared to have the effect of stoking Sandy's fire-hole, and which, after being partially smoked, were ruthlessly cut up and stuffed into the stumpy pipe which seldom left his lips.

"You don't appear to think much of those"—remarked the Baron, evidently nettled at seeing his expensive cigars unappreciated.

"Oh, andeet, an' they're note thet bad"—replied the unsophisticated Highlander, "but they're na sae seeckenin'* as the perrique"—and hacking away at a chunk of the black, mollasses-sodden tobacco in which his soul delighted, Sandy resumed his headlong career.

But in vain he spied every nook, goyle, and cleeve, round High Tor, Black Tor, and Three Barrows—not a beast was

* Strong, full-flavoured—derivation obvious.

to be seen. The Baron was now beginning to lose his temper at being sent out on what he half-suspected to be a wild-goose chase, and vowed that nothing should ever again induce him to go tramping after 'a d——d mountain-cow,' as he disparagingly denominated the lord of the forest, so at length I suggested that we should try the rough ground to the north of Cranhead—for, strange as it may appear, I had an idea that the object of our search would be found in that direction.

We had almost reached the highest level of Cranmoor when Sandy clutched me by the arm, and dropping on his knees amongst the fern and heather, drew me down beside him—at the same time motioning to the Baron to imitate our example. His quick eye had detected some animals feeding near the head of the valley, but upon a closer inspection they proved to be some of the half-wild ponies which roam the moor.

"You'd better have a good look amongst those rocks just below the skyline while you're about it"—I suggested. "It looks a likely place for a stag to lie, and it's our last chance."

"I haf them, I haf them!"—suddenly exclaimed Sandy, his voice trembling with excitement and his eye glued to the telescope. "See yon patch o' brecken to the Wust o' the pownies. Follow the bit burnie tell ye come to a beg grey ston. Then carry yere ee East aboot five huntert yards in a line wi' the beg ston, and ye'll see anither patch o' brecken. He's leein' aboot fefty yards to the No'th of et, close to a sma' roke. A'm thenkin' he's more than a ro-yal and the vulvet's ofe his hornes, but a'm note seein' any hinds whateffer. We'll get back oot o' his secht, or that black bonet o' the Bar'n's 'll pit him awa'"—and suiting the action to the word, he snatched up the rifle and crawled away downhill, beckonin' to us to follow him.

Despite the facts that crawling in tight trousers headfirst down a steep bank on hands and knees, on a broiling September day, is a form of exercise which does not usually commend itself to middle-aged men of a full habit, and that his physical conformation was better adapted to a rotatory than to a serpentine mode of progression, the Baron imitated the stalker's movements to the best of his ability, and having reached a more secluded spot, a council of war was held. According to Donald, it appeared that the stag, of malice aforethought, had as usual selected a most impregnable position for taking his noonday siesta, as whatever breeze was stirring blew down to him from the moor above, while the draught from the hollow in which he was lying was drawing up to him—our only chance being to make a long detour and approach him on a side-wind from the right and risk a snap-shot.

Then the real business of the stalk began, and a hot, dirty job it was—alternately skirting patches of treacherous green morass, leaping from tussock to tussock, tramping ankle-deep through the black, crumbly soil of the peat-bogs, or crawling on hands and knees across some heathery knoll exposed to the full blaze of the afternoon sun, and before we reached the shelter of the 'bit burnie,' the bridegroom-like character of the Baron's toilette had undergone considerable modifications.

"Ye'd best pit thet black bonet in yere poket, Bar'n"—remarked our guide, "he can see it twa mile awa, an' we'll be in his secht directly"—so the obnoxious Glengarry was handed over to me, and on we crawled as before—Sandy leading, the Baron next, and your humble servant bringing up the rear. But, suddenly, to our dismay, as we were crossing a hollow, a small, wild-looking head with pricked ears and long, shaggy mane, rose above the nearest skyline, and a loud snort proclaimed that the vigilant ponies—who must have shifted their position—had discovered our whereabouts.

"'Od tam the beasties"—cried the stalker, shaking his fist at them as they scampered off, "they'll pit him awa for certain. Come along. Rin, mon, rin!"—and he broke into a long, slinging trot, slipping the rifle out of its cover as he went.

"Now look here, my good chap"—exclaimed Jansen who, although dead-beat, crimson with exertion, and drenched to the skin with peat-water and perspiration, was, as far as any traces of excitement were concerned, as cool as the proverbial cucumber, "if you think that I'm going to run after you up a hill like the side of a house, you make a very great mistake, and please to remember that I've got to do the shooting, not you, so it isn't any use your hurrying yourself."

This was undeniable, so poor Sandy, like a greyhound in the slips, with difficulty restraining his ardour, and inwardly anathematising the foreign 'shentlemans,' was compelled to accommodate his pace to that of the panting but phlegmatic Baron. We were now within a couple of hundred yards of where the stag had been lying—his head and neck just visible above the heather—and the greatest caution was necessary. Motioning us to halt, Sandy crept forward until he reached the brow of a small knoll, and carefully parting the bents of heather and peering through the aperture, his face lit up again.

"He's there yet. I can see the white tips to his hornes, but, andeet"—looking dubiously at the Baron's glistening cranium—"a 'm thenkin' we'll note get any nearer to him; the sen iss shinin' on yere hedde joost like a pla-ate."

"Cuss your impudence"—growled the irate Jansen, who very naturally resented the comparison, "just shove along and leave my head alone, you hare-brained, herring-gutted son of a bare-breeched, whisky-swilling Highlander!"

"'Deet, then, an' I wass meanin' no harrum, whateffer"—whispers Sandy apologetically, and peace having been temporarily restored, we resume our crawl. At last our leader pauses behind a huge grey rock.

"He's aboot saxty yards, an' leukin' awa from us. Wull I whustle him up, or wull ye tak him as he lees? A'm thenkin' ye'll note get a better chance"—he whispers huskily, as, trembling with excitement, he pushes back the stop and hands over the rifle to the Baron.

"Bless your soul, man"—replies Jansen, "I'd hit a five-dollar piece at that distance. I'll aim at his neck and bet you a sovereign to nothing I kill him." Bang!—and as the smoke clears away we see that the proud head and branching antlers have sunk down amongst the purple bells of the heather. We spring to our feet.

"Weel dune! Weel dune!"—screams Sandy excitedly, patting the successful sportsman on the back and executing an extemporary *cancan* in the exuberance of his delight, "he's deed enough, I heerd the boolet strike"—and drawing his clasp-knife he bounds away, while the Baron follows at a more leisurely pace.

But why does Sandy start back as if he had seen the ghosts of all the lairds of Strathdhu? Why does he dash his stalking-cap upon the heather and give vent to a copious flow of Gaelic which, if done into English, would cause the cheek of a Billingsgate fish-hawker to pale with envy? Why does the expression of complacent satisfaction vanish from Jansen's purple face, and why is the pure atmosphere of Cranhead defiled by a perfect salvo of blasphemy?

The reason is only too obvious. In place of the noble form of the monarch of the glen outstretched upon the heather, 'gigantic still in death,' the crimson life-blood welling from a small hole in the neck, while a blue film overspreads the rapidly-glazing eye, there lies at the Baron's feet a dusty old deer-skin—which had long graced the servants'-hall at Netherleigh—roughly stitched together with twine, stuffed with heather, and cunningly kept in position by two or three hazel wands, the points of which are firmly fixed in the ground like the rods of a Gipsy's tent. Beside it, with its glass eyes staring vacantly at its would-be destroyer, lies the head of a magnificent stag from Netherleigh Chase—on temporary leave of absence from the main staircase—very indifferently set up by the Netherton bird-stuffer.

Let us draw a veil over the remainder of the painful scene, including my well-simulated indignation at the hoax of which we had been made the innocent victims, the Baron's return to the Court, his suspiciously cordial welcome by the conspirators, and their wild dance round the remains of the slaughtered stag in the Banqueting Hall after dinner.

"Dam-me, sir!"—cried Jansen, purple with rage, turning sharply on Mr. Standish, between whom and himself there was but little love lost, "if this had happened in the States, I'd have had you quivering on a daisy before breakfast to-morrow morning!"—but this savage outburst only redoubled the mirth of his tormentors, who wound up the evening by turning a freshly-caught badger into his bedroom, after the disappointed stalker had retired to rest in high dudgeon, and then screwing up his door on the outside; having previously substituted an evil-smelling compound—

the principal ingredients of which consisted of patent boot-polish, bird-lime, and rancid butter—for the *cosmetique* with which their victim was in the daily habit of renovating the evanescent hues of his carefully-dyed moustache.

And here, lest it may appear as if Jansen was rather too roughly treated, let me assure you that this was very far from being the case. In sketching his character I have been most careful to prevent my personal antipathy to the man from over-colouring the picture, and if I were at liberty to mention certain things respecting him which came to my knowledge during his visits to Netherleigh, I think you would admit that he deserved all he got—and more.

CHAPTER XXXII.

The Baron Takes Me into His Confidence.

TO resume the thread of my story. One day, during the winter of the year 184—, while returning from the cottage which my wife occupied, I was accosted by the Baron's sour-faced valet James Wilson, who informed me that his master—who had arrived unexpectedly from town the previous evening—would like to have a little conversation with me, and would meet me at four o'clock in the summer-house by the salmon-pool below the falls, at the end of the north garden, adding, for my encouragement, that I should 'find the Guv'nor all right and needn't be afraid of opening my mouth'—which was highly reassuring, to say the least of it.

It was a typical November afternoon, dark, damp, and chilly, and as I hurried along the gravel-walk between the dripping masses of rhododendron in the direction of the river, I wondered what could possibly have induced the comfort-loving Baron to exchange the luxurious atmosphere of the smoking-room, for the draughts and discomfort of the little arbour on the banks of the Cran. On the occasion of his last visit to Netherleigh in the autumn, he had presented me with a five-pound note on leaving, and as I was well aware that he was not in the habit of throwing his money away—being what, among servants, is usually termed a 'bad parter'—I racked my brains in a vain endeavour to guess the probable nature of his little game.

I found the Baron seated on the rustic table in the centre of the arbour, smoking one of the big, full-flavoured cigars which he affected, and apparently occupied in tracing patterns on the sandy floor with the point of his gold-headed Malacca cane. His brows were knit in thought and he was evidently engaged in working out some intricate mental problem, but as soon as he caught sight of me, his features resumed their wonted expression, and in answer to my apologies for keeping him waiting, he replied in his usual free-and-easy style :—

"Not at all, Loveridge—not at all. As you know, I'm a bit of a Cockney and seldom see a salmon off the slab of a fishmonger's shop, and I've been watching those beggars jumping at the fall and knocking their silly heads against the rocks—like certain friends of mine—with a good deal of interest. To tell you the truth "—'Here comes a corker,' thinks I to myself—" I've often wanted to have a quiet chat with you about your adventures in the States, but I've never found an opportunity, so sit down and make yourself comfortable, and before going any further let me give you a cigar."

I think I have already mentioned that after my poor mother's death I had given up smoking, but as Adams was very fond of a weed, I accepted one of my companion's big regalias without any scruples. He then went on to congratulate me upon the judgment I had displayed in the selection of 'my wives'—as he was pleased to call them—with a good deal more to the same effect—evidently wishing to make me believe that he considered me to be one of the shrewdest individuals of his acquaintance. However, I was rather too old a bird to be caught with a bit of cheap flattery, and as, after satisfying his curiosity, the conversation began to languish, I rose to depart. As I was about to leave the summer-house, he called me back, and pressing a couple more cigars wrapped up in a Bank-note into my hand, said:—

"I hope, Loveridge, you won't be offended by a little proof of my appreciation of the trouble you have always taken to make me comfortable when I've been staying here, but I'm off to London early to-morrow morning, and I daresay I mayn't see you again for some time. By-the-bye"—he continued—"there's a little matter which I'd almost forgotten to mention"—'Now we're getting warm,' thinks I—"and upon which I should like your opinion. We're both of us men of the world and understand each other, and I feel sure that I may rely upon your keeping anything I may say to yourself—although, as a matter of fact, it's more or less of an open secret, and I daresay you've talked it over in the housekeeper's-room a score of times. No doubt you've already guessed that I refer to the state of things up there?"—pointing with his cane in the direction of the house.

I hadn't the faintest notion as to what he was alluding, but I nodded my head, and he continued:—"As a general rule these fine old county families—as they are so fond of calling themselves—have a fine old county skeleton carefully hidden away in some cupboard, only waiting for somebody possessed of a little perseverance and penetration to unearth it, and, unless I'm very much mistaken, our friends up there are no exception. As I daresay you'll admit, I'm not exactly what you'd call a flat"—'That's the solid truth, and no mistake,' thinks I to myself—"and I can put two and two together as well as most. As of course you've heard, there's supposed to have been a bit of hanky-panky about Sir George's marriage, and as soon as ever the old cock passes in his checks you may bet your bottom dollar there'll be an all-fired ruction."

Now I should explain that I'd never even heard the subject mentioned before, and was, consequently, taken quite aback, but I nodded my head sagaciously, as if I could tell him a thing or two if I had a mind—just to *tadder leste.** Jansen paused as if expecting me to make an observation—for we were both on the same lay, each trying to find out

* Draw him out.

how much the other knew—but as I kept silent, he flicked the ash off the end of his cigar with the point of his cane, and resumed:—

"Of course, we all have our theories about it, but I expect that mine is as near the truth as anybody's. If I'm mistaken, just tell me why there were no festivities when Geoffrey L'Estrange came of age?"

I had an answer to this, at all events, the fact being that Mr. Geoffrey kept his twenty-first birthday when staying at Buonavista, near Georgetown, and I told the Baron so.

"That's all very fine"—he persisted, "but why was he sent abroad just as he was coming of age, and why didn't the tenantry have a blow-out, and fireworks, and all the rest of it, if it wasn't that the old man didn't want the subject opened up again? Sir George's health? Bunkum! I've been having a talk with that consumptive-looking devil-dodger"—I had noticed him on more than one occasion walking with Father Considine—"and although he's as close as an oyster, I'll get it out of him before I've done. You mark my words"—lowering his voice and speaking impressively—"the priest is playing a waiting game, but his hand may be forced at any moment, and, in the meanwhile, there's no earthly reason why we shouldn't have a cut-in ourselves. It's a hundred to one that the baronet has got some compromising letters or documents stowed away somewhere—these sentimental old buffers always have—and if things are as I suspect, and you can manage to lay your hands on them, we shall be able to put the screw on both parties and name our own terms."

The cat was out of the bag at last, with a vengeance. Thought I to myself, 'I suppose you take me for as big a blackguard as yourself,' and I had two minds to up and tell him as much; but prudence prevailed, and I sat tight. The Baron got off the table, brushed the cigar-ashes off his trousers, and settled his cravat.

"Anyhow"—he continued, "it's worth thinking about, so keep your eyes skinned and a quiet tongue in your head. Don't forget to drop me a line if anything turns up. Earl Street, St. Jermyn's, will always find me. And now I must be toddling, for I've got a little matter of business with the old gentleman before I go, and I suppose this will be about the best time to catch him "—and suiting the action to the word, the quick-witted scoundrel jerked the end of his cigar through the open window and bustled out of the arbour, leaving me to digest the information at my leisure.

My first impulse was to go straight to Sir George and tell him all about it, but on second thoughts I came to the conclusion that it would be better to hold my tongue, as the Baron would be sure to deny everything, and I might very likely get myself into trouble. It was quite true that I had heard the subject of Sir George's marriage discussed in the housekeeper's-room, but beyond a bit of harmless gossip about her ladyship having been an actress, no allusion to any deeper mystery had ever been made in my presence. As soon as the Baron and his valet had taken their departure, I took the first opportunity of pumping Mrs. Barry and Adams on the subject, but I found that although they were familiar with the circumstances attendant upon the arrival of Lady L'Estrange and her child at Netherleigh, they were no better informed than the rest of the world as to the events which had immediately preceded the marriage.

As far as regarded Father Considine's connection with the matter, it had never entered into my head to suspect him of any deeper design than that of establishing and enforcing his authority over the rather laxly-conducted household—the natural outcome of an energetic and ambitious disposition—but viewed by the side-light which Jansen had thrown upon the subject, his presence in the house and line of action were open to a very different interpretation.

Mr. Geoffrey, as I have mentioned, had lately shown a very strong inclination to take the bit between his teeth, and, when I came to think of it, it now seemed pretty certain that, in the natural course of events, upon his accession to the title and property, Father Considine's sway would come to an end; while it was quite on the cards that one of the finest estates in Devonshire, with its broad acres and heavy rent-roll, would pass entirely out of the control of the Catholic Church. Looking at it from this point of view, the stake was certainly a heavy one, and the players could hardly be said to be evenly matched, although, at this period of the

THE BARON TAKES ME INTO HIS CONFIDENCE. 373

game, the strong cards had declared themselves in the hand of the novice.

On one side of the table was an outspoken and rather hot-headed young gentleman, with no turn whatever for intrigue, and, moreover, head over ears in love with a very pretty young lady belonging to one of the oldest Protestant families in the county. On the other, an ambitious and self-contained priest—a member of a Society notorious for the unscrupulous and far-reaching nature of its policy—whose faculties had been developed in that sternest of all schools, a Jesuit Seminary. According to the Baron's theory—as far as I could judge from the hints he had let drop—Mr. Geoffrey's right to the title and Netherleigh estates—the Irish property not being entailed—was open to question, and Father Considine was already endeavouring to detect the flaw, but what gave colour to this supposition was the fact that Mr. Francis was a thorough-going Catholic, and, in the event of his succeeding to the baronetcy, the priest—or, rather, the party he represented—could rely upon his support in carrying out whatever views he might happen to entertain.

It must not be supposed that I arrived at these conclusions quite as quickly as I am able to write them down, or that I was one of those precious clever gentry who are able to tell a horse's age by the length of his tail—on the contrary, it took me weeks and months, and even then I shouldn't have been much the wiser if it hadn't been for my wife. She always had more brains in her little finger than I had in the whole of my body, had Mantis, but I had just sense enough to know that two heads are better than one as a general rule—and I only wish I'd stuck to it through life.

And now let me relate the result of the Baron's interview with Sir George 'on a little matter of business,' after his unexpected disclosures in the arbour. During his frequent visits to the Court he had set himself seriously to work to captivate the affections of the eldest Miss Blount—who was a considerable heiress—but finding that he was wasting his time in that direction and that very little more was to be squeezed out of Mr. Geoffrey—whom he had been initiating into the mysteries of picquet—he severed his connection with the family by persuading Sir George, who had asked his advice on the subject of certain investments, to purchase some shares which a friend of his owned in a really genuine concern. Upon receiving a cheque—amounting to some thousands—for the purchase-money, Jansen started the following morning for London, promising to deposit the securities with Sir George's banker. As, however, several weeks elapsed without anything more being heard of the Baron or the securities, my master instituted inquiries in the proper quarter, and, as the result of his investigations, it transpired that in the meanwhile the shares had been sold, and the securities handed over, to another purchaser.

It might reasonably have been supposed, at first sight, that by this act Jansen had placed himself within the clutches of the law, but to entertain such a supposition, even for a moment, would have been to do our friend a very great injustice—he was just a *leetle* too clever for that. It appeared that the securities—which really belonged to Jansen—had been registered in the name of a third party, whom we will call Mr. John Straw, and the Baron, producing a receipt from the latter for the purchase-money entrusted to him by Sir George, protested that he had been made the dupe of the perfidious Straw, who had sold the shares twice over.

Needless to add that when the legal screw was applied, Mr. Straw—who was a mere tool, rather than an accomplice, of the Baron's—floated airily over to Boulogne, while Jansen, the impersonification of conscious rectitude, strutted about St. James' Street with an extra-large-sized gardenia in his button-hole, the immaculate purity of which should of itself have been sufficient to disarm suspicion.

I am not sure that I have told the story quite correctly, for business details are rather out of my line, but the main facts are as I have given them. Shortly afterwards Mr. Geoffrey, on his way to dine with a friend at the Two Services, happened to run against the perfidious Jansen in the entrance-hall of the Club. The Baron was talking to some mutual acquaintances, and as my master approached, he turned round, and holding out his hand as if nothing had occurred, addressed him in the familiar style which he usually affected.

"Halloa, Geoff, my boy!——" he began, but my master, with difficulty keeping his temper, stared him straight in the face and passed on without taking the slightest notice of him. There the matter would probably have ended, but on leaving the Club after dinner they found our friend waiting for them outside the hall-door. Being blessed, as I have already had occasion to remark, with a pachydermatous hide and not easily rebuffed, he approached Mr. Geoffrey—who was in the act of lighting a cigar—and tapping him playfully on the shoulder, began:—"Look here, old man, you mustn't——" but, for once in his life, he had miscalculated the limits of human forbearance. If there was one thing my master detested more than another, it was being 'pawed about,' as he called it, and catching the astonished Baron by the shoulder, he swung him round and incontinently kicked him down the Club steps into the street—where he narrowly escaped being run over by a passing cab.

* * * * *

Having lost sight of the Baron, his disclosures soon ceased to occupy my mind, for besides my regular duties at the Court, I had my own domestic affairs to attend to. I was the proud father of two dark-eyed, olive-skinned youngsters—named, respectively, after my kind friend the Parson of Netherleigh and Sir George—and in addition to the trouble the young rascals gave their mother, we were annoyed by periodical visits from that *vafodi poori grasni*, my *stiffi-dye* Cinerella Lovell—I'd most forgotten my Romany. She used to come whining to us for money, for, according to her account, her amiable son, Mr. Solomon, had never altogether recovered from the effects of a clip on the head which he had received on a certain frosty night in March some six or seven years ago, but my pretty sister-in-law, Trainette, set our minds at ease on that score by attributing his impoverished circumstances to intemperate habits combined with a constitutional aversion to anything in the shape of regular work.

My dear old Granny was sleeping peacefully in the little churchyard of Loxhoe—where she had been buried according to her express desire—a tiny hamlet on the very verge of the cliffs, where the short-cropped herbage was watered by the salt spray from the Atlantic, and the strong-winged grey gulls chattered to their brown-speckled young ones within a stone's-throw of the old Gipsy's resting-place. Of the elders who, in former days, used to sit round the camp-fire in the Combe, Neptune alone remained. The old man was no longer able to do much in the way of trapping or fishing, but he was well looked after by his sons, Perin and Pharez, and managed to earn a living by hawking red and silver sand, earthenware, dried fish, etc., and being a perfect compendium of the gossip of the neighbourhood, he had become quite an institution in a county where news travels but slowly.

After my handsome but uncertain-tempered cousin Vester had been jilted by pretty Lementina Boswell on his return from Exeter gaol, he left the West of England for good and all, and changing his name for one which was destined to figure prominently in the annals of the Prize Ring, joined some of the Coopers and Ayres, and earned a precarious livelihood by attending fairs and race meetings, where he looked after horses, sparred in the booths, and acted as tout or runner to the four-in-hands upon their arrival on the course.

It so happened that at Ascot, just as the drag belonging to the Grenadier Guards—then stationed at Windsor—was leaving the course after the last race, an altercation arose between Vester and the sergeant in charge of the commissariat department, who, upon their arrival on the course, had roughly ordered my cousin to go about his business when he offered to help to unharness the horses.

Now the sergeant in question enjoyed the reputation of being the best man in the Service, and had been taken over to Ascot for the express purpose of getting up a little fight on the quiet, and at the prospect of a bit of fun Lord W——, who was driving, pulled his team out of the line of homeward-bound vehicles, and brought the coach to a standstill— the wheels were blocked with empty champagne bottles, and the preliminaries quickly arranged. In the meanwhile half-a-dozen other drags had followed Lord W——'s lead, a level piece of turf was selected, and a purse amounting to upwards of twenty pounds collected in a few minutes.

The news of the impending fight spread like wild-fire, and some five or six hundred spectators, consisting of country-gentlemen, betting-men, hooked-nosed Sheenies, flash Gentiles, prigs, touts, welshers, and a strong contingent of the Gipsies camped about the Heath, soon formed a respectable-sized ring within the outer circle of the drags. I was not present myself—being at that time in Mr. Shice's employment in Westport—and am, therefore, only able to speak from hearsay, but Horace Ayres told me that when the men stripped in the ring, as far as weight of metal went, it looked a pound to a penny on the sergeant—a powerfully-built man and a trained athlete into the bargain. On the other hand, Vester was by no means a novice at the game, although a bit too light in the opinion of the amateurs, but what there was of him was all wire and whipcord, while his graceful figure and confident bearing, combined with the easy way in which he put up his hands, strongly impressed the spectators in his favour—contrasting, as it did, with the rather constrained attitude of the military hero who, making the most of his height, held his head up as if on parade, keeping his left hand stiffly extended on a level with his hip and his guard too close to his body.

Any doubts, however, as to the sergeant meaning business were very quickly dispelled, for walking straight up to his opponent without any preliminary sparring, he drove him back among the crowd and lifted him clean off his legs with a terrific upper-cut, thereby causing the betting, which opened at evens, to change to 6 to 4 on the soldier, who was strongly supported—as in duty bound—by the Grenadiers, while the Blues—whose horses Vester had taken out and watered—backed the Gipsy.

During the first three rounds my cousin was twice knocked off his pins—for the spectators crowded in so that it was impossible to get away—but in the fifth and sixth the beef on the sergeant's ribs and chest began to tell its inevitable tale. It was the old story. Youth and condition had to be served, Vester began to knock holes through the big 'un, and at the end of the tenth round Cannon—who, very appropriately, had been picking up the soldier—was obliged to chuck up the sponge.

The chance encounter on the Heath proved the turning-point of my cousin's career, for, as luck would have it, Mr. L—— H——,—a well-known Hebrew financier and a staunch patron of the Prize Ring,—happened to be standing in Vester's corner, and taking a liking to the Gipsy's style and finding that he could use his head as well as his hands, he personally assisted old Abraham Cooper in sending his man up to the scratch. Mr. H—— was the largest winner over the fight, and at its conclusion he presented Vester with a ten-pound note and insisted upon his accompanying him back to London, where he put him on a liberal allowance of butcher's meat and a tap of strong ale, and employed him as carman at his place of business in Bermondsey. At the end of six months Vester was a very different man from the half-starved 'bushman' who had all his work cut out to beat the muscular but beefy sergeant, and before parting company with him, he amply vindicated Mr. L—— H——'s judgment, and repaid his generosity, by winning three fights off the reel against good men.

In the meanwhile pretty Lementina Boswell had married old Ben Lee, of the firm of Lee and Robinson, the well-known Refreshment Contractors, and upon his death my cousin Vester who, by a series of brilliant successes—marred but by one defeat, and that more honourable, under the circumstances, than a dozen victories 'on the cross'—had achieved a record second to none in the history of the Ring, sacrificed his chances of the championship in order to marry his old flame. As, however, we shall meet Vester again before long, I will leave him for the present.

To bring the family history up to date, I should state that my uncle Sylvester—who, upon the expiration of his seven years' sentence for the assault on Inspector Lougher, had returned to his old haunts—finding that *loorin' foki* with his *gryor** was not a paying game in the long run, forsook the green Devonshire lanes for the smoke and dirt of the Metropolitan Gipsyries, and was shortly afterwards knocked down and killed by a nervous young horse that he was leading back from Barnet Fair.

* Taking people in with his horses.

CHAPTER XXXIII.

A Fine Old County Skeleton.

AS month succeeded month and winter gave place to summer, the suspicions which had been aroused by the Baron's strange communication were gradually lulled to rest, and I began to look upon that usually well-informed individual as a bit of a failure in the Cassandra-like *rôle* which he had so unexpectedly assumed, although, at the same time, I was altogether at a loss to account for his unwonted liberality. No fresh complications had arisen between Father Considine and Mr. Geoffrey to ruffle the placid surface of existence at Netherleigh—the latter was in London, while the former seemed to be completely absorbed in the congenial task of cataloguing the large and valuable collection of manuscripts and rare books which had been amassed by Sir George's predecessors.

With the exception of one unpleasant incident—which, although it has no direct bearing upon my story, is, perhaps, worthy of mention—the domestic horizon appeared to be as serene and unclouded as the summer sky without, from whence the sun was now pouring his full splendour upon the bright-coloured *parterres* of the south-front and the masses of crimson geraniums which were disposed at intervals in *jardinières* along the terrace, causing the peacocks to retire to the comparative coolness of the shady courts and corridors at the back of the house, and driving the blackbirds and the rest of the feathered songsters to the shelter of the hanging woods which sloped abruptly down to the river.

Some two hundred feet below the south-west terrace, the

Cran, reduced to a mere brown thread, was brawling over the stickles, while every stone in the river's bed was distinctly visible to the naked eye and resembled an intricate piece of mosaic work. I had come out to look for Sir George, and as I leaned over the parapet and gazed down into the valley below, some tiny dark specks came in sight, creeping like ants along the narrow white streak which marked the course of the Netherton road. As they gradually grew more distinct, I was able to distinguish the familiar outlines of my uncle Neptune's old blue *vardo,* preceded and followed by the usual straggling array of men, women, and children—vans, horses, and dogs. As they wound along the opposite bank of the river, an occasional shout or laugh came floating upwards through the still summer air, causing a strange feeling of yearning to pass through my breast.

When, later in the day, I went with some of the men-servants for our daily swim in the deep Orchard Pool beyond the north garden, we found the whole of the dusky crew—amongst whom were my cousins Perin, Frank, and Pharez—splashing, swimming, and diving in the cool water, or whooping, yelling, and chasing each other along the further bank after precisely the same primitive fashion as prevailed amongst us when I sojourned with my kinsmen in leafy Fernleigh Combe. I swam across and had a long chat with my cousins, and after hearing all the family news and the gossip of 'the road,' I hurried back to the house, arriving just in time to assist my master to dress for dinner—a formality which he invariably observed even when dining in solitary state, but on this particular occasion he was joined, as usual, by Mr. Frank and Father Considine.

And now, in order to give you an insight into some of the conditions which tended to regulate my master's state of health, it might, perhaps, be as well if I were to explain the incident to which I have alluded at the commencement of this chapter.

In addition to the family plate, of which there was a very large quantity, there were several sacramental vessels—chalices and patens, as they were called—which were used in the chapel services, and which were celebrated throughout the West of England for their delicate workmanship and antiquity—in fact they were so old, and worn so thin, that the slightest pressure would bend them out of shape, and the funny part about it was that when they were shown by the chaplain to visitors, no lady was ever allowed to touch them.

Now at that time we had a footman—his name was George, and he was a nephew of old Dan Hurley, the stud-groom—who was the best chap to clean plate I ever saw. It wasn't any particular plate-powder, brush, or leather, that he used which made him turn out his plate different to the others—it was the interest he took in his work. It seemed a perfect pleasure to him, and instead of coming out into the park to play cricket with the other men of a summer's evening or whenever he had an hour to spare, he preferred to stop indoors polishing up his plate—especially when, as happened now and again, Father Considine sent for him to the sacristy to clean the great silver candelabra and the communion-plate.

Well, one morning when the housemaids went into the library, they found that the room had been broken into,—a hole having been cut through the shutters and the fastenings removed from the outside. The false bookcase had been opened and an attempt made upon the safe; but either they had been disturbed at their work, or the old-fashioned strong-box had proved too strong for the thieves. But when the time came for morning service, it was found that the chapel had also been broken into, and that all the communion-plate, etc., was gone.

You may imagine what a sensation the event created in our quiet household, and all of us men-servants rushed off to the chapel in a great state of excitement. We found that the heavy flag-stone, which covered the entrance to the family vault, had been removed, several of the coffins had been broken open, and all the silver coffin-plates and metal ornaments wrenched off. As one of our proverbs says:—"*Saw moosh man jal te congri yeck divvus* or the *vauver*,"* but I should strongly recommend any person afflicted with a weak stomach to postpone his visit to his final resting-place until circumstances beyond his control render it unavoidable, for—especially when burglars or body-snatchers have been at work—I can assure you from personal experience that a

* "Everybody must go to church—be buried—one day or another."

family vault is not the pleasantest place in the world even on a fine morning in May.

The coffins had been tossed about anyhow, and the Baron might literally have had his pick of 'good old county skeletons,' but amongst all the disorder and horrors, one very curious thing was noticeable. I must explain to you that when the last Lady L'Estrange died, some twenty years previously, something had been done to the body to prevent decay—embalming, I think they call it. Before she was buried, those of the servants who wished to do so were allowed to see her as she lay in her coffin, and I have often heard Mrs. Barry relate how beautiful she looked with her hands crossed upon her breast and all her rings—some of which were very valuable—sparkling in the light of the tapers. This had given rise to a report that she had been buried in her rings, but it was altogether incorrect, as they had been all removed before the leaden coffin was soldered down.

Having lit some candles, we proceeded to take a look round, and we found that the outer shell of her ladyship's coffin had been broken open, the silver memorial-plate wrenched off, and the inner coffin of lead—in which the body had been confined—cut through with a sharp instrument and prized open. But the thieves had all their trouble for nothing, for, as I have explained, the rings had been removed, but the effect of the embalming had been to cause all that was mortal of the late Lady L'Estrange to crumble away to an impalpable powder upon contact with the air, while, strange to say—and unless half-a-dozen others beside myself had seen it, I would scarcely ask you to believe it—the luxuriant masses of golden-brown hair which had been the poor lady's principal ornament during life, remained just as bright and silky as the day she died, and seemed, literally, to fill the coffin with a flood of light.

Very fortunately, Sir George had not yet left his room—he seldom made his appearance downstairs much before luncheon-time—and Mr. Francis gave strict orders that not a word was to be said before him about the vault being broken open; but what does Father Considine do but go and tell my master all about it, and, as you may imagine, the news almost killed the old gentleman, and a doctor had to be sent for from London.

But the worst remains to be told. The footman who used to clean the plate so well had lately become rather queer and depressed, and Sir George had given him permission to go and stay with some relatives near Exeter. Well, a day or two after the burglary, the poor fellow came back to Netherleigh and asked to see Sir George, but was told that the baronet was too ill to see him. From the way he went on, it was evident that he had got it into his head that people suspected him of being connected in some way with the robbery, and a few days afterwards his body was found in the river.

It may easily be understood that these two occurrences were calculated to exercise a very prejudicial effect upon my master's health. Upon the same afternoon that I swam across the river for a chat with my relations—about a month after the event I have just related—Sir George had been complaining of the excessive glare and heat of the last few days, and after making a very poor dinner, he retired to the library rather before his usual time. It was my duty to bring him his bedroom candle at half-past ten precisely, and to let in the brace of Clumber spaniels that always slept upon the hearth-rug in his bedroom. As usual, just as the clock struck the half-hour, I knocked at the library-door, but receiving no reply, I entered and found my master lying back in his arm-chair as white as a sheet and apparently lifeless. He had evidently been writing when the attack seized him, for the pen had dropped from the nerveless hand on to the carpet, while open letters and account-books were scattered about the table. I therefore concluded that, feeling better after dinner, he had set to work to overhaul some of his correspondence and accounts, and that the exertion, combined with the unusually oppressive atmosphere, had brought on one of the fainting fits which had caused his medical advisers such anxiety.

I ran at once to the bell, and ringing loudly, proceeded to throw both the French windows wide open, while the spaniels, taking advantage of the opportunity, rushed frantically out into the darkness in quest of their hereditary enemies the peacocks, between whom and themselves there existed a feud of long-standing respecting a right of way on the terrace. I then loosened my master's collar and cravat, and upon Adams's arrival we wheeled him to the open window and proceeded to apply the restoratives which the doctors had prescribed, and which were always kept in readiness for emergencies. It was some time before he showed any signs of vitality, and, upon his return to consciousness, he remained in such a feeble condition that we were obliged to carry him to his bedroom with the assistance of the footmen.

As we slowly made our way upstairs, Father Considine—who had probably been roused from his studies by the ringing of bells and the trampling of feet—met us at the head of the staircase, but finding that his assistance was not required, he returned to his study.

My poor master, who, in spite of his occasional fits of irritability, was invariably most considerate and disliked giving unnecessary trouble, would not hear of my sending a groom at that time of night for Mr. Hill—the village doctor who was in the habit of attending him, and whose treatment had met with the approbation of the eminent London physician who had been summoned in consultation. He appeared much more comfortable after we had put him to bed, and having given him his basin of arrowroot with an extra lacing of brandy in it, I sat up with him until he dozed off to sleep. I am unable to say exactly how long I remained in Sir George's room, as I may have nodded a little myself, but I was aroused by hearing the spaniels scampering up the passage in their usual breathless, helter-skelter fashion, and knowing that they would begin to whine and scratch at the door if refused admittance, I got up and let them into the dressing-room—which opened out of my master's bedroom—where I was in the habit of sleeping whenever Sir George was ill.

The fact was that I had forgotten all about them. I had taken it for granted that Adams would have seen that the library windows were fastened up and the door locked before going to bed, but it was evident that he had omitted to do so, or the dogs would have come upstairs before, so after waiting for perhaps half-an-hour longer to make sure that Sir George was sound asleep, I lit a bedroom candle and went downstairs with the intention of seeing that all was safe for the night.

As I descended the main-staircase, my feet sank at every step into the thick pile of the carpet, but as I crossed the entrance-hall, where the moon was shining brightly through the stained glass of the heavily-mullioned windows, my footsteps rang out distinctly upon the flagstones.

Before I had taken ten steps along the corridor which led to the library and dining-room, the library door was thrown open, and the tall figure of Father Considine, carrying a lighted candle in one hand and a book in the other, emerged from the darkness and advanced to meet me. There was nothing the least unusual in this, for he was in the habit of visiting the library in search of some favourite author or book of reference at all hours of the day and night, but as the flickering light of the candle played upon his features, I fancied that I noticed an unusual brightness in the deep-set eyes and a complacent smile about the thin lips, which, contrary to his usual habit, he seemed at no pains to repress. It might have been the effect of the candle-light, but at all events he appeared to be in an unusually good humour, for as I stood aside to allow him to pass, he stopped to inquire how Sir George was going on, and after asking me two or three more questions, wished me 'Good night' quite pleasantly and proceeded on his way along the corridor, and crossing the moonlit hall, mounted the staircase in the direction of his private apartments.

I watched the retreating figure until it was lost to sight, and then entered the library. Knowing the priest's dislike to night air, I was not surprised to see that the windows had been closed, and I noticed that the shutters had been drawn together as closely as was possible without actually putting up the bars—a set of new-fangled contrivances with spring-catches, which had been fixed since the burglary, and which were very apt to pinch your fingers if you weren't in the habit of handling them. Having fastened the shutters and seen that everything was safe, I collected the letters and papers which were lying scattered about the table, and having placed them under a letter-weight, I was about to leave the room, when I noticed that the false-bookcase between the windows was slightly ajar, and crossing over, I found Sir George's bunch of private keys hanging from the lock of the strong-box, or safe, which, when closed, the shelves of handsomely-bound imitation-books effectually concealed.

Not being gifted with an undue amount of inquisitiveness—I don't count reading letters which have been left in clothes sent down to brush, for if gentlemen don't want them read, they shouldn't leave them about, and if I hadn't taken the trouble to look through Mr. Geoffrey's correspondence pretty regularly, I should never have known what arrangements to make for the day or what things to pack up or put out, he was that careless, but opening letters by steaming them over a kettle is a thing I never did hold with, not considering it honourable, though more often done than some people think,—I was going to turn the key in the lock when my eye fell upon a small, flatly-folded packet of greyish-blue paper about four inches square which was lying on the floor at my feet, in the crevice between the base of the safe and the thick carpet. The little packet exactly resembled, both in size and shape, those in which makers of fishing-tackle are in the habit of enclosing their artificial flies, and my piscatorial instincts being aroused at the sight, I was unable to resist the feeling of curiosity which prompted me to investigate its contents.

On picking it up and turning back the last fold, I was surprised to find that, instead of fishing-tackle, the packet contained a lock of light-brown hair which, from its texture, might have belonged to a woman, but which, from its shortness, seemed more likely to have been cut from the head of a school-boy. It was twisted into a figure-of-eight and knotted together in the centre with a piece of ribbon which had once been blue, but which the lapse of years had turned to a greenish white. Underneath the lock of hair lay a still smaller packet containing a number of those downy and almost microscopic hairs which—as experience had lately taught me—are wont to adorn the human cranium at a very early stage of existence.

Upon the inside of the smaller packet were the initials G. A. B. L'E. in a peculiarly scratchy but distinct handwriting which I had no difficulty in identifying as that of

Sir George, nor did it require the exercise of any very exceptional ingenuity to arrive at the conclusion that the initials were those of my master's eldest son—Geoffrey Adrian Barrington L'Estrange. But the lock of brown hair was a puzzler. It might have belonged to Mr. Geoffrey when he was a boy—it certainly never came off Mr. Frank's head, for that was very much darker—but for a golden gleam in it which I had never noticed in his curly wig, and which reminded me more of her ladyship's beautiful hair which I had lately seen under such peculiar circumstances; or it might have belonged to fifty other people. If it had not been for the events which immediately preceded it, there would have been nothing very startling in the discovery of the packet itself, but I remembered the expression of ill-concealed satisfaction which Father Considine's face had worn as he passed me in the passage, and coupling with it the hints which Jansen had thrown out in the course of our interview in the summer-house, I jumped to the conclusion that the priest might possibly have stumbled across a missing link in some chain of evidence which he had been industriously piecing together.

Had it not been for the Baron's hints, I should most certainly have replaced the packet in the safe and locked it, laid the keys on the table, and gone back to my room without the least suspicion of there being anything wrong, but supposing the safe to contain any private papers capable of throwing a light upon the subject of Sir George's marriage, I felt sure that no conscientious scruples, or nice feeling of honour, would prevent my friend 'the Bat' from taking advantage of the opportunity which my master's sudden illness might have thrown in his way. Of course, I might be wronging the man, but I didn't think so. It was true that the same source of information was open to both of us, but I had no clue to guide me. I felt that I was in the position of a traveller groping his way in the darkness across a wild and pathless moor, while the priest—unless Jansen was mistaken, and I was beginning to think I had underrated his acuteness—was pressing steadily onward along a well-beaten track which grew broader and smoother as he neared his journey's end, and although I possessed a cool head and my fair share of the craftiness which is the birthright of every true-born Rom'nichal, I was, nevertheless, fully aware that in the event of an encounter between the polished blade of the Jesuit's highly-trained intellect and the rough cudgel of my natural astuteness, it would be long odds on the former.

Although my ideas were a bit hazy, I was not slow to recognise the fact that I stood face to face with an emergency, and that the events of the next few hours might powerfully influence the future prospects of a family which had always shown me the utmost kindness. As these thoughts coursed rapidly through my brain, I reflected that time was on the wing, and that I was liable to be interrupted at any moment by the priest's return, so, having assured myself that the coast was clear for the time being, I ran up to Sir George's room to see whether he was sleeping quietly, and then, returning to the library, locked the door on the inside, and hanging my coat on the key so as to prevent anybody from looking through the keyhole, I opened the false-bookcase and set to work to investigate the contents of the safe.

Upon throwing back the heavy inner door—which still bore the marks of the burglars' tools—I found that everything was arranged with almost mathematical precision, in accordance with the love of order and neatness which was one of Sir George's most pronounced characteristics. His private papers were separated from those which referred to the household and estates, while all were neatly docketed and laid in their respective pigeon-holes. There were countless packets of old letters, receipted bills, and small, red-backed books containing old banking-accounts. In one corner stood an iron casket that had formerly contained some valuable jewellery—which after the attempt on the house had been removed to the Bank at Exeter—while two or three of the drawers were entirely filled with shabby shagreen and morocco cases containing old-fashioned bracelets, brooches, rings, etc., of very little intrinsic worth. In fact, there was little to repay a professional burglar for his expenditure of time and labour, and I might have rummaged for hours amongst the letters and papers without becoming any the wiser, had not my attention been attracted by one little trace of disorder, which was all the more noticeable when contrasted with the prevailing neatness.

Upon the top-shelf was a row of books of almost uniform size, and differing only in the colour of the leather in which they were bound. Upon the backs of some of them the dates of certain years—ranging from 1809 to 1823—were stamped in faded gold numerals, while others bore no date or distinguishing mark whatever. One of these books appeared to me to have been taken out and replaced lately, for its back projected about half-an-inch beyond the others, and was slightly out of the perpendicular, its upper edge being correspondingly elevated, while the almost imperceptible film of dust with which the others were coated had been brushed or shaken off. My attention was insensibly attracted by the comparatively disorderly appearance of this particular book, and taking it down from the shelf, I noticed that it opened of its own accord at a certain page—the leaves being creased as if a letter or book-marker had been tightly pressed between them.

All at once an idea flashed across me, and taking up the small paper packet which I had picked up off the carpet, I found that it exactly corresponded with the impression. Something or other seemed to tell me that I was on the right track, and this feeling was strengthened when I found that the volume—which was in manuscript—contained Sir George's Diary for the years 1816-17.

My bedroom candle had burned down and was flickering in the socket, so, placing the book on the table, I lighted the reading-lamp and proceeded to examine it at my leisure. I had less hesitation in reading the Diary—which was in Sir George's unmistakable handwriting—since I reflected that its contents were no longer a secret, and as I spelled my way laboriously through page after page of cramped and faded handwriting, I marvelled at the thoughtlessness which had permitted my master to preserve this dangerous record of his early life, while my respect for the Baron's penetration and knowledge of human nature was correspondingly increased.

As far as my memory serves me, I will endeavour to give a summary of that portion of the Diary which relates to the question of my master's marriage. I have already described the circumstances under which Sir George—then Mr. George L'Estrange—made the acquaintance of Mdlle. de Gonidec at Bordeaux, but until this evening, in common with the rest of the world, I had never heard the true story of his infatuation for, and subsequent marriage with, the beautiful young actress. I had simply heard it stated that my master had been married in France and that Mr. Geoffrey had been born in Ireland and christened at Kilmore Castle, but I will now give a few of the most important facts, bearing directly upon the subject, in their proper order.

Upon leaving Bordeaux, the Paris company to which Mdlle. de Gonidec belonged, proceeded upon its provincial tour, visiting, amongst other towns, Limoges and Orleans, and it was at the latter of these two places that the marriage took place. Unquestionable as were his young wife's antecedents, as far as birth was concerned—for the De Gonidecs belonged to one of the oldest families in Brittany—Mr. L'Estrange was well aware that his father would be furious when he heard of the marriage, and partly, no doubt, out of consideration for his father's delicate state of health, my master resolved to keep the matter a secret for the present, and in order to prevent any communication between his father-in-law—Colonel De Gonidec—and Sir Pierre, he persuaded his wife not to enter into any details, but merely to inform her family that she had married an English gentleman and left the stage.

The young couple then proceeded to Paris, and my master took an opportunity of paying a flying visit to Netherleigh with a view to broaching the subject of his marriage, but the moment was not propitious, and having rejoined his wife in the French capital, they travelled down to Italy and spent the winter near Genoa. In the spring of the following year—1817—they returned to Paris, and then made their way by Dreux, Alencon, and St. Malo to Jersey, as Mr. L'Estrange had lately received some very disqueting reports of Sir Pierre's health, and wished to be within reasonable distance of Devonshire.

So far everything had turned out as well as could possibly have been expected, and, judging from the general tone of the Diary, they had lived in a lovers' Paradise of their own, 'the world forgetting, by the world forgot.' But, unfortunately, this blissful state of things was not destined to last, for Mrs. L'Estrange received a letter at St. Heliers from one of her sisters, with whom she had opened a correspondence, informing her that her father—whose suspicions had been aroused by the secrecy which had been maintained—had instituted inquiries at Orleans and had ascertained that, owing to some technical informality in the civil ceremony, the validity of the marriage was open to question. The letter concluded by warning her that the Colonel was furious at the deception of which—as he had every reason to believe—she had been made the victim, and having ascertained the L'Estranges' present address, was on the point of starting for Jersey, armed with a varied assortment of lethal weapons and threatening the direst vengeance on his daughter's deceiver, etc., etc.

Colonel de Gonidec, it should be explained, although a brilliant soldier, was a man of violent temper, and, moreover, enjoyed the reputation of being a *mauvais sujet*. After retiring from the army he had lost all his money in imprudent speculations and had lately taken to drink, and although altogether unable to support his family, he had quarrelled with his daughter Lucille for going on the stage. Apart from the statement which the letter contained relating to her marriage—which might, or might not, prove well-founded—the prospect of a visit from her fire-eating progenitor was, of itself, well calculated to terrify a rather delicate young wife who soon expected to be a mother, and rather than face the interview and expose her husband to the alternative of mortal combat or black-mailing, Mrs. L'Estrange persuaded my master—very much against his better judgment—to leave Jersey for England.

After a good deal of difficulty they succeeded in making terms with the skipper of a trading-brig—which was due to sail the same day—bound for Cork, who engaged, for a handsome consideration, to land them at Falmouth. This, as will be seen, proved a most fatal step. It was about the time of the equinoctial gales—March, 1817—and before they had been five hours at sea, a strong south-easterly gale sprang up, and the rascally skipper—who was probably only too glad of an excuse for breaking his contract—altered his course, allowing the brig to run before the wind under close-reefed topsails, and towards the evening of the second day they were off the Irish coast. As soon as my master discovered the trick that had been played upon him, he went straight to the captain's cabin, and a violent scene ensued. If he had seen as much of trading skippers as I subsequently did, and had sailed with such gentlemen as Captain Jack of the *Maria* or Captain Rogers of the *Swallow*, he would have known that threats and blandishments were equally thrown away and would quietly have accepted the situation, for, within a few hours, they were sailing up the sparkling waters of Cork harbour.

My master could hardly have been in a proper frame of mind to appreciate the beautiful scenery of the Cove, for, to add to his embarrassments, his companion was in anything but a condition to undertake the rough voyage, and within a few hours of their settling into furnished apartments in T—— Street, Mr. Geoffrey made his appearance in this world of sorrow rather unexpectedly. A nurse was procured for the child, but the unfortunate lady remained in such a critical condition—her illness having turned to brain-fever, brought on, probably, by the worry and uncertainty which her sister's letter had occasioned her—that the doctor ordered all her beautiful hair to be cut off, and strongly recommended Mr. L'Estrange to send at once for Sir Maurice Redmond, the recognised head of the medical profession in Dublin. This was done, and owing, possibly, to Sir Maurice's skilful treatment, Mrs. L'Estrange began slowly to improve, but it was evident that the doubt as to the legality of their marriage was weighing heavily on her mind, and my master—as honourable a gentleman as ever stepped—at once put the matter in the hands of a private-enquiry agent in Paris, and ascertained beyond doubt that, owing to some trifling omission in his declaration of nationality before the Mayor, according to the strict letter of the law the marriage was null and void.

The birth of the child only served to make confusion worse confounded, and it was during this period of doubt and despondency, intensified by the dangerous illness of the lady who, in the sight of heaven, was his wife, that my master—a prey to the deepest anxiety and remorse—cut off the lock of hair which had puzzled me so, and which he placed between the leaves of the Diary, where it had remained undisturbed up to the present time.

The child, who at first had not been expected to live, now began to thrive wonderfully under the care of his Irish nurse, and as soon as his mother was strong enough to be moved, the whole party left Cork for Youghal, and after passing a couple of days at that picturesque but untidy little seaport, made their way to Cappoquin, where they lived in the greatest retirement.

My master had now to choose his line of action. Three courses were open to him. To repudiate both his marriage and the child—as many a man would have done in his position—to go through the ceremony again and acknowledge the illegitimacy of his son—undoubtedly the wisest course—or to be remarried as privately and speedily as possible, concealing the exact date of the child's birth and trusting to the chapter of accidents to escape detection. Unfortunately for all concerned, my master chose the latter alternative, and knowing, as I did, his proud and sensitive nature, I can well imagine the struggle it must have cost him to stoop to deception.

Keeping the result of his enquiries as to the validity of the Orleans marriage a profound secret from the unfortunate lady, he professed to treat the whole matter as a joke, suggesting that, in order to make things safe beyond the possibility of a doubt, they should be privately remarried as soon as possible. This had the desired effect of reassuring his companion, and leaving the child with his nurse at Cappoquin, they proceeded to Dungarvan, where they were quietly married—for the second time—in the Roman Catholic church, without anybody being the wiser. The south coast of Ireland at that time of year was as good a place as could well have been selected by anyone desirous of living in seclusion, so, sending for the nurse and child, the L'Estranges took a small house near the little fishing village of Ardmore.

I ought, perhaps, to mention, that in order to keep his father-in-law quiet, my master forwarded him a properly-attested copy of the Dungarvan marriage, at the same time pointing out that nothing was to be gained by making it known that the legality of the Orleans marriage was open to question, and offering to pay him an annuity so long as he refrained from annoying them or communicating with

Sir Pierre. This offer was accepted, and the terms, presumably, adhered to, since nothing further appears to have been heard of Colonel de Gonidec, who died at Dinan in the year 1822.

Finding that the strong Atlantic breezes soon had the desired effect of bringing the colour back to the young mother's cheeks, my master—who had received no news of his father for some time—crossed over from Waterford to Bristol, and made his way down to Devonshire, leaving his wife perfectly happy and contented with the child and nurse.

His first step upon his arrival at Netherleigh, where he found his father in a very critical condition, was to inform his old friend, the Rev. Mark Sealy, of his marriage with Mdlle. de Gonidec—without, however, giving any particulars as to date or locality—and of the birth of a son and heir. With some difficulty he persuaded the Parson to break the news to Sir Pierre, but whether the message was conveyed or not, did not transpire from the Diary, for within a few hours of his arrival at the Court, Sir George found himself master of Netherleigh.

As soon as the necessary formalities had been observed, he hurried back to Ireland, and proceeded with his wife—now Lady L'Estrange—to visit his Kilmore Castle estates. Here the child was christened, amidst the rejoicing of the tenantry, by Father Dennis Massy—at that time parish priest of Kilmore—and after passing the summer on the West Coast, they returned to Devonshire.

Such were the principal facts of interest contained in the Diary—the remaining particulars I am able to supply of my own personal knowledge. I have already mentioned that, upon their return to Netherleigh, the L'Estranges were rather coldly received by the neighbouring families, but, luckily for themselves, they possessed resources, both pecuniary and intellectual, which rendered them independent of county society. Their experience of domestic happiness and tranquillity was, however, destined to prove a brief one, for within a few weeks of the birth of their second son Francis, the bright-eyed mistress of Netherleigh was laid in her last resting-place beneath the chancel of the old chapel. Sir George—as I have already told you—never quite recovered from the effects of the shock occasioned him by his wife's sudden death, and, strangely enough, he appeared to have taken a dislike to his second son, and withdrawing himself more and more from society, devoted himself to the education of his eldest boy.

    *   *   *   *   *   *

The secret of Mr. Geoffrey's birth had been well kept, and up to the time of Father Considine's arrival at Netherleigh, it is probable that nothing had transpired to cause my master any further anxiety respecting his son's succession to the title and estates.

CHAPTER XXXIV.

I am Entrusted with an Important Commission.

I HAD now learned almost as much as I cared to know, so, carefully restoring the little packet to its former resting-place between the leaves of the Diary, and replacing it on the shelf, I locked the safe, and turning down the lamp, crept quietly upstairs, taking the keys with me.

The rooks were already beginning to stir amongst the elms outside the dressing-room window, and feeling that sleep was out of the question, I looked into Sir George's bedroom in order to assure myself that he was sleeping quietly, and as the grey morning light stole in through the curtains and lit up the thin, high-bred face, pinched and drawn by illness and worry, but now resting so peacefully upon the pillows, I no longer wondered at the harassed look which I had so often remarked about the eyes, or at the deep lines with which secret troubles and anxieties had furrowed the broad forehead.

Returning to the dressing-room, I threw myself half dressed upon the bed and racked my brains in a vain endeavour to puzzle out the situation. In thinking over the events of the past night, one or two things struck me particularly. Unless Father Considine had taken the book off the shelf, the only explanation which occurred to me by which to account for the presence of the paper packet on the floor, was that Sir George had, himself, had occasion to refer to the Diary—whether or not this was the case could only be ascertained by consulting him. If, however, the priest had taken it out of the safe, the important point was how much or how little of it he had read, and this, again, depended entirely upon the time at his disposal.

Now you can get through a good deal of print in a short time, but when it comes to manuscript, it is a different thing altogether. It had taken me four hours of close application to extract the information a summary of which I have given, and although Father Considine was, probably, a much quicker reader, he could scarcely have gone over the same ground in less than two hours at the very least. Allowing that he had slipped down to the library the moment we had got Sir George to his bedroom, he would only have had two clear hours at his disposal—supposing him to have known exactly where to put his hand upon the Diary. But I felt convinced that the priest had not passed more than half-an-hour in the library,—and for this reason.

It will be recollected that when I threw open the windows to let in some fresh air, the spaniels rushed out on to the terrace, and they had not returned when Adams and I—with the assistance of the footmen—carried Sir George upstairs. Knowing their habits so well, I reasoned that they would probably trot about the terrace for awhile, then take a turn round the garden, and after a skirmish with a stray cat or a scurry after an outlying rabbit, re-enter the library through the open windows. Finding the room deserted and the door shut—for both the drawing-room and library doors were furnished with self-closing springs—they would coil up on the hearth-rug. As soon as they heard Father Considine's footsteps in the corridor, they would jump up and wait just inside the door with their heads on one side and their ears cocked, and, the moment it opened, they would

I AM ENTRUSTED WITH AN IMPORTANT COMMISSION.

bolt past the priest and come scampering up to my master's bedroom as hard as they could lay legs to the ground.

According to this reasoning, Father Considine would have entered the library only a minute or two before the spaniels had roused me while dozing by my master's bedside, and as I went down to the library about half-an-hour afterwards, I calculated that he could not have read very much in so short a time.

From my experience of former attacks I calculated that Sir George would sleep on until nine or ten o'clock, so, as soon as it was light, I made my way to the stables, and waking one of the grooms, got him to unlock the saddle-room, and having saddled a hack, rode off to the village—ostensibly to fetch the Doctor, but in reality with a view to consulting my better-half.

A secret, like a kiss, is—as we say in Romany—'*Kooshto for chichi till it's pordered amen dui*,'* and I had a very high opinion of my wife's practical common-sense, nor was it the first time that her sharp wits had helped us out of a tight place.

I was all for letting well alone, for I knew that Sir George would be furious with me for meddling—albeit with the best intentions—with his private affairs, but Mantis was of a different opinion.

"You'd best go to the master, Sam"—said she, "and make a clean breast of it. He may cut up rough at first, but when he comes to hear how it all came about, he'll be thankful to you in the end, and rather than let that image of a priest get the *juckni vast*,† I'd up and tell him myself, that I would"—so, of course, that settled it. I got back to the Court just as Mr. Hill drove up, and having ascertained from him that Sir George was as well as he was likely to be for some time to come, I determined to broach the subject as soon as possible—for I felt that if it was to be done at all, there was not a moment to be lost.

At twelve o'clock I was in the habit of taking a glass of port-wine and a biscuit to my master in the library. Knocking at the door, I found him seated at the writing-table, busily engaged with his accounts. This was altogether contrary to the Doctor's orders, but it was just like my master

* 'Good for nothing till it's shared between two.' † "Whip hand."

all over—a more contrary gentleman never breathed. Naturally most kind and considerate, since his health had broken down he couldn't bear the least approach to contradiction. Adams' way of managing him was never to answer him, or, at any rate, to agree with him in everything—for the word 'No' was like a red rag to a bull.

"Adams"—he would say, "did Mr. Hill say what time he would call to-morrow?"

"I will inquire, Sir George"—the butler would diplomatically reply, retreating at the same time in the direction of the door.

"But didn't you show him out yourself?"

"Yes, Sir George."

"Then you must know what he said?"

"Yes, Sir George."

"Upon my word, Adams, I think you get more stupid every day"—my poor master would exclaim.

"Yes, Sir George"—the imperturbable Adams would reply, making good his escape and closing the door noiselessly behind him.

That was Adams' notion of managing him. I knew him pretty well by this time, and if I wanted him to do a thing, I used, as a general rule, to suggest just the opposite; but on this occasion, for the life of me, I didn't know how to begin, and I loitered about the room pretending to put things straight, until he should have finished his port, as I hoped that it would put him in a good humour. At last he emptied the glass and leaned back in his chair, so thinking the moment a propitious one, I refilled the glass and opened the subject by telling him that I had found the safe unlocked the previous night and a small paper packet lying on the floor.

"Oh, yes, very likely"—he replied, "I remember opening the safe, and I suppose I must have left the keys in the lock. But what sort of packet was it, and where did you put it?"

Then it all came out, bit by bit. The fat was on the fire and no mistake, but, on the whole, he took it much quieter than I could have expected. First of all he jumped up, knocked over the wine-glass, and stood leaning against the back of the chair, trembling all over, while the blood mounted to his cheeks and then left them paler than before. I picked up the glass, refilled it, and he drank it off at a gulp, but his hand trembled so that he spilled some of the wine over his cravat. Then he sat down again, his head resting on his hand, and his face turned away from me.

After a while he roused himself, and told me to go on with my story. I began by telling him of my interview with the Baron in the summer-house the previous November, and of the proposition which that enterprising individual had made me. Then I told him how I had seen Father Considine leave the library: how I had picked up the little paper packet at the foot of the false-bookcase: how I had opened it out of curiosity, under the impression that it contained fishing-tackle of some sort or other: how the Baron's hints flashed across me: how I had noticed that a certain book appeared to have been taken off the shelf and replaced in a hurry: how my suspicions had been confirmed by the discovery that the packet containing the hair had been lying between the pages of the book: and, finally—and this was the worst part of it—how I had been tempted to read the Diary in order to find out whether there was any truth in Jansen's statements. I took my wife's advice and told him everything just as it had happened, finishing up by begging my master, under the circumstances, to overlook the great liberty I had taken, and assuring him that I was ready to do anything in the world to serve him or Mr. Geoffrey.

To my surprise, beyond wincing slightly when Jansen's name was mentioned, Sir George evinced comparatively little emotion at the news, but as I brought my story to a conclusion, the listless look disappeared, and setting his right hand firmly on the table, he pushed back his chair and faced me.

"Loveridge"—he began, and at first his voice trembled slightly, but grew steadier as he proceeded, "you must have been in my service now some ten or twelve years, and during that time I, personally, have had no cause to complain of you, but, rather, the contrary. I have known you ever since you were a boy not much higher than this table, and I have taken a good deal of interest in your career. I believe that you were the means—under God—of saving my son's life when prostrated with fever in Demerara, and for that reason, and that alone, I am disposed to overlook the unwarrantable liberty you have taken in prying into my private affairs. It is true that there are some excuses to be made for you, and I, of all men, have no right to judge you harshly. Chance has placed the one secret of my life in your hands, but I am willing to credit you when you say that you will not only respect it, but are willing to go through fire and water to further my son's interests."

Rising from his chair, my master began to pace restlessly up and down the room, then, reseating himself, he continued in a lower voice:—

"I daresay you are surprised at my taking things so quietly, but the knowledge that I might have to face the emergency at any moment has enabled me to meet it calmly and resignedly. About seven years ago I became aware that Father Considine had his suspicions as to the true state of affairs, and, since then, I have never known what it is to have a peaceful moment. My health has gradually given way beneath the strain, I feel that circumstances are too strong for me, and I have neither the power or the inclination to prolong the struggle."

Now, although I was glad to be let down so easily, this helpless tone was by no means reassuring. It was evident that a reaction—consequent upon the late excitement—had set in, so I poured out another glass of port. I pointed out that if—as I felt sure—Father Considine had only spent half-an-hour in the library, he could not possibly have learnt much from the Diary, and endeavoured, by taking a sanguine view of the case, to cheer up the despondent old gentleman.

"Well, well, Loveridge"—said Sir George wearily, "there may be something in what you say, but I am inclined to let matters take their course. And now," he added, getting up and walking to the window, as if to close the interview, "have you anything more to tell me or any suggestion to make?"

"If you ask me, Sir George"—I replied, "I should say that the first thing is to destroy the Diary before Father Considine takes possession of it—as he probably will if he gets another chance—but, before doing so, I wish to call your attention to one of the entries."

"Take the keys"—said my master, "unlock the safe, and bring me the book. You know where to find it,"—he added, with a bitter smile. "And now"—he continued, as I placed the Diary on the table, "what is it that you want to know?"

I asked him to turn to the month of April 1817, where the following entry had attracted my attention. 'April 21st. L appears to get daily weaker, and O'B. not so sanguine. Went with O'B. to meet mail, but found Redmond could not arrive before morning. G.A.B.L'E. bap^{td}.'

"Yes"—said my master resignedly, "you have put your finger on the weak point, and as you have detected it, it is not likely that it can have escaped Father Considine's notice. It was all owing to Doctor O'Brien's good-natured officiousness that it came about. He assured me positively that the child was not likely to live, and advised me to have it baptised at once. I had not yet heard, officially, whether the marriage ceremony at Orleans was legally valid or not: I was worried to death with anxiety and worn out with sitting up night after night: my brain was in a whirl, and at last I told Dr. O'Brien to do whatever he thought right—the result being that a priest was sent for and the child baptised, the people who kept the lodgings acting as sponsors, in accordance with the requirements of our ritual. From that moment his health seemed to improve, and it was not until I received the information from Orleans which necessitated a second marriage at Dungarvan, that I became alive to the consequences which the existence of a record of his birth or baptism might entail in years to come. Neither Dr. O'Brien or the priest who performed the ceremony knew anything about us. To them we were merely stray tourists, and being, both of them, busy, hard-working men, they probably never gave the matter a second thought. I have ascertained that Dr. O'Brien died in 1832, Sir Maurice Redmond in 1827, and the priest—whose name I forget, but who was an older man than either of them—is not likely to have survived them. T—— Street, where we lodged, has been enlarged and partially rebuilt, and as I have never been able to trace the people who kept the lodgings—their name was Blake—I imagine that they must also be dead, since they were an elderly couple at the time. A year or two later the nurse, Ellen McSweeny, emigrated with her husband to America, and I believe that, with the exception of the baptismal register—if, indeed, such a record has been preserved—no proof exists that my son was born prior to the second marriage. Upon my return from England after Sir Pierre's death, we spent some months at Kilmore, where, in order to divert suspicion, he was publicly baptised—in reality, for the second time—by Father Dennis Massy, the parish priest. Since then twenty-eight years have elapsed, and until Father Considine's arrival nothing had ever occurred to give me the least cause for anxiety, and although I have never been able to ascertain the exact extent of his information, I feel certain that, up to last night, he never suspected the possible existence of a baptismal record in Cork."

The gong now sounded for luncheon, and immediately after, by Sir George's desire, I returned to the library and remained closeted with my master for two or three hours, during which the matter was discussed in all its bearings. Like many people who suffer from general debility rather than from any specific complaint, Sir George was a different man altogether after lunch. It was evident that the necessity for exertion was acting like a strong tonic on the worn-out system, and I was delighted to find that he seemed disposed to fight the matter out to the bitter end.

I first of all suggested that he should consult Mr. Sealy —but no, he would consult nobody. His apathy had given place to a nervous excitement which was painful to witness. His step grew firmer, his eyes brighter, the colour mounted to the wasted cheeks, and as he paced restlessly up and down the room he looked, for the moment, quite ten years younger.

The same idea was, doubtless, uppermost in both our minds, but we refrained from putting it into words. Pride kept Sir George silent, while I—well, there was just a little awkwardness in the position, and where so much had, of necessity, to be left to chance, what was the use of entering into details?

As the result of our interview it was understood that I was to start at once for Cork, " to see how the land lay," but before I left the library I asked Sir George whether it was not possible that some official or duplicate record of Mr. Geoffrey's first baptism might exist in the Government Record Offices in Cork, Dublin, or elsewhere.

"No"—said my master decidedly, "beyond any memorandum or record of the transaction which the officiating priest may have made at the time, and which may or may not have been preserved, I am positive that there is nothing of the kind. I have made it my business to ascertain at the Public Record Office, Four Courts, Dublin, and by application to the Registrar-General, that no official records of the births of Roman Catholic children are preserved. And now, how much money will you require?"

"Two hundred pounds ought to cover all expenses, I should think"—I replied.

"Here is a cheque for three hundred"—said Sir George. "I would willingly give three thousand, or thirty, for the matter of that, to know——" Then breaking off abruptly in the middle of the sentence, he resumed:—"You had better see Hurley and get him to drive you over to Norton with the brown mare, where you can get post-horses to Exeter, and if you lose no time you ought to catch the night train to Bristol. But before you go, just light the fire."

"A pity you hadn't done it twenty years ago"—thought I to myself as I struck a match—for I knew, well enough, that it wasn't for the sake of the warmth that Sir George wanted the fire lit that blazing-hot summer day.

Before leaving the Court I had a confab with Adams in his sanctum, and over a bottle of port from his private bin I explained to him that I was going away on 'the Governor's' business, and that, for certain reasons, it was desirable that no letters of Father Considine's addressed to Ireland should leave Netherleigh during my absence. The butler—who, with the exception of myself, was the only Protestant servant in the establishment, and between whom and the priest there was but little love lost—winked significantly and assured me that I might make my mind easy on that score, and half-an-hour later saw me rattling out of the stable-yard seated in the high dog-cart beside Hurley the stud-groom.

"Hurry now, Sam"—cried old Dan, as we pulled up at my wife's cottage to get a certain suit of clothes that I particularly required and two or three other things, "'tis the divil's own diversion I'll be having to kape the mare from rarin' an' tarin,' wance she's started"—and so it proved, for when I came out five minutes later, the brown mare was on her hind legs, pawing the air wildly with her fore-feet. Tossing my small portmanteau—which had travelled a good many miles since Passon Mark gave it me—into the trap and scrambling in after it as best I could, I waved 'Good-bye' to Mantis and the youngsters, old Dan chirruped to the mare who, after two or three frantic plunges which threatened to snap the traces, laid herself down to her work, and we were soon bowling along the road at the rate of some sixteen miles an hour.

We did the eighteen miles to Norton under the hour-and-a-half, and ordering out a pair of posters from the Porchester Arms, I started again without delay and reached Exeter with an hour to spare. The line from Exeter to Bristol—or, to speak more correctly, from Exeter to Taunton—had been opened the previous year, and with a commendable but mistaken view to economy I took a third-class ticket. It was my first experience of railway travelling in England, and I shall never forget the horrors of that journey.

With the exception of a few benches for the accommodation of passengers, the third-class carriages were built upon precisely the same lines as the cattle-trucks of the present day, and being open at the sides, they afforded scarcely any protection from the wind and rain. The smoke, sparks, and smuts from the engine came driving into our faces in blinding columns, while the jolting was terrible, and to add to our discomforts we ran into a heavy thunderstorm soon after leaving Taunton. We were detained between Bristol and Bath, and again at Reading, owing to some accident to the machinery, and did not reach London until half-past six in the morning.

I drove straight to my cousin's house in Westminster, where I found a sleepy-looking pot-boy engaged in taking down the shutters. Upon expressing a desire to see the master of the house, I was told that 'the Guv'nor' would be down soon, and, an hour later, I was tackling a square meal in the snug parlour behind the bar in the company

I AM ENTRUSTED WITH AN IMPORTANT COMMISSION.

of my cousin, my old playmate Lementina—now a comely matron of eight and thirty—three or four dark-eyed youngsters, and a young lady whose head, at a short distance, presented the appearance of being enveloped in surgical bandages, which, however, on a closer inspection, proved to be nothing more formidable than a heavy crop of curl-papers. Her manners were subdued, and in the languid and, truth to tell, rather washed-out damsel who faced me at Vester's hospitable board, the young bloods who used the house would have experienced some difficulty in recognising the scornful and supercilious beauty who, at a later period of the day, condescended to work the beer-engine and dispensed mild ale and sparkling repartee amongst her numerous admirers.

His improved circumstances, combined with the softening influences of matrimony, had effected such a marked improvement in Vester's manners and appearance, that in the jovial landlord of the King's Head I had some difficulty in recognising the beetle-browed *kooromengro** who, just ten years previously, had sprung lightly over the ropes after lowering the colours of the second best man in England.

As soon as breakfast was finished, we retired to the large club-room at the back of the house, where the ropes and stakes were set up on sparring nights and where we could talk without fear of interruption, and I at once proceeded to acquaint my cousin with the object of my visit. Without mentioning any names, I told him of my projected trip to Ireland, and asked him whether he could put his hand on someone who would be able to help me to get hold of any document which might happen to be locked up where I couldn't get at it.

"*Tatcho, mi pal*"†—replied Vester, "if you're not above working with a cross-cove, I can spot the very man to suit you in once. Jem Wood's his name, but his *bongo navior's* ‡ Snide Lurk and Dustman—and that's what he most in general goes by. I done him a turn once when the cops were after him down at Hampton, and since then I've often employed him 'working-back' betting-*lils*, russias, *chordi-jookos* and *oras*.§ If you make it worth his while and

---

* Prize-fighter. † "Right you are, my brother." ‡ "Nicknames."
§ "Recovering betting-books, note-cases, stolen dogs, and watches."

can only manage to keep his head out of the bucket, he'll *keeravit* the *kerrimus* his *kokero vast*.* It's no use to look for him this time of day, but between three and five he's generally to be heard of at the Dolphin in Cheapside or at his house of call in St. Giles. Meantime you'd best take a turn between the *coppas*,† then have a bit of a snack, make your terms with Jem, and be off to Bristol by the night mail, so's to catch the Cork boat in the morning."

As I had not taken off my clothes for the last two nights, I was not sorry to follow Vester's advice, and in spite of the unaccustomed noise of the traffic, was soon sound asleep.

CHAPTER XXXV.

Some Passages from the Life of Mr. James Wood.

MY time being necessarily limited, at two o'clock, sharp, Vester's sporting-looking turn-out—consisting of a high-seated gig with a skewbald trotting-cob between the shafts, silver-plated harness, and leopard's-skin rug—came round to the door, and we were soon rattling away city-wards. I reached the Bank just in time to cash Sir George's cheque, and having entrusted the notes to the safe keeping of the mistress of the King's Head, we started again, bound, this time, for Cheapside, in search of my future ally, Mr. James Wood.

Having drawn the Dolphin blank, we left the trap in charge of a bright-eyed Jew boy at the corner of Little Earl Street, and plunged into the seething tide of ill-savoured humanity which, at all hours of the day, ebbs and flows

* "Do the job on his own responsibility." † "Blankets."

along the narrow footways of Monmouth Street. The bulk of the resident population appeared to consist of Jews, who lurked, spider-like, within the dark interiors, keeping watch and ward over vast accumulations of second-hand boots and shoes, cast-off wearing apparel, and dingy theatrical costumes. The younger representatives of the favoured race were busily occupied in selecting choice specimens from the rich collection of vegetable and other refuse which obstructed the gutters, while slipshod, sallow-skinned Rebeccas squatted on the doorsteps, basking in the sun and satisfying the more immediate requirements of the infant Benjamins. Groups of sturdy Irishwomen, their heads enveloped in shawls and their arms akimbo, were gossiping and quarrelling at the entrances of the courts and alleys, while below the level of the footway was a row of dark cellars where whole families herded together in one room like rabbits in a burrow—occasionally coming to the surface for a breath of fresh air, but contenting themselves, for the most part, with a kaleidoscopic view of the ankles of the passers-by from the lower rungs of the short ladder which formed their only means of communication with the world above.

Leaving the comparative respectability of Monmouth Street, we crossed Bainbridge Street and threaded our way through the maze of tortuous alleys and reeking slums known to the *habitués* of St. Giles' as 'the Rookery.' With the exception of a few dolly-shops,* provision-stores, and an occasional gin-palace, the commercial element was conspicuous by its absence, the houses consisting, for the most part, of the lowest class of pratting-kens, where lodgings might be obtained for the moderate charge of threepence a night, and where the 'two-penny rope' was a recognised institution amongst the more economically inclined. The gutter-sinks were choked with garbage which had been allowed to accumulate for days and weeks. Stagnant pools of liquid filth filled the interstices of the disjointed pavement, and from each of the dark entries which opened like drains into a main-sewer, there issued an effluvium which differed only in the degree of its penetration and virulence from that of its precursors and successors. The greasy door-posts were blackened and polished from constant contact with the

* Rag and bone shops kept by unlicensed pawnbrokers.

shoulders of the pallid-faced, puffy-eyed loafers who, with hands deep-buried in their trowser-pockets, leaned listlessly against them, smoking short pipes and occasionally calling to one another across the street in a shibboleth of their own.

After the noise and bustle of Monmouth Street, where the commercial element was predominant, the silence and general air of depression was very noticeable. The men and women seemed but half awake—like a poacher's dog in the daytime—while the children, instead of playing with one another, lounged about the doorways in unconscious imitation of their elders and eyed us suspiciously as we passed.

Vester informed me that we were then in the very worst part of St. Giles', and that notwithstanding the quietude which prevailed, nearly every lodging was occupied by professional thieves. Some of the men recognised the ex-prize-fighter and shouted their criticisms upon his appearance and condition across the street as we passed, while others evidently took us for a brace of plain-clothes D's, and gave us plenty of elbow-room.

Crossing Broad Street opposite the Church, we shouldered our way through a crowd of slatternly women and juvenile candidates for the hempen cravat clustered about the portals of the Hen and Chickens, listening to a ballad-singer who was droning out the 'Transport's Farewell,' or some equally inspiring ditty, in a dismal nasal monotone, and entered the abode of the redoubtable Mother Clavering. The long bar was crowded with customers whose orders were being attended to by the widow herself, assisted by a couple of energetic pot-boys, while groups of men were seated at small tables, engaged in playing cards, dominoes, or rattling the bones. The atmosphere was thick with tobacco-smoke, but, with the exception of an occasional oath, the proceedings were perfectly orderly and not a man or woman appeared to be the worse for liquor.

The Mother, herself, was a tall, athletic-looking female with shoulders like a grenadier and strongly marked features whose masculine outlines were accentuated by a dark fringe upon her upper lip and chin—her general appearance fully corroborating Vester's assertion that, in the event of a row, the widow thought nothing of vaulting over the bar, seizing a couple of the ringleaders by their neckcloths, and rattling their closely-clipped heads together like castanets, preparatory to ejecting them neck and crop, while the fighting pot-boys could be reckoned upon to clear out the balance.

My cousin had been here before on a similar errand, so, finding that the individual of whom we were in search was not in the house, the landlady invited us to wait in her private room behind the bar, through the glass partition of which she was enabled to keep a sharp eye on her customers. We ordered spirits and cigars for the good of the house, and proceeded to make ourselves as comfortable as circumstances permitted, but, before we had been seated five minutes, a hubbub arose in the front bar-room, and one of the pot-boys came flying in to deliver his report.

"If you please, 'M—" he began, "there's some on 'em says 's how they won't have no strangers a'settin' inside there, where they can spot all as comes and goes, and others says if so be as square-coves is allowed the use of the house, they'll take their custom somewhere else. I told 'em 's how it were only a couple of gents of the Fancy, but they says 'Square-coves is square-coves, and if'——"

"They said that, did they?"—interrupted the fiery dame. "Square indeed! I'll square the chatty flymps"—she continued, as she shook out her cap-ribbons, kilted her skirts, and rolled up her sleeves, displaying a forearm which a blacksmith might have envied. "I'll precious quick make 'em granny who's omee* here"—and she sailed out of the parlour with colours flying, closely followed by her trusty lieutenant.

The situation was scarcely a pleasant one for a nervous man, but Vester and I were both pretty well able to take care of ourselves, so, following the landlady into the front bar, we prepared for a bit of sport. What might have been the upshot I can only guess, for as the tumult was at its highest, the double ground-glass doors swung open and the man of whom we were in search entered the room. Hearing the hubbub he paused for a moment, irresolute, upon the threshold, keeping his hand upon the door-handle, as if undecided whether to advance or retreat, but catching sight of Vester he nodded familiarly to him: the landlady

---

* "Make them understand who is mistress here."

dropped the man she had collared: the thieves returned to their benches and resumed their games, and once more harmony reigned supreme.

In place of the brawny, black-muzzled, pilot-jacketed, cat-skin-capped, heavy-booted ruffian of the Bill Sykes type, whom imagination had conjured up, I saw a dapper, slightly-built man, rather long in the reach and, if anything, less than the medium height, who might have passed for a third-rate 'pro,' a tout, or a dog-fancier in easy circumstances. His smug face was clean-shaven, his well-pomatumed hair had been coaxed into a couple of carefully-trained curls which lay flat on either cheek and showed that for some months, at least, he had escaped the attentions of the prison barber, and there was a comical twinkle in his one sound eye which made the fixed and stony glare of the artificial one all the more perceptible. A curly-brimmed white beaver hat with a black band—known in sporting parlance as 'butcher's mourning'—was jauntily cocked over his left brow, so as almost to conceal the damaged optic: a belcher handkerchief, secured by a gaudy scarf-pin, protruded from the lapels of a stylish brown Chesterfield which, in turn, covered a rather dilapidated cutaway coat, and under his left arm he carried a weak-eyed black-and-tan terrier whose bodily weight did not exceed two or three pounds.

As soon as the necessary introductions had been effected, we adjourned to the landlady's sanctum, a fresh relay of spirits and cigars was brought in, and this time we were allowed to carry on our negotiations unmolested. It struck me that Mr. Wood was inclined to give himself considerable airs on the strength of his professional reputation, and throughout the interview, with all the vanity of a first-class thief, he treated us to an amount of flash patter which might have delighted a philologist, but which, for the most part, was double Dutch to me.

"Come, cheese your patter, Jem, and let's get to business, for there's no time to spare"—growled my cousin, who was beginning to lose patience at the ostentatious and unnecessary display of the cracksman's linguistic resources, but as he still continued in the same strain, Vester and I began to talk in Romany, which very soon had the desired effect.

To cut matters short, after a long palaver in the course

of which, to judge from the bill, an astonishing amount of spirits and cigars must have been consumed, it was arranged that Mr. James Wood should accompany me to Ireland in a strictly professional capacity, upon the understanding that he was to receive £5 *per diem* and all expenses paid, with a bonus of £50—to include hire of tools and incidental expenses—and his return fare to London if his services should be required and the job brought off to my satisfaction. In pursuance of this plan he was to return to his lodgings in Bloomsbury to pick up his 'tools,' and having given certain necessary instructions to the lady who presided over his household and shared his fortunes, he was to join me at Paddington in time to catch the night mail.

I had just time to bolt a hurried mouthful of dinner, when the trap came round and we were off again to the station, which we reached a few minutes before the train was due to start—but in vain I searched the platform for any traces of my working-partner. At last, just as the porters were slamming the doors and I had given him up, Mr. James Wood, carrying a small but apparently heavy carpet-bag, emerged from some lurking-place where he had been lying *perdu*, and entered the compartment in which I was seated—and I was not sorry to see that he had discarded his flash toggery in favour of a close-fitting pea-jacket and a low-crowned hat. I handed him his ticket as he passed me, and was talking to Vester through the window, when an officer in plain clothes came to the door of the carriage and recommended me to change into another compartment, as I was travelling in bad company. As the train was just moving off, I thanked him for the information and told him that I would keep an eye on my neighbour, and, if necessary, take an early opportunity of shifting my quarters.

A hearty shake of the hand and "*kooshto bok!*" from Vester, and as the station lights flashed rapidly past, then faded away one by one, finally abandoning us to the semi-obscurity of a flickering oil-lamp, I began to realise for the first time that I had not only embarked upon an undertaking of an extremely dubious character, but that I had as travelling-companion an individual as to whose character and occupation there could be no sort of doubt whatever—and the reflection that I carried about my person notes and gold to the amount of three hundred pounds scarcely tended to alleviate my anxiety.

My confederate, on the contrary, was in the highest possible spirits at the prospect of a job. 'Copping a register,' as he termed it, was, literally, a little holiday to him, and curled up in a corner of the carriage with a cigar in full blast and his business eye twinking merrily, he alternately puffed and pattered away to his heart's content, and, once started, I found that there was no such thing as stopping him.

"You sonnied the bloke as tharied* you jest as the rattler was startin'? Rowland's his name and a dead nark he is—always a-tryin' to queer my pitch. Thought I was going to touch for your thimble or russia,† I'll be bound. I'll Rowland his Holiver for him one of these fine nights! Did you stag the milingtary-lookin' swell with the 'starchios and Piccadilly-veepers, as run his rule over you in the push by the brief-jigger? ‡ Not you, I'll bet a kervorten, nor yet didn't Rowland. A near miss he 'adn't a 'wired you,§ but that wouldn't a-suited my book and I give him the fisno straight. Capting Beresford's his name and a tip-top gun he is—most in general works the South Coast lines on the mag,‖ but I reckon he's readered ¶ there, or he wouldn't be going our way. Third class? Not much. Travellin' fust with the Dook o' Bluefort or the Bishop o' Barth and Wells. It's straight, I tell yer."

"You want 'er know how I come to get my lurk darkened? Well, I'll tell you, altho' it aint a subjec' as I'm pertic'lar fond o' gassin' about, and to give you the full strength of it, I suppose I'd best begin at the beginnin'. The old 'un was an antem-cackler **—what they calls a Baptist—and lived at Monmouth, and altho' you'd 'ardly credit it to look at me, I was brought up to the ministry. But I was an idle young shaver and couldn't stand the psalm-singin' and the preachments—let alone the water-

---

* "You noticed the man who spoke to you." † "Watch or note-case."
‡ "Felt you over in the crowd by the ticket-office."
§ "Picked your pocket."
‖ "A magsman is a fashionably-dressed swindler who relies upon his appearance to disarm suspicion. The arrival-platforms of the tidal trains are his favourite hunting-grounds."
¶ "In the *Police News.*"   ** "Dissenting minister."

cure—and instead o' goin' to chapel I used to pal in along of the poachin' lot as used to 'ang about the bridges of a Sunday."

"Poor old dad! He didn't mean no 'arm, but he was jest a bit too 'ard on me. One of his favourite capers was to baptise 'em in the river, and on a Good Friday, or one of them re-ligious orlidays, they'd meet on the banks of the Wye, and then I'd give the other young shavers the horfice, and we'd go and 'ide ourselves in the bushes somewhere 'andy. You sh'd a-seen the old 'un wade in right above his middle when, as like as not, there'd been a sharp frost overnight and a heast wind a-blowin' fit to freeze the boko off of a cast-iron monkey. Then he'd call to the pore shiverin' things as were a-singin' 'ims on the bank, and 'tice 'em in one by one, men and women—blimy! we'd most bust ourselves a-larfin' to see the gals' faces when they felt the cold water—and then he'd put one harm round 'em to keep 'em from sinkin'—for, mind you, there were a stiffish current runnin' and the water were as cold as workus charity—and he'd push 'em back'ards under water three times, and the third time they'd go right out 'er sight and no herror, and come blobbing hup agen a-ketchin' at their breath and a' splutterin' like a cat in a cold barth. And then he'd come ashore and wring the water out 'er his coat-tails, and they'd sing another 'im or two, and go to some cottage as were 'andy, and change their wet things and take a little spiritool conserlation—and they wanted it bad enough, I'm sure."

"When I was about fourteen I slung my 'ook and joined some travellin' Barks*—turnpike-sailors and silver-beggars, most of 'em—and stalled the monkery † with 'em for two or three year. A rough lot they were, and a rough time I 'ad of it—reg'lar keyhole whistlers the lot of 'em, skipperin'‡ it for choice when they'd got the price of a doss about 'em. When I was seventeen I got a charge of small shot in my legs and a treemoon o' reesbin for bluey-crackin',§ and when I come out 'er steel I padded the hoof to Start." ||

"S'elp me never, I *was* down on the knuckle when I got there, and no herror—could cut my toe-nails without takin'

* "Irish." † "Travelled the country."
‡ "Sleeping under a haystack or in a barn."
§ "Three months' imprisonment for stealing lead off the roof of a house."
|| "London."

my trotter-cases horf, and bein' jest a bit too 'andy with my myliers,* I 'adn't been there a fortnight before I got rumbled and pinched. The beak let me go with a caution, and as I was leavin' the Court, a reg'lar 'igh-flyin' shickster come up and told me 's how she'd spotted me workin' in the Strand, and if I'd like to come and live along of her and her fancy-man, they'd put the kibosh on me in no time."

"I lived a matter o' two year along of the Brennans, and 's long as we kep' friends I'd nothink to complain of. They give me what money I wanted, togged me out kiddily, and I'd always plenty to eat and drink. I was a smart, well-mannered young chap then, and could talk and be'ave myself well enough when I wanted to—and can now, for the matter of that, as you can see for yourself. I used to prac-tize wipe-hauling, tail-buzzing, and thimble-twisting, on Jack and Rose for an hour or two hevery day, and when I was pretty puffec at the job I'd go hout with Rose and work the pushes and barneys† till I'd got a nerve on me. When Rose'd finished with me, Jack took me in 'and, and I used to go wirin' in the main-thoroughfares with the Brennans to stall back and front.‡ But one day I'd a fall-out with Jack. He 'cused me o' playin' Ananias and Sapphira—pinchin' the reg'lars,§ as we call it—and swore as he'd get me put away if I didn't turn up more, and as I knew he'd be as good as his word, I done my bilk and joined a black-faced mob ‖ in the Midlands. For some years I tooled and wired about the monkery with different mobs. When one place got too sultry, we'd shift to another, travelling' inter Scotland, Wales, or wherever there 'appened to be anythink goin' on in the way of fairs, races, 'Sizes, reviews. and such like, but as soon as I became a reg'lar first-class cracksman, I got swished,¶ and from that day to this I've worked single-handed and kep' myself to myself."

* "Fingers." † "Crowds."
‡ "When a juvenile prig attains to the dignity of a 'single-handed wire,' he is usually accompanied during 'working' hours by two comrades who act, respectively, as 'front' and 'back stalls.' The duty of the 'stall' is to keep a sharp look-out for the police, to relieve the operator of any watches, purses, etc., which he may acquire, and to create a diversion in his favour if he happens to get collared."
§ "Keeping back part of the plunder."
‖ "A mob or gang of burglars who blacken their faces to conceal their identity and trust to violence rather than to skill."   ¶ "Married."

I have necessarily omitted Mr. Wood's more emphatic asseverations and expressions, but during the latter part of our conversation my companion's language had become a little more parliamentary, while his accent had improved in proportion—as if to carry out his assertion that he could talk aud behave himself well enough if he liked. To my no small relief he appeared to have forgotten his promise of telling me how he had lost the use of his sinister optic, and, in spite of my forebodings, I had just composed myself for a comfortable nap in my corner of the carriage and had already begun to nod, when the train pulled up at a station, and Jem awoke me with an intimation that he would like to 'moisten his chaffer' with a pull at a certain black bottle which Vester had thoughtfully provided in case of emergencies. The raw spirits disappeared down his capacious gullet like water, and having temporarily satisfied his craving, he very politely offered me a drink, and, upon my declining it, proceeded to transfer the bottle to his own pocket—but remembering my cousin's warning and being determined to nip any communistic tendencies in the bud, I at once called his attention to the little omission.

"Right y'are, Capting"—he replied, not in the least abashed, "I'm apt to be a trifle habsent-minded at times. And now, if you'll oblige me with a light, I'll tell you how I come to lose my peeper."

"About four year back I went down to Wales for Llandaff Fair, and there I 'appened to run agen a pal by the name of Alf Palmer—a chiv, blink, and snell-fencer *—as said 's how he could put me up to a real soft thing. Alf were a putter-up † by perfeshion, and told me 's how a sportin', flashy sort 'er gent by the name of Griffin—as owned a brewery near Newport—'ad a snug little crib 'bout four mile out'er town on the Chepstow road, where heverythink were done right up to the knocker. The she-flunkey'd told him that whenever any of the quality 'appened to look in on their way 'ome from 'untin', plenty of fizz was brought in on a gold salver, and whenever he gave a blow-hout, the sideboard were covered with gold and silver plate."

* "Knife, spectacle, and needle-hawker."
† "A man who calls at gentlemen's houses, ostensibly for the purpose of disposing of his wares, but, in reality, with a view to acquiring any information which may prove of service to his patron, the professional burglar."

"Well, I tell you, I thought at fust it sounded jest a bit too clush, but, howsomedever, when I was in Newport I trots hout and has a look round the premises, finds as Griffin allus dined in town on Wednesdays, and comes back dead sweet on the plant. I took a extry bit o' trouble about the job, and on the Wednesday night I 'ires a trap and a fast-trottin' tit, and drives my missus—as fly a bewer, she were, as ever chucked a stall, a reg'lar tip-top tamtart and A1 at gladderin', truckin', and sallyin', and though she brought me nothink but a Whitechapel fortin',* she were worth her weight in gold, and that weren't no bloomin' trifle, pore thing."

Here Mr. Wood's feelings threatened to overpower him, and necessitated a second application to the bottle. Gulping down his emotion and a liberal dose of the best brown British, he pulled himself together and resumed:—"As I were a-sayin', I drives my missus hout to the village, where Alf were to meet us and 'old the 'orse, while she were to crow.† It ended by my doin' little snakesman‡ for my nibs and back-jumpin' the carsey,§ and I gets clean off with the scawfer ∥ and 'bout 'er thirty quid in single-pennifs ¶ and silver. We made a long round back to vile,** and the night bein' cold and windy I pulled the blyhunker†† hup under a wall and lit the darkey to sample the swag before goin' any further—which I allus makes a p'int o' doin'."

"A fine show it made in the moonlight as it come hout 'er the sack, for hevery piece of it were hengraved and stamped all hover with dragons—bein' the fambly crest, I take it—and motters, but you'll 'ardly credit it when I tells you 's how, when I put the hacid on it, hevery bloomin' hounce were snide,‡‡ and not worth cartin' away. Straight. S'elp my bloomin' never you might 'er knocked me down with a 'ammer! I felt all hover alike and touchin' nowhere, and the missus started on Alf a good 'un. There were nothink to be done but get scat of the lot, somehow, so I cuts the quad under the shoulder with the flail, and we starts back to

---

* "A clean apron and an umbrella." † "Keep watch."
‡ A boy who is introduced through some small opening and unfastens the door or window from the inside.
§ "Breaking into the house by a back-window." ∥ "Plate."
¶ "Bank-notes." ** "Town." †† "Horse." ‡‡ "Base metal."

vile at a gallop. But heverythink turned up crabs that night. Before we 'd gone a mile, the blank tit shies at a Gipsy tent in the moonlight and runs us off the tober, the trap turns hover, and I was chucked into a ditchful o' brambles with the missus and Alf atop o' me."

"'Gorblimy!'—I begins, but before the word were well hout 'er my mouth—s'true as I 'm sittin' here a-talkin' to you—a blessed thorn or sutthink runs inter the corner of my bloomin' eye, and blind I become, sure enough, within a fortnight—what the old 'un 'd a-called a reg'lar wisitation o' Providence. I couldn't tell you how we got back to Newport that night—I was that bad—but as we crossed the bridge over the Usk, my missus and Palmer got down and heaved the sackful o' shoful * into the river, and fust thing next mornin' I were obligated to go to the orspital."

"I dessay you 'd 'er thought 's how that 'd 'er finished it, but it didn't, not by chalks, for on Monday 'Liza—that's my missus as was—comes to the ward where I were lyin', and 'Jem'—says she, 'the vile 's readered all hover with these 'ere stiffs,'†—and she read hout, 'Fifty Pounds Reward.—Whereas on Wednesday night last certain evil-disposed persons broke into Mr. Griffin's house at Llanbedhr and carried off a valuable service of gold and silver plate and a considerable sum in notes and gold, the above reward will be paid to any person, not actually concerned in the robbery, who may give information leading to the recovery of the plate or the conviction of the thieves.'"

"Well, it seemed a reg'lar rum start, and look at it which way I would, I couldn't tumble to it nohow. To think that a downy cove like Griffin should hoffer fifty quid reward for a lot o' duffin' stuff as wasn't worth runnin' into the meltin'-pot, beat me altogether, so I sends 'Liza off to Nat Hart—him as kep' the billy-fencing shop down in Jamaica Street—to see what he could make of it. Old Father Nat swore I must'er been scammered and 'ad made a mistake in samplin' the wedge,‡ but next mornin' he gets a boat and goes hout at daylight and drags up the sack hout'er the mud with the grapplin'-'ooks—and shoful it were, right enough, hevery bloomin' hounce."

"Then he come and seen me, and we 'as a talk, and he

* "Base metal." † Posters. ‡ "Silver."

'ires a trap and drives hout to Llanbedhr and takes the 'ole bloomin' lot back to Griffin, just as it were—sack, mud, and all—and tells him 's how his kids 'ad a'seen it stickin' out'er the mud at low tide. Old man Nat said s'how when Griffin seen the plate turn hup agen like a snide midgic,* his face were a picter, for he'd never dreamed of it bein' worked back, and 'd honly hoffered the reward as a cheap chyike to his credit—which were a bit rocky. Fust he tried to bounce the old-'un, but Nat stuck to him like a tick to a dead nigger, and it hended by his writin' a cheque for thirty-five quid, two quid ready, a box o' cigars, and a dozen o' fizz."

"'And now, Mr. Griffin, sir'—says Nat, 'what 're you a-goin' to give me to keep my mouth shut?' That were what I call hartful, and it hended by his givin' of him another fiver. I touched two-thirds and Nat and Alf napped their reg'lars, but, as you may suppose, it didn't pay me for the loss of my peeper. The next time I passed through Newport I heerd 's how Griffin 'ad hoffed it to America, howin' his creditors some thousands o' pounds. And that 's how I come to get my lurk darkened."

Jem proved a most entertaining companion, and during the journey to Bristol I acquired quite a fund of information respecting the habits of the criminal classes—little imagining, at the time, that I was, myself, destined to see the inside of a convict prison. Amongst other things he explained that the tip-top cracksmen and magsmen never consorted with the second or third-class thieves, or worked with any of the 'mobs,' but always endeavoured to live as quietly as possible—generally occupying respectable furnished apartments in the suburbs of some large town, and never visiting the thieves' quarter in order to avoid being 'spotted by the Ds.'

"'S long as I worked with a mob"—he said, "we used to keep together as much as possible—'cos we was all well known to the perlice, and it weren't no manner o' use tryin' to pass for square-coves. We'd our reg'lar tradesmen, prattin'-kens, and lush-cribs, and when we made a bit, we used to well it with the omee.† We've got our signs and passwords jest the same as you swell Romanys—I knows a few words of Romany and tinkers' patter through travellin'

---

* Bad shilling.　　　† "Bank it with the landlord."

along of Larry O'Neil and his gang, and I grannied some of what you were a-tharyin' to your cousin at the Chickens—and if I was to go to Newcastle or New York to-morrow, I sh'ld find a sure pal and a safe kradyin'-ken * before I'd been two hours in the vile. They don't forget to lump it on for our 'commodation, but's long as we can keep ourselves to ourselves we don't objec'."

Talking of detectives, he told me that a clever one could tell at a glance whether a house had been broken into by a first or second-class thief, according to the neatness of the work or the reverse, while in some cases he could name the operator right off from some peculiarity of style or from the use of some particular tool. Until he had lost his eye, he had always worked single-handed, going for nothing but plate, jewellery, notes, or gold, and never resorting to violence, if it could by any possibility be avoided. In the case of a heavy 'plant' or 'put-up job,' not being a powerfully built man he was forced to employ an assistant—suggestively termed a 'nasty-man'—whom he hired by the job to do the heavier work. Since his accident, he had been obliged to give up all single-handed jobs, but managed to get a livelihood by 'working-back' stolen property when a reward was offered or a conviction seemed inevitable: by hiring out his tools which, he assured me, were the most complete set in London: by working on jobs, which required skilled labour, for second or third-class cracksmen: by acting as snide-witness in *alibi* cases, and by screeving 'shams' and 'delicates' † for begging-letter impostors and other vagabonds.

After favouring me with a few practical illustrations of his manual dexterity in the performance of such delicate little operations as 'cross-fanning,‡ 'screwing-up,'§ and taking a letter from the inside breast-pocket of my coat—in which, as the conjurers at the fairs say, 'the quickness of the 'and deceives the heye'—my mercurial companion took a final pull at the bottle, and curling himself up in his corner, was soon fast asleep.

* "Lodging-house."
† "Preparing false testimonials, subscription-lists, certificates, etc."
‡ Stealing a scarf-pin or watch from behind, or with the right arm passed beneath the left elbow, while a race is being run.
§ Garrotting.

After a little hesitation, excusable, perhaps, under the circumstances—for I reflected that Mr. Wood might possibly take advantage of my somnolent condition to screw me up in sober earnest—I proceeded to follow his example, and slept soundly until the train ran into Bristol station.

CHAPTER XXXVI.

I Find Out 'How the Land Lies.'

I ASCERTAINED upon my arrival at Bristol that the Cork boat was not due to sail until the following day, so I determined to make the journey *viâ* Waterford. It was then about 2 a.m., and as the packet did not start until 6.30 a.m. I drove with Jem to the Docks and went on board at once. Having been forewarned as to his bibulous propensities, I determined not to lose sight of my companion, and securing a cabin to ourselves, persuaded him to turn in. To judge from his snoring, he was asleep almost immediately, so, having taken the precaution of hiding his boots in a spare berth, I followed his example.

Some hours later I was roused by the trampling of the passengers overhead, and as I sat up and rubbed my eyes, it slowly dawned upon me that the berth lately occupied by my professional friend was vacant.

There was no doubt about it. The bird had flown and the nest was cold, and as his boots had also disappeared, I came to the conclusion that the wily Jem had been playing 'possum all the time. Under the circumstances I was agreeably surprised to find that my money was still safe, and as he had left the carpet-bag containing his precious tools behind him, I concluded that he had merely stepped out to satisfy his craving for drink—but in the meantime I thought it just as well to look after him.

In vain I searched every hole and corner of the vessel, but at last I ascertained from one of the sailors that my friend had asked him the way to the nearest tavern, and here, sure enough, I found him, just five minutes before the boat was due to start. The rascal was the centre of an admiring audience composed of sailors, cattle-drovers, and 'lumpers,' and had evidently been making the most of his time. As he flatly refused to move and appeared inclined to show fight, I took him by the scruff of the neck, and, with the assistance of the friendly sailor, ran him down to the boat, getting on board just as the hawsers were being cast off and the paddles began to revolve. During the bustle and confusion which reigned on board I managed to smuggle him down the companion without attracting attention, and hustling him into the cabin, locked the door on the outside and went on deck.

The weather was bright and fine as we steamed down the muddy waters of the Avon—past the rocky gorges and green slopes where the hawthorn blooms perfumed the air, covering the bushes like newly-fallen snow tinged a warm pink by the rays of the setting sun. I was not sorry to be once more on board ship, but off the Welsh coast we ran into a dense fog-bank, and were obliged to feel our way at half speed to the dismal accompaniment of the fog-horn.

About mid-day, as I was chatting with one of the passengers, I noticed a small crowd collected under the hurricane-deck, and going forward, found my versatile friend limply reclining against a coil of rope, nursing a half-empty gin-bottle and relating, with tears in his eyes, the pathetic narrative of how he had been decoyed away from his happy home. Skipping the intermediate stages—the dignified and the amorous—he had evidently passed from the pugnacious to the imbecile, and was now crying-drunk.

I afterwards found out that he had turned the key in the lock of the cabin-door, from the inside, by means of an ingenious instrument termed the 'American tweezers,' and making his way to the refreshment-bar, had purchased a bottle of his favourite 'satin.'

Under the circumstances, the only thing to be done was

to disclaim any connection with him, and an hour later I found, to my relief, that he had relapsed into a state of drunken stupor. As soon as the passengers had all left the boat at Waterford, I got the sailors to turn the ship's hose over his head and shoulders. This energetic treatment had the desired effect, and as soon as ever Mr. Wood was able to walk, I had him conveyed to the Coach Inn, where he was securely locked into an empty room until the mail was ready to start.

The Coach Inn was kept by an Irish gentleman of good family, who combined the avocation of hotel-keeper with that of horse-dealer. As we had four hours to wait until the coach started for Cork, I amused myself during the interval by overhauling the set of house-breaking implements contained in Jem's bag—a description of which I will attempt to give for the benefit of householders in general.

First and foremost, lying just inside the mouth of the carpet-bag, came the pair of very delicately-fashioned but powerful forceps to which I have already alluded, and which are known in the profession as American tweezers. By means of this instrument the operator is enabled to get a firm grip of the ward-end of any key which may have been left in the lock, and to turn it almost as easily as if he held the handle in his hand.

Then came a tin box containing a varied assortment of skeleton-keys with wards at both ends, termed 'double-enders,' and a bunch of wire pick-locks known in the trade as 'spiders,' and warranted to open anything—except, perhaps, a patent Chubb or Brahma.

The remainder of the outfit comprised a slender wax-taper, twisted into a coil: a bull's-eye lantern, or 'darkey': several gimlets, files, and chisels, of different sizes: a powerful, crow-footed 'jemmy' about fifteen inches long, which, in the hands of the 'nasty-man,' must have proved a formidable weapon: a large cold-chisel, called the 'sergeant-major,' for cutting through metal plates: a heavy-headed, short-handled hammer, or 'monkey-driver,' with its business end protected with leather to deaden the sound, for driving the aforesaid 'sergeant-major': a thin-bladed palette-knife, such as artists use, for pushing back the spring catch which fastens together the sashes of a window: a glazier's diamond, for cutting out a pane of glass: a 'neddy,' or life-preserver: some 'dumb sparklers,' or silent matches, wooden and steel wedges, and a number of odds and ends.

At the bottom of the bag were the more complicated and highly-finished instruments, upon the construction of which a considerable amount of mechanical ingenuity and skilled labour must have been expended. These consisted of a revolving panel-cutter, worked by a two-handed lever: a mechanical drill for cutting through iron plates, worked by a powerful lever and propelled by a slow-motioned screw: a leather case containing a set of 'bits' of various diameters, belonging to the drill: and a powerful but compactly-made instrument, familiarly termed the 'Jack-in-the-box,' for wrenching off any locks which might turn a deaf ear to the blandishments of the 'double-enders' or remain obdurate to the insinuating advances of the 'spiders.' The latter was the tool used by Sullivan and Jordan to break open the iron safe in the bonded-warehouse on Custom House Quay in the autumn of 1834, when diamonds to the amount of £6,000 —the property of a Spanish countess—were stolen.

All the tools were carefully packed in tow and oil-rag to keep them from rusting, and no doubt formed a profitable source of income to Mr. Wood who, when not employed on the job himself, was in the habit of hiring them out to such professional gentlemen of his acquaintance as were unprovided with mechanical appliances of their own.

At length the Cork coach drew up to the door and my bibulous companion was unceremoniously hustled into the interior, along with a couple of sturdy graziers who were in a precisely similar condition, while I managed to secure the box-seat—the roof being crowded with cattle-dealers who had been attending a neighbouring fair. The well-appointed, dark olive-bodied coach, with its slashing team of three matching blood-bays and a clever-shaped roan wheeler that looked like carrying fourteen stone over a big country, bore testimony to our landlord's judgment in horseflesh, but it struck me as rather incongruous that a turn-out which would have done no discredit to Piccadilly, should have no more suitable load than a mob of noisy, frieze-coated cattle-dealers. A whisky-bottle circulated freely, the men lit their *dhudeens*, and the fun grew fast and furious—a superabundant supply of native wit and humour making ample amends for the rough exterior and uncouth manners of my fellow-passengers.

We stopped to change horses at Dungarvan, and the sight of the chapel where Sir George had been married to Mdlle. de Gonidec more than a quarter of a century previously, seemed to bridge over the lapse of years and brought back to my mind the occurrences of the past few days, which the bustle of the journey, combined with the change of scene, had momentarily banished, while Jem Wood's husky, gin-and-watery voice, now hiccupping out the sentimental ditty 'Why did she leave him because he was poor', —now raised in angry dispute with the occupants of the interior, reminded me forcibly of the serious nature of the enterprise to which I stood committed.

Leaving Dungarvan, we stopped at Cappoquin—where my master had lived in retirement after leaving Cork—and Lismore, with its picturesque castle overhanging the Blackwater. Skirting the woodcock-haunted coverts which stretch away to the river, we reached Fermoy, where we changed again, and after a square meal, started with a fresh team of well-shaped greys, and before long came in sight of the handsome park-lodges and trimly-kept villa residences with their terraced gardens, which overhung the beautiful valley of the Lee.

As I did not wish to be seen with Jem Wood near the scene of our prospective operations, I took a room at the Imperial in the name of Lester, and sent my companion—who had slept off the effects of his debauch—to look for a 'sure pal and a kradyin'-ken' in charge of one of the ragged-coated gentry who crowded round the coach on its arrival. Notwithstanding a few handsome public buildings and some fine streets, a more poverty-stricken place than the fair city of Cork in the year of grace 1845 it has seldom been my lot to visit. The streets literally swarmed with beggars of every description, while the district in which my companion had taken up his quarters was infinitely worse than anything I had seen in St. Giles'—which is saying a good deal.

Next morning I met Jem by appointment on St. Patrick's Bridge and accompanied him to his diggings, where I exchanged my everyday clothes for the fashionably-cut suit which I had worn home from Charleston, and by the addition of a false moustache which my companion had procured for me in London, and a drab-coloured beaver with a black band, I flattered myself that I had sufficiently altered my appearance as to minimise the probability of detection in the event of subsequent inquiries being instituted.

So far I had carried out my hastily-conceived scheme without let or hindrance. I had arrived upon the scene of action with an ally in whose skill I had the greatest confidence, and I had now to ascertain whether a certain entry was still in existence, or ever had existed, and in the former case to obtain possession of it by hook or by crook—for notwithstanding that I had received no definite instructions on this point, I knew, well enough, that this idea had been uppermost in Sir George's mind, although pride kept him silent. The programme was a sufficiently comprehensive one, while the time allotted for its execution was limited by the possible arrival at any moment of one of Father Considine's emissaries bound on a similar mission.

It must be remembered that, with the exception of the name of the street—now rebuilt and improved beyond all recognition — in which my master — then Mr. George L'Estrange—had lodged, and of the parish—St. Bridget's—in which that street was situated, I had little or nothing to guide me in my researches, and as I had no time to waste in making cautious enquiries, I determined to take the bull by the horns and go straight up to the first priest I chanced to meet in the street whose appearance inspired me with confidence, instead of setting to work in a more roundabout fashion.

With this object in view I strolled leisurely up Patrick Street, but although there were plenty of priests about, the majority of them did not strike me as being likely subjects for a 'plant.' They all seemed cut from one pattern, being, for the most part, commonplace, shrewd-looking men, chiefly remarkable—as compared with the refined, well-dressed ecclesiastics who performed the services in the neighbourhood of Netherleigh—for their stubbly chins, shabby surtouts, greasy hats, and a general absence of clean linen—some sallow and cadaverous, some florid and burly, some dark, some fair, some jovial, some ascetic, all brisk and energetic, but none of them quite what I wanted.

But at length virtue, or, at all events, patience, brought its reward. A portly, fresh-complexioned gentleman of commanding presence, arrayed in the finest of broadcloth and speckless linen, came picking his way, Agag-wise, along the filthy sidewalk, looking, what with his rosy, clean-shaved cheeks, ivory-handled ebony walking-cane, well-cut clothes, shiny boots, and a general air of prosperity, for all the world like a well-fed dignitary of the Church of England, and presenting a pleasing contrast to the hollow-eyed spectre of famine and destitution which haunted every crowded street, seething slum, and reeking alley. He was what they called, over there, 'a fine figure of a man,' and walked with a firm, deliberate step, carrying his head high and acknowledging the cringing salutations of the corner-boys, car-drivers, and beggars by a slight elevation of the ebony cane, and the nods and smiles of the ladies in the private cars by a courtly sweep of his well-brushed beaver.

He was evidently a swell of some sort, so, concluding that such a prosperous-looking gentleman would not be of a suspicious disposition, I determined to follow and accost him at the first opportunity. Perfectly unconscious that he was being shadowed by a stranger of foreign aspect whom a plain-clothes D. from 'the Factory' would most assuredly have catalogued as 'suspicious,' the worthy churchman continued his perambulations at the exasperating rate of some two miles an hour—the most difficult of all paces to follow without attracting attention—now halting for a stare into a shop-window, now pulling up for a confab with a friend, but at last, to my relief, he entered a Post Office and tendered a money-order for change.

"Now or never"—thought I, as I ranged up alongside him at the counter, and pulling out my pocket-book as a guarantee of my respectability, and assuming a strong American accent, asked the clerk whether he could oblige me with change for a ten-pound note—at the same time artlessly displaying a sheaf of similar vouchers from the Bank of England.

Strange as it may sound to English ears at the present date, the sum mentioned was just three pounds more than the officials could muster between them, and I was about to retire, when my clerical friend solved the difficulty and opened the conversation by producing a well-filled purse, and offering, in the most courteous manner, to cash the note.

"I gather, sir"—he remarked, with the least taste in life of a brogue, as we left the office together, "as much from the surprise you manifested just now as from your appearance, that you are a stranger to Ireland, and are possibly unaware that we have lately passed through a crisis of the greatest agricultural and commercial depression, and I very much doubt whether you would succeed in cashing a ten-pound note at any one of the principal shops, without their having to send to the Bank for change—such is the scarcity of ready money."

In reply, I expressed my regret at this lamentable state of affairs, and at once proceeded to broach the subject which lay uppermost in my thoughts. Apologising for troubling him—a perfect stranger—with my private business, I told him that I had come all the way from America for the express purpose of proving the birth or baptism of a Roman Catholic—a relative of mine—which, as I had reason to believe, had taken place in Cork some eight and twenty years previously, winding up by asking him whether he would kindly put me in the way of prosecuting my enquiries.

"Twenty-eight years ago! Whew—that's a long way to go back"—he replied. "To the best of me belief there was no such thing as an official or compulsory registration of birth, although, if the child had been baptised by the parish priest, he would probably have made an entry at the time. But men come and go, and things get mislaid and lost. Still, there's always a chance. I think ye said T—— Street, St. Bridget's? See here, now: take this kyard"—producing a card-case and pencil—"your name, I think ye said, is—— ?"

"Colonel Leonidas B. Lester: L-e-s-t-e-r, Flemington Fencibles, New Jersey, U.S.,"—I answered without the least hesitation—for I had previously rehearsed the scene in my imagination and had provided myself with a name to suit the occasion.

Handing me his card with a few lines scribbled on it in

pencil, Canon Power recommended me to call at the Mission House in St. Bridget's and enquire for Father Shanahan, who would no doubt do his utmost to assist me.

"If there is anything more I can do for ye"—he continued, "ye've only to call at that address, and I shall be happy to give any information in me power. No thanks at all. Only too glad to be of use to a stranger, and especially to an American"—and raising his hat, the good-natured priest resumed his walk in the direction of the Mall.

Placing the worthy Canon's card of introduction in my pocket-book, I at once jumped on a car and drove down to the Mission House in St. Bridget's. A portion of the parish seemed to consist of narrow, dirty streets, in which were situated business-premises, warehouses, and a few wretched shops, while the remainder was inhabited by what appeared to me to be the very scum of the population. The Mission House was in Nelson Street, and there I found Father Shanahan in his shirt-sleeves selling—or, rather, distributing, for the price appeared to be nominal—rice and oatmeal to a swarm of ragged, gaunt-eyed applicants who crowded round the little man, clamouring, gesticulating, and snapping and snarling at one another like a pack of famished hounds, and who were with difficulty kept at bay by a verger, or sacristan, armed with a stout walking-stick belonging to the priest.

The Mission House was nothing more or less than an old, dismantled warehouse, the walls of the largest room on the ground-floor having been roughly distempered and hung with a few gaudily-coloured prints of scriptural subjects. The greater portion of the floor was occupied by a number of rush-bottomed chairs in an advanced state of decrepitude, and at the further end of the room, partitioned off by a stout handrail, was a temporary altar fashioned out of three or four office-desks nailed together and covered with an altar-cloth, upon which were placed several tall wax-candles and a large crucifix.

In order to gain admission to the interior, it was necessary to pass through a small door, or wicket, in one of the massive warehouse gates, which were kept permanently barred and bolted. On stepping through the wicket I found myself in a small yard paved with cobble-stones, just sufficiently large for a dray to turn and surrounded on three sides by gloomy warehouses, the walls of which were pierced with narrow, iron-barred windows. To the left was the two-storied warehouse, the lower floor of which was used as a temporary Mission House. To the right were two or three doors which probably led to the counting-house and clerks' offices, and above my head was an archway from which swung a rusty iron crane.

An old brown retriever with grizzled muzzle, lack-lustre eyes, and a coat like a workhouse doormat, had discovered the only ray of sunlight which illuminated the gaol-like precincts, and was lying stretched out at full-length, patiently waiting until Father Shanahan should have succeeded in satisfying the wants of his ragged flock.

Following the dog's example, I seated myself upon an empty barrel and watched the crowd of beggars of both sexes as it surged round the door of the Mission Room. It seemed ages before the last applicant emerged, holding in one hand a tattered handkerchief containing a modicum of rice, and clutching a squalling brat to her half-naked breast with the other arm, but at length the ancient retriever—who was evidently well acquainted with the ways of the place—got up, stretched himself with a prolonged yawn, and trotted into the Mission Room, and for the second time I followed his example.

Canon Power's card proved the best of passports. "Ye'll find everything here at sixes and sivins"—panted the perspiring ecclesiastic as he struggled into his coat and proceeded to mop his forehead with an enormous red and yellow Bandana, "but, the Saints be praised, we're only here while the new Church's buildin', and that'll be complated next month as ever is. Meanwhiles I'll do me best for ye. Hurry now, Spillane"—to the sacristan—"lock up and be aff to yer dinner. If ye'll jest step acrass the yard I'll have a hunt among the ricards. Down, ye schamer!"—to the dog—"'tis hungry y'are. 'Tis an ould watch-dog we found chained up to a bar'l and half-starved, when we took over the primises."

The old retriever threw up his head and went through the pantomime of barking, but the sound died away in his throat, and he contented himself with preceding us, corkscrew-fashion, across the yard in the direction of one of the before-mentioned doors. Taking a bunch of keys from his pocket, Father Shanahan unlocked the door, and we found ourselves in a small outer office, or porter's lodge, the one window of which overlooked the street, and which contained no furniture with the exception of a deal table, a couple of rush-bottomed chairs, and a row of pegs—upon one of which an old frieze-coat was hanging. Directly opposite the one by which we had entered, was another door, covered with moth-eaten green baize and studded with brass-headed nails.

Father Shanahan hung up his hat on a peg and laid his stick across the table, while the dog curled himself up in front of the empty fireplace.

"If ye'll sate yerself"—said he, pushing a chair towards me, "I'll jest run upstairs and have a hunt among the ricards, but I'm doubtful of finding what ye're wantin'. Eighteen-sivinteen I think ye said, and the name?"

"George Albert Bartholomew Lester"—I replied, for I had—very cunningly as I thought—selected both Christian and surnames resembling as closely as possible those of which I was in search, under the impression—mistaken, as it proved—that the entries would be arranged in alphabetical order.

The priest proceeded to unlock the baize-covered door, and passing through, closed it behind him. I listened intently as he crossed the bare boards of the room beyond. Then came the creaking of another door and, finally, the sound of footsteps ascending what appeared—from the dead sound of the footfall—to be a flight of stone stairs. Cautiously turning the handle of the door through which Father Shanahan had made his exit, I peeped into the next room, which had evidently been the clerks' office or counting-house. Besides the one through which I had entered, I noticed two other baize-covered doors, one of which was slightly ajar and revealed a flight of stone steps leading, apparently, to an upper story—but the dog's pricked ears and the patiently anxious expression of his eyes, which were fixed upon the entrance-door, had warned me that I might be interrupted at any moment, and my investigations were brought to an abrupt termination by the entrance of Spillane with a bowl of broken victuals for his four-footed pensioner.

I FIND OUT 'HOW THE LAND LIES.'

It must have been fully twenty minutes before I caught the sound of descending footsteps, and, a moment or two later, Father Shanahan entered the room carrying three dust-covered books with blue edges and dingy, brown-mottled leather bindings.

"There"—he cried, banging them down on the table with a grunt of relief. "They're the only ones I can find of about that date. There's sixteen and part of sivinteen in them. The most of eighteen's missin', and part of nineteen, and then comes twenty-one—but ye're not needin' that."

Taking up the books, one by one, and 'sissing' the while like an ostler, he held them at arm's length and clapped the covers together, causing the accumulated dust to fly out in clouds, then, seating himself at the table, he gave them a final polish over with the Bandana, and drawing a pair of horn-rimmed spectacles from a case, announced himself as ready to begin.

"April, 1817, I think ye said? Well, we'd best begin with January, to make sure. There's mar'ges, baptisms, and parish accounts all of a jumble together. What name did ye say, Cornel, and is't a mar'ge or a baptism ye're wantin'? James Albert Bartholomew, was't? Ah, to be shure! George Albert Bartholomew Leicester. L-e-s-t ——? 'Deed, thin, that's a quare way. I mind there was a Meejor by that name lived down at Blackrock when I came here these fifteen year back—a tall man, he was, with grey whiskers and an eyeglass—but, to be shure, he was a Protestant and spelt his name different. Let's see now, January 5th, George Edward Lenny and Mary Ellen Finucane—ah! that's a mar'ge, but Father McNulty's fist's for all the world as if a daddy-longlegs'd dhrownded himself in the ink-bottle and gone stravagin' over the pages to dhry himself. George Cohen, George Alfred Lashmar, Albert Eugene Leahy—there's no end to Georges, but sorra a Lester at all, at all"—rattled the garrulous priest, as he ran his stumpy forefinger down the columns, page after page, translating any likely entries into English—or, rather, Irish—from the queer sort of dog-Latin in which they appeared to have been written.

"Now we come to April. Massy—Chris. Bartholomew—that's not it. Chearnley—Patrick George. Barrington

L-e-s-t—no, L'Estrange—Geoffrey Adrian. That's nearer, any way. Did ye spake?"

I had been standing behind the priest, looking over his shoulder, my left hand on the back of his chair, my right holding my hat and stick, and as he stumbled and hesitated over the familiar name, and I caught sight of the fatal entry, the existence of which I had come so far to verify or disprove, despite my utmost efforts at self-restraint and the strong curb I was putting on myself, I felt the blood rush to my head, while my grasp tightened on the back of the chair and an involuntary exclamation escaped me. Luckily Spillane had left the room and Father Shanahan was unable to see my face.

"I thought you had skipped a page, that was all"—I replied, steadying my voice with an effort, "but I see that I was mistaken."

"It's eager y' are"—remarked the priest with a good-natured chuckle, "and small blame t' ye after comin' all that way. Maybe there's money dependin' on 't?"

"A matter of a hundred and fifty thousand dollars"—I answered as coolly as possible, for my composure had returned now that I had seen all that I required.

At length Father Shanahan brought his investigations to a conclusion—needless to say without further result—and having told Spillane to replace the books and lock up everything, he put on his hat and we left the Mission House together. Having thanked the good-natured priest for the trouble he had taken, I parted from him at the corner of Nelson Street and made my way back on foot to Jem Wood's quarters, and after a prolonged confabulation with that worthy, I resumed my everyday clothes and returned to the Imperial.

CHAPTER XXXVII.

The Mission House in Nelson Street.

THE following morning I again met Jem by appointment, and he at once proceeded to deliver his report. After I had left him the previous day he had made his way down to Nelson Street, and had dropped into a grocery store, where liquor was sold, situated almost opposite the Mission House and commanding a view of the entrance gates.

A few minutes before six o'clock Father Shanahan, accompanied by another priest, had let himself in by the small wicket in the warehouse gates, leaving it open behind him. Later on a few people had entered the Mission House for evening service, and Jem—who, despite his Methodistical training, was no bigot—had followed them in with a view to taking a quiet look round the premises. At the conclusion of the service the two priests had left, followed, shortly after, by Spillane, and the wicket had been closed and locked behind them by a man who lived on the premises and acted as caretaker.

This man's name, he had ascertained from the proprietor of the grocery-store, was Patrick Doolan, and it was with him that we should ultimately have to reckon. Doolan, it appeared, was an Army pensioner, and being of a sociable disposition, was in the habit of spending his evenings at a small *shebeen* called the Four-Leaved Shamrock. About nine o'clock the caretaker had opened the wicket-gate, and having locked it after him and placed the key in his pocket, had betaken himself to his usual haunt, followed by the old retriever.

As soon as he had seen him safely tiled down at the Shamrock, my trusty ally had doubled back and had taken an impression of the lock of the wicket by means of a blank key made of tin—one side of which was coated with wax. He had then returned to the Shamrock and had entered into conversation with Doolan, finding him as 'sweet'* as possible, and in his anxiety to create a favourable impression had wound up the evening by getting very drunk.

It was now Thursday morning, and Jem told me that he had found a pal who had undertaken to get a key made to pattern and finished off by Saturday at mid-day.

"Doolan"—he said, "'ll be goin' to the Shamrock 'tween nine and ten to-morrow night, for I've made a 'pintment to meet him there and sample the Irish, and my pal 'll get his bewer to crow for us while he keeps him sweet for an hour or two, and from what you tells me, we 'ad ought 'er jump the crib, cop the cherpin, and misli † in an 'our and a 'arf—with luck, that's to say."

This would, of course, depend upon the accessibility of the place where the records were kept, but I had no reason to suppose that it was anything more formidable than an ordinary cupboard or lumber-room, and I remarked that it seemed to me that we ought to do the job in less than half the time.

"Now look'ee 'ere"—replied Mr. Wood reproachfully, "I jest want 'er arst you whether you or me's agoin' to boss this 'ere job? There's more ways o' killin' a pig than cuttin' 'is throat, and when I takes a contrac' in 'and, I likes ter work it out shipshape and Bristol fashion 'cordin' to Cocker. It ain't no manner o' use goin' to the hexpense of bringin' a fust-class cracksman hall the way from Start to Barkshire ‡ if you means ter work it like a black-faced mobsman. There's sech a thing as perfeshional pride, and if we sh'd 'appen to get rung or pinched, I sh'ldn't like ter 'ave it brought up agen me that I'd coopered the job. Now there's three or four doors to be opened at least—'cordin' to your 'count—and if I was ter bust the locks hoff with the Jack, Doolan 'd be bound to report it next mornin', and then the narks 'd be turnin' heverythink hupside down to find us. Now if we picks the locks, halthough it may take more time, when he hopens the premises on Sunday mornin' for the priests to come in and finds hall the doors onlocked, it's ten

---

* "Unsuspicious."
† "Break into the house, get hold of the book, and be off."
‡ From London to Ireland.

to one he'll think he was scammered overnight, and 'll muffle his clapper for fear o' losin' his shop, and they won't very likely miss nothink for weeks ter come."

As there seemed to be a certain amount of plausibility in Jem's arguments, I bowed to his superior judgment and allowed him to go about the job his own way—promising to meet him at his lodgings at nine o'clock sharp on Saturday evening.

Although I had seen some rough work in my time, burglary, flavoured with a dash of sacrilege and a strong probability of homicide, was an altogether novel experience, and on the eventful evening, as the hands of the coffee-room clock pointed to half-past eight, I must confess that I felt just the least bit queer, and as Dutch courage is no bad substitute for the genuine article at a pinch, I fortified myself with two stiff go-downs of brandy and water before leaving the hotel.

On reaching the slum where Jem had taken up his temporary abode, I exchanged my clothes for an old pea-jacket which had seen some service, and my hat for the same old fur travelling-cap which had stood me in such good stead on a certain memorable occasion in the Lovers' Walk near Netherton, and which had been found and brought back to MacAlister's by some children who had been gathering primroses near the river. The tools had undergone a thorough overhauling, and the carpet-bag having been packed, we muffled up our throats so as to conceal the lower part of our faces, and crossing the noisy court where a free fight was in progress between some drunken tinkers armed with soldering-irons, made our way towards the Mission House in Nelson Street, and entering the store on the opposite side of the road, called for two bottles of porter and seated ourselves near the window which commanded a view of the warehouse gates.

About half-past nine the caretaker made his appearance at the wicket in his shirt-sleeves, and after taking a look up and down the street, turned on his heel and re-entered the yard. It was close on ten o'clock before he showed again, but this time he slipped through the wicket, followed by the dog, closed and locked it after him, placed the key in his pocket, and having lit his pipe, sauntered off up the street with the air of a man who has finished his day's work and intends to enjoy a pleasant evening.

"That's a bit of luck"—I remarked to my companion, pointing to the old retriever who, after deliberately seating himself in the gateway as if he meant to stay, on second thoughts got up, scratched his mangy hide, and finally trotted off up the street after the caretaker.

"M' yes—for the dorg"—replied Jem, reflectively rubbing his stubbly chin. "I carnt never a-bear to injure a dumb hanimile—'specially dogs, through bein' in the Fancy myself and naterally fond on 'em."

As soon as Doolan disappeared round the corner, I paid for the porter and followed my leader—who was already on his track—until we saw the caretaker enter the hospitable portals of the Shamrock. Jem then called my attention to a man who was lounging carelessly against the doorpost, smoking a short pipe and talking to a woman, and who, as soon as he caught sight of us, took off his hat and replaced it with a peculiar flourish, and then entered the tap-room leaving the woman outside.

"Bone"—said Jem, "that's my pal and the crow"—and turning on his heels, he led the way at a rapid pace back to Nelson Street. It was now past ten o'clock, and as there was no lamp nearer than the street corner a hundred yards or more away, there was not much fear of our operations attracting the attention of the passers-by. As soon as we reached the warehouse gates, my companion halted, and producing the newly-finished key from his pocket, unlocked the wicket, and stepping through, we found ourselves in the yard, with the Mission Room on our left and the offices on our right. Jem quickly locked the door after him, leaving the key in the lock and giving it an extra half-turn to prevent it being pushed out.

"There"—he cheerfully remarked, "that'll stop the bloke from onlockin' it, onless he 'appens to be pervided with a pair of 'Merican tweezers, but if he should come back and begin 'ammerin' at the gate and kickin' up a rumpus before we've finished, as soon as I slips the door open, and he bends his 'ead to step through the wicket, you jist curb his nibs on the pea* with the jemmy and pull him inside, and then

* "Strike him on the head."

we'll rope him up and shove a gag in his mouth while we finish the job; but if we've done, we'd best nammus different ways."

My companion evidently regarded the 'curbing' of the unsuspecting Mr. Doolan on 'the pea,' as he termed it in his quaint but expressive phraseology, as a mere business detail scarcely worth discussion, and it may be imagined that the immediate prospect of having to play 'nasty-man' to Mr. Wood's burglarious lead, was scarcely calculated to place an amateur at his ease.

"Fust of hall"—he continued, "we'll jest see where he dosses, and whether he's left any keys about that might come in 'andy."

We had little difficulty in discovering Mr. Doolan's sanctum, and there, as if to vindicate the correctness of Jem's surmise, we found two or three keys, with one of which we were enabled to unlock the door of the outer office. Having relocked it on the inside, Jem placed the carpet-bag on the table at which Father Shanahan had seated himself while engaged in searching the records, and opening it, he produced a small bull's-eye lantern which he lit with a silent match—but before doing so he made things safe by nailing the old frieze-coat across the small window which overlooked the street.

He then produced some goloshes which he drew over his shoes, and having provided me with a pair of loosely-fitting woollen socks for the same purpose, he proceeded to examine the door which separated us from the inner office, and which, as I suspected, proved to be locked. Giving me the lantern to hold, Jem took the 'double-enders' from their tin box and laid them in a row on the floor within reach. As, with difficulty restraining my impatience, I stood silently watching his operations, every second seemed a minute, while every footstep in the street heralded—to my excited fancy— the caretaker's return. It was, nevertheless, impossible to help admiring the dexterous and methodical manner in which, without the least sign of flurry or nervousness, my companion applied key after key to the obstinate wards, but just as he had settled down to his work, we heard someone slowly pacing along the pavement outside, and as the footsteps came to a halt beneath the window, Jem shaded the bull's-eye and suspended his operations, while I held my breath until I could hear my heart thumping against my ribs.

In a minute or two, to my intense relief, the footsteps moved off up the street, but I noticed, to my surprise, that in the meanwhile Jem was going through a rather impressive piece of dumb-show. Taking the 'neddy' from the carpet-bag, he hung it from his wrist, and handing me the jemmy, crept on tiptoe to the door, which he unlocked and held open, listening intently the while. A moment or two later the wicket was shaken violently, the light of a lantern gleamed on the cobble-stones beneath the entrance-gates, and a bell—which I had not noticed—hung immediately over our heads, went 'jingle, jingle' and made me jump nearly out of my skin.

It was a critical moment for a novice, and though not exactly what you would call a coward, I would have given all I was worth and a year's wages into the bargain to have been back in the pantry at Netherleigh. For a minute all was silent—then the footsteps moved off again with the heavy, measured tread which, in my boyhood, I had learned to associate with the advent of the village *baulo*. My companion gave vent to a grunt of relief.

"Nothink but a blank watchman wantin' to step in and 'ave a glass and a chat with Doolan"—he grumbled, "that's about the size of it"—and unshading the lantern, he went back to his work. "More 'urry, less speed"—he continued, "a little hoil wouldn't do this lock any 'arm"—producing a small compressible oil-can and a feather—"heasy does it all the world hover, and there she goes"—the 'double-ender' turned in the lock, the door opened, and crossing the inner office, without further delay we transferred our attentions to the door at the foot of the staircase which the priest had mounted. Here the same operations were repeated, the keys being arranged on the floor as before and a good deal of precious time wasted—as it seemed to me—in order to gratify Mr. Wood's professional vanity.

But at length the lock yielded to the blandishments of an insinuating 'spider'—the key-hole being too small for the double-enders—and as the door swung open, revealing a steep flight of stone stairs, something sprang between us and disappeared in the darkness, causing me to jump back a couple of yards.

"Come along"—said Jem, who, although but a poor creature in the morning, seemed to have a nerve of iron at night, "it's honly the blank masheen.* Let's 'ave a suck at the monkey, for by the look of these stone steps we've got a thickish job afore us"—and so it proved.

At the head of the stairs was a short passage flagged with the same stone as the steps. On either side of this passage were two or three half-open doors of the ordinary size and pattern, but our attention was irresistably attracted to a smaller one at the end of the passage facing the head of the stairs, apparently of solid oak studded with iron nails and clamped with rivets. The other doors—as I have said—stood open or ajar, but this particular one was locked and opened inwards, offering no purchase for a crowbar, its jamb being deeply sunk in the solid masonry, while the lock, protected by a strong metal plate securely rivetted to the tough oak of which the door was composed, was flush with the surface of the iron-sheathed woodwork.

Deceived by Father Shanahan's careless, easy-going manner, I had jumped to the erroneous conclusion that 'the ricards'—as he called them—would be found lying about in some dusty cupboard or disused lumber-room, but my illusions were at once dispelled by the sight of the un-compromising-looking barrier which evidently guarded the strong-room where the former occupier of the warehouse had very possibly been in the habit of keeping his ledgers, cash-box, or securities.

"Well, that's a twister and no herrer"—ejaculated the perplexed cracksman, after trying skeletons and picklock to no purpose, "one of these 'ere blankety, blank himproved patents as the locksmiths keep a-bringin' hout jest'er aggeriwate a cove. I sh'll 'ave to try the Jack on it, arter all."

The ingenious piece of mechanism termed the Jack-in-the-box was then fished up from the bottom of the bag and denuded of its tow and oil-rag coverings, the hammer-shaped head inserted in the keyhole, and the lower screw turned by means of the lever-handle until the instrument

* "Cat."

was firmly clamped to the iron plate which protected the lock. The lever-handle was then shifted to the powerful upper-screw, and a couple of turns brought a tremendous pressure to bear on the lock plates, but at the third or fourth revolution of the screw, something inside the lock gave way, and the instrument, losing its fulcrum, was instantly rendered useless.

"Jest as I thought"—exclaimed Jem with an oath which would have been dirt-cheap in any police-court at seven shillings, "false plates and hall the latest fakements. The drill's our last chance, and that's no bloomin' ketch this 'ot weather—and no elber-room, neither."

The Jack was then returned in disgrace to the bag, and the various pieces of which the drill was composed were taken out of their oil-rag wrappers and rapidly fitted together. A three-inch 'bit' was selected and inserted, the T-shaped head of the centre-pin fixed in the keyhole as before, and the set-screws adjusted. Jem stripped to his shirt, rolled up his sleeves, and buckled to like a man, putting his chest into his work, and at every turn of the lever-handle the three-inch 'bit'—propelled by a slow-motioned screw—eat deeper and deeper into the iron covering-plate. The plate proved to be a quarter-inch one, slightly corroded on the inner side, and the perspiration was running off my companion in streams before he had completed the first hole.

The drill was then shifted, and I took my turn at the lever-handle, and in this manner five concentric rings, each three inches in diameter, were cut through the covering-plate in a circular pattern—the circumference of each hole just touching that of its neighbour, like the beads of a necklace. Upon the completion of the fifth hole the central portion of the iron covering-plate came away, leaving several inches of the surface of the inner lock-plate of hardened steel exposed to view. It then became necessary to break up this inner case with the punch before the lock ifself could be destroyed, and this was by no means the easiest part of the job.

It took us an hour and twenty minutes by my watch, working spell by spell, to reach the bolts, and owing to the close atmosphere and the entire absence of ventilation, although stripped to our shirts the perspiration ran off us in streams and we were both pretty well cooked before the door yielded to our united efforts.

My companion's share of the work was now over, so, leaving him to pack up the tools, I lit the wax-taper and proceeded to investigate the contents of the strong-room. The room itself was about fifteen feet by twelve, and was roughly fitted up with drawers and shelves, upon which was piled a most miscellaneous assortment of rubbish, resembling odd lots of theatrical properties more than anything I can think of.

Soiled vestments and other garments of a less distinctly sacerdotal character depended from nails driven between the interstices of the masonry, while wreaths, banners, plated candlesticks, crucifixes, wax-candles of abnormal proportions, cheap, highly-coloured prints of the Virgin and most of the saints in the calendar, together with odds and ends of all sorts, were mixed up in inextricable confusion with bags of rice and meal, old boots, and other packages which would have seemed less out of place in a marine-store dealer's establishment. Such of the upper shelves as were not otherwise occupied were loaded with dust-covered volumes of every description, including manuscripts, copy and account-books, dog-eared, well-thumbed breviaries, registers, and books of instruction and reference—the only objects of any value in the whole of the collection being a small silver crucifix, and a canvas bag which, on inspection, proved to contain upwards of six pounds in silver and copper.

The fact of their being comparatively free from dust attracted my attention to the three volumes which had recently been searched and replaced by Father Shanahan, and taking down from the shelf the one which contained Father McNulty's list of the baptisms and marriages which had taken place in the parish of St. Bridget's during the years 1816-17, I hurriedly scanned its pages until I came to the entry of which I was in search. There was no mistake about it. The ink was faded and the flimsy paper discoloured and time-stained, but the entry was there, right enough, and, as if to make matters worse, the date of the birth was recorded as well as that of the baptism.

Taking a pen-knife from my pocket, I carefully detached from the string with which the pages were sewn together, the double leaf which bore on one of its sides the fatal record, in such a manner as to afford no evidence—the pages not being numbered—beyond a gap in the sequence of entries, of the register having been tampered with. Then, having stowed away my unwelcome prize and having restored the book to its original position on the shelf, I pulled open the drawers, disarranging the contents, slipped the silver crucifix and the bag of money into my pocket—for, as we had been compelled to break open the door, I thought it advisable, if possible, to put the gentlemen in black on the wrong scent—and rejoined my companion, whose temper had not been improved by the heavy work and who was swearing continuously to himself, like a cat purring, as he ruefully passed his fingers over the edges of the 'bits,' which had been turned by coming in contact with the inner lock-plate of hardened steel after penetrating the iron covering-plate.

"Copped?"—he laconically inquired. "Well, hall's well as hends well, and now my deal's a-goin' to misli.* It's jest like my blanked luck to come hall the way to Barkshire and then run agen a reg'lar patent-safety when I thought I 'ad the job thin and silky."

We then set to work to pack up the tools and 'tidy up,' sweeping the iron filings, fragments of lock-plates, etc., into the strong-room, and having closed the door—which bore Jem's sign-manual indelibly impressed upon its rugged surface—after us, we descended the stairs, locked the outer office—replacing the key in the caretaker's room—and having unlocked and relocked the wicket-gate which opened into the street, made our way through a labyrinth of back slums and alleys to my companion's quarters.

Here I had another look at the baptismal entry, in order to be sure that I had made no mistake in the excitement of the moment, and having satisfied myself that it was only too correct, notwithstanding Jem's advice to the contrary, I tore off the part which concerned Mr. Geoffrey and placed it carefully in my pocket-book, destroying the rest of the double page.

"And now, Jem"—said I, when I had changed my clothes, "if you'll make my things up into a small bundle

* "Now I'm off."

and meet me on St. Patrick's Bridge in an hour's time, I'll square accounts with you, for I shall lie close to-morrow and leave next week by the first packet for Bristol. But before leaving, I should like to know your plans."

Mr. Wood then gave me to understand that he had determined to prolong his stay in the Emerald Isle with a view to making a professional tour with a new-found pal, who had informed him that there were two or three places of interest in the neighbourhood which would repay a visit. "And now as I've got the tools inter workin' horder, it'd be a pity to let 'em get rusty"—he added significantly.

Jem was punctual at the trysting-place, and, according to agreement, I handed him over fifty pounds for the job and thirty pounds for the week's engagement, and as our little business had been so successfully carried out, I made the sum up to a hundred, receiving, in return, Mr. Wood's most solemn promises of eternal secrecy—which, to his credit be it related, he kept in the face of great temptations —and having shaken hands cordially, we parted mutually satisfied with each other.

The following Tuesday saw me on board the Bristol packet, and after a terribly rough passage, followed by a tedious railway journey, I once more found myself safe back at Netherleigh, having brought a rather hazardous enterprise to a successful conclusion.

CHAPTER XXXVIII.

"Koosbto Bok!" *

AFTER travelling some roughish roads, the old *vardo* is nearing its journey's end. Starting from Camford, it has carried us in safety to Netherleigh Combe: from the Combe to the Parsonage: from the Parsonage to Westport: from the old town back to Netherleigh Court: from the Court to Camford again: from the University town to Demerara, the West Indies, and America: from the *Nevvi Tem*† back to Netherleigh Court—to say nothing of our trip to Ireland—and it is but fair that the *chauro pooro gry*‡ should be indulged with a *dant* of *chaw* § and a roll by the roadside.

If I had my own way I should like to finish up by describing Mr. Geoffrey's marriage to Miss Winifred Blount, drawing special attention to the beauty of the bride, the toilettes of the bridesmaids, the size of the wedding-cake, Mr. Cecil's capital speech at the wedding-breakfast, the pleasant picture presented by Sir George walking up the aisle arm-in-arm with old Mr. Blount, the shower of rice, satin-slippers, and all the rest of it—finally bringing my tale to a conclusion amidst a blaze of fireworks and the rejoicings of the tenantry. I should like to add that they lived happily ever after, but, unfortunately, this is not a fairy-tale but an o'er true story with a moral—according to Dr. Carew—if not exactly a moral story, and I must confine myself to a brief statement of facts in the order in which they occurred.

Upon turning over the back pages of these Recollections, I find that they have already attained proportions certainly never contemplated at the outset. One thing has led to another, and although I have resisted, to the best of my ability, the temptation to stray—like an artful old van-horse

---

* "Good luck!"—the Gipsy, equivalent to "Good-bye."
† New World.   ‡ Poor old horse.   § Bite of grass.

—from the dusty roadside of matter-of-fact statement to the pleasant clover-fields of old-time reminiscences, I feel that I must have taxed your patience to the utmost. My excuse must be that the mental occupation thus afforded me has proved the best possible antidote to acute physical suffering, and in relating the few remaining incidents of my connection with the family of Sir George L'Estrange, I will endeavour to confine my narrative within the narrowest possible limits.

It would serve no useful purpose, were I to give the exact particulars of the interview with my master which followed my return to England—suffice it to say that I found him in one of his tantrums. It appeared that one of the footmen—a new importation and unacquainted with Sir George's little peculiarities—had objected to being called a thick-headed idiot, or something of the sort, and had 'up and given the Master as good as he gave'—the result being that I just came in for the tail-end of the storm, and got snapped up very short upon attempting to go into details. Upon my producing the little silver crucifix, I thought the poor old gentleman would have had a fit, but he calmed down by degrees and told me to see that it was returned without delay—which was done through the medium of my cousin Vester.

The fact was, that Sir George resented being under an obligation to an inferior, and could not help showing it, but in a day or two it had all passed off. From a pecuniary point of view I had no reason to complain of my treatment, and I fancy that Father Shanahan and the poor of St. Bridget's lost nothing in the long run through the burglary at the Mission House.

In the autumn of the same year, Father Considine accompanied Mr. Frank to Italy as usual, his duties being undertaken during his absence by a very nice gentleman named Father Eustace Fazackerley—a relation of the Fazackerleys of Erleigh. The new-comer was a great friend of Mr. Geoffrey's, and being—like his cousin Sir Grenville—a first-class horseman and fond of all outdoor amusements in which his cloth allowed him to participate, they soon became almost inseparables. I have no doubt that the young priest did his best to dissuade my master from turning Protestant, but when once Mr. Geoffrey had made up his mind, it was waste of time arguing with him, and his engagement to Miss Winifred Blount clinched the business.

Whether or not Father Considine received a hint from Sir George that his room would prove more acceptable than his presence, I am unable to say for certain, but, at all events, Mr. Frank came home by himself, and, in the natural course of events, Father Fazackerley stepped into the vacant berth—very much to the satisfaction of all parties concerned, with the exception, perhaps, of Mr. Frank, who was very much attached to his tutor.

Soon after Mr. Frank's return from the continent, Mr. Geoffrey was married—as I have already hinted—to Miss Winifred Blount in Netherleigh parish church, the ceremony, needless to remark, being performed by the Rev. Mark Sealy.

After his marriage we saw very little of Mr. Geoffrey at Netherleigh, and things became desperately dull at the Court. At Christmas, he always brought down a party for the shooting, and whenever his parliamentary duties necessitated his presence in Netherton, he made the Court his head-quarters; but during the greater part of the year the house was practically shut up, as far as the outer world was concerned, and Passon Mark was almost the only visitor—the two old gentlemen passing a good deal of their time together.

It will be remembered that, in former days, Sir George had shown a dislike—amounting, indeed, to positive aversion—to the society of his second son, but time had cicatrised the wound which her ladyship's death had inflicted, while Mr. Frank's slight physical deformity had grown less noticeable with advancing years, and now that the march of events had broken down the barrier of prejudice which had hitherto tended to keep father and son apart, the morbid feeling of reserve—so characteristic of ultra-sensitive natures—had gradually given place to an intimacy which a similarity of tastes went far to augment.

Sir George himself, relieved of the incubus which had weighed him down like an Old Man of the Sea, appeared to have shaken off again—for the time being, at all events—the effects of the malady under which he had been labouring, and which constant anxiety and worry had, no doubt, served to increase.

In proportion, however, as his bodily health improved, the old baronet's naturally proud and independent spirit began to reassert itself in a variety of ways, and I could not shut my eyes to the fact that my presence in the house served as a perpetual reminder of that grisly skeleton—lately transferred from the cupboard to the family vault—whose existence Baron Jansen had so shrewdly suspected. On the other hand, we were very comfortable, and I should have been well content to have stayed on as long as my services were appreciated, but now that my master appeared anxious to dispense with my personal attendance as much as possible, and to avoid me, after I had been in his service so many years, I could not help feeling hurt—for servants have their feelings like other people.

Matters were, however, brought to a head in the following manner. Mrs. Vester still retained a considerable share in Lee and Robertson's business in right of her late husband, and it having come to her knowledge that a vacancy in the post of sub-manager was likely to occur, she promised my wife to use all her influence with the other partners to obtain the place for me, provided only that I could manage to scrape together enough money to qualify—it being a rule of the firm that both the acting and sub-managers should invest a certain sum in the business. How the money was to be obtained was a mere detail, and scarcely worth discussion, according to these good ladies, and things might have gone on as they were for some time to come, had not my wife received a letter from Mrs. Vester, informing her that the sub-manager was under definite notice to leave, and advising me to send in my application without delay.

Now, as I need scarcely tell you, when one's wife and her bosom friend lay their heads together and determine on a certain course of action, the wisest thing to do—if you care for a quiet life—is to knuckle under at once, and look as pleasant as circumstances permit. The following afternoon I walked over to the Parsonage and had a long talk with Mr. Sealy, the upshot of which was that, within a week, my application for the post of sub-manager was forwarded to London, strongly backed up by testimonials from my old tutor, the member for Netherton, and Sir George—who behaved very handsomely as far as money was concerned—while Mr. Geoffrey was good enough to persuade some of his friends in London to use their influence with the firm; the result being that in the course of a few weeks I received an official intimation to the effect that I had been appointed to the post of sub-manager.

My final interview with Sir George was rather a painful one, but satisfactory on the whole. He spoke very kindly, saying that he was sorry to lose my services, but that he was inclined to agree with me that, for several reasons, it was better that I should make a fresh start in life. I, on my part, was sorry to go, for I had lived in and about the old place as man and boy for nigh on five and thirty years, and had been treated by my masters—Mr. Geoffrey especially—more as a friend than a servant. My wife and I went over to Mr. Sealy to tell him of my good luck and thank him for his kindness, and after saying 'Good-bye' to everybody about the place, we at length got our belongings packed up and started for M—— Street, City, the head-quarters of the firm, who also had a branch establishment in Birmingham.

My salary now amounted to £200 per annum, exclusive of all expenses of travelling, living, etc., and, for the next six or seven years, my wife—who developed a wonderful aptitude for the business—and I were fully employed in superintending the refreshment department at the principal race-meetings, passing the winter partly in Birmingham and partly in London.

My first start in my new capacity was upon the town-moor at Doncaster in the year when Cossack was made such a hot favourite for the Leger, but the party having backed something else—I forget what—the Derby winner was allowed to make his own running throughout, and Marson, coming with a wet sail, landed the Middleham horse—Van Tromp—an easy winner by a couple of lengths.

During the Chester meeting of Teddington's year a curious thing happened, which gave me a bit of a turn at the time and showed, plainly enough, which way the wind was still blowing. On the concluding day I was accosted by Jansen—whom I had often seen at different meetings but had never spoken to—who asked me to make an appointment the following week in London, as he wished to introduce me to a gentleman who had an important proposal to make which might turn out very much to my advantage. As I had no particular objection, I agreed to meet them at the Baron's rooms in Earl Street, St. Jermyn's, and there the matter dropped.

At the time appointed, I called at Jansen's rooms and found him in conversation with a rather mysterious-looking individual whom I at first took for a detective, but before long discovered to be a priest of some sort, and from the deference with which our astute friend treated him, evidently a man of some mark. In stature he was short and rather inclined to be stout. His face—or what I could see of it, for he kept his hat on during our interview, wore a long sort of Inverness-cape, and sat with his back to the light—reminded me strongly of pictures of the First Napoleon, but with more of the prize-fighter about the jaw, and he spoke in a quick, decided manner, and kept twirling a large seal attached to a horse-hair watch-guard round his finger.

He opened the conversation by telling me that he believed me to be in possession of certain information, and that if I chose to fall in with his views, I might practically put my own price on it. To my surprise and consternation, he then gave a detailed account of my visit to Cork in the summer of 1845, supplying particulars which I had almost forgotten myself.

"On the night of the 20th of June"—he went on to say, "the Roman Catholic Mission House in Nelson Street was broken into and certain articles abstracted; including a page in a parish-register believed to contain a record of the baptism of Geoffrey Barrington L'Estrange, the eldest son of Sir George L'Estrange of Netherleigh Court ——"

Upon my interrupting him by telling him that he was altogether mistaken as far as I was concerned, as I had gone to Ireland upon some private business of Sir George's connected with the Kilmore Castle estate, he stopped me at once, and continued—

"We have reason to believe that this document is now in your possession. We are not disposed, for the present, to enquire too closely how it came there, our object being to verify its existence. Should you be disposed to assist us in the matter, we are in a position to offer very liberal terms, but should you endeavour to thwart us by destroying the document or denying its existence, you must be prepared to take the consequences of a criminal prosecution. You can take three months from to-day during which to make up your mind, and at the expiration of that term we shall apply for a warrant against you, and one James Wood, for burglary and abstracting a portion of a register and other articles from the Mission House in Cork. In the meanwhile Baron Jansen is empowered to treat with you on our behalf. I don't think, Mr. Loveridge, that I need detain you any longer."

I again denied all knowledge of the matter and left the room, preceded by Jansen, who attempted to enter into conversation with me, but I pushed him aside and slammed the street-door in his face—for I was just mad at being caught like a rat in a trap, without any notice of what was coming.

And now, in order to enable you to understand the drift of the priest's communication, I must go back to my visit to Cork, and clear up a little matter which requires a word or two of explanation.

While knocking about the Channel on the return voyage, it occurred to me that, in my master's present state of health, he could not be relied on for any length of time. As long as he remained fairly well, I could count on his firmness, but, as soon as he became ill again, I dreaded the influence of such a man as Father Considine working upon his conscientious scruples, and it struck me that if I handed over the paper to Sir George's keeping, all my work might be thrown away, and I might find myself in Queer Street into the bargain. What I had done, I had done out of gratitude to Mr. Geoffrey, who had been a friend as much as a master to me, and like most people in my position, I looked upon the baptismal entry, or register—or whatever you like to call it—as the sole proof of his illegitimacy, instead of as merely a more or less important accessory. Acting upon this assumption I determined, if practicable, to retain possession of it instead of handing it over to Sir George or destroying it—both of which courses appeared to be equally open to objection.

Upon my return to Netherleigh I found my master in one of his tantrums—as before related. From the first, as I knew very well, he had felt, bitterly enough, the necessity of taking me into his confidence—for, unlike Mr. Geoffrey, he was as proud as Lucifer and never permitted the slightest approach to familiarity—and during my absence he had had time to repent of having sanctioned the course which I proposed to take. Upon this occasion he cut our interview as short as possible, scarcely allowing me a word of explanation, and I left him at the time under the impression that the original certificate had been destroyed, but, as a matter of fact, it still lay hidden away in an old tobacco-pouch which had once belonged to my poor father, and which I had kept in rememberment of him among the few odds and ends of any value which I possessed, and I had almost forgotten its existence.*

Jansen's principal—as I will call the mysterious stranger for want of a better name—had kindly allowed me three months in which to make up my mind, but more than a year had passed without my hearing anything further from him, when an event occurred which relieved me of all further responsibility in the matter by severing my connection with the L'Estrange family for good and all.

Upon our return to town from the Epsom meeting after a very heavy week's work, I found a letter at the City office in an unknown handwriting and bearing the Exeter postmark. The only person in that neighbourhood with whom I was in the habit of corresponding, was Adams, the Netherleigh butler—for whom I sometimes executed some small commissions—and I was therefore surprised to find that the letter was from Mr. Bullen—of the firm of Bullen and Wadham, Sir George's solicitors—and urged me to come down to Netherleigh without a moment's delay, as my presence was required upon business of the *utmost importance*.

Now I must plead guilty to a constitutional and, perhaps, not altogether ill-founded aversion to law and distrust of lawyers, and I am ashamed to say that I resolved to take no

---

* This is Loveridge's explanation of the incident, but Sir George's solicitor appears to have taken an entirely different view of the matter. The accompanying facsimile—see frontispiece—of the original baptismal certificate, as produced in the case of *L'Estrange v. L'Estrange and others*, is published by kind permission of Messrs. Bullen and Wadham.

notice whatever of the letter, which had been lying at the office for a couple of days; but within twelve hours it was followed by the arrival of a gentlemen who introduced himself as Mr. Bullen's managing clerk, and who—not without some resistance on my part—obtained leave of absence for me, packed up my clothes, hustled me into a railway-carriage, and carried me off to Exeter, *nolens, volens*. On reaching the old town, it appeared that Mr. Bullen had gone on to Netherleigh, and without further ado my captor ordered out post-horses at the Pack Horse Stables and hurried me off again, arriving at the Court at two o'clock in the morning.

I was thoroughly disgusted with the whole proceedings, for I had scarcely had a mouthful to eat, and not a particle of information could I extract from my companion, beyond eliciting the fact that Sir George was very ill and not expected to live. My first step on arrival was to knock Adams up, and from him I gathered the following particulars—that my poor, old master had been taken suddenly ill about a week previously: that he had sent at once for Mr. Sealy, who had remained with him for several hours: that Mr. Geoffrey had been summoned from London, and had arrived a short time before me with a well-known specialist: that Father Fazackerley was still acting as household chaplain, and that Mr. Bullen was sleeping in the house.

Next morning, as I was taking a turn in the rhododendron walk at the back of the house, I nearly ran against Mr. Geoffrey, or, to speak correctly, he nearly ran against me, for his hat was pulled down over his eyes and his head was bent—a rather unusual thing for him. When he looked up, I was perfectly startled at his altered appearance, for his face was worn and haggard, his eyes were bloodshot and heavy, as if from want of sleep, and he seemed at least ten years older than when I had last seen him about a month previously, and had made the remark that there were few better-dressed or better-looking gentlemen about town than my former master.

At first he appeared not to recognise me, but pulling himself together with a visible effort, he shook hands, giving my fingers a squeeze which made them tingle, and then, to my surprise, passed on without a word. Now all this would have been intelligible enough, under the circumstances, had it not been for Mr. Bullen's letter, which made me think that something must be wrong, and after my recent experience with the Baron and his friend, I determined to be upon my guard.

In the course of the morning I received a message to the effect that I should be wanted in the afternoon, and at three o'clock the library bell rang, and Adams accompanied me across the hall and along the corridor which I knew so well; finally ushering me into the room which I had entered with my uncle Neptune for the first time some thirty years previously. How well I remembered every detail of that scene—the dog-whip sticking out of Passon Mark's pocket, the rings on Lady L'Estrange's fingers, Sir George's velveteen coat and turquoise-headed pin, my uncle's white beaver hat, the black boy with the silver collar round his neck, and the ape who still leered at us from the tapestry in dangerous proximity to King Solomon's swelling calves. The only persons in the room upon the present occasion were Mr. Sealy, Mr. Bullen—who sat in Sir George's chair at the writing-table—and Mr. Geoffrey, who was leaning against the shutters of one of the windows with his arms crossed, his head bent, and his back to the light.

The solicitor opened the proceedings—they always like to have the first word, and the last too, if they can get it—by apologising for the inconvenience to which I had been put, and after 'supposing that I had heard of Sir George's dangerous illness, etc.,' he suddenly sprang the mine under my feet—as he imagined—by asking me in a very peremptory tone whether I remembered all the incidents of my journey to Cork in the year 1845.

Now, I was just a trifle too wary a bird to be caught twice, within a few months, by the application of a pinch of salt to my caudal appendage. I began by reminding Mr. Bullen that I was not in the witness-box, and then proceeded to fence and parry his questions until he fairly lost his temper, for I soon tumbled to the fact that, compared with Jansen's principal, the solicitor knew nothing about my movements or of my connection with Mr. James Wood, and for all he would have got out of me he might have gone on till Doomsday, had not Passon Mark come to his rescue.

"It appears to me, Samson," said the old gentleman, "that you and Mr. Bullen are at cross-purposes, owing to some misunderstanding on your part, and I hope that a few words of explanation may set things straight. When Sir George was taken dangerously ill a few days ago, he sent for me, as his oldest friend, and asked my opinion upon some very important matters connected with the baronetcy and entailed estates. My advice to him was to put all the facts connected with the case into black and white, and, in accordance with this advice, Mr. Bullen took down Sir George's statements in the form of a deposition, which has been duly signed and witnessed. It was by Sir George's express desire that you were sent for, as being the person best able to throw light upon certain important details, and generally to corroborate the statements contained in the deposition; and if he were present, he would be the first to impress upon you the absolute necessity of telling the truth, the whole truth, and nothing but the truth. Both Mr. Geoffrey and myself quite understand and appreciate your reluctance to make any statement which may appear to you to be damaging to his interests. Nothing that you can say will affect the result in the face of Sir George's deposition, but if, by your assistance, the principal facts can be proved beyond the shadow of a doubt, the affair may be settled more or less privately, whereas, if a technical difficulty should arise, there are certain parties interested who would not scruple to drag the whole matter into court. Geoffrey, I am sure that you will corroborate what I have said?"

"I am most anxious"—replied poor Mr. Geoffrey, "that Samson should quite understand that he will best serve my interests by telling everything he knows about it."

"And let me add"—said Mr. Bullen pompously, "that I am in a position to guarantee him an immunity from any ulterior consequences which may arise in connection with any statements which he may make."

"Thank you, gentlemen"—I answered. "I think I quite understand, but as it is not my business, I suppose there can be no objection to my seeing Sir George first?"

"That is only reasonable"—said Mr. Sealy. "If you will ring the bell, I will inquire whether he is able to see you"—and in a few minutes Adams returned with a message from Dr. Hill to the effect that Sir George was asleep and must not be disturbed, but that he would probably be able to see me about seven o'clock.

The interview was accordingly adjourned until the hour indicated, and at seven o'clock I accompanied Mr. Sealy to my old master's room. Father Fazackerley, who was sitting reading in an arm-chair, and who, as I had heard, had insisted upon sitting up night and day to help the nurse, rose as we entered the room, and after exchanging a few words with Mr. Sealy, left us alone with Sir George.

My poor old master was propped up amongst the pillows, looking more like a waxen figure than a creature of flesh and blood, so absolutely still did he lie, so clean and speckless was he, from the silvery hair, most carefully brushed and parted, to the tips of the filbert-shaped nails—so transparent and colourless was the hand which rested upon an open book of devotions. Upon a table beside the bed stood a reading-lamp with a green shade, the effect of which was to intensify the ghastly pallor of his wasted features—the only indication of life being the light which still lingered in the deep-set eyes.

As we drew near the bed, he stretched out his hand, which Mr. Sealy took, and showed that he recognised me by slightly bending his head.

"I have brought Loveridge here"—said Passon Mark, "in order that he may hear from your own lips whether or not it is your earnest desire that he should give Mr. Bullen all the information in his power respecting the baptismal entry at Cork, and other matters. If it is your wish, tell him so at once, and we will not disturb you again."

The answer was scarcely audible, but the intention was unmistakable:—"Yes, yes, Samson. Tell everything—everything"—and the words died away as the head sank wearily back upon the pillows.

After dinner, I met the gentlemen again in the library and told them everything—or nearly so—from my visit to my cousin Vester, to the abstraction from the St. Bridget's parish register of the double-page containing the entry of baptism.

"And what became of this page?"—Mr. Bullen asked,

"for I understand that you did not hand it over to Sir George."

Now, rightly or wrongly, I had got the notion into me head that, without the original baptismal record, it would by impossible to prove Mr. Geoffrey's illegitimacy, and I answered—as I thought—with every appearance of truth:—"I tore it up"—for if I hadn't, I meant to, as soon as ever I got back to town.

"Dear me"—says Mr. Bullen, scratching his head, "I'm afraid that complicates matters a good deal"—and I was beginning to congratulate myself at having bluffed the lawyer, when, to my dismay, up gets Passon Mark and comes 'limpety, limp' across the room to where I was stood, and propping himself up with his crutch-handled stick—just as he always did, since he broke his thigh, whenever he was going to take a snap-shot at a rabbit—places his hand on my shoulder.

"Samson"—he began, and I noticed a comical sort of twinkle in his eyes as he exchanged his formal way of speaking for the old familiar style which I knew so well, although his voice was grave enough, "that may go down all right enough with a stranger, but as a boy you were never what I should call a good liar, and you don't seem to have improved with age. *Pen o tatchopen*, Samson, *ta kair o pooro Beng aladge*"*—and he patted me encouragingly upon the back.

I suppose it is no use attempting to explain to a Gorgio the effect which that short sentence in Romany—heard after an interval of so many years—produced on me, any more than I can convey, in words, the power or fascination—call it what you please—which Passon Mark's manner enabled him to exercise, when he chose, over rough natures like mine. I was simply knocked all of a heap, my self-possession deserted me, and, turning to Mr. Bullen, I blurted out:—"I've got it safe at home, sir, and I'll send it to you as soon as I get back to London."

The effect upon the solicitor of this sudden transformation in my demeanour was ludicrous in the extreme. He sat staring, first at the Parson and then at me, with his mouth wide open and blinking like a great owl—then, pulling himself together, he wiped his spectacles, and said in

* "Tell the truth, Samson, and shame the Devil."

his nasty, sarcastic sort of way—" H'm, just as I expected, you felt that you had a hold over your master, and you meant to make the most of it."

"Oh, come now, Bullen"—expostulated the Parson, " I think that's scarcely called for"—but the spell was broken, and interrupting him, I let the lawyer have it—straight. I told him that if I had wanted to make money of it, I should have done so long ago: I described my interview with the mysterious stranger in Jansen's rooms, and wound up by telling him that unless he apologised I would burn the blessed thing as soon as ever I got back to town.

Sir George passed away very peaceably about daybreak, and I went back to London, but returned to Netherleigh by Passon Mark's desire, in order to be present at the funeral and the reading of the will, which had been made only a few days previously. It was a very short one, Mr. Sealy and Father Fazackerley being appointed joint executors, and the whole of the late baronet's property, real and personal—with the exception of the entailed estates, a few legacies, and annuities to old servants, etc.,—being left " to my eldest son, Geoffrey Adrian Barrington."

The title, of course, passed to Mr. Francis, together with the Netherleigh estates, but Mr. Geoffrey found himself a rich man, for Sir George had saved a great deal of money during his lifetime, and in addition to Kilmore Castle and the house-property in Paris, everything—with the exception of the entailed estate—went to him.

As soon as he had completed his arrangements for the sale of the Irish and French properties, Mr. Geoffrey Barrington—as he was henceforth called—emigrated with his wife and family to New Zealand, where he purchased a large tract of country not a hundred miles from Christchurch. *

A good deal of the land, which was bought for a few shillings *per* acre, is now valued at £20, and my eldest son—who went out to them and is now helping to manage the estate for poor Mr. Geoffrey's widow—told me in his last

* Poor Geoffrey Barrington was killed by treacherous natives on the Kaikora Range during an exploring expedition up-country, and his name helps to swell the long list of adventurous spirits who have nobly sacrificed their lives in the interest of scientific research. Young George Loveridge was the only European of the party who escaped, and he rode over 100 miles with a broken arm and a spear-head firmly fixed below the shoulder-blade.

letter that out of some 200,000 acres, they have 12,000 under corn, and that the live-stock consists of 50,000 sheep—chiefly Merinos and Cotswolds—500 well-bred horses, and about 2,000 shorthorns, which are sold by auction every month.

And now that I have brought the story of my connection with the L'Estrange family to a conclusion, little remains to be told, but for the benefit of anybody who may be curious to know what became of me, I may say that, in the autumn of 1854, I received a strong hint from head-quarters that unless I devoted more of my time to looking after the interests of the firm, and less of it to looking on at the racing, they would be compelled to secure the services of another manager; and as I considered the reprimand undeserved, I foolishly sent in my resignation on the spur of the moment, withdrew my money from the business, and acting once more upon my cousin Vester's advice, took over the lease of the Pembroke Arms—a well-known sporting house at the back of St. James' Street—which happened to be vacant.

Hitherto, notwithstanding the fact that my business compelled me to attend all the principal race-meetings, and that I was daily brought into contact with a vast number of sporting men of all ranks and conditions, I had the good sense to abstain from betting, but now that I was my own master, the same necessity no longer existed, and I was foolish enough to fancy that I was going to make my fortune on the Turf.

As, however, the leading events of Turf history have been described over and over again, I will pass to events which more immediately concerned myself. When, in the spring of the year 1856, the Rev. Mark Sealy was laid to rest in the little moss-grown churchyard of Netherleigh, I knew that I had lost my best friend, and, curiously enough, from that very day my luck—hitherto pretty good—underwent a change, and before the end of the year I had lost, not only my winnings, but all that I had made in business. Yellow Jack cost me a lot of money, while Melissa—whom I had backed heavily—only failed to win the Oaks through the incapacity of her jockey. Sly had been given the mount in order to recompense him for having been taken off Clementina colt in the Leger, and Lord Clifden's first jockey—Job Marson—was forced to look on at the race, which, as he bitterly remarked, he could have won blind-fold.

After a cruel bad season, which caused the retirement of three or four well-known owners and a host of lesser lights, following the example of a good many others, and notwithstanding that I had been advised by his owner to back Malacca, I went for the gloves with a Vengeance, and after seeing Mr. Parr's horse beat the favourite by a couple of lengths, I took my final leave of Newmarket a wiser but a poorer man.

I was, of course, unable to settle, and becoming implicated the following year in a discreditable transaction connected with a trotting-horse, by which a gentleman was defrauded of a considerable sum of money, I was compelled to give up the Pembroke Arms, and took a restaurant in the neighbourhood of Leicester Square, where I made the acquaintance of the men who eventually proved my ruin.

And now, as I have already hinted, I think that the *chuvveno, pooro gry*, collar-galled and lame as he is, may very well be indulged with a roll by the wayside, if not with a summer's run at grass. As for the moral which—according to Dr. Carew—my story was intended to convey, if it has not been self-evident throughout, I am afraid that no words of mine will suffice to point it, but if these rambling Reminiscences have served to while away an idle hour or two, or have tended to throw any light upon, or awake any interest in, the habits of my people, they have more than fulfilled the object with which they were written, and it only remains for me to say "*Kooshto rarde, ta Kooshto bok!*"

THE END.